"Tony Merida and Danny Akin have writt[en] [one] of the best commentaries on the Psalms [and it provides] a great balance of giving insight into the [text while] being accessible to the everyday reader. [If] [you're] a pastor looking to preach through the Psalms, or simply a layperson desiring to grow in your knowledge of one of the most beloved books of the Bible, this is your commentary"

Dr. Matt Carter, lead pastor, Sagemont Church, Houston, Texas

"All of Scripture is God's word to us; Psalms is God teaching us what words to say to him. And since God's final word to us is Jesus Christ, so also Christ should be the center of our words to God. This commentary series is rightly named 'Christ-Centered Exposition,' and this volume on Psalms 101–150 beautifully fits into that pattern. Authors Danny Akin and Tony Merida explain the text with wonderful clarity and excellent ordering, always seeking to apply it directly to our twenty-first-century lives. But their top priority always is bringing their readers to a stronger faith in Jesus Christ. I am truly thankful for their Spirit-led work in this volume!"

Andrew Davis, senior pastor, First Baptist Church, Durham, NC

"Danny Akin and Tony Merida have combined to produce a practical and warm-hearted exposition, pointing people to Jesus Christ in Psalms 101–150. This book will guide readers to see Israel's hymn-book in fresh ways, recognizing these psalms as wonderful resources of Christian worship and praise. The commentary is characterized from beginning to end by faithful exposition, serving as an exemplary model for those who will teach and preach these psalms in the days to come. I am confident that this work will serve pastors and church leaders well as they thoughtfully and prayerfully reflect on these final fifty psalms. It is a joy to recommend *Exalting Jesus in Psalms 101–150*."

David S. Dockery, president, International Alliance for Christian Education, and Distinguished Professor of Theology, Southwestern Baptist Theological Seminary

"For years I've read the entire Bible at least once a year. In my reading plan, I actually read the Psalms twice a year. The Psalms always point me to Jesus. In Psalms I behold Jesus as 'my Shepherd' (Ps 23), 'the Rock of my salvation' (Ps 89), the Lord who sits at the right hand of the Father (Ps 110), and the One from whom my help comes (Ps 121). In this excellent, new work, *Exalting Jesus in Psalms 101–150*, Dr. Danny Akin skillfully points all of us to Jesus. I believe you will be more like Jesus if you read and study this Christ-exalting book by my dear friend."

Steve Gaines, pastor, Bellevue Baptist Church, Memphis

"Students of theology have been in need of a scholarly exploration of the Psalms. Dr. Merida and Dr. Akin's effective exegesis and brilliant exposition provide a robust and vibrant theological reflection that highlights the central nature of God and his character. Their interpretations are comprehensive, challenging, and Christ-centered. This is an accessible tool for every Bible student and will serve as a blessing to both the church and the academy for many years to come."

Doug Logan, president, Grimké Seminary, Richmond, Virginia

"As one who serves in both the church and the academy, I recognize the increasing need for commentaries that are Christ-centered and spiritually enriching. In *Exalting Jesus in Psalms 101–150*, Akin and Merida help us behold the majesty of God and the mercy of Christ found in the Psalter. This volume will lead you to drink deeply of the wells of God's grace and will equip you to see Christ in all of Scripture. I highly recommend this commentary to anyone who desires to increase in their love for Christ and to proclaim the glories of his kingdom."

Aaron L. Lumpkin, Associate Dean of Students, Missouri Baptist University; elder of Church of the Redeemer, Saint Louis, MO

"Pastors, teachers, and Christians longing to know God's Word more will find this latest installment of the Christ-Centered Exposition series on the Psalms a treasure. These scholars and teachers offer in this commentary a clear and Christ-centered exposition of the Scriptures that reflects their combined years of faithfulness to Christ and his church. This volume will lead you to worship, as well as to learn."

R. Albert Mohler, Jr., president, The Southern Baptist Theological Seminary

"Here's why I will read any commentary Dr. Tony Merida contributes to: he writes biblically rich, gospel-soaked commentaries to pastors, from a pastor. Like each of the other works in this series, I always come away with an angle on the text that I hadn't seen before. Covering Psalms 101–150, this commentary is written with solid exegesis, helpful pastoral insights, and thoughtful applications that make it a must-have tool in the hands of any pastor or student of the Bible. If you're working through the Psalms, this book needs to be on your shelf."

Adam Ramsey, lead pastor, Liberti Church, Gold Coast, Australia; network director, Acts 29 Australia & New Zealand

"Daniel Akin and Tony Merida have joined to walk readers through Psalm 101–150 looking for Jesus the Christ. The authors serve as guides, expertly revealing Christ in this volume of the Scriptures. This book is a necessary companion for those seeking to understand, identify, and apply the practical and recognizable responses and cries of the psalmists while walking in the footsteps and becoming the image of our Savior."

Dr. Robert Smith Jr., Charles T. Carter Baptist Chair of Divinity, Beeson Divinity School, Samford University

"This volume on the Psalms is full of light and heat. Preachers will find nuggets for their sermons, Christians will find it helpful for their devotional life, and Bible studies will benefit from the questions at the end of each section. The psalms are God-ordained prayers for his people. Tony Merida and Danny Akin help us navigate the Psalms for reflection, understanding, and delight in God. I love the Christ-Centered Exposition Commentary series."

Harvey Turner, lead pastor, Redeemer Burbank; Acts 29 US West leadership team

"The psalms are a treasure chest of Christ-centered truth. Merida and Akin are gladly sharing the treasure map with their walkthrough of these psalms in a way that is both readable and insightful. These reflections will help you to rejoice in Christ from the Psalms and to preach Christ from the Psalms."

Dr. Scott Zeller, executive pastor, Redeemer Church of Dubai; emerging regions network director, Acts 29; global leadership team, City to City

CHRIST-CENTERED

Exposition

OT / COMMENTARY FEATURING

AUTHORS **Daniel L. Akin and Tony Merida**

SERIES EDITORS **David Platt, Daniel L. Akin, and Tony Merida**

CHRIST-CENTERED

Exposition

EXALTING JESUS IN

PSALMS 101–150

HOLMAN
REFERENCE
NASHVILLE, TENNESSEE

SERIES DEDICATION

Dedicated to Adrian Rogers and John Piper. They have taught us to love the gospel of Jesus Christ, to preach the Bible as the inerrant Word of God, to pastor the church for which our Savior died, and to have a passion to see all nations gladly worship the Lamb.

—David Platt, Tony Merida, and Danny Akin
March 2013

AUTHORS' DEDICATIONS

To my former colleagues and friends Russ Bush and Michael Travers, both of whom are now in heaven. Their love for the book of Psalms was a model and inspiration to us all.

Daniel L. Akin

Kimberly is the musician in our home, and she has put several psalms to music recently, as we have been enduring the Covid-19 crisis. Singing the psalms is a great way to memorize Scripture; it has served to encourage our souls in this challenging time; and it has been a wonderful way to stay connected to others in the church who have been participating in her songwriting activities. I dedicate this commentary to my true companion, Kimberly.

Tony Merida

Due to the length and complexity of Psalm 119
as well as its prominence in the Psalter, we felt it better served readers
for this psalm to be given further treatment in a separate volume:
Christ-Centered Exposition: Exalting Jesus in Psalm 119

TABLE OF CONTENTS

DA = Daniel Akin
TM = Tony Merida

ACKNOWLEDGMENTS

Many thanks to Mary Jo Haselton, Kim Humphrey, Kimberly Rochelle, and especially Devin Moncada for their excellent work and assistance on this series of studies in the Psalms.

—Daniel L. Akin

I must say thank you to some people who made this commentary possible. First of all, thank you to Imago Dei Church for allowing me the privilege of preaching through these "sacred songs." We have dipped into the Psalter throughout our short history as a church, and these particular Sundays have been extremely edifying. I'm so thankful to have a congregation that enjoys substantive exposition and that encourages their pastors so consistently and thoughtfully.

Thanks to the elders of Imago Dei Church. What a privilege it is to labor with you. In the highs and lows, you have served faithfully and joyfully. I don't take having such a unified elder team for granted. Praise be to the Chief Shepherd for this grace.

I must also say thank you to Dr. Danny Akin for showing me abundant kindness in many ways, including the gracious invitation to be part of this commentary series. It has been a labor of love, and I'm thankful to be part of it. I do pray that these commentaries continue to bless Jesus's people.

To David Stabnow, thank you for your hard work of editing these commentaries. You have been a pure pleasure to work with.

Finally, I must "give thanks to the LORD, for he is good; his faithful love endures forever!" (Ps 107:1). "You, oh LORD, have done great things for us, and we are glad" (Ps 126:3, author's translation). "I will bless you every day; I will praise your name forever and ever" (Ps 145:2).

—Tony Merida

SERIES INTRODUCTION

Augustine said, "Where Scripture speaks, God speaks." The editors of the Christ-Centered Exposition Commentary series believe that where God speaks, the pastor must speak. God speaks through his written Word. We must speak from that Word. We believe the Bible is God breathed, authoritative, inerrant, sufficient, understandable, necessary, and timeless. We also affirm that the Bible is a Christ-centered book; that is, it contains a unified story of redemptive history of which Jesus is the hero. Because of this Christ-centered trajectory that runs from Genesis 1 through Revelation 22, we believe the Bible has a corresponding global-missions thrust. From beginning to end, we see God's mission as one of making worshipers of Christ from every tribe and tongue worked out through this redemptive drama in Scripture. To that end we must preach the Word.

In addition to these distinct convictions, the Christ-Centered Exposition Commentary series has some distinguishing characteristics. First, this series seeks to display exegetical accuracy. What the Bible says is what we want to say. While not every volume in the series will be a verse-by-verse commentary, we nevertheless desire to handle the text carefully and explain it rightly. Those who teach and preach bear the heavy responsibility of saying what God has said in his Word and declaring what God has done in Christ. We desire to handle God's Word faithfully, knowing that we must give an account for how we have fulfilled this holy calling (Jas 3:1).

Second, the Christ-Centered Exposition Commentary series has pastors in view. While we hope others will read this series, such as parents, teachers, small-group leaders, and student ministers, we desire to provide a commentary busy pastors will use for weekly preparation of biblically faithful and gospel-saturated sermons. This series is not academic in nature. Our aim is to present a readable and pastoral style of commentaries. We believe this aim will serve the church of the Lord Jesus Christ.

Third, we want the Christ-Centered Exposition Commentary series to be known for the inclusion of helpful illustrations and theologically driven applications. Many commentaries offer no help in illustrations, and few offer any kind of help in application. Often those that do offer illustrative material and application unfortunately give little serious attention to the text. While giving ourselves primarily to explanation, we also hope to serve readers by providing inspiring and illuminating illustrations coupled with timely and timeless application.

Finally, as the name suggests, the editors seek to exalt Jesus from every book of the Bible. In saying this, we are not commending wild allegory or fanciful typology. We certainly believe we must be constrained to the meaning intended by the divine Author himself, the Holy Spirit of God. However, we also believe the Bible has a messianic focus, and our hope is that the individual authors will exalt Christ from particular texts. Luke 24:25-27,44-47 and John 5:39,46 inform both our hermeneutics and our homiletics. Not every author will do this the same way or have the same degree of Christ-centered emphasis. That is fine with us. We believe faithful exposition that is Christ centered is not monolithic. We do believe, however, that we must read the whole Bible as Christian Scripture. Therefore, our aim is both to honor the historical particularity of each biblical passage and to highlight its intrinsic connection to the Redeemer.

The editors are indebted to the contributors of each volume. The reader will detect a unique style from each writer, and we celebrate these unique gifts and traits. While distinctive in their approaches, the authors share a common characteristic in that they are pastoral theologians. They love the church, and they regularly preach and teach God's Word to God's people. Further, many of these contributors are younger voices. We think these new, fresh voices can serve the church well, especially among a rising generation that has the task of proclaiming the Word of Christ and the Christ of the Word to the lost world.

We hope and pray this series will serve the body of Christ well in these ways until our Savior returns in glory. If it does, we will have succeeded in our assignment.

David Platt
Daniel L. Akin
Tony Merida
Series Editors
February 2013

Psalms 101–150

Twelve Marks of a Wise and Trustworthy Leader

PSALM 101

Main Idea: A person of God will pursue the highest standards of holiness and godliness in himself and his co-laborers.

I. The Person of God Will Praise the Lord for His Goodness (101:1).

II. The Person of God Will Walk in the Way of Integrity (101:2).

III. The Person of God Will Continually Acknowledge His Utter Dependence on the Lord (101:2).

IV. The Person of God Will Guard His Heart as He Leads His Home (101:2).

V. The Person of God Will Keep His Eyes from Anything That Is Worthless (101:3).

VI. The Person of God Will Hate What Is Wrong and Will Not Let It Get Hold of Him (101:3).

VII. The Person of God Will Not Welcome Evil Persons into His Inner Circle (101:4).

VIII. The Person of God Will Give No Place to Slander and Gossip (101:5).

IX. The Person of God Will Seek Out the Humble, Not the Prideful (101:5).

X. The Person of God Will Look to Surround Himself with People Who Are Faithful and Have Integrity (101:6).

XI. The Person of God Will Have Nothing to Do with Liars and the Dishonest (101:7).

XII. The Person of God Will Not Grow Weary in the Battle of Good and Evil (101:8).

There is little question that honesty, ethics, and integrity are essential foundations for faithful, long-term leadership, regardless of the profession. Unsurprisingly, the Bible places a premium on integrity:

> *The one who lives with integrity lives securely, but whoever perverts his ways will be found out.* (Prov 10:9)

The integrity of the upright guides them, but the perversity of the treacherous destroys them. (Prov 11:3)

Righteousness guards people of integrity, but wickedness undermines the sinner. (Prov 13:6)

Better the poor person who lives with integrity than the rich one who distorts right and wrong. (Prov 28:6)

Those of us called to the office of the pastor, the overseer and elder, will also know that 1 Timothy 3:2 reminds us that we must be men "above reproach." Titus 1:6 adds that we "must be blameless."

Psalm 101, which King David penned, speaks directly to the issue of leadership and integrity. Its eight verses highlight trustworthiness and wisdom. Warren Wiersbe says Psalm 101 is "Leadership 101" (*Bible Exposition Commentary*, 273). Willem VanGemeren says it addresses a "Commitment to Excellence" (*Psalms*, 743). The great reformer Martin Luther even wrote an eighty-page exposition of this psalm. It is a royal psalm of the king, and the qualities it accentuates find an echo in Isaiah 11:1-5. Both texts are a prophetic portrait of Messiah Jesus. Only our Savior could perfectly fulfill the awesome expectations of the leader described in this psalm. Allen Ross says,

> What it adds up to is a description of the ideal King, for none of the Kings of Israel were able to live up to this. But as a royal psalm, the description also looks ahead to the ideal King who will reign with righteousness, the promised Messiah. (*Psalms 90–150*, 198)

The eight verses highlight twelve marks of a wise and trustworthy leader.

The Person of God Will Praise the Lord for His Goodness
PSALM 101:1

This psalm contains several "I will" statements. Verse 1 has two of them and begins the psalm on a note of praise and joyful gladness. Twice David says, "I will sing." He sings of the Lord's *chesed*, his "faithful love," and he sings about the Lord's "justice." These two attributes of our God are twin pillars we should always keep together. They provide the foundation for our own leadership. Calvin says, "To sing therefore of mercy [faithful love] and of judgment [justice] is equivalent to declaring in solemn terms, that he would be a just and an upright king [leader]" (*Psalms 93–150*, 87).

"Faithful love" means we act mercifully and graciously in covenantal love. "Justice" means we act righteously and fairly. As we celebrate and sing of the perfection of these qualities we see in our God, we also pursue them as essential qualities in our own lives as faithful and fair leaders in covenant with our people. Spurgeon says, "He singeth best who worketh best for God" (*Metropolitan Tabernacle Pulpit*, 229).

The Person of God Will Walk in the Way of Integrity
PSALM 101:2

Praise for our Lord's faithful love and justice should find a companion in our commitment to live and act toward others in faithful love and justice. David says in verse 2, "I will pay attention to the way of integrity," an idea emphasized three times in the psalm (v. 2 [twice], v. 6). The phrase "I will pay attention" could be rendered "I will be wise." He gives his attention and his heart to "the way of integrity."

A faithful and just leader will be a Psalm 1 person, a 1 Timothy 3:1-7 person. He is above reproach and blameless in his conduct. He does not listen to the advice of the wicked; rather, his delight is in the teachings of the Lord. He thinks and meditates on the Word of God.

This person lives life wisely by living with healthy transparency. He avoids the places of evil. He says no to the things that can enslave him or cause others to stumble. There is no dishonesty, duplicity, foolishness, or compromise in this person. His public life and his private life are the same. When only God is watching, he is the same person as if ten thousand were watching.

The Person of God Will Continually Acknowledge His Utter Dependence on the Lord
PSALM 101:2

Verse 2 contains a brief but powerful prayer: "When will you come to me?" It is a humble and sincere acknowledgment of our need for the Lord's presence and power if we are to live a life of integrity and to lead well. There is an important implication here. To lead well, we must pray well. To lead well, we must know our strengths and our weaknesses. We must know we are utterly dependent on our Lord for any true success in ministry. Oswald Sanders says, "The spiritual leader should outpace the rest of the church, above all, in prayer. . . . Prayer is indeed the Christian's vital breath and native air" (*Spiritual Leadership*, 99). Pastor Dee Duke adds,

> Almost everyone believes that prayer is important. But there is a difference between believing that prayer is important and believing it is essential. "Essential" means there are some things that will not happen without prayer. (Quoted in Newell, *Expect Great Things*, 225)

The Person of God Will Guard His Heart as He Leads His Home
PSALM 101:2

In verse 2 David identifies the home as a specific area where integrity is essential for spiritual leadership. David says a leader must live with a heart of integrity in his home. Paul said much the same thing in 1 Timothy 3:4-5. Likewise, James Boice is right when he says, "The only way to lead a blameless life is to have a blameless heart" (*Psalms 42–106*, 820). The person of integrity will order well his private world. His life of integrity will be most evident to those closest to him. He will be faithful to his spouse with whom he has entered a divine and sacred covenant before God in marriage. He will love and care for his children, bringing them up "in the training and instruction of the Lord" (Eph 6:4).

He will also avoid, like a deadly and infectious virus, the flirtatious and home-destroying woman of Proverbs 5. He will heed the wise words of Randy Alcorn:

> Whenever I feel particularly vulnerable to sexual temptation, I find it helpful to review what effects my action could have: grieving the Lord who redeemed me; dragging his sacred name through the mud; one day having to look at Jesus, the righteous judge in the face, and give an account of my actions; following the footsteps of people whose immorality forfeited their ministries and caused me to shudder; losing my wife's respect and trust; hurting my daughters; destroying my example and creditability with my children; causing shame to my family; losing self-respect; forming memories and

flashbacks that could plague future intimacy with my wife; wasting years of ministry training; undermining the faithful example and hard work of other Christians in our community; and on and on. ("Consequences")

Wise and godly leaders will care for their homes. They will not ignore their families, nor will they take them for granted.

The Person of God Will Keep His Eyes from Anything That Is Worthless

PSALM 101:3

David says, "I will not let anything worthless guide me" (v. 3). The CSB notes that a literal translation of the Hebrew is, "I will not put a worthless thing in front of my eyes." The word *anything* speaks of the absolute and comprehensive nature of this commitment and conviction. The word translated "worthless" (NIV, "vile") is literally "a thing of Belial." That which is wicked and worthless, David will not set his eyes on. He knows the intimate relationship that exists between the eyes and the heart. Because this commitment follows on the heels of the end of verse 2, Job 31:1 is an appropriate warning in this context: "I have made a covenant with my eyes. How then could I look at a young woman?" To properly guard our eyes, we should regularly recall the words of Jesus in Matthew 6:22: "The eye is the lamp of the body. If your eye is healthy, your whole body will be full of light [i.e., goodness]." And again, we should remember the counsel of the Proverbs:

> Wisdom is the focus of the perceptive, but a fool's eyes roam to the ends of the earth. (Prov 17:24)

> My son, give me your heart, and let your eyes observe my ways. (Prov 23:26)

> There is a generation that is pure in its own eyes, yet is not washed from its filth. There is a generation—how haughty its eyes and pretentious its looks. (Prov 30:12-13)

The Bible says not to put your eyes on what is worthless. Instead, we ought to put our eyes on what is worthy. Hebrews 12:1-2 is a good word here: "Let us run with endurance the race that lies before us, keeping our eyes on Jesus, the pioneer and perfecter of our faith."

The Person of God Will Hate What Is Wrong and Will Not Let It Get Hold of Him
PSALM 101:3

Having nothing evil before his eyes, a wise and trustworthy leader will hate the work of those who walk away from the truth. David says that we are to "hate the practice of transgression." The wise leader will maintain his personal purity, in part, by hating and not tolerating evil. The word translated "transgression" carries the idea of falling away, "doing apostasies" or "acts of unfaithfulness" (Ross, *Psalms 90–150*, 201). If he has people in mind, David is saying he will not put faithless people on his team. It does not matter how charismatic, gifted, or talented they are, they are not welcome in his world. They "will not cling to [him]." Their sin and unfaithfulness to the things of God, as an ongoing lifestyle, disqualifies them. Spurgeon is right: "Hatred of sin is a good sentinel for the door of virtue" (*Treasury*, vol. 2b, 240).

The Person of God Will Not Welcome Evil Persons into His Inner Circle
PSALM 101:4

A wise and godly leader must know and embrace a biblical theology of the heart. Repeatedly, he will recall the wisdom of key Scripture passages that speak to this issue of the heart, especially as he considers those he would invite into his inner circle.

> *The heart is more deceitful than anything else, and incurable—who can understand it?* (Jer 17:9)

> *God, create a clean heart for me and renew a steadfast spirit within me.* (Ps 51:10)

> *Guard your heart above all else, for it is the source of life.* (Prov 4:23)

> *A wise heart accepts commands, but foolish lips will be destroyed.* (Prov 10:8)

> *The heart of a wise person instructs his mouth; it adds learning to his speech.* (Prov 16:23)

> *As water reflects the face, so the heart reflects the person.* (Prov 27:19)

Brood of vipers! How can you speak good things when you are evil?
For the mouth speaks from the overflow of the heart. (Matt 12:34)

But what comes out of the mouth comes from the heart, and this defiles
a person. For from the heart come evil thoughts, murders, adulteries,
sexual immoralities, thefts, false testimonies, slander. (Matt 15:18-19)

David said that a godly leader must hate the practice of transgression and not allow it to cling to him (v. 3). He now says in verse 4 that a godly leader will not come close to "a devious [NASB, "perverse"] heart." It "will be far from me," he says. Indeed, David declares, "I will not be involved with evil." David begins with himself, but he also speaks concerning those he would consider his close confidants. Integrity is crucial all around. A devious or perverse heart is a twisted heart. Its affections are warped, and the choices it makes will inevitably be evil. They are not reliable or trustworthy. They will harm the people of God and infect morale.

Although not a book about the Bible, *Good to Great* by Jim Collins offers a wealth of wisdom, particularly for team building. Collins writes that good leaders get the right people on the bus and the wrong people off the bus. When in doubt, they do not hire. They keep looking. And when they know they need to make a change, they act. Collins writes, "The old adage 'People are your most important asset' turns out to be wrong. People are *not* your most important asset. The *right* people are" (*Good to Great*, 13).

Spurgeon said there is "the need of extreme care in the choice of our intimates" (*Treasury*, vol. 2b, 249). The people you surround yourself with can make or break you. Be the right person and pursue the right people. The two go together.

The Person of God Will Give No Place to Slander or Gossip
PSALM 101:5

Verse 5 has strong and direct language. The poetic nature of the psalm serves as a helpful guide, especially in our application of the text. Verse 5 is a specific example of verse 4. Because David "will not be involved with evil," he will "destroy anyone who secretly slanders his neighbor." *The Message* says this: "I put a gag on the gossip who bad-mouths his neighbor." Alec Motyer renders the verse, "One covertly slandering his associate—him I will exterminate" (*Psalms by the Day*, 282).

A secret slanderer is an evil gossip who spreads lies. He is a whisperer of untruth. He has an agenda to hurt others and will stop at nothing to destroy a pseudo-friend. He does not mind making a false accusation or ruining someone's reputation. Calvin says a slanderer is "like one who administers poison to his unsuspecting victim, [he] destroys men unawares" (*Psalms 93–150*, 91). Scripture says,

> Do not go about spreading slander among your people; do not jeopardize your neighbor's life; I am the LORD. (Lev 19:16)

> Whoever spreads slander is a fool. (Prov 10:18b)

> Lying lips are detestable to the LORD, but faithful people are his delight. (Prov 12:22)

Wise leaders will not run with cowards and losers. They will reject liars, separate themselves from gossips, and have nothing to do with slanderers.

The Person of God Will Seek Out the Humble, Not the Prideful

PSALM 101:5

There is a threefold criterion of the prideful in verse 5: they are those who slander, who have haughty eyes, and who have an arrogant heart. Notice the reverse order connection. An arrogant heart will lead to haughty eyes (an arrogant swagger), which will give way to a lying tongue! The godly leader will not tolerate this sin in himself or in others. He will walk with integrity and expect the same in others. He will silence slanderers and refuse to run with the prideful and arrogant. He will set them aside to negate their cancerous influence in the community of God's people.

Haughty eyes are the outward expression of an arrogant heart. Arrogant and ambitious people are notorious for looking down on others and oozing an air of superiority. The opposite of pride is humility, something God prizes and extols as one of the Christian's most important virtues. Oswald Sanders says, "Humility is the hallmark of the spiritual leader" (*Spiritual Leadership*, 61).

In the context of character traits for leaders, Peter's words are instructive:

In the same way, you who are younger, be subject to the elders. All of you clothe yourselves with humility toward one another, because God resists the proud but gives grace to the humble. Humble yourselves, therefore, under the mighty hand of God, so that he may exalt you at the proper time. (1 Pet 5:5-6)

"Humility," as Rick Warren writes, "is not thinking less of yourself, it is thinking of yourself less" (*Purpose Driven Life*, 148).[1] Humility is crucial for all Christian activity. John Flavel adds, "They that know God will be humble, Isa. 6:5; and they that know themselves cannot be proud" (*Method of Grace*, 487). Finally, Augustine is often attributed with saying, "If you plan to build a tall house of virtues, you must first lay deep foundations of humility."

The Person of God Will Look to Surround Himself with People Who Are Faithful and Have Integrity
PSALM 101:6

There is a common saying in business that A leaders hire A leaders and B leaders hire C leaders. David says the person of God will be on the lookout for particular people for his team. He says, "My eyes favor the faithful of the land so that they may sit down with me." Then, in typical Hebrew parallelism, he adds, "The one who follows the way of integrity may serve me." Verse 6 stands in stark contrast to verse 5, and it returns to the theme of the eyes from verses 3 and 5. David will not allow anything worthless before his eyes, and he will not surround himself with those who have haughty eyes. He will seek out with his eyes the faithful and those who have integrity.

Notice the word "serve" (ESV, "minister") at the end of verse 6. Set your eyes on servant-leaders, individuals with a servant's heart. Look for people who do not expect or ask of others what they do not expect or ask of themselves. Here are some hints for what to look for in a servant-leader:

Look for a person who has worked as a janitor or custodian.

Look for a person who has worked as a server.

---

[1] This quote is regularly, though incorrectly, attributed to C. S. Lewis; however, Lewis never stated these words in any of his books (O'Flaherty, *Misquotable C. S. Lewis*, 8–9).

Look for a person who is kind and generous in a restaurant.

Look for a person who gladly gives attention to children and the elderly.

Look for a person who is gracious to those who can do nothing to further his or her agenda.

Look for a person who treats others like they are the most important people in the world.

Mark 10:45 reminds us of how central to the gospel being a servant-leader is: "For even the Son of Man did not come to be served, but to serve, and to give his life as a ransom for many."

The Person of God Will Have Nothing to Do with Liars and the Dishonest
PSALM 101:7

Verse 7 has the language of the king and his court, and it still provides application for anyone in Christian leadership. Verse 5 advises to confront and deal decisively with slanderers and the arrogant. Now, verse 7 says to do the same with the one "who acts deceitfully" and "who tells lies." Such a person is not welcome in David's house, and he will not receive his counsel.

Those who are dishonest and destructive, deceitful and deceptive, are not allowed a seat at the table of leadership. They cannot have access to the leader's court. The disloyal, dishonest, unfaithful, hypocritical, lying, gossiping, and divisive are not welcome. The person of integrity will take inventory of his own life, watching out for himself so that he can avoid temptation (Gal 6:1), and he will consider carefully who his trusted counselors and advisors are.

Ross is right: "No liar should ever be put in a position of authority or honor" (*Psalms 90–150*, 203). And Calvin makes a direct application to those called to leadership. A wise leader, he says, "will exercise discretion and care, that, instead of taking persons into his service indiscriminately, he may wisely determine each man's character, so as to have those who live a life of strict integrity as his most intimate friends" (*Psalms 93–150*, 93). The people we listen to and spend time with are certain to influence who we are and how we live.

Spurgeon pointedly adds, "If David would not have a liar in his sight, much less will the Lord; neither he that loves nor he who makes a lie shall be admitted into heaven. Liars are obnoxious enough on earth; the saints shall not be worried with them in another world" (*Treasury*, vol. 2b, 241). Revelation 21:8 confirms Spurgeon's words.

The Person of God Will Not Grow Weary in the Battles of Good and Evil
PSALM 101:8

Followers of the crucified and risen Lord Jesus do not fight for victory. We fight *from* victory. We have read the last book of the Bible and know that our God wins! The war is won, but battles will remain until that day. Vigilance in the fight is a necessary characteristic of God's people. We must not grow weary in well-doing.

In verse 8 David declares, "Every morning [ESV, "morning by morning"] I will destroy all the wicked of the land, wiping out evildoers from the LORD's city." This is strong but necessary language cast poetically. In the ancient world, judgment usually happened in the morning. The Lord's city was Jerusalem. The person of God in a position of spiritual leadership will confront evil and wickedness day after day. If God will not tolerate evil, neither can we whom he has called to lead and shepherd his people. We will be on guard against the figurative dogs, pigs, and wolves of Scripture. We will protect the flock of God. At the same time, we will speak prophetically against evil whenever and wherever we see it. We will not play either the coward or the hireling!

Conclusion

The faithful servant of King Jesus believes Christian witness should permeate all of culture. Living out the kingdom ethics of Scripture, we are to be salt and light to a wicked and darkened world as we share and display the gospel. We should oppose racism, bigotry, greed, selfishness, all forms of sexual immorality, and pornography. We should help the orphaned, the needy, the abused, the aged, and the helpless. We should contend for the sanctity of all human life from conception to natural death. The person of God does not care who is in the White House or Congress. He does not care whether it is a Democrat, Republican, Libertarian, or Independent. His allegiance is to the King, not a president. His hope and assurance are in Calvary's hill, not Capitol Hill. Evil is evil. Wrong is wrong. Wherever he sees it, he must speak and act. He cannot be silent. He cannot remain inactive.

Reflect and Discuss

1. When the psalmist refers to God's "faithful love," what acts of God is he referencing? Where in the New Testament and in your own life do you see evidence of God's faithful love?

2. This section teaches that living wisely means having "healthy transparency." What do healthy patterns of transparency look like? What would unhealthy transparency look like?

3. Have you seen a difference in your prayers when you believe prayer is *important* and when you believe it is *essential?* What was different between the two?

4. Sexual immorality is a sin where by spiritual leaders often fall. Why is this the case? What are proactive ways godly leaders can pursue integrity?

5. Have you ever evaluated the people you have close to you? Do they match what you would say you want to have around you? What is present and what is missing?

6. At what point does your conversation become gossip? What can you do in those moments to bring the gospel truth into those conversations?

7. What are some actions that might be culturally acceptable, even in the church, but are evidence of an "arrogant heart"?

8. What other hints of a servant-leader would you add to the list in this section?

9. Should Christians associate with nonbelievers who sin in the way this psalm describes? Why or why not?

10. List examples of wise and faithful spiritual leaders you have known personally. What about their leadership and lives would you want to emulate?

A Prayer of One Afflicted

PSALM 102

Main Idea: The psalmist teaches us how to cry out to God desperately, honestly, and confidently during dark seasons of life.

I. In Affliction, Pray Desperately (102:1-2).
II. In Affliction, Pray Honestly (102:3-11).
III. In Affliction, Pray Confidently (102:12-28).
    A. God's eternal kingship (102:12)
    B. God's compassion (102:13-14)
    C. God's sovereignty (102:15)
    D. God's power (102:16)
    E. God's condescension (102:17)
    F. God's faithfulness (102:18-22)
    G. God's immutability (102:23-28)
    H. God's Son (Heb 1:10-12)

Nearly one-third of the psalms are laments. Not everything in the Psalter is "happy-clappy" because not everything in life is happy-clappy! Life is hard. There are times of grief, mourning, sorrow, frustration, despair, anxiety, confusion, and many other forms of suffering. For this reason, we need to know what to do in such dark times. How will we bear trials?

One way we learn to endure is by learning from the psalms of *lament*. We learn how to pray desperately, honestly, and with God-centered, Christ-filled confidence and hope. Psalm 102 is one such psalm. Leslie Allen summarizes it: "A desperately sick man turns to Yahweh as his only hope" (*Psalms 101–150*, 14). We have much to learn from this desperate psalmist.

Though this psalm has traditionally been classified as a penitential psalm (a song confessing sin and seeking forgiveness), along with Psalms 6; 32; 38; 51; 102; 130; and 143, that is really a misclassification. Psalm 102 receives that designation because of its traditional usage in the Christian community. VanGemeren rightly states, "The psalm exemplifies the literary genre of an individual lament" ("Psalms," 644). This individual lament also has the whole community of faith in view. The context seems to be exilic. The psalmist is crying out to God as one exiled from the promised land.

We must also add that this lament is unique. It includes a "prophetic-hymnic section" (VanGemeren, "Psalms," 645), which provides future hope to God's people. In fact, this psalm has a powerful Christological focus. The writer of Hebrews cites Psalm 102:25-26 explicitly in Hebrews 1:10-12, using this psalm to praise Jesus as the preexistent Lord. The writer of Hebrews uses these verses as the Father speaking about the Son, through whom the universe was made (Heb 1:2) and who is "sustaining all things by his powerful word" (Heb 1:3). Kidner adds that one may read the entire psalm messianically, saying that the Hebrews' reference to Psalm 102 "implies that the sufferer throughout the [whole] Psalm is also *the Son incarnate*" (*Psalms 73–150*, 362; emphasis added; see also Wilcock, *Message*, 114).

What types of affliction are you encountering? Ligon Duncan helps us relate present situations with this psalm. Like a careful surgeon, Duncan attempts to care for the souls of his people:

> Have you known affliction? Deep and intense? Unrelenting affliction? A darkness where there is no light at the end of the tunnel? Have you brought it here with you today?
>
> Perhaps it's in your job and your vocation . . . your profession. You have with integrity sought to earn a living, do what is right, and yet there is someone—a client, a partner— who had betrayed you and is raking your good name through the mud, calling into question all of your integrity, threatening your livelihood and the well-being of your family as well as ruining your reputation. And when you go home, late at night you want to lay your head on the pillow and close your eyes and forget about it, but you cannot. There's no escaping it. Everywhere you go that reality is there, and there is no relenting in its pursuit of you.
>
> Or maybe it's in a family estrangement; one to whom you would give great joy, and from whom you would receive great joy, has plunged a knife into your own soul and there is no relief. It may be your husband or your wife or a child, or your own mother and father, or some close relative. And in the very place where we're meant to have security and joy there is in

fact the deepest of affliction, because there is no one who can hurt us like those who are closest to us.

Or maybe it's just that you are living in a yawning loneliness . . . surrounded by frenetic activity in work, surrounded by numerous acquaintances, but no one who really knows you and loves you or would care about you if you were gone; no one to stick with you to the end.

Or maybe it is that you carry within your own body a disease that is killing you.

Or maybe there is an unbelieving child who has broken your heart.

And I could go on and on and on, and not end the list of the afflictions that are here today. My friends, it is one of the supreme truths of God's word . . . that He speaks to us precisely in these places and that He dares to say to us, "Write down your afflictions and pray them to Me. In fact, I am going to give you words in My word so that you can pray back to Me your broken heart in the midst of your affliction, and so that you can bring to Me your complaint." (Duncan, "A Prayer")

Betrayal. Grief. Sorrow. Loneliness. Physical disease. A loved one's unbelief. Confusion. These are real experiences. How does one endure them? Praise God, he has given us his Word to help us not only to understand this broken world but also to pray his Word back to him. I (Tony) want to point out three ways the psalmist helps us pray in our afflictions.

In Affliction, Pray Desperately
PSALM 102:1-2

The superscription gives us the feel of desperation: "A prayer of a suffering person who is weak and pours out his lament before the LORD." Obviously, this person needs divine help, so he cries out to God. The opening verses include a rich vocabulary of prayer. The psalmist uses various words to convey the passion and depth of his supplication.

The psalmist's language reflects much of the language of the Psalter, as the supplicant seeks God's presence and help through prayer. In verse 1 the afflicted one seeks Yahweh's attention: "hear my prayer" (v. 1a; cf. 39:12; 65:2). He continues by humbly asking for God to graciously allow his "cry for help [to] come before [him]" (v. 1b; cf. 18:6). Verse 2a includes a negative plea: "Do not hide your face from me in the day of trouble" (cf. 13:1; 27:9). Then he asks God again to hear his prayer: "Listen closely to me; answer me quickly when I call" (v. 2b; cf. 31:2; 71:2; 88:2; 56:9; 69:17).

The psalmist feels alienated. The popular singer Adele's hit song "Hello" comes to mind. In it, she is trying to communicate with someone special in order to reconnect, but she feels like she is calling from the "other side" or from the "outside." Do you feel like that? Do you feel like an outsider? Learn from the psalmist: persist in prayer; be desperate in prayer.

Despite this dark season of his soul, the suffering saint is also demonstrating a sense of confidence. He knows God hears the prayer of the afflicted; otherwise it would make no sense to call to him persistently and desperately. Later in the psalm he says, "He will pay attention to the prayer of the destitute and will not despise their prayer" (v. 17). Be encouraged if you find yourself in a similar season of affliction. God hears the prayers of the destitute! Call on him desperately in times of affliction.

What's most striking to me about this opening plea is *the passion* of the afflicted one. This is not a soft, casual, perfunctory prayer. In the ESV there are three exclamation points in these first two verses! This guy is calling on the Lord passionately, and he will not give up until he has God's ear. The Puritans used to say, "Pray until you've prayed." If you're a Christian, you know what they meant. Don't get off your knees until you have communed with the Father. Press in to know him and meet with him.

As I (Tony) was reading commentaries on this psalm last Sunday night, my family was watching the movie *War Room*, which is about prayer. An older saint is teaching a younger Christian woman about how to seek the Lord earnestly. I greatly appreciated the passion with which this older saint prays. She has her little prayer room, her prayer lists, and her verses, and she has a living faith. Do you have a prayer closet? Do you have some place where you can cry out to God? Piper says, "Until you know that life is war, you cannot know what prayer is for" (*Let the Nations Be Glad!*, 2007, 69).

In Affliction, Pray Honestly
PSALM 102:3-11

Next, the psalmist acknowledges his desperate situation. In verses 3-11 he expresses his anguish to God honestly. Sometimes we call friends when we're in trials and say, "Can I vent for a moment?" You might call verses 3-11 "holy venting." The psalmist pours out his complaint to God. This is a good example for us. You should vent to God before venting to others.

In verse 3 he feels **his transience**: "my days vanish like smoke" (cf. 37:20; 68:2; Isa 51:6; Hos 13:3; Jas 4:14). Throughout this psalm the psalmist feels that his days are few and they are losing meaning (vv. 11,23). In dark seasons, one often becomes more aware of his or her mortality.

Next, the sufferer acknowledges that his "bones burn like a furnace" (v. 3b), which is perhaps a reference to inflammation or a **feverish anxiety** (VanGemeren, "Psalms," 646) if this is meant to be a real physical description of his condition (cf. Job 30:17; Lam 1:13).

In verse 4 the afflicted man speaks of his "heart" (his "self"), saying that it's "suffering" and "withered like grass." In other words, he feels **dried up inside** (Williams, *Psalms 73–150*, Kindle). Have you ever experienced this? Maybe we should ask, "Are you experiencing this right now?" Do you feel spiritually dry? If so, pray with the psalmist! Express your anguish to God!

As a result of his spiritual dryness, the psalmist has experienced **the loss of appetite** (v. 4b; cf. v. 9). You have a real problem when you don't even remember to eat (cf. 1 Sam 1:7-8). If you've been in the hospital or visited there, you often find both patients and visitors forgetting to eat lunch or dinner because they're overcome with affliction.

Because of his suffering and lack of appetite, the psalmist adds, "my flesh sticks to my bones" (v. 5; cf. Job 19:20). We can picture a tormented man with a great **loss of weight**. I think of Tom Hanks in the movie *Castaway*. He was abandoned, alone, afflicted, tormented, and terribly skinny on that desert island. Fortunately, the psalmist could talk to God in his affliction. Tom Hanks only had an imaginary friend made from a volleyball! That movie highlights humanity's need for companionship and community. We weren't made to be alone. We were made for God and people.

In verses 6-7 he adds more poetic descriptions of his condition. He says, "I am like an eagle owl" (v. 6a). The precise identity of this bird is unknown. Some translate it as a "pelican" (NASB). A pelican is a coastal bird and would obviously be out of place in the dry wilderness. Further, owls were unclean (Lev 11:17). The psalmist essentially says that he's **lonely and rejected**.

Due to the loneliness and rejection, the psalmist is **restless** (v. 7). Misery often includes an inability to sleep.

In the psalmist's culture, ill health was regarded as punishment for sins (Allen, *Psalms 101–150*, 14). So then, the sufferer is **enduring persecution** because of his negative situation (v. 8). People taunt him and mistreat him. They may even include the taunt, "Where is your God?" (cf. Pss 22:7-8; 42:3,10; VanGemeren, "Psalms," 646), thus multiplying his suffering.

The psalmist seems to agree with his enemies (vv. 9-10). What's the reason for his tears and his diet of ashes? He seems to think it's the result of God's anger and wrath. Behind his pain is a theology that says sin brings suffering (cf. John 9:2; Jas 5:16). In other words, he **feels like the victim of divine punishment** (v. 10). As a result, mournful ashes become part of his life as he hopes to divert God's displeasure (Allen, *Psalms 101–150*, 14).

But no sin is ever mentioned in this psalm. And the psalmist offers no prayer of confession. Allen says the psalmist leaves unexplained his reference to divine wrath, not linking it with personal wrongdoing but mentioning it virtually as an "amoral force" (ibid.). Some classify this as a penitential psalm because they associate his sin with his feeling of divine punishment. However, this is questionable. Is he denying sin? Is he ignorant of sin? We don't know for certain. We know he feels abandoned and under the anger of God. Perhaps the mystery is really only resolved in the Messiah, the Suffering Servant who bore God's wrath for no fault of his own but on behalf of sinners. Whatever the cause for verse 10, the psalmist knows where to turn for relief (vv. 12-22).

The psalmist concludes with an additional line about the brevity of life and the feeling of alienation (v. 11). This provides a nice transition into the next section, in which the psalmist contrasts his fleeting existence with the permanence and faithfulness of God.

Before looking at verses 12-22, we should mention something about the suffering of a Christian. Remember this: "unexplained suffering" doesn't mean "meaningless suffering" (Duncan, "A Prayer"). All of your sufferings are, in a sense, unexplainable. God's inscrutable ways are not always revealed to us. But no suffering in the Christian life is meaningless. In the end all will be clear, but for now we live by faith in God. Prayer is an act of faith. It's an act of trust in the goodness, wisdom, and power of God. In the middle of your affliction, learn from the psalmist and express your heart to God *honestly*. The psalmist doesn't have all the answers, but at least he's talking to God. He's not turning *from* God; he's turning *to* God. This serves as a pattern for afflicted saints.

In Affliction, Pray Confidently
PSALM 102:12-28

The psalmist next teaches us to pray with confidence in God. Though the supplicant's condition is dark, he's not hopeless. He has confidence not only in the character of God but also in the future work of God. He has confidence that God will restore the city to universal acclaim at a time of God's own choosing (Wilcock, *Message*, 113).

The contrast between the psalmist's condition and the Lord's character is made emphatically when he says, "But you, LORD" (v. 12). What do you do with your affliction? You need a "But you, LORD" in your vocabulary! You must see beyond your circumstances to the unchanging character of God. This type of emphatic transition happens throughout the Psalms. For example, in the famous messianic Psalm 22, we read of this type of pivot three times (Ps 22:3,9,19). If we can get our eyes off of our ourselves and consider God's character, we will find not only divine help but also an intimacy with God that we wouldn't otherwise know (cf. Phil 3:10-11). Samuel Rutherford used to say that when he found himself in the cellar of affliction, he found that the Great King keeps the best wine in the basement (in Piper, "Where the Great King Keeps His Wine")!

During his trial the psalmist considers eight characteristics of God. If you are in the cellar of affliction, drink of God's grace found here in these verses.

God's Eternal Kingship (102:12)

We may pass away like the grass, but the Lord reigns forever (v. 12a; cf. Rev 1:8). In times of grief, you must remember that God is still enthroned above all. He rules over all things, including your affliction. In contrast to the psalmist's feeling of hatred and wrath, he can say of God that he will be glorified by countless generations of people (v. 12b). Our afflictions will not thwart this unstoppable reality.

God's Compassion (102:13-14)

Next, the psalmist prays with confidence because of God's grace and favor. The psalmist believes God will rise up and have compassion on his holy city, not because the psalmist or the people deserve it but because God is faithful and compassionate. Specifically, the psalmist knows God will be compassionate because God is faithful to his Word. The psalmist is probably speaking of the passing judgment of the Babylonian exile (cf. Isa 40:1). God had an "appointed time" (v. 13b) for deliverance, which would usher in a season of restoration. He would graciously fulfill his promises.

In verse 14 the afflicted man reminds Yahweh of the ruined condition of Jerusalem in order to move him to compassionate action. "Your servants" appeals to God's faithfulness to his covenant people. Thus, God's faithfulness and compassion give the psalmist confidence in prayer.

In times of despair, it's sometimes hard to believe in God's goodness and love. But we must not put our feelings over God's Word; we must submit our feelings to God's Word. What we find is that nothing will separate the believer from God's love (Rom 8:31-39). He loves us with an everlasting love. We may doubt this fact at times; so when we do, we must go to God's Word and fill our minds and hearts with this medicinal truth.

God's Sovereignty (102:15)

Next, the psalmist draws our attention to God's absolute sovereignty. As God restores Zion, the nations will also come to revere his name. The psalmist sees his affliction in the midst of the larger story of redemption. God is bringing a people to himself. That sovereign plan will not be thwarted. The nations will glorify his name. When we read the New Testament, we know even more of that global plan than the psalmist knew. Through faith in Israel's Messiah, the nations will come to know the true and living God (cf. Isa 60:3; 62:2).

While God doesn't need us to accomplish his global mission, he uses us. We must see that our endurance in our many afflictions helps to contribute to the outworking of this great plan. We don't fight as pathetic victims but as victors in an unstoppable mission.

God's Power (102:16)

Further, the psalmist can pray with confidence because he trusts in God's ability to execute his plans. The psalmist knows that his future and the future of the city are entirely dependent on God. And because he depends on God, he has every reason to hope. Since Almighty God has promised to rebuild the city, he can find comfort (cf. Isa 40:5; 60:10; Jer 31:38-40; Mic 7:11).

In the midst of affliction, we must remember God's power. He has the power to rebuild our lives, homes, churches, and cities. He can turn mourning into dancing. He can make bones live. He can bring beauty out of ashes. Trust in his power.

God's Condescension (102:17)

Moreover, the psalmist has hope because he knows of God's divine humility. This great and magnificent God also hears the prayers of his people—in this case, an afflicted people praying for the deliverance from exile! This cry for deliverance is reminiscent of Israel's slavery in Egypt. We read of that moving situation in Exodus 2:

> The Israelites groaned because of their difficult labor, they cried out, and their cry for help because of the difficult labor ascended to God. God heard their groaning, and God remembered his covenant with Abraham, with Isaac, and with Jacob. God saw the Israelites, and God knew. (Exod 2:23b-25)

Israel groaned and cried out to God. And God saw. God heard. God knew. God acted. He still sees, hears, knows, and acts. Cry out to him in times of grief and trial.

God's Faithfulness (102:18-22)

The psalmist continues praying with confidence because he knows the future is in God's hands. He speaks of God's faithfulness. This is a particularly sweet part of the passage. The psalmist wants God to look down (v. 19), "hear a prisoner's groaning," and "set free those condemned" (v. 20). Again, the Exodus 2:23-25 passage comes to mind. But why does he desire God to act? It's so generations to come might glorify God (vv. 18,21-22; cf. Isa 43:15). The psalmist is saying, "Lord, hear my cries so generations after me may hear of your faithfulness." He wants God to use his afflictions for the good of others.

When you read the story of Job or Hannah or the exodus, you have the privilege of knowing how the story ends. But none of them did. Their stories serve as a testimony to God's faithfulness. Their stories tell us that the future is in God's hands, and we can trust him. We see that their sufferings might have been unexplainable, but they weren't meaningless.

When you ask God to act on your behalf, don't make it all about you. Ask the Lord to act for the glory of his name and so that others may hear of God's faithfulness.

This prophetic vision in verses 18-22 takes us from restoration from exile to the full restoration of God's kingdom (VanGemeren, "Psalms," 649). This newly "created" people is striking (v. 18). Kidner says,

> This verb [*created*] points to a great act of God, either in renewing a dead Israel or in making the Gentiles "God's own people," who were "once . . . no people" (1 Pet 2:9). The translation, "a people yet unborn," does less than justice to this. (*Psalms 73–150*, 363)

For all eternity the redeemed from every tribe and tongue will testify to the Lord's faithfulness.

God's Immutability (102:23-28)

The psalm ends with the psalmist once again reflecting on his own mortality and God's unchanging being and purposes. In verses 23-24 the sufferer seems to think his affliction will shorten his already short life, not allowing him to see God's future work of restoration. Verse 23 restates his condition. He is weakened by trials. He feels the brevity of life. At the same time, because the psalmist has a relationship with God ("my God"), he cries out for God to spare his life (v. 24). It's a simple prayer. But it's honest and genuine.

As the psalmist ponders his frailty, he immediately thinks of God's eternality. The Puritan Thomas Watson said, "When God lays men on their backs, then they look up to Heaven" (Thomas, *The Golden Treasury*, 18). The psalmist considers God's unchanging nature and purposes. In the midst of darkness, he stops and considers that the preexistent God created the world (v. 25; cf. Ps 90:1-2). If God can create the world and sustain it, he can sustain us in our trials! Further, the psalmist depicts the creation as a garment—something that will change (v. 26). It will be transformed (2 Pet 3:10). But God is unchanging (vv. 26-27). God's faithfulness will outlast the world. Finally, the psalmist shows us that we must remember God's unchanging purposes in our grief. He will keep his people so that they may worship him forever (v. 28).

When you feel like giving up, or like you're drying up, remember that God never grows weary and never gives up. He not only never gives up, but he also never loses. He will accomplish his purposes. His character never changes, and his purposes never change.

God's Son (Heb 1:10-12)

But we're not finished. The psalmist speaks not only about the greatness of God to his generation but also about something so great he couldn't even grasp it entirely. The writer of Hebrews cites Psalm 102:25-27, not with the psalmist addressing God but with God addressing the Messiah (Heb 1:5-12). In Hebrews 1 the writer uses Old Testament texts as proof of the Son's deity. Jesus is Lord (John 1:1; Phil 2:10-11; Col 1:16). The author of Hebrews draws attention to the Son's deity later in his letter with language from Psalm 102: "Jesus Christ is the same yesterday, today, and forever" (Heb 13:8).

Furthermore, Wilcock says, "Already before the time of Christ there were those in Israel who understood Psalm 102 to be messianic" (*Message*, 116). One could read the entire psalm as pointing to Christ, the afflicted One, who was wounded for our transgressions (Isa 53). The psalm foreshadows the sufferings of a Greater One. In verses 1-11 it's easy to see abandonment and the bearing of God's wrath (at no fault of his own) in Christ (cf. Ps 22). In verses 12-22 we can see Christ's life cut short and the new city of God and its recognition among the nations. Finally, in verses 23-28 we can see the anguished prayer of Christ and the Father's assurance of his eternal glory.

Suffering Christian, take heart. Don't quit. Your Savior knows affliction. Not just because he knows all things but because he also experienced suffering. Your Savior bore the wrath you deserve (cf. Isa 53). Even though your affliction may be great, he already took the greatest affliction for you! He rose from the dead, conquering your greatest enemies. He now gives us access to the Father, allowing us to cry out for grace in our times of need (Heb 4:14-16). Through Christ, we can approach the throne of grace "with confidence" (Heb 4:16 ESV). He will grant us grace to endure our many afflictions, and afterwards the risen Messiah will "bring many sons and daughters to glory" (Heb 2:10). He stood in our place, and now he intercedes for us (Heb 7:25). One day we will stand with him in a new city, where suffering will be no more (Heb 13:14). So while we suffer, let's offer the sacrifice of praise to him (Heb 13:15) and pour our hearts out to him.

Augustine once said, "God had only one Son without sin, but He has no sons without affliction." Don't be surprised by suffering. Learn to pray in the midst of it. Learn to see Christ as your unshakable hope to endure it and your great hope for getting to the other side of it. Remember that this psalm of lament, and the other psalms of lament, should lead us to say, "Maranatha! Come Lord Jesus!" Soon our faith will end in sight, and laments will be no more. Laments will be replaced with loud shouts to the triumphant Lamb (Rev 15:3).

Reflect and Discuss

1. Are you going through deep affliction presently, or do you know someone who is? How does this psalm relate to these afflictions?
2. Does it encourage you that there are so many psalms of lament? Why or why not?
3. What do verses 1-2 teach us about prayer?
4. Do you find it easier to "vent" to people rather than first pouring out your problems to God in prayer? What does this psalm teach us about praying honestly before God?
5. Why is the transition in verse 12 so important? What does this pivot teach us about the life of faith and the practice of prayer?
6. What does this psalm teach us about God's sovereignty?
7. What does this psalm teach us about God's compassion?
8. What does this psalm teach us about the nations?
9. How does this psalm point us to Jesus?
10. Take a few moments to pray with the psalmist, praying desperately, honestly, and confidently to God.

Bless His Holy Name

PSALM 103

Main Idea: In this beloved hymn of praise, the psalmist blesses the Lord for the many redemptive benefits displayed to God's people.

I. What Benefits! Forgiven, Healed, Redeemed, Crowned, Satisfied (103:1-5)
II. The Lord's Character: Righteousness and Justice, Grace and Mercy, Magnified (103:6-10)
III. The Father's Love—like Immeasurable Distances—So High and Wide (103:11-14)
IV. The King's People, though Feeble, because His Love Endures, They Will Survive (103:15-19).
V. Bless the Lord, in Heaven and on Earth; Bless the Lord, O My Soul, and Be Revived (103:20-22)!

A few years ago I (Tony) traveled with a group to Nigeria. One night our local leader introduced me to a Nigerian minister. His Nigerian name was difficult to pronounce, so the leader gave me its meaning: "bless his name." I was a bit jealous of that! I said, "It's nice to meet you, Reverend Bless His Name!"

In Psalm 103 David calls himself and others to bless the Lord for the many redemptive benefits the Lord has displayed to his people. This psalm introduces a series of psalms of praise grouped together in Psalms 103–107 (Allen, *Psalms 101–150*, 21).

David begins and ends the psalm by preaching to himself about the need to praise God, using the expression "My soul" (103:1-2,22b). This inward dialogue, or "gospel self-talk," appears in various places in the Psalms (Pss 42; 43; 62:5; 116:7; 146:1). In Psalm 42 the psalmist preaches to the downcast soul; in Psalm 103 David focuses on the mind and memory in this self-exhortation.

We too may shake off gloom and apathy by reminding ourselves about the nature and work of God. When we think rightly about God and consider his grace, it engenders gratitude. If we aren't praising God truly, we aren't thinking about God rightly and deeply.

In between these self-talk bookends (vv. 3-22a), David preaches to the community and to all creation. With echoes from the book of Exodus, David reminds everyone about who God is and what God has done. He provides numerous reasons to bless the Lord. So then, while he begins with himself, this psalm isn't individualistic. It's personal *and* communal, just like authentic Christianity is.

Inspired by H. F. Lyte's famous hymn, "Praise, My Soul, the King of Heaven," I put together a few lines to serve as our outline:

> What benefits! Forgiven, healed, redeemed, crowned, satisfied;
> The Lord's character: righteousness and justice, grace and
>   mercy, magnified;
> The Father's love—like immeasurable distances—so high and
>   wide;
> The King's people, though feeble, because his love endures,
>   they will survive;
> Bless the Lord, in heaven and on earth; bless the Lord, oh my
>   soul, and be revived!

My son Joshua said I don't need to write a poem about this psalm since it's already a poem in the Bible! I told him that I wrote it not to impress but to help us remember this amazing psalm. I'm trying to draw attention in particular to the glory of God's *complexity*. God is the Loving One, Judge, Father, and King. Some people have a one-dimensional vision of God. But Psalm 103 shows that God is each of these. And if we don't hold each of his attributes together, we will end up with an errant view of God. Motyer comments: "The blend of changeless fatherly care and endless sovereign rule is the distinctive stress of this psalm" (*New Bible Commentary*, 552).

What Benefits! Forgiven, Healed, Redeemed, Crowned, Satisfied
PSALM 103:1-5

David begins exciting his affections with a threefold call to bless the Lord (vv. 1-2). Twice he calls his "soul" to bless the Lord. He knows the Lord, whose name is "holy," deserves *whole-person worship*—"all that is within me" (v. 1). The psalm begins with a call to our inmost being, and it ends with a fourfold call to the uttermost of beings (vv. 20-22).

David adds, "Do not forget all his benefits," which is the first phrase of many that echo Moses (cf. Deut 6:12; 8:11). It's vitally important for believers to remember the blessings of God and to live in constant gratitude to God. Ingratitude flows from an arrogant heart and is something we should repent of (see, for example, Hezekiah in 2 Chr 32:35). We often talk about the "benefits package" when discussing jobs. If you do the work, you get the package. Here, we find undeserving people receiving the most important and most glorious benefits package ever! These benefits don't come from a heavenly employer but a heavenly Father. Consider this list of "hymnic participles" (Allen, *Psalms 101–150*, 19): "forgives . . . heals . . . redeems . . . crowns . . . satisfies" (vv. 3-5). What benefits! We need to remind ourselves of these blessings constantly, for David tells us that by doing so we will experience eagle-like spiritual renewal (v. 5b).

Scripture shows us numerous examples of the how the Lord **forgives** and **heals**. In the days of Moses, rebellious Israel certainly needed to be forgiven of wicked idolatry (Exod 32). In the days of David, the king certainly needed pardon (e.g., 2 Sam 11; Ps 51). In our day we need forgiveness repeatedly. In Psalm 25 David reminds us of the God-glorifying nature of divine forgiveness: "Lord, for the sake of your name, forgive my iniquity, for it is immense" (Ps 25:11; cf. v. 18). God forgives, and God gets the glory for that.

In the exodus narrative God declares that he is "the Lord who heals" (Exod 15:26). From the story of the paralytic in Mark 2, we learn that Jesus both forgives and heals (Mark 2:1-12). He prioritizes forgiveness and previews the day in which all the lame will be healed in the new heavens and new earth. In his kindness the Great Physician sometimes provides a foretaste of that great day by touching the sick and restoring their health.

In thinking of David's sin with Bathsheba, we find a difference between the way God forgives and the way God heals (Kidner, *Psalms 73–150*, 364). God granted forgiveness to David immediately, but the healing of his son was denied (2 Sam 12:13-14). God invites sinners to repent and find immediate forgiveness. But while sinners may fast and pray for healing, they aren't necessarily granted it. The timing for healing is up to God, and sometimes that means healing is delayed until the life to come (Wilcock, *Message*, 118). But this shouldn't discourage the believer. Instead, it should point us to what matters most: *our relationship with God*. Sin *destroys our relationship with God*, but God stands ready to forgive (Neh 9:27); sickness may *deepen our relationship with God* (Rom 8:23; Heb 5:8; 12:11), and in seeking healing and strength, we enjoy the grace of knowing God better (Phil 3:10-11).

Next, David reminds us that the Lord **redeems** our lives from the pit (Ps 103:4). At one level this expression could refer to rescue from deadly dangers in life, but David probably has in mind the idea of being rescued from death itself (resurrection). We find examples of this longing in Psalm 49 (vv. 7-9,13-15) and Psalm 16:9-11. As we widen our gaze even more to the New Testament, the redemption experienced through Jesus Christ gives us an even greater appreciation for the Lord who redeems sinners from the pit (Rom 3:24; Col 1:13-14).

The Lord not only redeems us but also **crowns** us, exalting us by granting us undeserved royalty. Even though we deserve humiliation because of our sin, our gracious Redeemer makes us part of his royal family. Such an act is attributed to the Lord's "faithful love and compassion" (v. 4b). It's not attributed to our goodness, faithfulness, or achievements. In our culture one gets crowned for exceptional performance; in the kingdom of God, we get crowned because of Jesus's performance and his bestowal of grace (Eph 2:7).

David rounds out the opening section by reminding himself and the community that the Lord **satisfies** and **renews** his people (103:5). He satisfies us with the best of things—that is, forgiveness and a right relationship with him. He satisfies our thirst for joy, meaning, significance, and beauty. Like a strong eagle, he renews our spirits (Isa 40:31), as we ponder who he is and what he has done for us. The eagle is a picture of tireless strength—quite a picture of renewal!

The Lord's Character: Righteousness and Justice, Grace and Mercy, Magnified
PSALM 103:6-10

After speaking of the Lord's goodness (vv. 2-5), David now reflects on more attributes of God. He makes a general statement first, with a probable allusion to Israel's bondage to Egypt (v. 6). The Lord doesn't tolerate injustice but executes perfect righteousness and justice. His rule is just and righteous, and he rights wrongs. The Lord's righteousness "is the stamp of all his actions" (Moyter, *New Bible Commentary*, 552). He considers the plight of the oppressed, comes to their aid, and deals with the oppressors justly.

In verse 7 David reflects on the works and ways of the Lord revealed to Moses. These works weren't limited to the exodus miracles but occurred throughout the wilderness experience and at Mount Sinai. Through this journey the Lord trained his people (Kidner, *Psalms 73–150*, 366; cf. Deut 8:2).

Verse 8 contains an almost direct quote of Exodus 34:6-7. After Israel worshiped the golden calf in wicked idolatry, the Lord spoke these words about himself. The Lord passed before Moses, revealing his name/character to him. David summarizes the Lord's self-portrait with four attributes: "The LORD is compassionate and gracious, slow to anger and abounding in faithful love" (Ps 103:8). These four perfections are repeated throughout the Scriptures (cf. Pss 86:15; 145:8; Neh 9:17; Jer 3:12; Joel 2:13). This statement, given first to Moses, is one of the most important statements in Scripture about the character of God.

God defines who he is. No one else gets to decide what he's like. He revealed himself to us. We must resist the temptation of worshiping the God of our imaginations; instead, we must worship the God of revelation.

Further, David doesn't pull this statement out of the air. He proceeds to list four corresponding acts of God that are tied to these attributes of God (vv. 9-10). God didn't simply say that he is merciful and compassionate; he shows that he is! As you read the book of Exodus, for example, you find this to be the case.

Contrast this with Islam for a moment. In the Quran, each of the 114 chapters (with one exception) begins like this: "In the name of Allah, the Merciful, the Compassionate." While Allah may be called this, he deals with people on the basis of their performance, not according to grace. One may call Allah "merciful and compassionate," but does he actually show mercy and compassion in the Quran itself? No. The Bible is clear about the nature of God. He is Redeemer. He is Forgiver. He is the Loving One. These attributes are displayed with *actions* throughout Scripture and across human history. He has dealt with us on the basis of grace. God revealed the magnitude of his love by sending his Son to die for sinners (cf. Rom 5:8). He didn't merely declare that he is gracious; he demonstrated it!

In verse 9 "accuse" translates a term used for disputes and for nursing grievances (Kidner, *Psalms 73–150*, 366). The Lord is justly angry at sin, but he doesn't maintain his anger forever. Have you known people who just look for reasons to be angry? They nurse grievances.

They stay mad all the time. God isn't like that, though he actually has good reasons for being angry. Marvel at the reluctance of his anger (Duncan, "Grace").

Recently, my (Tony's) favorite basketball team, the University of Kentucky Wildcats, played the Duke Blue Devils. The Cats triumphed, and this game was particularly sweet for me since two Duke fans watched the game with me! One of these guys happens to live with me (only the gospel could bring us together!). I told this "Dukey" that the replay would be shown all week long in the living room. It would be a festival of sorts.

Now, why do UK fans dislike Duke so much? There are many reasons, but it began in the days of Duke superstar Christian Laettner. In 1992 he played a perfect game against UK and did so with his typical bully-like behavior. In the final seconds, he beat UK with an unbelievable shot, which sports networks repeatedly play during basketball season. The sentence "I still hate Laettner" appears today in documentaries and on T-shirts. My son even went around class the day after our recent victory over Duke telling his classmates, "I still hate Laettner." This funny example illustrates the idea of "keeping your anger forever." Kentucky fans can't let it go.

Do you have ongoing bitterness or anger against someone? How would you fill in the blank, "I still hate _____"? Learn from the character of God here. He is slow to anger and abounding in steadfast love; he doesn't keep his anger forever. Praise God!

Further, in God's mercy, he "has not dealt with us as our sins deserve or repaid us according to our iniquities" (v. 10). This truth reminds us of Psalm 130, where we read that if God kept a record of our iniquities, we couldn't even stand up (130:3-4). Can you imagine if all of your sins were displayed for all to see? Today people talk about police wearing cameras in order to hold them accountable. Imagine if we had cameras on us at all times, and people could just watch us all the time (a recent novel called *The Circle* includes this kind of concept). Here's the deal: God knows it all. We hide nothing from the One who matters most, yet he doesn't deal with us according to our sins! He doesn't give us what we deserve! Kidner says that God tempers not only his wrath (103:9) but also his justice (v. 10)—and that at great cost to himself, as the New Testament reveals in the death of Christ (*Psalms 73–150*, 366). In his holiness God dealt with our sin; in his love, he provided his Son as atonement.

Bless his holy name for such patience, mercy, and grace. May the Lord empower us to imitate his mercy with others! May the Lord make us slow to anger and abounding in love for others!

The Father's Love—like Immeasurable Distances—So High and Wide
PSALM 103:11-14

How can one describe God's great love? David attempts to use immeasurable distances to get the point across. Paul does something similar in the New Testament (Eph 3:18-19). First, David goes **vertical** (v. 11; cf. 36:5; 57:10; Isa 55:9). Words fail to convey the magnitude of God's love. So the massive love of God, the loyal love of God, displayed to unworthy Israel is compared to the grandeur of the heavens. Whenever you look into the clear blue skies or behold a distant star, remind yourself that God's mercy is greater still (Williams, *Psalms 73–150*, Kindle).

In Jesus's high priestly prayer, he prayed that believers would experience the greatness of God's love (Duncan, "Grace"). He asked the Father that the world would know the Father loves us even as he loves the Son (John 17:23). We're in Christ, so we're loved with a love that surpasses explanation. For all eternity we will marvel at the magnitude of God's love.

Be warned, though, that this love must not be taken lightly. Recipients of this love respond in awe and holy respect. We read of this response three times in the psalm with the phrase "those who fear him" (vv. 11,13,17; cf. 34:79; 85:9; 102:15; Rom 8:28). Don't presume upon God's love; stand amazed by it. Respond with a life of worship and obedience (Rom 12:1-2).

The Lord's pardoning love for Israel needs another directional illustration, so David goes **horizontal**, east to west (v. 12; cf. 139:9-10). Remind yourself daily of the comprehensiveness of God's forgiveness (Isa 43:25; Mic 7:19).

Some wounded people constantly bring up past offenses. They play the "past offense trump card" in present conflicts. David tells us here that God—though his memory is perfect and is never at fault—never plays this card. He doesn't say to forgiven people, "Do you remember that time you turned your back on me? Do you remember that time you ate that fruit?" (Duncan, "Grace"). Praise God, he removes our sin as far as the east is from the west!

Once again, we need only look at the New Testament to have an even greater appreciation for the immeasurable love of God, which we experience in Jesus Christ. The Savior has removed our guilt. There is no condemnation. We are free and forgiven forever. May our gracious Savior enable us to forgive others the way we have been forgiven (Eph 4:32)!

From great distances David turns to the Lord's **nearness** (vv. 13-14). The Lord not only liberates us but also draws us in as family. The Hebrew word for "compassion" here (translated sometimes as "pity") is an emotional, visceral word. It conveys the deep feeling of a true parent (Kidner, *Psalms 73–150*, 366). Isaiah uses it to speak of motherly love (cf. Isa 49:15). It's also used in 1 Kings 3:26 in a story displaying the emotional intensity of a mother. God isn't distant and detached but filled with emotion for his kids. The prodigal son narrative illustrates the Father's emotional compassion (Luke 15:20).

The Lord adopted Israel (Rom 9:4). He made them his children. The New Testament unpacks the doctrine of adoption even more gloriously (Rom 8:12-17; Gal 4:4-7). J. I. Packer states, "Adoption is the highest privilege that the gospel offers" (*Knowing God*, 206). Such a privilege should cause us to praise God (1 John 3:1). Even if your earthly father wasn't or isn't compassionate to you, your Abba Father is. If your earthly father was or is compassionate toward you, it's only a shadow of the heavenly Father's compassion (Duncan, "Grace").

The next verse magnifies another feature regarding the Father's tender love. The Father knows us completely, yet he still loves us! If you ever think no one knows you, he does. He who knows us the best, loves us the most. While the Father calls us to holiness, he knows our weaknesses. He knows that we are but "dust" (v. 14; cf. Gen 2:7; 3:19). We're broken, needy sinners, but we're still loved. Lest we doubt such love, we need only look to the cross (Gal 2:20). There we're reminded that we're more broken than we've realized but more loved than we have ever dreamed.

The King's People, though Feeble, because His Love Endures, They Will Survive
103:15-19

The psalmist now considers an even broader vision of God. He considers the everlasting nature of God in verses 17-18 and portrays him in verse 19 as the great King over all. He also reminds us of our frail state in verses 15-16 and of the hope we have in the everlasting love of God. Sir Robert Grant's classic hymn, "O Worship the King," is more associated with Psalm 104 than Psalm 103, but one stanza reflects this section of the latter:

> Frail children of dust, and feeble as frail,
> In thee do we trust, nor find thee to fail;
> Thy mercies how tender, how firm to the end,
> Our Maker, Defender, Redeemer, and Friend.

Regarding our transient nature, in verses 15-16 the psalmist says that, like a wildflower, we flourish, but we fade (cf. Matt 6:28-30; Isa 40:6-7; Job 14:2); like the grass we're here, and then we're gone (cf. Pss 90:6; 92:7; Isa 51:12). If we're so fleeting and fragile, what hope do we have? The next two verses tell us.

Our God endures. His love is permanent. In Psalm 90:2 we read, "From eternity to eternity, you are God." Here in Psalm 103:17-18, God's everlasting love shines with glory. Our lives are brief and unpredictable. God's steadfast love lasts forever. His righteousness is unchanging. All who respond to him in fear—that is, those who know him in a covenant relationship, who live under his Word—have the assurance that they will dwell with him forever.

Have your friends ever let you down? Have you ever been betrayed or forgotten? People will let you down and hurt you, sometimes even when they don't intend to do so (Duncan, "Grace"). David tells us God never lets his people down. He never betrays his people. He will not ever. From eternity to eternity, he is our faithful, loyal Father.

This promise of life forever with God is also held out to the generations to come, to "grandchildren" (v. 17b). Mary declared, "His mercy is from generation to generation on those who fear him" (Luke 1:50). Though our lives are transient, and though salvation is ultimately owing to the mercy and grace of God, we can impact the coming generations by living godly lives and by faithfully teaching the gospel (cf. Exod 34:7a; Pss 100:5; 102:28).

In verse 19 the psalmist takes up the subject of God's kingship. Psalms 93–100 expound this theme powerfully. Marvel at the breadth of his kingship. He rules over all. Because our God is King, he deserves wholehearted worship and total allegiance. Because he rules over all, we can rest peacefully. Spurgeon rightly says, "This matchless sovereignty is the pledge of our security, the pillar upon which our confidence may safely lean" (*Treasury*, vol. 2, 282).

Bless the Lord, in Heaven and on Earth; Bless the Lord, O My Soul, and Be Revived!

PSALM 103:20-22

David concludes his meditation by calling on all of heaven and earth to praise God. He gives a fourfold call to praise in verses 20-22.

With language similar to Psalm 148:1-4, he begins by addressing the angelic host (v. 20). These supernatural beings surround the throne and do the Lord's bidding. They worship him day and night and obey his word (cf. Luke 1:11,19; 2:9).

The angelic armies of God are part of the celestial court (v. 21; Luke 2:13; Matt 26:53). They exist to do *the Lord's will* for his glory. Jesus echoes this idea in the Lord's Prayer (Matt 6:10), saying that we should pray for God's will to be done "on earth *as it is in heaven*" (emphasis added). So then, this angelic army serves as an example to us. We exist to do God's will for God's glory.

Next, the psalmist calls the rest of creation to follow suit (v. 22a). In Jesus's triumphal entry to Jerusalem, the people declared, "Blessed is the King who comes in the name of the Lord!" (Luke 19:38). The Pharisees were upset by this action and told Jesus to rebuke his disciples. Do you remember what Jesus said to them? He said, "I tell you, if they were to keep silent, the stones would cry out" (Luke 19:40). Creation exists to magnify the King.

Finally, David returns to his original audience, namely, himself: "My soul, bless the LORD!" (v. 22b). Thus every creature in heaven and on earth, including himself, is charged with the same assignment: to bless the Lord. In light of who he is and what he has done, how could we not join in this chorus of praise?

Learn the importance of reflecting on the character and work of the Lord so that you may truly and deeply bless the Lord.

Reflect and Discuss

1. What does this psalm teach us about both the personal and the communal nature of our faith?
2. What does it mean to preach the gospel to myself? Why is this beneficial?

3. This psalm shows that statements about God's *attributes* correspond with God's *actions* in history. Why is this significant?
4. Why is an eagle a fitting analogy for spiritual renewal? How do we experience such renewal?
5. Go back and read Exodus 34. Consider the surrounding context. How does this context shed light on Psalm 103?
6. How are the characteristics of God revealed in Psalm 103 reflected in Jesus's life and ministry?
7. How should you imitate in your own life and ministry the characteristics of God revealed in Psalm 103?
8. What does this psalm teach us about our weaknesses? How does this impact you?
9. What does this psalm teach us about the permanence of God's love? How does this encourage you?
10. What does this psalm teach us about God's sovereignty? What are the implications of his sovereignty for your life?

How Great Thou Art

PSALM 104

Main Idea: In this hymn of praise, the psalmist celebrates the way the created order glorifies the Creator.

I. **The Lord Is Clothed in Splendor and Majesty (104:1-4).**
II. **The Lord Rules the Land and the Waters (104:5-9).**
III. **The Lord Provides for His Creation (104:10-18).**
    A. The springs and the rain (104:10-13)
    B. Mankind in the midst of creation (104:14-15)
    C. Homes for creatures (104:16-18)
IV. **The Lord Governs the Rhythm of Day and Night (104:19-24).**
V. **The Lord Delights in His Creatures (104:25-26).**
VI. **The Lord Gives and Takes Away (104:27-30).**
VII.**The Lord's Glory Endures Forever (104:31-35).**

The famous British philosopher Bertrand Russell sadly stated the result of a godless worldview: "There is darkness without and when I die there will be darkness within. There is no splendor, nor vastness anywhere; only triviality for a moment and then nothing" (in Piper, *When I Don't Desire God*, 198). Contrast his words with those of theologian John Calvin, who said, "The world is a theatre of God's glory." The reformer also credited the creation of the world to *God's goodness*:

> Moreover, if it be asked what cause induced him to create
> all things at first, and now inclines him to preserve them, we
> shall find that there could be no other cause than his own
> goodness. (Calvin, *Institutes*, 2007, 1.5.6.)

Indeed, in the Genesis account we read repeatedly that the Lord saw his creation and declared that it was "good." Psalm 104 reveals much about the goodness of God and the glory of God, which should win our affections to God.

So let's think about one of the most astonishing things God has ever done: create the world. And what a world it is! It is full of splendor and beauty because it reflects the splendor and beauty of God!

Psalm 104 begins and ends the same way Psalm 103 begins and ends—with an inward call to "bless the Lord." In Psalm 103 David focuses on *redemption*, but the unnamed author of Psalm 104 focuses on *creation* as the subject of his self-exhortation. With wonder and detail, the psalmist reflects on the Creator King in order to stir his own soul to worship. He reflects in particular on how God enjoys his creation and how he invites us to enjoy the world and to glorify him.

We should indeed reflect on creation deeply in order to worship our Creator joyfully and gratefully. In verse 34 the psalmist says, "May my meditation be *pleasing to him*; I will rejoice *in the LORD*" (emphasis added). The psalmist is meditating on *God* as he considers the breadth and variety and detail of God's creation. A lot of people today are attracted to creation but often fail to meditate on *the Creator*. Paul teaches in Romans 1 that many worship created things rather than Creator—to their own destruction. We should instead join the psalmist in meditating on God and rejoicing in God while reflecting on his amazing creation.

Psalm 104 contains many echoes of the account of the days of creation in Genesis 1 (see Kidner's breakdown, *Psalms 73–150*, 368), and there's also an overlap in vocabulary. But there are some differences. Genesis 1 is logical and schematic, whereas Psalm 104 is exuberant and free and employs a rich vocabulary (Allen, *Psalms 101–150*, 31). There's also a difference in order. Psalm 104 mentions animals and mankind earlier than the account in Genesis 1 (ibid.). Finally, there's a difference in how much is said about each day of creation (Wilcock, *Message*, 121). However, the most significant difference may be that Genesis 1 reflects on the beginning of creation; Psalm 104 celebrates *the way creation works presently* (ibid., 122).

Often scholars bring up the similarity between Psalm 104 and Egyptian sun hymns, like the "Hymn to Aten" (see Allen, *Psalms 101–150*, 29–31). But Psalm 104 worships the Maker of the sun, not the sun. If the psalm is alluding to one or more of these ancient sun hymns, the reason may be for making that point. In other words, the message is this: don't worship the sun; worship the Maker of the sun! Again, the focus of one's meditation on creation must not culminate with marveling at created things but with rejoicing in Creator God.

I (Tony) love the psalmist's account of creation because today there are endless debates around Genesis 1. These debates are important, but what tends to happen when we constantly debate things like the age of the earth and the length of a day is that the grandeur of creation gets lost. Consequently, the greatness of God gets lost. Psalm 104, as a poet's version of creation, stirs up our souls with awe and wonder. Don't just debate creation; celebrate creation!

Further, the focus on the way the creation *presently* works stands out as a practical feature of this psalm, which supplies us with needed motivation to get outside daily and behold the wonders of creation. It also shows us why all of the things we see exist, namely, to glorify God. In Psalm 148 the psalmist says, "Praise him, sun and moon; praise him, all you shining stars. Praise him, the highest heavens, and you waters above the heavens" (148:3-4). Do you talk like this? "Come on, you bright yellow sun, praise God! Praise God you big blue sky! Praise God you little spider!" Creation reveals the incomparable wisdom of God, the unrivaled power of God, and the breathtaking goodness of God. Learn to see it!

Let's join the psalmist now in meditating on the greatness of God. Since the Creator is the primary focus of the psalmist, I will begin each section of this exposition with reference to him.

The Lord Is Clothed in Splendor and Majesty
PSALM 104:1-4

After preaching to his own soul, the psalmist declares, "LORD my God, you are very great" (v. 1). This expression sets the tone for the rest of the psalm. The following verses magnify God's greatness. The psalmist calls God "my God," showing that only a person in a relationship with God will view God as great and greatly to be praised.

The psalmist then uses metaphors to convey the glory and power of God. As a sign of God's royalty, the Lord is "clothed with majesty and splendor." The King's splendor is conveyed with similar language elsewhere in the Psalter (cf. Pss 8:1; 21:5; 93:1; 96:6).

God's divine glory is expressed with the phrase, "He wraps himself in light as if it were a robe." Recall that John tells us that "God is light and there is absolutely no darkness in him" (1 John 1:5). Light is vital to life, hence we read about it in day one of creation (Gen 1:3-5); God is covered in light. He is full of light and life, and he gives life to all his creation.

Verses 2b-4 echo day two of creation. The psalmist says that God spreads out the sky "like a canopy," which transitions his focus from Creator to creation. God made the heavens and controls them.

VanGemeren comments, "As a camper pitches his tent somewhere, so God without exertion prepared the earth for habitation" ("Psalms," 658).

Next, God lays "the beams of his palace on the waters above" (v. 3). The word for "palace" is used again in verse 13: "He waters the mountains from his palace." Kidner says, "The dizzy height of 'the waters above the firmament,' or the clouds, is pictured as but the base of God's abode" (*Psalms 73–150*, 369). God is enthroned above the waters above the firmament (cf. Gen 1:7; Pss 29:3; 148:4). With this choice location, the poet expresses how God is involved with, yet separated from, the world (Amos 9:6).

With more poetic exuberance, the psalmist adds that God makes "the clouds his chariot, walking on the wings of the wind" (v. 3b). God, not Baal, drives the clouds, as a driver directs his chariot! Remember that Jesus was taken up from earth in a cloud (Acts 1:9) and will return "in clouds with great power and glory" (Mark 13:26). "Walking on the wings of the wind" also expresses God's sovereignty over nature and symbolically conveys God's transcendence.

God not only directs the winds but also rules over the angels. The psalmist says that God makes "the winds his messengers, flames of fire his servants" (v. 4). Modern translations take this phrase to describe God's rule over nature. But many scholars prefer to interpret it as referring to the angelic host, viewing the sentence the other way around—that is, God "makes his messengers [angels] winds, his ministers a flaming fire" (ESV). Kidner says that this suits the Hebrew word order better and that Hebrews 1:7 quotes it with this meaning (*Psalms 73–150*, 369). The implication is that God is also ruling his angelic hosts, who are wrapped in light and assume the form of the wind and lightning (ibid.). Williams asks, "Is it possible that these angelic presences account for the wind and fire on the Day of Pentecost?" (*Psalms 73–150*, Kindle). We should also consider how Hebrews 1 contrasts the angels with the greater glory of the enthroned Son of God!

The first four verses show us why the psalmist begins saying, "LORD my God, you are very great."

The Lord Rules the Land and the Waters
PSALM 104:5-9

Having considered days one and two of creation, the psalmist now considers day three: the formation of land (cf. Gen 1:9-10; Job 38:8-11). God "established the earth on its foundations; it will never be shaken" (v. 5). This is a poetic way of describing the security of God's creation. The waters covered the whole earth (v. 6; cf. Gen 1:2), forming a vast "deep," like a garment to be worn. The foundations of the earth were present but weren't separated from the waters. But then the waters receded at God's thunderous "rebuke" (v. 7). Mark may have had this verse in mind when he spoke of Jesus rebuking the wind (Mark 4:39).

The psalmist continues, "Mountains rose and valleys sank—to the place you established for them" (v. 8). Translations of this verse vary. VanGemeren prefers the NIV: "They flowed over the mountains, they went down into the valleys, to the place you assigned for them" ("Psalms," 660). In other words, the waters flowed over the mountains as the land appeared and went down into the valleys as streams coursing toward the sea. The "place appointed for them" (author's translation) shows God's sovereign control over them. The waters are held within bounds (v. 9a) that they may "never cover the earth again" (v. 9b). They may rage against the shore, but they cannot cross it so as to overwhelm the entire earth again (Goldingay, Psalms, 186).

From these verses we see God ruling his creation. The waters are no threat to God's sovereignty. God brings order out of chaos. He controls that which people fear, including the waters. He established a place for the waters; he sets the boundaries for the waters; and he reigns over the waters. In the New Testament we see that authority displayed by Jesus. In light of his sovereign power, we should trust in him wholeheartedly in times of personal chaos and disorder.

The Lord Provides for His Creation
PSALM 104:10-18

The Springs and the Rain (104:10-13)

Even though the waters have gone to the seas, God still provides the needed moisture for the earth. In verses 10-12 we marvel at the Creator's gentle care for his creatures. He not only creates them but also, as these verses show, sustains them. The Lord provides the water they need. The psalmist is apparently reflecting on the splendor of mountain rain with its impact on the plant and animal life (VanGemeren, "Psalms," 661). In God's causing springs to gush, the psalmist highlights God's control and care. The Lord not only prevents the waters from being dangerous but also puts them safely into a reservoir to serve creation (Goldingay, *Psalms*, 187).

These waters give life to "every wild beast" (v. 11a). The psalmist draws attention to "the wild donkeys" in particular, who "quench their thirst" with God's life-giving water.

At the same time, these waters supply the needs of the birds and provide for the growth of the trees (v. 12). In response to God's provision, the birds can peacefully sing among the branches (cf. Matt 6:26; 13:32).

In verse 13 we see that the creation is "satisfied" with the Lord's work of sustaining the world. Williams says, "He opens the windows and sends the showers" (*Psalms 73–150*, Kindle). VanGemeren marvels as well: "His watering is as effortless as that of a man watering plants or irrigating a garden" ("Psalms," 661). Goldingay quips, "Yhwh is acting as a celestial sprinkler operative" (*Psalms*, 187).

Behold, then, how God cares for his creation. He satisfies and sustains his creatures. As you observe nature personally, consider how he does all this, and make it an occasion to praise God. Allow these creatures to lead you in worship! You should also make it an occasion to rekindle your trust in God, for if he cares for the birds, how much more will he care for us (Matt 6:26)? In the words of Peter, entrust your soul to "a faithful Creator" (1 Pet 4:19).

Mankind in the Midst of Creation (104:14-15)

The psalmist continues to think about the Lord's providence, turning his attention to mankind in the midst of creation. The thought of water naturally flows to a description of the growth of vegetation (the second part of day three of creation, Gen 1:11-13). God provides for mankind both indirectly and directly. Indirectly, the Lord provides food for cattle (v. 14a). By so doing, he provides for man. These creatures aren't wild but exist for mankind. Then directly, the Lord provides "food" for mankind (v. 14b; cf. Gen 1:29).

Because of the Lord's work in creation, humans (day six of creation) are able to "cultivate" the land (v. 14). Man is thus set apart from the animal kingdom. Humans are farmers, not merely gatherers (cf. v. 28). God provides vegetation (e.g., grain, the vine, and the olive tree), and man has the ability to create things from these crops. Humans are made in God's image; part of our uniqueness is the ability to create things, reflecting our Creator. God made us *makers*.

Further, these gifts of God—wine, oil, and bread—are expressions of God's *goodness* (cf. Deut 7:13). The whole psalm shows his goodness. Here in particular we see that the Lord in his goodness gives bread for our sustenance (Gen 18:5), wine to lift the spirits (Judg 9:13; Eccl 10:19), and oil to protect, cleanse, and beautify the skin (Ps 92:10; Luke 7:46). These were basic products in the biblical period. From God's provision of these things, we see that God gives us what we need to survive, but in his goodness he also gives us things to *enjoy*.

Recall that Jesus's first miracle involved turning water into wine at a wedding! God is not a cosmic killjoy. He's the giver of all good things (Jas 1:17). We should eat, drink, and bathe to the glory of God, who "richly provides us with all things to enjoy" (1 Tim 6:17). We must avoid all abuses of God's gifts—gluttony (Prov 23:20-21; Titus 1:12), drunkenness (Titus 1:7; 2:3), addictions, and conceit. Kill these sins. Pursue self-control (Gal 5:23). Spiritual maturity involves enjoying and using God's gifts with self-control and responsibility and not as an end in themselves. The ultimate end is to enjoy the gifts of God with gratitude to God (1 Tim 4:3-5).

God could have made a world that was boring and mechanical. All food could have tasted like rice cakes, and we could just drink water all the time. But God created us with palates, and he created plants to cultivate, meat to eat, bread to nourish, wine to enjoy, and oil to refresh us. We enjoy all of this now, even though the world is under the curse. One day the curse will be reversed and paradise will be restored, and we will enjoy the new creation with our King Jesus (Rev 21:1-7). Here's to that day!

Homes for Creatures (104:16-18)

The psalmist moves from grass and food to the trees. The Lord planted and sustains trees in Lebanon. The region of Lebanon was proverbial for its cedars. God gives the birds homes in these majestic trees (v. 17). The psalmist includes the "stork" as an example who builds her home in the "pine trees" (v. 17b, "junipers," NIV). The juniper was another tall, impressive tree that flourished in Lebanon (Goldingay, *Psalms*, 188). Then there are the hills, which serve as homes to "wild goats," with the cliffs serving as refuge for "hyraxes" (v. 18).

One of the problems with the technological age is that many spend too much time looking at a screen and not enough time looking at creation. Let's embrace the value of beholding the works of the Lord.

The Lord Governs the Rhythm of Day and Night
PSALM 104:19-24

Our attention now shifts to the regularity of the created world. The psalmist teaches us that the Lord governs the sun and moon (day four of creation, Gen 1:14-19). The psalmist gives examples of some common patterns in creation related to the sun and moon. He once again highlights the fact that the moon is not God, nor is the sun. God rules over them (v. 19). At night the "animals stir." When the sun rises, they return to their dens. Humanity's work pattern is the reverse.

The idea of the lion preying on other animals (v. 21) shows that the psalmist is accepting the way things currently work in the world. Now they have to be tamed, but in the end the lion will dwell with the lamb and eat only hay (Isa 11:6-7; Goldingay, *Psalms*, 190).

In verse 24 the psalmist pauses for a moment of worship. This verse is transitional. It looks back at all that has been said and looks forward to what is yet to come. Of particular interest to the psalmist is God's wisdom. Recall the author of Proverbs saying, "The LORD founded the earth by wisdom and established the heavens by understanding" (Prov 3:19; see 8:22-31). God's wisdom is revealed in all the ways his creatures exist and dwell under his sovereign care. They reveal the work of the Master Craftsman. We too should marvel at the wisdom of God in creation and give him glory.

The Lord Delights in His Creatures
PSALM 104:25-26

The psalmist turns our attention now to the wonder of the seas (day five of creation, Gen 1:20-23). The psalmist highlights the vastness of the seas and the innumerable creatures in these waters. I love Eugene Peterson's paraphrase:

> *What a wildly wonderful world, GOD!*
> *You made it all, with Wisdom at your side,*
> *made earth overflow with your wonderful creations.*
> *Oh, look—the deep, wide sea,*
> *brimming with fish past counting,*
> *sardines and sharks and salmon.*
> *Ships plow those waters,*
> *and Leviathan, your pet dragon, romps in them.* (vv. 24-26 *The*
> *Message*)

Indeed, it is a "wildly wonderful world, God!" And he made it all.

The mention of the ships traveling these seas obviously reveals a post-Edenic reflection on the world. This fact also draws attention to humanity as the pinnacle of creation. Man can use seas for his own purposes. Because man is a maker, being made in the image of God, he can create a vessel to cruise the dangerous waters.

As people travel the waters, they discover new creatures, and one mysterious, sportive creature is mentioned here: "Leviathan" (v. 26). The psalmist says that Leviathan was formed to "play" in the sea. We don't know what this creature was. You can imagine sailors coming back from trips trying to explain a magnificent sea creature we know, like a whale.

Some refer to this unknown creature as "God's pet" or as God's "pet dragon." Humans loving their own pets also display their being made in God's image! God created us not only for rest and work but also to play and enjoy life.

So then, from the sea monster we can observe that chaos has been tamed, and God's pets play in the seas. Job puts it this way:

> *Can you pull in Leviathan with a hook*
> *or tie his tongue down with a rope?*
> *Can you put a cord through his nose*
> *or pierce his jaw with a hook?*
> *Will he beg you for mercy*
> *or speak softly to you?*
> *Will he make a covenant with you*
> *so that you can take him as a slave forever?*
> *Can you play with him like a bird*
> *or put him on a leash for your girls?* (Job 41:1-5)

God not only rules his creation but also takes pleasure in it. John Piper unpacks this idea in his classic work, *The Pleasures of God*. Regarding the sea monster, Piper says,

> Why did God create sea monsters? Just to play, to frolic in
> the ocean where no man can see, but only God. The teeming
> ocean declares the glory of God and praises him a thousand
> miles from any human eye. (*Pleasures*, 74)

Consider that some magnificent flowers grow, display glory, and provide wonderful fragrances but will never be seen, felt, or smelled by any human. They exist for the mere pleasure of God. The psalmist doesn't know what's going on in the deep. He just knows that creatures exist for God's enjoyment and glory. There are millions of creations we will never observe—things that crawl, walk, blow bubbles, make homes, etc. that exist to glorify God. When the blue whale smacks his tail and sailors hear it three miles away, God can say, "Did you see that? I did that! That's my whale!" (Piper, "The Pleasure of God in His Creation").

Piper suggests that *Ranger Rick* magazine inspires more praise than most theological journals! This is because it records man's discovery of incredible phenomena in nature that until recently have only been enjoyed by God for thousands of years (*Pleasures*, 74). In commending this magazine, Piper is showing how creation should make the believer worship the Creator with wonder. He says, "We should pray for the eyes of children again, when they saw everything for the first time" (*Pleasures*, 76). I (Tony) read that sentence and thought about a little boy in our congregation, Jai, who brings his toy sharks with him to our gatherings. The creatures of the deep fascinate him! That's a good thing. That's a God thing.

When we behold this wildly wonderful world of God, we should shout, "How countless are your works, Lord!" (v. 24)

The Lord Gives and Takes Away
PSALM 104:27-30

God is the source of life for all creation. These verses show how the whole creation is totally dependent on God (v. 27; Gen 1:29-31). Regularly, they live in reliance on God. They "live and move and have [their] being" in God (Acts 17:28).

In verses 28-30 the poet emphasizes the Lord's actions: "You give . . . you open your hand . . . you hide . . . you take away . . . you send . . . you renew." The creation merely gathers what the Lord gives them (v. 28a). When the Lord opens his hand generously, they are filled with good things (v. 28b). This idea expresses God's common grace in the world (Matt 5:45; Ps 145:9).

However, if the Lord expresses disfavor (hides his face), perhaps through pestilence or famine, the creation is "terrified" (v. 29). Likewise, if the Lord should "take away their breath" (v. 29b), they die, returning to the dust (Gen 2:7; Job 34:15).

The Lord grants life by his life-giving spirit: "When you send forth your Spirit, they are created" (v. 30a ESV). He also preserves and renews it. Each passing generation is replaced by the next. God didn't merely create and take his hands off. He is active in sustaining his creation. God's renewing power over creation will be on full display in the new creation, and even now creation groans for that day (Rom 8:22). In the *Book of Common Prayer*, the latter part of Psalm 104 is one of the readings for the Day of Pentecost, a fitting text for reflecting on the Spirit's renewing work in the lives of people.

The Lord's Glory Endures Forever
PSALM 104:31-35

In this final section, the poet praises God with one final burst. Kidner says, "The Psalm from first to last, hallows the name of God" (*Psalms 73–150*, 372).

In verse 31 the psalmist is really praising God for something that will happen: the Lord's glory will endure forever. The heavens declare the glory of God now (Ps 19:1-2), and the glory of God will also cover the whole earth like water covers the sea (Num 14:21; Hab 2:14).

Regarding the Lord's rejoicing in his works, we see that in the beginning God declared that his creation was good. He took pleasure in creation (Gen 1:31; Prov 8:31). Commenting on Psalm 104:31, Piper says,

> God does take pleasure in his creation—things like water and clouds and wind and mountains and thunder and springs and wild asses and birds and grass and cattle and wine and bread and cedars and wild goats and badgers and rocks and young lions and sea monsters. God delights in all the works of his hands. (*Pleasures*, 66–67)

The Lord's absolute control of creation is seen in verse 32. Tumult results when he merely "looks" and "touches." The language reflects God's great glory and power (cf. Ps 144:5; Exod 19:18; Amos 9:5).

In the final three verses, we find three ways we should respond to the Lord's glory.

First, respond with songs of praise. For as long as we live, we should join creation and praise the Lord (v. 33; cf. 146:2). While we have breath, let us praise our Creator! The proper response to beholding God's glory is praise. It completes our enjoyment.

Second, respond with joyful meditation. The psalmist asks that his meditation would be sweet to God (cf. Ps 19:14), as he rejoices in who God is and what God has done. We too should reflect on this world that we may worship our God. Remember Psalm 111:2: "The LORD's works are great, studied by all who delight in them." Study God's works (i.e., the things he has made) that you may be drawn into worshiping this great God.

Third, respond with gospel hope. Almost out of nowhere, we read about sinners vanishing from the earth (v. 35). The psalmist wants the wicked gone! Why is this statement here? VanGemeren puts it well: "The psalmist is not vindictive in his prayer against the wicked but longs for a world fully established and maintained by the Lord, without outside interference" ("Psalms," 664).

This longing is really a longing for the new creation (see Rev 21:1–22:6). We must never forget that creation is tied to the gospel. Michael Bird states, "God's act of creation is the presupposition of the gospel, while the new creation is the ultimate goal of the gospel" (*Evangelical Theology*, 140). The creation will be comprehensively restored, and sinners will be no more. So then, let all who have not bowed the knee to Jesus Christ, the Lord of creation, do so now. In grace, God is able to make sinners new creations in Christ Jesus (2 Cor 5:17) so that they may later enjoy God's new creation. Then we will behold even more glory! Then we will enjoy even more of creation than we do now! My friend Nate says, "I'm going to ride dolphins in the new creation!"

As we behold the glory of creation now, allow your reflections to point you ahead toward the glory that will be revealed later. Allow this gospel hope to encourage you. Preach to yourself, "My soul, bless the LORD!" (v. 35b), as you reflect on a world with no conflicts, cancer, death, or brokenness. Such reflections can cause the most dejected to shout, "Hallelujah!" (v. 35c).

So, who is correct: Bertrand Russell or John Calvin? I prefer the latter's perspective: creation is a theater of God's glory. Behold it with wonder now and anticipate greater glory in the future. Such a hope is made possible through the redeeming work of the Lord Jesus Christ, who took the place of sinners that we may have a place in the coming kingdom. Bless his holy name.

Reflect and Discuss

1. Why would Calvin call the world "a theatre of God's glory"? How does Psalm 104 support this concept?

2. How are Psalms 103 and 104 similar? How are they different?
3. What strikes you the most about the nature of God in verses 1-4? Why?
4. How do we see the goodness of God revealed in Psalm 104?
5. Should we enjoy creation? Why or why not? If you answered yes, how should we enjoy it?
6. What are some of the ways we see the doctrine of the image of God illustrated in Psalm 104?
7. How does creation reveal God's wisdom?
8. Does God take pleasure in his creation? Explain.
9. How does this psalm show creation's dependence on God?
10. How does the psalmist teach us to respond to the glory of God's creation? How is the gospel related to creation?

Praise the Lord of History

PSALM 105

Main Idea: This historical psalm celebrates God's faithful works done on behalf of his people, reflecting primarily on episodes found in the Pentateuch.

I. **What: Worship the Lord (105:1-6).**
II. **Why: He Is the Lord of History (105:7-45).**
    A. The Lord's promise to Abraham (105:7-11)
    B. The Lord's protection and providence: from Canaan to Egypt (105:12-23)
    C. The Lord's protection: in Egypt (105:24-36)
    D. The Lord's promise fulfilled: from Egypt to Canaan (105:37-45)
III. **Wow: Marvel at the Lord of History.**

Why do you believe in Christianity? There are many answers to this commonly asked question. (I hope your church is a safe place for people to ask such questions.) While the intent of the author of Psalm 105 is not necessarily to answer this question, we do find many important answers here. The most obvious answer is that Christianity is rooted in *human history*. The characters in the Bible existed. The first coming of Christ happened. The bloody death and bodily resurrection of Jesus really took place. Christianity is married to human history. Our skeptical friends may not be persuaded of the historical record, but that shouldn't stop us from making this point. And it's a truth that should reassure believers in their faith.

Do you enjoy history? Perhaps you love it. Maybe you find it boring and uninteresting. Those who like history and those who don't are often distinguished by whether they view history as *spectators* or as *participants*. I (Tony) grew more interested in history as a student when I found myself connected to it. As an American, I find our nation's history interesting because it's my history. And even more importantly, I find biblical history interesting because I'm a Christian. If you're a Christian, the history of the people of God is *your history*. We shouldn't view redemptive history as casual observers but as active participants in the ongoing mission of the redeemed.

The following three psalms teach us much about the history of the people of God. There are both positive and negative lessons to learn (Ps 105 is positive; Ps 106 is negative). In Psalm 105 the author traces Israel's journey from God's covenant with Abraham to their possession of the promised land. In tracing this history, Allen says the psalmist has a triple goal in mind: to *inspire God's people to praise God*, to *encourage them in the faith,* and to *exhort them to live in accordance with his will* (*Psalms 101–150*, 42). Keep these goals in mind as we journey through the psalm.

The use of the psalm was appropriate for various celebrations of God's faithfulness, as in the case of David's bringing the ark to Jerusalem. First Chronicles 16:8-36 is clearly associated with Psalm 105, as the first fifteen verses of Psalm 105 are quoted in 1 Chronicles 16. The hymn should also be used as an aid in our moments of worship as we ponder God's faithfulness to us today.

Psalm 105 is a longer psalm, but it's easy to follow. The writer surveys the sequence of events from Genesis to Joshua, with the majority of time spent on the events in the Pentateuch. After providing some opening exhortations in verses 1-6 to worship God and remember his works, the writer proceeds in verses 7-45 to exalt the Lord of history, who accomplished his will in various time periods. The psalmist actually gives the application of redemptive history—*worship the Lord*—in the beginning of the psalm before unfolding the reasons for doing so. After we trace the psalm, I will collect some of the truths about God that should cause us to marvel at him.

What: Worship the Lord
PSALM 105:1-6

In verses 1-6 the psalmist calls on the people to praise God, giving a string of imperatives that call for various expressions of praise: "Give thanks, . . . call on his name; proclaim his deeds. . . . Sing to him, sing praise to him; tell about all his wonderful works! Boast in his holy name; . . . rejoice. . . . Seek. . . . Remember." These imperatives provide a rich understanding of worship.

Verses 1-2 express the *verbal acts of worship*. The redeemed should say so! They should make known the glory of God in personal praise, corporate praise, and global witness.

Verse 3 reminds us of *the gravity of worship,* as the psalmist calls us to focus on the nature of God, whose name is "holy." To boast in his name means to make his name the most important thing—in your life, work, parenting, service, prayers, recreation, rest, eating and drinking, dating, marriage, studies, and so on. All of life should be lived for the glory of his name. All our sin problems are worship problems—a failure to have God in his rightful place in our "hearts." Resist living a life of faith that focuses on knowledge and skill but is disconnected from the heart. Minister out of the overflow of a healthy, humble, happy heart.

Verse 4 draws attention to *our need for worship.* We are told to seek the Lord presently, that we may find strength. Though the psalm will describe events in the past, the psalmist emphasizes that the Lord is at work presently (cf. Eph 3:14-21). Therefore, let us seek his "face"—his presence—for we need his power, as the people of God expressed when the ark was brought into Jerusalem.

Verses 5-6 set the tone for the rest of the psalm. The writer highlights *the relationship between remembering and worship.* He urges the saints never to forget all that God has done for his people so that they will live a life of praise. The people are called to remember God's "wondrous works" and "wonders" (cf. Pss 9:1; 96:3; Deut 4:34) and his "judgments" (cf. Exod 6:6; 7:4; 12:12).

Memory is a significant part of our faith, as many of the psalms demonstrate (e.g., 103:2). Our Christian pilgrimage includes various mountain peaks where we have encountered the Lord in powerful ways. I (Tony) can remember vividly the night I submitted to the lordship of Jesus as a sophomore in college and committed my life to following him. I have never been the same. I remember packing my bags and flying to New Orleans to begin seminary. I remember pivotal events: from my first summer camp serving as a camp pastor, to the day I took Kimberly's hand in marriage, to my first Sunday as a pastor, to adopting our children, to planting our congregation and meeting for the first time on a Sunday, to baptizing my father and some of my children. These types of moments are to be remembered. Don't forget all that God has done for you! Paul tells Timothy not to forget the Savior: "Remember Jesus Christ, risen from the dead and descended from David" (2 Tim 2:8a). How could Timothy possibly forget the Savior? Paul knew that we are prone to drift away from our first love, prone to get busy with things, even good things, and slowly drift away from sweet communion with the Lord who redeemed us.

Further, each verse draws attention to *the object of worship*: the Lord. And *the subjects of worship*: the people of God. The rest of the Bible shows that all Christians today are included among the offspring of the patriarchs (Gal 3:6-9; 4:28-31). We have inherited this rich history (Kidner, *Psalms 73–150*, 374), so we can sing with the psalmist as participants in this story. It's a gift of God's grace to be able to worship him.

This string of imperatives could be used in a variety of ways. You could use them this week for personal worship, simply reading them each day, allowing them to give some structure to your praise to God. When was the last time you slowed down to remember the mighty acts of God and give him thanks and praise? Sometimes we have to force ourselves to give thanks to God because our hearts grow cold. Make yourself recount the grace of God and thank God. (We're commanded to give thanks, whether or not we feel like it!) Perhaps journaling will help you. Maybe a prayer walk will assist you, as you get outside and behold creation.

You could also use these verses for family worship. You might read a verse per night this week, asking the family to give thanks for particular blessings, to sing, and to seek the Lord's strength.

You could also use these verses in corporate worship, reading a verse and then pausing for a time of personal reflection, followed by a corporate action that corresponds with each verse.

The fact is, God's people are to be a worshiping people. Our worship centers on who God is and what God has done. Our worship is both personal and corporate. And our worship should carry over into global witnessing. For we should not only remind one another of God's deeds but also make his deeds known among the nations (105:1; cf. Pss 96; 76:7,12).

We should remember that non-Christians are also worshiping people. Humans worship what we value, serve, rejoice in, sacrifice for, and spend time/money/energy on. The big question in life is, Whom are you worshiping? The rest of the psalm will unfold *why* we should value the Lord above all.

Why: He Is the Lord of History
PSALM 105:7-45

The psalm breaks down into four main sections. In streamlined fashion the writer shows the faithful works of God in early redemptive history.

This large section of Scripture carries a note of gratitude throughout. The psalmist isn't merely teaching; he's leading people in worship to the Lord of history.

The Lord's Promise to Abraham (105:7-11)

The psalmist begins by noting the Lord's covenantal faithfulness to his people, which magnifies the grace and faithfulness of God. God protected the family line that led to the coming of Christ. These verses are the psalm's central verses, for everything else mentioned is the fulfillment of God's promise to Abraham.

The writer calls the Lord "our God" (v. 7) and says the Lord "remembers his covenant forever" (v. 8). A covenant is a "stunning blend of law and love," more intimate and loving than a contract and more enduring and binding than a personal affection alone (Keller, *Preaching*, 104). The psalmist reflects on God's covenant with Abraham, Isaac, and Jacob (vv. 9-10). We read of this covenant, this blending of law and love, in Genesis 15:18; 17:2-8; 22:16; 26:3-5; 28:13-15; and 35:12.

This covenant is described everlastingly, "for a thousand generations" (v. 8). Remembering here implies more than memory; it involves action. God actively remembered his covenant in sending his Son, Jesus, who has made us heirs of a new covenant (Luke 1:72-73). He protected this holy genealogy. If he can protect the line to Christ, he can protect us until we arrive in glory (Phil 1:6).

In verse 11 the psalmist draws particular attention to the land promise associated with the covenant. This particular aspect of God's promise is fulfilled at the end of the psalm. A promised new creation now awaits the redeemed from every tribe and tongue, when an uncountable number of people will have bowed the knee to Abraham's ultimate offspring, Christ. God's fulfilled promise of the land should give believers today great assurance of this new creation to come. God keeps his word. He speaks and he acts.

Why do you believe in Christianity? Here's another reason: the Bible is a unified book of redemptive history, a book of promises made and promises kept.

The Lord's Protection and Providence: From Canaan to Egypt (105:12-23)

This set of verses describe first how Abraham's family lived in Canaan as nomadic strangers and how they then migrated to Egypt (Wilcock,

Message, 129). The psalmist underscores God's protection of the patriarchs (vv. 12-15) and God's providence in Joseph's life (vv. 16-23).

Protection (vv. 12-15). In the beginning of Israel's history, they were "few in number" (v. 12). There weren't many members of the covenant community. They were also unstable. The psalmist says they were "resident aliens in Canaan" (v. 12b), who were "wandering" around from nation to nation, kingdom to kingdom (v. 13). For three generations they lived as nomads.

Nevertheless, the Lord protected them (v. 14). The Lord used plagues and dreams to rebuke those who threatened his people. For instance, Pharaoh (Gen 12:17), Abimelech, and his son (Gen 20:3; 26:11) did not prevail against Abraham and Isaac.

In the Lord's eyes the Hebrew people were his "anointed" (v. 15a), so he made sure they weren't touched. And the Lord guided them and guarded this band of nomads in the midst of political and moral pressures of their day. The Lord also called them "my prophets," a statement here that's generalized to apply to all three patriarchs (VanGemeren, "Psalms," 667). For more on this abbreviated history, read Genesis chapters 12–35. The psalmist covers many chapters in four verses to highlight the Lord's protection.

We should be reminded that our ultimate protection is found in the Lord as well. We may do a lot of good and wise things to protect ourselves from danger, but ultimately we rest in the Lord's protection.

Providence (vv. 16-23). The next section contains a description of God's remarkable providence. As the story line of the Bible is unfolded, the writer includes a famine next. The Lord summoned a famine (v. 16; cf. Gen 41:54), which was "destined to be the pivot of all events" (Kidner, *Psalms 73–150*, 375). But because the Lord had a good plan in mind, he sent Joseph ahead of time to Egypt (v. 17a; cf. Gen 45:5,7; 50:20).

Joseph's life was Israel in miniature; the path to glory came through suffering (Allen, *Psalms 101–150*, 43). It was also an anticipation of Jesus's life and ministry. Glory came to Jesus through suffering—suffering in many ways like Joseph. For the Christian, this too is a paradigm for us. We will reach glory only through suffering (Mark 8:31-38; Rom 8).

The psalmist reminds us that Joseph endured an unjust imprisonment and the humiliation of slavery (vv. 17b-18; cf. Gen 39:20). He dwelt in slavery until "his prediction came true" (105:19a), which is probably referring to Joseph's God-given ability to interpret dreams (Gen 40:5-23; 31:12-13). His earlier dreams included two referencing his exalted

status; these dreams proved to be God's word of promise (Gen 37:5-11).
But until "the word of the LORD" proved true, Joseph was "tested" and
tried (Ps 105:19).

Joseph endured because the Lord was with him (Gen 39:2-3,21;
Acts 7:9) as he worked out his sovereign purposes through him. In the
end, Joseph understood the big picture and rejoiced in God's providence. Here are two classic statements he made regarding them:

> *Then Joseph said to his brothers, "Please, come near me," and they
> came near. "I am Joseph, your brother," he said, "the one you sold into
> Egypt. And now don't be grieved or angry with yourselves for selling
> me here, because* God sent me ahead of you *to preserve life. For the
> famine has been in the land these two years, and there will be five more
> years without plowing or harvesting.* God sent me ahead of you *to
> establish you as a remnant within the land and to keep you alive by a
> great deliverance. Therefore* it was not you who sent me here, but
> God. (Gen 45:4-8a; emphasis added)

> *You planned evil against me; God planned it for good to bring about
> the present result—the survival of many people.* (Gen 50:20)

These verses should encourage us! The Lord will accomplish his purposes, even if the means are messy. Trust him in hard times, for he is
working out his good will for his people.

In verses 20-22 the psalmist reflects on how Joseph was released
from prison, and Pharaoh made him the "master of his household"
(Gen 41:14-40), similar to the secretary of state (VanGemeren, "Psalms,"
668). Joseph administrated all of Pharaoh's "possessions" (v. 21b; cf.
Acts 7:10). All would recognize the incredible wisdom of Joseph, and he
would be given the opportunity to instruct leaders (v. 22).

Here are more evidences of God's providence that should inspire
praise. God can work through evil kings and leaders, and God can place
his servants in strategic places to accomplish his sovereign purposes.

In God's providence, the writer says, "Israel went to Egypt," also
known as the "land of Ham" (v. 23). There they lived as "an alien" in the
land. That's how they got to Egypt: the Lord directed them there.

One of the main themes of the Bible is suffering. This should encourage us because life is filled with it! In that great theological movie, *The
Princess Bride*, the Man in Black responds to Buttercup's statement, "You
mock my pain!" by saying, "Life is pain, Highness. Anyone who says differently is selling you something."

Why do you believe in Christianity? Here's yet another reason to do so: the Bible provides the best explanation of suffering. One of the main themes of the Bible is suffering. The early chapters of Genesis describe how evil and suffering came into the world. Joseph's life was filled with suffering. The book of Exodus is about release from slavery. The Wisdom books provide reflections on suffering. The Psalms offer prayers for help in suffering. New Testament books like Hebrews and 1 Peter deal greatly with suffering. Above all, the hero of Scripture, Jesus Christ, was a man of sorrows. He was the Suffering Servant.

God isn't unaware of your suffering. Jesus can identify with you in it and provide grace for you to endure it, all with the promise of one day eradicating it. One day he will wipe away our tears.

While the problem of suffering is a turnoff for many nonbelievers, faithful Christians know that a richness and joy come only in knowing Christ in the midst of suffering (Phil 3:10). Be encouraged by the life of Joseph. God is with you. God is at work. God will accomplish his plans. Don't grow angry in suffering. Learn how to live in the midst of it by trusting, praying, fellowshipping, weeping, and hoping (see Keller, *Walking with God*).

The Lord's Protection: In Egypt (105:24-36)

In verses 24-25 the writer summarizes Exodus 1. Israel multiplied as a result of the Lord's providence, and Pharaoh's anger intensified, resulting in increased hardship for Israel. The psalmist, however, skips over any details of their hardship in Egypt because his focus is on the Lord's protection and mighty acts (VanGemeren, "Psalms," 669).

Moving on from Abraham and Joseph, we now read of Moses, the Lord's servant, and Aaron, whom the Lord had chosen to be Moses's mouthpiece (v. 26). God used both of these men, displaying his power through them (v. 27; cf. Exod 10:2; Jer 32:20). Exodus 3–4 describes this "sending" at length. The story of Moses's commission shows how God can use ordinary, weak human vessels to accomplish his purposes.

The writer then proceeds to highlight how God demonstrated his power in Egypt by noting eight of the ten plagues or "signs" and "wonders." His list is not complete, nor is it chronological. He states it in poetic form. The plagues are framed between the ninth plague (105:28) and the tenth plague (105:36), that is, between *darkness* (Exod 10:21-28) and the *death of the firstborn* (Exod 11:4-8; 12:29). Below is a chart comparing the orders in each passage (compare also Ps 78:44-51):

The Order in Exodus 7–12	The Order in Psalm 105:28-36
1. Blood	1. Darkness
2. Frogs	2. Blood
3. Gnats	3. Frogs
4. Flies	4. Flies
5. Livestock	5. Gnats
6. Boils	6. Hail
7. Hail	7. Locusts
8. Locusts	8. Death of the firstborn
9. Darkness	
10. Death of the firstborn	

The change in ordering has no bearing on the historicity of what happened in Egypt (VanGemeren, "Psalms," 670). The reason for mentioning darkness first might be because this was the decisive act for the Egyptian people. Pharaoh's counselors were advising Pharaoh to come to terms with Israel, so we read, "They did not rebel against his words" (v. 28 ESV). By the tenth plague Pharaoh surrendered.

The psalmist doesn't even mention Pharaoh; his intent is to show God's action. Notice the verbs: God "sent" darkness (v. 28); "turned" the waters into blood (v. 29); "spoke," and there came swarms of flies (v. 31); "gave" them hail (v. 32); "struck" their vines and fig trees (v. 33); "spoke," and the locusts came (v. 34); "struck" all the firstborn (v. 36). The psalmist doesn't want the people to forget what *the Lord* accomplished for them.

As God executed judgment on Egypt (and on its gods; Num 33:4), he was revealing to everyone that he alone is God. Woven throughout Exodus 7:5–11:10 is this central theme: "that they may know that I am Yahweh." This theme appears especially in the section on the plagues. God wanted both Israel (Exod 6:7) and the Egyptians (Exod 7:5) to know that he alone is worthy of worship. God's judgment, then, was mingled with mercy. Israel saw and believed and praised God. Egypt rejected Yahweh.

The Lord passed judgment on Egypt and Egypt's gods but protected his people. He protected them from threats in earth, sky, and sea. We should look to him for protection from all threats in this life.

The exodus event was the major redemptive event in the Old Testament. It's displayed in a greater way with the salvation we have now in Christ. Here's another reason to believe in Christianity: grace. Only Christianity offers free redemption. God offers new life as an expression of his grace.

The Lord's Promise Fulfilled: From Egypt to Canaan (105:37-45)

As in the case of the previous eras, the story of Israel's return to Canaan is also summarized and stated in the most positive light. The author doesn't mention the length of the journey or the sins of Israel during the forty-year wandering. The giving of the law and the tabernacle (positive elements) are also omitted. So then, what does the author include in this short summary of a long period of time?

He first highlights *the wealth and well-being of the redeemed* (vv. 37,43). The Lord not only delivered his people out of Egypt but also sent them with valuable supplies! This gold and silver provided for their needs in the promised land (Exod 3:21-22; 11:2; 12:35-36). In verse 43 he uses the verb "brought . . . out" again. When the Lord delivered them, they not only had supplies but also were filled with joy and singing.

Next the writer includes *a definite break with Egypt* (v. 38). After enduring the plagues, Egypt was happy for Israel to leave.

In addition, the psalmist notes how *the Lord graciously sustained his people with his presence, protection, and provision.* We read of the pillar of cloud and fire (v. 39; Exod 13:21-22). For 40 years the Lord demonstrated his presence with his people with these miraculous signs. The pillar of cloud and fire provided *guidance and protection* for 40 years (cf. Ps 78:14; Exod 14:19-20; Num 10:34-36).

God also miraculously provided *food and water.* God's provision included quail and bread from heaven (v. 40), along with water from the rock (v. 41; cf. Ps 78:15-16,24,27-28; Exod 16:13-16; 17:1-6)—all wonders of God's grace!

Notice the responsiveness of the Lord, as well. "They asked, and he brought . . . satisfied. . . . He opened a rock" (vv. 40-41). Not only did God meet the needs of his people, but his provision was also abundant (v. 41; cf. Isa 41:18; 48:21). There is no mention of Israel's murmuring, just the Lord's gracious activity.

Be reminded that the Lord continues to feed his people physically and spiritually through Jesus Christ and that God is not only *with* his people today but also *in* them (John 14:16-18). He continues to guide us through the presence of the Holy Spirit.

Here we may add to our list of reasons to believe: the Holy Spirit has invaded our lives. He has changed us from the inside out. He has opened our eyes to embrace Jesus for who he is—the Rock, the Bread of life, the Son of Abraham.

Moreover, the writer highlights *God's commitment to his covenant* (v. 42). Abraham was God's servant, and his descendants are called God's "chosen ones" (v. 43; cf. v. 6). God brought out his chosen ones "with rejoicing" and "shouts of joy" (v. 43) and fulfilled his word by bringing them into the promised land (v. 44). It was a land with an indigenous population of as many as seven idolatrous nations (v. 44; cf. Ps 78:55; Gen 15:19-21; VanGemeren, "Psalms," 671). Through conquest they took possession of cities, vineyards, orchards, cisterns, and various material benefits (ibid.). In Deuteronomy 6:10-12 God promises such inherited blessings but warns Israel about forgetting all his benefits, and he urges them to fear him and worship him alone (Deut 6:13-15).

That leads us to the final verse of the psalm. This is how salvation works. God saves us and grants us every spiritual blessing in Christ Jesus, but that privilege comes with a calling to holiness (1 Pet 1). It comes with a calling to live our lives under God's Word with happy submissiveness. It comes with a calling to walk after the Spirit, not after the flesh (Rom 8:4).

This is *why God's grace abounded* (v. 45; cf. 78:7). The writer notes this calling to holiness before making one concluding exhortation: "Hallelujah!"

Wow: Marvel at the Lord of History

This psalm teaches us so many truths about the Redeemer that should incite praise, provide encouragement, and propel us to holiness. Allow me to collect and apply some of the truths we have mentioned.

First, the Lord saves. Beginning with verse 8, scan the page to see what God does:

- Verse 8: "He remembers."
- Verse 9: "He made [a covenant] with Abraham."
- Verse 10: "[He] confirmed [it] to Jacob as a decree."
- Verse 14: "He allowed no one to oppress them."
- Verse 14: "He rebuked kings on their behalf."
- Verse 16: "He called down a famine against the land."
- Verse 25: "He turned [their hearts] to hate his people."

- Verse 26: "He sent Moses."
- Verse 28: "He sent darkness."
- Verse 29: "He turned their water into blood."
- Verse 31: "He spoke, and insects came."
- Verse 32: "He gave them hail."
- Verse 33: "He struck their vines."
- Verse 34: "He spoke, and locusts came."
- Verse 36: "He struck all the firstborn."
- Verse 37: "He brought Israel out."
- Verse 39: "He spread a cloud."
- Verse 41: "He opened a rock."
- Verse 42: "He remembered his holy promise."

What does all this teach us? It teaches us that "salvation belongs to the LORD" (Jonah 2:9). The Lord redeems. The Lord acts. We can't save ourselves. The Lord saves. Don't ever forget it! Marvel at his grace and favor.

Second, the Lord speaks. We should marvel at this fact as well. The recounting of Israel's early history begins and ends with God's promise made and kept. The Bible is a book filled with promises made and kept.

God spoke creation into existence, and by his word he brought his people into existence. We need to remember the privilege of having God's Word and its power. We need to remember that God builds his church by his Word. You can build a crowd on personality, but not a true church. The people of God are brought forth by and sustained by the Word of God.

Third, the Lord sends. We're reminded in this psalm of his sending of Abraham, Joseph, and Moses. God is a sending God. Jesus would later say to his disciples, "As the Father has sent me, even so I am sending you" (John 20:21 ESV). As his people, we're not only saved but also sent. We're commissioned to make disciples among all nations (Matt 28:18-20). Marvel that the Lord uses people like Moses—and people like us—to accomplish his redemptive purposes.

Fourth, the Lord uses means. The Lord achieves his purposes in a variety of ways. In Psalm 105 we're reminded that sometimes God will use unpleasant means to accomplish his agenda (Wilcock, *Message*, 132). He caused a famine in order to propel Jacob's family to Egypt. He sent Joseph ahead to Egypt in preparation for the famine. Joseph endured the hardship of prison so that he would eventually be at the right place and right time to save the lives of many people (ibid.). Likewise, from Egypt to Canaan the Lord used messy means to accomplish his redeeming plan on behalf of his people. We need to remember that we don't know the whole story of our lives. As believers, we must simply trust that God may be using unpleasant means to accomplish wonderful ends. He is sanctifying us. He is making us like Jesus. He is making us long for an arrival in the new creation.

Fifth, the Lord sustains. In the stories of both Joseph and the exodus, we find that God's presence is sufficient. God provides, protects, and enables his people to endure hardship. So while we may face various trials in this life, we aren't left alone. God is with us and in us. Let that encourage you!

Finally, the Lord remembers his covenant forever. This promise made in verse 8 is fulfilled through the coming of Abraham's ultimate offspring, Jesus. Matthew opens his Gospel by showing us God's faithfulness to his word, as he records the genealogy from Abraham to Jesus. His Gospel begins, "An account of the genealogy of Jesus Christ, the Son of David, the Son of Abraham" (Matt 1:1). The incarnation of the Son of God is one massive reassurance that God keeps his promises.

We who are in Christ Jesus have a better hope than a promised land. Canaan was a shadow of the reality of a heavenly home promised to us (Heb 3:7–4:1; 11:13-16,39-40). Here's a final reason to embrace Christianity. Christianity offers you an answer to the inner ache of homesickness. C. S. Lewis stated, "If I find in myself desires which nothing in this world can satisfy, the only logical explanation is that I was made for another world" (*Mere Christianity*, 137). Psalm 105 points us in the direction of our final destination. One day the saints will be home. Remember this truth in the midst of struggle and suffering, and go on running the race of faith with your eyes fixed on Jesus until you arrive in his presence.

Reflect and Discuss

1. Why is history important to the Christian faith?
2. What are some of the expressions of praise mentioned in verses 1-5? Which expression strikes you the most, and why?
3. Why is remembering important for the Christian life?
4. What is a covenant? Why is God's covenant with Abraham important? How is it tied to the gospel?
5. How is Psalm 105 related to the coming of Christ?
6. What are some of the lessons we learn from the life of Joseph?
7. What are some of the lessons we learn from the exodus?

8. Why did God bring his people out of Egypt?
9. Identify all the things God did in redemptive history, as recounted by the psalmist. How should these acts encourage you personally?
10. Take a few moments to seek the Lord's strength in prayer (v. 4) in light of all that this psalm teaches us about our Redeemer.

Sin and Grace

PSALM 106

Main Idea: This historical psalm recites a series of events from Israel's past, magnifying God's faithful love toward a sinful people and teaching valuable discipleship lessons.

I. **Disciples Worship with Their Lives, Not Merely with Their Lips (106:1-3).**
II. **Disciples Care about God's People, Not Merely Themselves (106:4-5).**
III. **Disciples Practice Repentance, Not Self-Righteousness (106:6-46).**
    A. Unbelief (106:7-12)
    B. Discontent (106:13-15)
    C. Jealousy (106:16-18)
    D. Idolatry (106:19-23)
    E. Grumbling (106:24-27)
    F. Unfaithfulness (106:28-31)
    G. Rebellion (106:32-33)
    H. Corruption (106:34-46)
IV. **Disciples Glorify God, Not Themselves (106:47-48).**

In the previous psalm I tried to do a bit of "blue-collar apologetics." May I continue? Here's a common question: Why do you believe the Bible is true? We could give many answers. We can point to *external* evidence, *internal* evidence, and *experiential* evidence.

Externally, we Christians can talk about matters like archeology and manuscript reliability. Both give us good reasons to trust the Bible.

Internally, we can talk about (1) textual consistency—that is, despite being written by more than 40 authors, during a period of more than two thousand years, the Bible is remarkably consistent in its message—and (2) the vast number of fulfilled prophecies contained in the Scriptures.

Experientially, we can talk about (1) how God has changed thousands of lives through the living and abiding Word of God, and (2) how God's Word bears the ring of truth and authenticity; it best explains the history of a world filled with sin and suffering, along with longing for redemption.

I bring this question up because Psalm 106 gives us a supporting point to the matter of authenticity. Psalm 106 contains a catalog of sins committed by God's people. If you were going to write your own history, you probably wouldn't include this! If you were going to write your family history, you probably wouldn't include certain scandals, of say, prostitution, murder, abuse, or religious violence. If a church wanted to write its history, it probably wouldn't contain all the moral scandals of its past. Consider yearbooks at high schools. What do they contain? They contain the highlights. You don't read about the kid who got expelled for bringing weed to school. But the Bible doesn't sugarcoat history. The Bible is filled with stories and examples of perverse sin. It's honest about the nature of broken humanity. It's authentic. And because it provides an honest and authentic picture of humanity, it gives us honest and authentic *hope* for the world. Because the good news of the Bible, and of Psalm 106, is that God's grace is greater than our sin! We need redemption, and praise God, we have a God who redeems.

Like Psalm 105, Psalm 106 is a historical psalm (perhaps written during some kind of exile, see 106:4-5,27,47). The psalmist recites a series of events from Israel's history, magnifying God's faithfulness and love toward a sinful people. Unlike Psalm 105, Psalm 106 catalogs a list of Israel's wrongdoings. Goldingay says, "In Ps. 105 the repeated theme was, 'We're in trouble, but Yhwh rescued us.' Here, the repeated theme is, 'We failed Yhwh, and Yhwh punished us, but then we were rescued'" (*Psalms*, 222).

We have much to learn from this psalm. It incites praise, but it also warns and instructs us about some basic discipleship themes.

What does this psalm teach disciples today? Obviously, it teaches us about the wonders of God's love. It teaches us about the unthinkable sins of Israel and the unrelenting love of God. But what should our response be to his steadfast love? The psalmist teaches us four critically important lessons.

Disciples Worship with Their Lives, Not Merely with Their Lips
PSALM 106:1-3

Worshiping with your *lips* does matter! Throughout the Psalms we're called to give verbal expressions of praise (e.g., 105:1-2). However, here the psalmist connects lips with *life*.

He opens with a call to praise, and he closes with a call to praise
(v. 48). This call to praise in verse 1 involves verbal expressions. It's a
call to praise God in particular for his *faithful love*. God's faithfulness,
goodness, grace, mercy, and love fly like banners over this psalm. The
psalmist will talk much about sin, but the great hope of the psalm is
found in the goodness, grace, faithfulness, and love of God. We should
never cease giving God verbal praise for these attributes.

In verses 2-3 the psalmist shows the relationship between words and
deeds. In verse 2 he asks the question, Who can worship genuinely? This
question gets asked elsewhere, as in Psalm 15, where the psalmist asks,
"LORD, who can dwell in your tent? Who can live on your holy mountain?" (15:1). Here's the answer: "The one who lives blamelessly, practices righteousness, and acknowledges the truth in his heart" (15:2). A
similar question is raised and then answered in Psalm 24:3-4. Likewise,
in Psalm 106:3 the psalmist gives the answer, connecting life with lips
with a little beatitude. Allen puts it well: "Right living must ever be the
preface to worship" (*Psalms 101–150*, 53).

If Israel had practiced justice, they wouldn't have gone into exile.
The prophets rebuked the people who participated in great worship
assemblies but failed to practice justice (Isa 1:11-15). Jesus, however,
obeyed where Israel failed. One of the great attributes of the Messiah,
promised in places like Isaiah, is that he will uphold *justice* (Isa 11; 61).
The world needs justice. Just watch the news! And when Jesus returns,
we will be stunned by his execution of justice. Peace and righteousness
will exist perfectly when our Messiah makes all things new. At Jesus's
first coming, he gave us a foretaste of that just rule. Now, the Spirit is
making us like Jesus. And one of the ways people should see Christ in us
is through righteousness and justice in all our actions.

The psalmist says, "At all times" (v. 3). The doing of justice (Mic 6:8)
includes doing that which honors God in all of life (cf. Job 29:14)—with
integrity in your vocation, finances, family, relationships, church membership commitments, social involvements, recreation, and so on.

Jesus connected life with lips when he said that if you're on your
way to worship and remember that your brother has something against
you, you should go be reconciled with your brother before you go to
worship (Matt 5:23-24). Peter connected life with *prayer*. He says to
everyone, "Be self-controlled and sober-minded for the sake of your
prayers" (1 Pet 4:7 ESV). To husbands in particular, Peter says they
must show honor to their wives "so that [their own] prayers may not be

hindered" (1 Pet 3:7 ESV). Our lives matter when it comes to worship and prayer.

Often churches put people on stage because they're gifted musically, even though they are not seeking to observe justice and walk in righteousness. Let's not make this mistake if we're in leadership. Understand, we aren't talking about moral perfection here. We're talking about pursuit of godliness. Something is wrong when a person can live like a total pagan during the week and then arrive on a Sunday morning and sing praise with great gusto and expression. This is hypocrisy. This doesn't honor God. This will not help the watching world.

So then, we should prepare ourselves for weekly worship by walking with God during the week. Ligon Duncan (whose exposition of this passage helped me tremendously!) reflected on the privilege he had as a young person in being able to sit under some of the best biblical preaching in the world. Sadly, it didn't impact him greatly. He didn't arrive on Sundays with expectancy or a sense of gratitude for the privilege of hearing God's Word. Instead, his mind drifted to other stuff. Why? Duncan said it was because he had been thinking about other stuff *all week*. He wasn't committing criminal offenses during the week; he simply wasn't thinking about God rightly and deeply. I appreciate his testimony. I can relate to it. Why does one person gets something out of a worship service and the other person doesn't? One reason is just this: the true worshiper worships all week long and arrives at corporate worship with expectancy and gratitude and need. The others come in with their minds on earthly things.

We must see all of life as an opportunity to honor God. In the mundane, ordinary experiences, learn to worship. When you do the dishes, do yard work, study, exercise, eat, drink, or spend time with friends and family, do it to the glory of God (1 Cor 10:31). In your day-to-day dealings, work honestly, keep your promises, be faithful to your spouse and children, and be mindful of the poor. Verse 3 is teaching us that true worship involves both lips and life.

Disciples Care about God's People, Not Merely Themselves
PSALM 106:4-5

Here's another needed corrective for worship. Many view worship and the life of faith *individualistically*. This is a common inclination for Westerners. But consider how the psalmist approaches God:

Remember me, LORD,
  when you show favor to your people.
Come to me *with your salvation*
so that I may enjoy the prosperity
of your chosen ones,
rejoice in the joy of your nation,
and boast about your heritage. (106:4-5; emphasis added)

The psalmist is seeking God's blessings *personally,* but he realizes that he wants to experience these blessings *within the context of the people of God.* He's not an isolated mystic. He recognizes that he's a participant in the ongoing story of the people of God, and he's seeking God's favor personally in view of that corporate reality. In this context he seems to look ahead to deliverance from exile (cf. Isa 49:8; 60:10). If deliverance comes, there will be renewed blessing, joy, and glory (Ps 106:5).

Many Christians either haven't been taught about the communal nature of the faith or are refusing to submit to it. Much of today's teaching is about God's blessing of individuals with health, wealth, and prosperity. It's a deadly combination of false gospel and individualistic consumerism. We need to revive the teaching of "the communion of saints," stated in the Apostles' Creed. This phrase means that the church includes a common union of believers in the Lord Jesus Christ. It includes the saints who have already entered heaven (the church triumphant) and the saints who still struggle on earth (the church militant).

Disciples understand that they are part of a larger story of God's people, and that story is going somewhere (Duncan, "Our Story"). At the end of Hebrews 11, we are told that the saints who have gone before us are waiting for the fullness of God's promises until we all *together* enjoy the fulfillment of those promises (Heb 11:40).

So then, how can we demonstrate a concern for God's people, not merely for ourselves? We should first recognize that God is redeeming a people (Titus 2:14). We should care about all of God's people. We should identify with them, rejoice with them, weep with them, do mission with them, and pray with and for them—both locally and globally. And practically, each of us should join a local, gospel-preaching, gospel-shaped church. God's plan has never been for a Christian to live apart from the community of faith.

Sometimes coaches have excellent players on their teams but have horrible teams because they are filled with ambitious individuals who simply want to make it to the pros. This dynamic is present in Christendom as well. Many want to be superstars but don't want to attend a small group. They want a platform but don't want to do child-care. They want accolades but don't want to care for the widows in their churches. They want to be on the ministry circuit but don't want to go to membership meetings. This version of Christianity is consumeristic, cheap, selfish, immature, and shallow. Reject it. Instead, let's love the people of God. Let's pray for the people of God. Let's serve with the people of God. Let's worship with the people of God. Let's pray for our own needs in light of the people of God.

Disciples Practice Repentance, Not Self-Righteousness
PSALM 106:6-46

Now the psalmist provides a detailed historical account of Israel's rebel-lion and God's relentless grace. Verse 6 provides the purpose for cata-loging theses sins and prepares us for the content of the next 40 verses. It includes a corporate confession: "Both we and our ancestors have sinned; we have done wrong and have acted wickedly." The psalmist identifies with his ancestors' failures and accepts that his contempo-raries have behaved like them. So he moves through a list of sins as a means of confession and repentance.

Repentance is a daily discipline for the Christian. This may sound negative and morbid, but only if one doesn't understand repentance. Here's something you need to know about the psalmist: he's happier than the person who refuses to repent (Ps 32:3-5). Repentant people find joy. Repentant people are happier than self-righteous people (Luke 15). The psalmist, even while acknowledging the sins that he and God's people have committed, knows that God's grace is greater than these sins! He knows that the kindness of God leads us to repentance (Rom 2:4). He knows that repentance leads to joy.

The psalmist values repentance over self-righteousness. Self-righteous people deny sin, shift the blame on their sin, redefine sin, or only talk about other people's sin. A true disciple acknowledges sin, confesses it, and daily experiences God's renewing grace. We come into the Christian life by repentance, and we continue walking in close fel-lowship with God and growing in the image of Christ through repen-tance. Therefore, this psalm is a tremendous gift to us because it serves as a guide for repenting disciples.

Before moving through this sin inventory, stop and consider the grace of God and the patience of God. Derek Kidner says, "God's extraordinary long-suffering . . . emerges as the real theme of the Psalm" (*Psalms 73–150*, 378). We should marvel at God's longsuffering. We should also seek to imitate God's patience and grace toward others. Praise God that he's patient with us! Praise God his mercy extends to us!

Let's seek God's mercy as we consider the psalmist's recounting of Israel's historical failures. We could label these sins with various descriptions. I have chosen eight terms, but each sin overlaps with other sins and includes other sins.

Unbelief (106:7-12)

The psalmist begins with the exodus event and points out Israel's history of unbelief. By the time the people had gotten to the Red Sea, they had already seen God's mighty power and faithful love displayed in Egypt, including the mighty plagues, but then they "rebelled by the sea" (v. 7). They were asking God, "What have you done for me lately?" At the first sign of danger, they didn't believe (cf. Exod 14:11-12). They didn't trust God. From the beginning, they seemed to have an "ingrained unbelief" (Wilcock, *Message*, 136).

Despite their unbelief, the psalmist goes on to say that God "saved them for his name's sake" (v. 8a; cf. Exod 14:18). The Lord did this to make his power known (v. 8b). He saved them through the Red Sea miracle (vv. 9-11; cf. Exod 14:15-22). What grace!

Following this miracle, the psalmist says, they "believed" and "sang his praise" (v. 12; cf. Exod 15). But this belief and praise proved to be short-lived. It was more emotional than authentic. Williams says, "It is one thing to praise God for his benefits. It is quite another thing to praise God as God" (*Psalms 73–150*, Kindle).

Let's go back to the rebellion in Egypt (v. 7). Notice the relationship between believing *with the mind* and rebelling *with the will* (Kidner, *Psalms 73–150*, 379). If we don't believe, we rebel. It's that simple. In fact, the sin list that follows includes expressions of unbelief-driven sin.

If we don't believe God will provide, we will be tempted to steal, cheat, lie, or freak out. If we don't believe that God is more satisfying than any pleasure in this life, we will indulge the flesh. If we don't believe our identity is in Christ, we will try to find our identity from our careers, from what people say about us, or from somewhere else.

At the root of rebellion is unbelief. Let's repent of not truly believing God's Word. Pray for grace to help your unbelief. He has raised Jesus from the dead. He has given us new life. You can trust his Word.

Discontent (106:13-15)

God provided miraculously and mercifully for his people in the wilderness, but they "soon forgot his works" (v. 13a). They "would not wait for his counsel" (v. 13b). Their impatience and discontent is described as a "wanton craving" (v. 14a ESV) that led them to test God.

So they displayed not only selfish desires but also godless *attitudes*. From the beginning of the journey, they made demands instead of offering humble requests to God (Exod 15:24; 16:3). They questioned God's goodness and grew tired of God's daily provisions.

The Lord Jesus obeyed where Israel failed in the wilderness. When Satan presented a similar temptation to Jesus, our Lord honored the Father with obedience (Matt 4:1-7).

In the book of Numbers, the people grew tired of manna and started thinking back to all the good things they had in Egypt, expressing their displeasure and discontent (Num 11:5-6). The result of Israel's discontent was tragic (Ps 106:15). The Lord's anger blazed. God gave them a sickening amount of quail; on top of that, he struck them with a plague (Num 11:10-34). They called this place "Kibroth-hattaavah" because they buried people there who "craved the meat" (Num 11:34).

Let's learn from Israel here. Resist discontent and the placing of demands on God. Learn to delight in God's will and to trust in your Father's provision. Remember that you don't find contentment by looking away from God's will but by walking in it. Jesus said, "My food is to do the will of him who sent me and to finish his work" (John 4:34). Let's repent of being discontent with God's actions and instead find satisfaction in doing his revealed will.

Jealousy (106:16-18)

Next the psalmist highlights the sin of jealousy. Dathan and Abiram shared in Korah's rebellion against Israel's leaders (Num 16). The psalmist identifies the cause of this revolt as envy (v. 16a) or jealousy (ESV). The envy led to Israel's grumbling (a sin mentioned in v. 5). Their grumbling against the leaders was actually a grumbling against God, who appointed the leaders. We may not take grumbling against God's appointed leaders seriously, but this story shows us that we should!

God brought a dramatic judgment against the people as a result. The earth opened up and swallowed the conspirators, and fire consumed those who tried to violate the priestly requirements (Num 16:31-35).

Men were jealous of other leaders. Sound familiar? Throughout Scripture, envy is underneath many sinful actions (Mark 7:22; Rom 1:29; Gal 5:21). Matthew even says that Jesus knew the people delivered him up to be crucified because they were filled with envy (Matt 27:18). Paul says one sin that characterized our lives prior to conversion was envy (Titus 3:3). Envy leads to problems in the local church (Gal 5:26). People can even be motivated in ministry by envy instead of love (1 Cor 13:4; Phil 1:12-18). Peter tells us what to do with this wicked sin: rid ourselves of it (1 Pet 2:1).

Idolatry (106:19-23)

Exodus 32 and Deuteronomy 9 tell us about Israel's sin of making a calf and worshiping this man-made, metal image (106:19). Of all places, they worshiped the calf in Horeb (Sinai, Exod 19:20) during the most stunning encounter with God discussed in the Old Testament (Wilcock, *Message*, 138). Allen says, "Israel's career of ingratitude reached an all time low, in the golden calf incident" (*Psalms 101–150*, 54).

In verse 20 you can hear a preview of the apostle Paul's words to the Romans. The psalmist says, "They exchanged the glory of God for the image of an ox that eats grass" (106:20 ESV). They sought to replace God with something else. In Romans 1 Paul says idolaters "exchanged the truth of God for a lie, and worshiped and served what has been created instead of the Creator, who is praised forever. Amen" (Rom 1:25). Idolatry involves making a foolish and deadly trade. Wilcock says, "When people abandon the God of Scripture, it is astonishing what foolish alternatives people choose" (*Message*, 139). Israel's foolishness is noted here: Why worship something that eats grass?

The psalmist connects Israel's idolatrous exchange to spiritual amnesia (v. 21). God had put his power on display in Egypt (v. 22). God had shown his supremacy over the gods of Egypt, yet the people made a golden calf to worship.

We make foolish exchanges when we fail to remember the Savior. When the grace of God doesn't arouse our affections for the Savior, we will go chasing other lovers. We will look to other things or people to give us what only Jesus can give us. So then, let's daily remember the gospel!

Because of their idolatry, the Lord would have destroyed Israel, but the psalmist says Moses interceded for the people (v. 23; cf. Exod 32:7-14,30-34). What grace again! This description shows us how the gospel works. We need a mediator and we have one! We have a mediator better than Moses, Jesus Christ, who not only turned away God's wrath but also actually absorbed it on our behalf so that we could be right with God. VanGemeren says, "The metaphor 'stood in the breach' derives from military language, signifying the bravery of a soldier who stands in the breach of the wall, willing to give his life in warding off the enemy (cf. Ez 22:30)" ("Psalms," 677). Jesus stood in the breach for us. He gave his life for idolaters like us that we may have life. Don't forget the Savior!

Fight idolatry not by merely resisting idols; fight idolatry by pursuing Jesus with great passion! Don't just say no to idols; say yes to the Savior. If your affections are filled with joy in the Savior, you will have no room for idols!

Grumbling (106:24-27)

The Scriptures have much to say about the sin of grumbling/complaining/murmuring (Phil 2:14; 1 Cor 10:10). Here the psalmist spotlights Israel's grumbling when they failed to obey God and take the promised land (Num 13–14).

At Kadesh Barnea the people rebelled again. They didn't believe the Lord could lead them to the promised land (stated here as "the pleasant land"). Twelve spies went to scout out the land (Num 13:32–14:38). Ten gave a bad report, leading Israel to fear and to decline to take the land. This was the moment of truth for Israel, and they failed (Kidner, *Psalms 73–150*, 380). They refused to believe God's word. Even though they believed God's promises at the Red Sea momentarily (Ps 106:12), they regarded them as insufficient in this stage of the journey (Deut 1:32). So, instead of believing and praising God (v. 12b), they "grumbled in their tents and did not listen to the LORD's voice" (v. 25 HCSB; cf. Num 14:1; Deut 1:27; 1 Cor 10:10). Stubbornly and cowardly, they stayed in their tents grumbling instead of taking the land. It makes you wonder how much of our grumbling is tied to cowardice. A relationship exists in this story.

As a result of their grumbling unbelief, a whole generation would die in the wilderness in fulfillment of God's oath (v. 26; cf. Num 14:32; Ps 95:8-11). The reference to "scattering their offspring among the nations" (v. 27 CEB) seems to refer to the fact that similar unbelief led Israel into (present?) exile (cf. Lev 26:33; Ezek 20:23).

Unfaithfulness (106:28-31)

Continuing this sad commentary, the psalmist turns to more idolatry and unfaithfulness in Moab (see Num 25). Israel joined itself to "Baal of Peor" (v. 28 ESV), the Canaanite fertility god. Peor was a mountain in Moab (Num 23:28). In Numbers 25:1 we read that Israel played the harlot with the daughters of Moab. Israelite travelers had reached civilization and had found a structured religion that was more appealing to them. It was more "comforting than the tiresome faith of Yahweh—comforting with the comforts of the whorehouse" (Wilcock, *Message*, 140). So they rejected the true faith and embraced a pagan religion.

The psalmist adds a detail. The people also "ate sacrifices offered to the dead" (v. 28b ESV). "The dead" could refer to "lifeless gods," but more likely it refers to Moabite rites connected to the dead (Kidner, *Psalms 73–150*, 381; Goldingay, *Psalms*, 232; cf. Deut 14:1; 18:11; 26:14; Isa 57:1-8). One aspect of Baal's activity included the realm of the dead.

Involvement in Moabite rites once again provoked the Lord to wrath. Israel was spared, however, because one man intervened: Phineas (v. 30). The Lord sent a plague, but Phineas's actions checked it. Interestingly, Phineas punished one of the idolatrous Israelites who was seeking to marry a non-Israelite and was turning with her to Baal to make the family fertile. Phineas put the offenders to death with a javelin (Num 25:6-9), making atonement and satisfying the call for judgment (Num 25:13). Though the plague was stopped by his intervention, a huge number still died during this time of unfaithfulness (Num 25:9). Phineas was "counted . . . as righteous" down through the ages for his zeal for Yahweh (106:31 ESV).

We must see the uniqueness of Phineas's actions here. He was in a sense protecting the whole future of Israel by executing judgment. We aren't called to throw javelins at people in the church! But we must pursue a life of faithfulness and holiness.

"Credited to him as righteousness" reminds us of Abraham's justification and ours (Gen 15:6; Rom 4:3,23-25). Kidner remarks,

> Happily it is Abram's faith we are to follow, not Phineas's zeal!
> But this is because the sentence has been executed (on the
> just, for the unjust), and atonement made, not in token but in
> full. (*Psalms 73–150*, 381)

Because Jesus has made us righteous, we have the power now to pursue practical righteousness.

Those who have been declared righteous through the work of Jesus Christ have no business participating in pagan religions. Christ is sufficient. Paul makes this argument forcefully in the New Testament (see 2 Cor 6:14–7:1).

Rebellion (106:32-33)

Or we could call it "more complaining!" Or "more unbelief!" The psalmist goes back now to Numbers 20, where God grew angry "at the waters of Meribah" (v. 24). In an earlier incident the people complained about a lack of water, and Moses struck the rock and water gushed out (Exod 17:1-7). Now, near the end of the journey, the people quarreled again with Moses over lack of water. This time God told Moses to speak to, not strike, the rock (cf. 1 Cor 10:4). But Moses, in anger, calling the people "you rebels" (Num 20:10), struck the rock twice (Num 20:8-11). As a result, God passed judgment on Moses, rejecting his entry into the land (Num 20:12).

Moses treated God's word and this symbol disrespectfully, with the same type of rebellion as the people. Interestingly, the psalmist draws attention to the people provoking Moses rather than to Moses's actions, saying that "Moses suffered because of them" (v. 32) and that they "embittered his spirit" (v. 33). This emphasis doesn't intend to excuse Moses's actions, but it does highlight the evil of driving another person to sin.

We should confess not only our rebellion to God but also the times in which we have helped others sin. By our words and actions, what have we done to drive someone, or enable someone, to sin? Our actions always affect other people. Let's be mindful of this reality. Let's ask God to help us love our neighbors, not cause our neighbors to stumble (Matt 18:5-6).

Corruption (106:34-46)

In verses 34-39 we see further corruption associated with the settlement in Canaan. It wasn't only the wilderness generation that was unfaithful. So were the people who crossed the Jordan River.

Once in the land, Israel disobeyed the Lord's command to drive out the nations (v. 34; cf. Num 33:53). Instead, they "mingled with the nations and adopted their ways" (v. 35). This corruption involved idolatry, insightfully described as "a snare" (v. 36).

This pagan worship included child sacrifices made to demons, and Israel participated (v. 37; cf. Lev 18:21; Deut 32:17; 1 Cor 10:19-21). As a result, "innocent blood—the blood of their sons and daughters," was shed as they "sacrificed to the idols of Canaan" (v. 38). This verse may bring to mind the unthinkable action of abortion, the brutal sacrifice of real sons and daughters.

The psalmist summarizes: "They defiled themselves by their actions and prostituted themselves by their deeds" (v. 39). God's response to this corruption is stated in verses 40-43. The Lord's wrath was kindled, as he considered them an abomination. God gave them into the hands of the Gentiles (v. 41), who oppressed the people (v. 42). Many times the Lord delivered the people, yet they continued to rebel (v. 43). This cycle is played out throughout the book of Judges: apostasy, a cry for help, deliverance, and then renewed apostasy.

However, judgment was not the last word, for hope arises in verses 44-45. As with Israel's cry to God in Egypt (Exod 2:23-24), the Lord heard the people's cry here (v. 44). God's sensitivity is tied to his covenantal commitment (v. 45), just as it was in Egypt (Exod 3:24). As a result, the Lord moved the hearts of Israel's oppressors (v. 46). This verse moves the biblical narrative ahead to a later time period, to exile and restoration (2 Kgs 25:27-30; Ezra 1:2-4). Solomon prayed for such clemency (1 Kgs 8:46-53), and the psalmist shows us God's compassionate response.

What's the point of this catalog of sins? God's mercy overshadows his judgment (Williams, *Psalms 73–150*, Kindle): "His faithful love endures forever" (Ps 106:1). Israel's only hope was found in this fact. And our hope as individuals and as churches is found in the steadfast love of God, too. Let his love lead you into repentance and praise. We can now consider the concluding prayer and doxology.

Disciples Glorify God, Not Themselves
PSALM 106:47-48

This psalm teaches us that God alone deserves glory. Were it not for his mercy, we would have no hope. God grants grace and mercy to rebels, and therefore he alone should be praised.

Corporately, the people cry out. Once again the psalmist identifies himself as part of the people of God. He is praying specifically that they may be delivered from the Gentiles and may return to the land (v. 47a).

The result of such salvation will be worship (v. 47b). The common cry throughout history is, "Save us." In Jesus, we have a Savior who delivers rebels! Concerning the birth of Jesus, the angel said to Joseph, "You are to name him Jesus, because he will save his people from their sins" (Matt 1:21).

Verse 48 provides a fitting end to this psalm. God's steadfast love is greater than even the people's perversity. As a result, all his people should praise him continually! This is an appropriate conclusion not only to Psalm 106 but also to Book IV of the Psalms (Pss 90–106).

So then, in light of God's steadfast love, let's worship with our lives, not just our lips. Let's stay concerned about the people of God, not merely ourselves. Let's practice repentance. And let's live for the God who saves sinners through Jesus Christ. Let's live faithfully before him until we see him and enjoy the new heavens and new earth, where this cycle of sin and rebellion will be no more and where total justice and peace will have no end.

Reflect and Discuss

1. Have you ever been asked, "Why do you believe the Bible is true?" If so, what are your typical answers? What does Psalm 106 teach us about the nature of Scripture?
2. What does this psalm teach us about worshiping with our *lips* as well as with our *lives*?
3. What does it mean to "uphold justice"? What verses would you use to teach someone about a biblical view of justice?
4. How does this psalm emphasize the communal/corporate nature of the faith? Why is this important?
5. Why should we practice repentance? What does this psalm teach us about repentance?
6. What does this psalm teach us about God's steadfast love?
7. What is idolatry? What are some common idols today?
8. What does Israel's history teach us about the sin of grumbling? Why is grumbling so evil?
9. What does this psalm teach us about God's covenant?
10. Take a few moments to reflect and pray through this psalm. Use it as a guide for repentance and renewal.

Give Thanks to the Lord

PSALM 107

Main Idea: In this historical psalm, the writer calls on the redeemed to give thanks to God, their Deliverer, for his faithful love.

I. **A Call to Give Thanks to God (107:1-3)**
II. **Reasons to Give Thanks to God (107:4-42)**
   A. Give thanks for his deliverance (107:4-32).
      1. The Lord delivers wanderers (107:4-9).
      2. The Lord delivers prisoners (107:10-16).
      3. The Lord delivers the sick (107:17-22).
      4. The Lord delivers the storm tossed (107:23-32).
   B. Give thanks for his sovereignty (107:33-42).
      1. The sovereign Lord passes judgment (107:33-34).
      2. The sovereign Lord restores (107:35-38).
      3. The sovereign Lord condemns princes and exalts the poor (107:39-42).
III. **An Appeal to Gain Wisdom (107:43)**

Psalm 107 is the first psalm in Book V of the Psalms (Pss 107–150). Despite this boundary marker in the Psalter, Psalm 107 is tied to Psalms 105–106, the final two psalms in Book IV of the Psalter (Pss 90–106). These three psalms (105–107) provide historical reflections on God's work on behalf of Israel. The opening line of Psalm 107 even begins with the same initial call to praise found in Psalm 106: "Give thanks to the LORD, for he is good; his faithful love endures forever" (107:1).

However, there are some obvious differences in this trilogy. Psalm 106 appears to include *a prayer for deliverance from exile*. Psalm 107 seems to be *a postexilic thanksgiving*, a hymn of praise to God for answering the prayer of Psalm 106.

While Psalm 107 is a lengthy historical psalm, it's easy to follow. After an initial call to give thanks in verses 1-3, the psalmist gives the reasons to do so in verses 4-42. Verses 4-32 contain four pictures of the Lord's deliverance, and verses 33-42 include praise to God for his sovereign work in the world. Finally, verse 43 contains an exhortation to gain wisdom.

A Call to Give Thanks to God
PSALM 107:1-3

The psalmist calls the people to praise God because "he is good" and "his faithful love endures forever" (107:1). God's goodness is displayed in manifold ways, both in creation and in redemption. The psalms are filled with expressions of praise to God for his goodness (cf. 25:8; 86:5; 118:1). Likewise, the psalmists celebrate God's "faithful love" throughout the Psalter (cf. 103:8; 87:5,13,15).

One of the signs of personal and corporate spiritual renewal is a proper vision of, and delight in, God's goodness, love, and faithfulness. These exiles were sent away because of their sin, but because of the Lord's goodness and faithfulness they were gathered back home. All glory should go to God.

This praise-filled acknowledgement of God's goodness and faithfulness involves more than mental assent. The psalmist calls the people to *say something* about God's redeeming love (vv. 2-3). The redeemed are to declare the glories of God's redemption because he has delivered them from the enemy and gathered them back into the land. This was no small act! All of the "redeemed of the LORD" (cf. Isa 62:12) should praise the Lord for the various ways (both physically and spiritually) he has rescued them. The "foe" here probably refers to Babylon, and "redeemed" is speaking of being delivered from exilic slavery.

God is Redeemer. In Christ Jesus God has provided ultimate redemption for those in need of salvation (Col 1:13-14). He has delivered us from our great foes: sin, Satan, judgment, and death. We who have been so delivered should say something! We should never tire of speaking about our great God and Savior in praise and in evangelism. "Redeeming love has been my theme, and shall be till I die" should be the anthem of every former slave to sin who has been made a child of God (Cowper, "There Is a Fountain").

We talk about things that matter to us. When a school's beloved sports team wins a game, students talk about it. When people enjoy a good book or movie, they recommend it to others. When people hear a good story, they share it. So then, we who have experienced the greatest of all acts, redemption, should want to make this news known in worship and witness. A silent Christian is a strange creature. Does such a creature exist? We should probably affirm that a silent Christian is no Christian at all. The redeemed sing, share, discuss, pray, and declare the glories of the Redeemer, even if they must do so through sign language.

Previously, in Psalm 106:47, the exiled people prayed for God to gather them back into the land. In 107:3 we read of that act. God gathered his people from various directions, from all over the Mediterranean. This is a foretaste of the day in which the Lord gathers people from every tribe and tongue (Matt 8:11; Rev 7:9). All the redeemed on that day will most certainly say so!

Reasons to Give Thanks to God
PSALM 107:4-42

The psalmist now tells us why we should be filled with gratitude for who God is and for what he has done. He first recounts four experiences of individuals who needed to be rescued (vv. 4-32) and then exults in the sovereign Lord's restoring grace (vv. 33-42).

It's possible that these four experiences (vv. 4,10,17,23) speak of one specific group of exiles, but more likely the psalmist is describing the experiences of four different groups of exiles that were scattered in various places. Whatever the case, the psalm describes the circumstances of exile and magnifies the Lord as Redeemer, Deliverer, and Rescuer who deserves wholehearted thanksgiving.

Within each of these four experiences, the psalmist says that the people "cried out to the Lord," and the Lord "rescued them" (vv. 6-7,13-14,19-20,28-30). They cried. He delivered. As a result, the Deliverer should be praised for such displays of his "faithful love" (vv. 8,15,21,31).

Give Thanks for His Deliverance (107:4-32)

The four pictures of deliverance can be divided into two parts: (1) suffering due to man's limitations: those lost in the desert or tossed at sea; and (2) suffering due to sin: prisoners and the sick (VanGemeren, "Psalms," 682).

The Lord delivers wanderers (vv. 4-9). Like those who wandered in the exodus, so now Israel needed the Lord to deliver them from their recent "desolate wilderness" (v. 4a). They were homeless, having no "city where they could live" (v. 4b). As desperate wanderers, they were also "hungry and thirsty" (v. 5a). Consequently, their "spirits failed within them"

(v. 5b). In other words, they were in great need both physically and spiritually. When people live purposeless lives, they grow discouraged and lose their passion for living.

Christians today can go through periods of spiritual wandering. The good news is that the Lord brings the wanderers home. How so? Verse 6 tells us. We see the first of four cries for help in the psalm. In their time of distress, Israel knew where to look. They called on the Lord, and he rescued them. He snatched them out of the grip of bondage and drew them to himself.

Robert Robinson's classic hymn "Come Thou Fount" expresses this cry for God to bring home our wandering hearts: "Prone to wander, Lord, I feel it, / Prone to leave the God I love; / Here's my heart, O take and seal it, / Seal it for Thy courts above." Be encouraged, dear wanderer, the Lord settles, secures, and satisfies those who cry to him for restoring grace.

The psalmist goes on to speak of how the Redeemer continues to work in the lives of his rescued wanderers (v. 7). He replaces wandering with a right path and their homelessness with a city in which to live (cf. Isa 62:12).

What's the proper response to such transformation? Our reaction to the Lord's intervening grace should be heartfelt thanks to him for his love and his works (v. 8). The psalmist then adds a supporting word to incite gratitude (v. 9). Previously they were hungry and thirsty, and their souls were fainting, but now they are satisfied, full, and flourishing.

What a picture of deliverance! The Lord met every need. He reversed every crisis (cf. Luke 1:51-53). He continues to make our paths straight (Prov 3:5-6), provide food, shelter, and water (Ps 104), retrieve wanderers (Luke 15:11-32; Jas 5:19-20), and renew our passion for living (Ps 103:5; Isa 58:10-11; Jer 31:25).

"All humanity" (107:8,15,21,31) experiences the Lord's common grace in various ways as they enjoy food, water, and shelter (cf. 145:9), but the redeemed have additional reason to give him thanks. They know the Redeemer *personally* and know that his steadfast love endures *forever*. For all eternity the redeemed will enjoy the riches of God's goodness.

The Lord delivers prisoners (vv. 10-16). The next condition involves imprisonment. The exiles sat in "darkness and gloom" (v. 10a). They endured "cruel chains" (v. 10b; cf. Isa 5:30; 8:22; 42:7; 49:9; Mic 7:8). Again, physical distress leads to spiritual distress. The people were crushed in both ways.

Why the hardship? The psalmist says it resulted from their rebellion "against God's commands" and refusal to submit to the Most High's "counsel" (v. 11). Israel had rejected God's authority, and because of their sin they suffered judgment.

The Lord broke Israel's stubborn hearts by making them endure "hard labor" (v. 12a). This labor caused them to "stumble," and they had "no one to help" (v. 12b). Then they realized the folly of their ways. Once again, we read that the people "cried out to the LORD" (v. 13a) and he "delivered them" (v. 13b ESV). What grace! Even though they had rebelled against the Lord, he heard their cry and reversed their lot (v. 14).

In light of his redemption, the people are called to express their gratitude (v. 15). Again, a supporting verse is then provided (v. 16).

These are powerful images of the Lord's deliverance. Throughout Scripture we see God delivering people from both physical and spiritual imprisonment (e.g., Mark 5:1-20; Acts 12:1-17; 16:25-34). All who are in Christ Jesus know the chain-breaking power of the risen Christ. He has liberated us from spiritual prison and brought us into the light (Luke 4:18-19). The words of Charles Wesley's hymn come to mind: "Long my imprisoned spirit lay fast bound in sin and nature's night; thine eye diffused a quickening ray; I woke, the dungeon flamed with light; my chains fell off, my heart was free; I rose, went forth, and followed thee" ("And Can It Be?").

The Lord delivers the sick (vv. 17-22). Because these rebellious people were "fools," they also "suffered affliction" as a form of judgment (v. 17). Here we find a direct relationship between sin and sickness. We read of their "rebellious ways" and "iniquities" (v. 17). Their sickness involved a sickness unto death in which food was no longer appetizing (v. 18). Sickness doesn't always come directly from sinful *choices* (sometimes it does), but it is always tied to living in a sinful *world.*

The good news is that the Lord rescues grieving people from their sicknesses. Again we read that the exiles cried out, and God delivered them (v. 19). Though the Lord had passed judgment on Israel, he was willing and able to heal her. He was able to give the people individual relief and also able to bring them into the land for corporate relief. How was this healing accomplished? The psalmist says, "He sent his word and healed them; he rescued them from their traps" (v. 20). God's word contained the promise of restoration and comfort (cf. Isa 55:11). God's Word is life giving and restorative. By the power of the Word and the Spirit's work, grieving sinners are restored today as well.

What should our response be? Gratitude (v. 21). A further description of thanksgiving is provided this time: "Let them offer sacrifices of thanksgiving and announce His works with shouts of joy" (v. 22 HCSB). The people are called not merely to voice thanksgiving but to demonstrate it with "thanksgiving sacrifices," a communal offering involving great songs of joy.

How much more should we who have received a new heart and the promise of eternal healing give thanks to God? Jesus Christ has made the final sacrifice, and now we should offer him unending praise with our lips and our lives (Rom 12:1; Heb 13:15). He can heal us from temporal sickness (Luke 7:22; 17:11-19; Jas 5:13-16), and he promises to take us to a place with no sickness (Rev 21:4). We should sing with the hymn writer, "My great Physician heals the sick, the lost he came to save; for me His precious blood he shed, for me His life he gave" (Eliza Hewitt, "My Faith Has Found a Resting Place").

The Lord delivers the storm tossed (vv. 23-32). The psalmist now turns to the sea. This particular crisis speaks not so much of human *guilt* but human *littleness* (Kidner, *Psalms 73–150*, 386). The historical context here is a bit of a mystery and may simply be a poetic construction to describe the need for deliverance in general. Alternatively, it could be speaking of exile in particular, likening exile to being storm tossed (cf. Isa 54:11).

The psalmist describes the scene. Merchants go down to the ships to do business on the great bodies of water (v. 23). As they engage in business, they observe the wonders of God's creation in the seas (cf. Ps 104:25-26). Next the psalmist describes the power of the Lord over the seas. He says first that the Lord has the power *to cause the storm*, not "Mother Nature" or some other god over the waters (107:25-27; cf. Ps 105:31,34). Recall the words of Jonah: "But the Lord threw a great wind onto the sea, and such a great storm arose on the sea that the ship threatened to break apart" (Jonah 1:4).

The psalmist paints the picture of the sailors' terrifying experience (v. 26). As a result, they become unstable and hopeless (v. 27). Such an occasion would tempt any of us to "cuss like a sailor"!

But then we read of the grace of God in hearing their desperate prayer (v. 28). Sailors cried. The Lord delivered. The Lord may bring us to our wits' end so that we may turn to him. Such crises are means of grace to us. We never know what the Lord may be doing in our trials.

Like scenes in Jonah and the Gospels (Jonah 1:15; Matt 8:26), the sovereign Lord displays his power now *to calm the storm* (v. 29). The waters grow quiet, and the Lord safely guides the sailors to their "harbor" (v. 30). Many hymns express the Lord's storm-calming power and his loving guidance: "Jesus, Savior, pilot me Over life's tempestuous sea: Unknown waves before me roll, Hiding rock and treacherous shoal; Chart and compass come from Thee, Jesus, Savior, pilot me!" (Edward Hopper, "Jesus, Savior, Pilot Me").

The once fearful but now happy sailors are called on to join the thanksgiving party (v. 31). In addition, the sailors are called to give thanks to the Lord in communal worship and in places of leadership (v. 32). They are called to tell their story of how the Lord delivered them not only to honor God but also to encourage others.

Consider the basic fears of people today. This psalm says something about where to look when facing such problems. In fact, this psalm points us ahead to Jesus. For example, in Mark 4–5 Jesus delivers people from four huge fears: storms, the demonic, sickness, and death. It's no wonder the disciples exclaim, "Who then is this? Even the wind and the sea obey him!" (Mark 4:41). Look to the Lord Jesus for ultimate rescue and peace.

Give Thanks for His Sovereignty (107:33-42)

The psalmist offers a final meditation on the Lord's work of judgment and redemption in these verses. His meditation includes three main sections, which highlight how the Lord has sovereignly chosen to work in history.

The sovereign Lord passes judgment (vv. 33-34). Because of the people's "wickedness" (v. 34), the sovereign Lord may use the ruining of the land as a sign of judgment (v. 34; cf. 1 Kgs 17:1).

The sovereign Lord restores (vv. 35-38). The scene is now reversed. As a sign of blessing and favor, the Lord may also choose to bless the land and its people. In the case of the returned exiles, they experience the Lord's reversing their plight as he feeds the hungry and gives them a city in which to dwell (v. 36). Now secure, the people may find "a fruitful harvest" (v. 37; cf. Ps 85). The psalmist adds that the creation command to be fruitful and multiply is now fulfilled in these seasons of blessing (v. 38a), and this blessing extends to the livestock (v. 38b).

All who repent of sin and turn to the Lord experience his restoring grace (Acts 3:19-20). When we hunger and thirst for righteousness, we find fulfillment and fruitfulness (Matt 5:6). Be encouraged; the Lord restores. Look to him in seasons of barrenness, that you may find great joy and renewal.

The sovereign Lord condemns princes and exalts the poor (vv. 39-42). The people now sing of the Lord's reversals. God is able to lift up the poor and the oppressed, and he will judge the wicked. This picture of God lifting up the broken and exiled Israel, along with his pouring out of contempt on the oppressors, should encourage the redeemed and incite praise. God will have the last word. He will shut the mouths of the unjust. He will bless the faithful poor. Praise him for his concern for the "nobodies."

Various Scriptures (e.g., Ps 113:5-9) echo this concept of God reversing the fortunes of the poor and afflicted in various places, perhaps most memorably in the songs of Hannah and Mary (1 Sam 2:1-10; Luke 1:46-55). The lesson here is obvious: endeavor to "walk humbly with your God" (Mic 6:8), that in due time you may "be exalted" (Luke 14:11). Avoid resisting the Word of God and trampling on people as a means to your desired end. The wicked may prosper for a season, but that time is short-lived and eternally foolish. Instead, follow in the steps of Jesus. Pursue a life of humility and godliness, though such a life may look strange to the world.

Paul tells the Corinthians of the ultimate gospel reversal: "For you know the grace of our Lord Jesus Christ: Though he was rich, for your sake he became poor, so that by his poverty you might become rich" (2 Cor 8:9). Because of the cross work of Jesus Christ, which looks foolish to some, we have found infinite spiritual riches. While we may experience poverty or hardship now, we know that the ultimate reversal is coming in the next life.

An Appeal to Gain Wisdom
PSALM 107:43

This final verse closes with an invitation to all who desire to live a meaningful life. Instead of playing the fool (v. 17) and rebelling "against God's commands" (v. 11) and despising his wise counsel, people are exhorted to consider the nature and work of God. He urges us to consider the many ways in which the Lord has displayed his steadfast love (v. 43). By meditating on the ways God works, one gains and grows in wisdom. Wise people know that God condemns sin and redeems the repentant. Wise people know God delivers helpless people who cry out to him. They know the Lord has the power to break the prison doors and calm the raging waters. They know the Lord can reverse one's fortunes. Wise people know the wicked will not ultimately prosper. They know to walk humbly with God and trust in his grace.

Where should we look today for wisdom? We look to Christ. Ultimately, wisdom is found in knowing a Person, not a set of useful principles. Paul says, "In him are hidden all the treasures of wisdom and knowledge" (Col 2:3). You learn wisdom when you know Christ and as you walk in him. So let us draw near to the Savior and give thanks to him, for his faithful love endures forever.

Reflect and Discuss

1. Why do we need to be told to "give thanks to God"?
2. How can you cultivate a more grateful heart?
3. What does it mean to be redeemed?
4. What are the four pictures of deliverance in Psalm 107:4-32? Which picture impacts you the most and why?
5. What does this psalm say about crying out to the Lord?
6. What do these "reversals" in verses 33-42 teach us?
7. Read Luke 1:46-55. How does Mary's song reflect the ideas in Psalm 107:33-42?
8. How does this psalm point us to Jesus?
9. Based on this psalm, how can we grow in wisdom?
10. Take a few moments to cry out to the Lord both for yourself and on behalf of others who need the Lord's rescuing grace.

The Warrior's Morning Song

PSALM 108

Main Idea: David shows us how to cultivate God-centered confidence when faced with challenging situations.

I. **Confidence through Songs and Prayer (108:1-6)**
   A. God-centered singing (108:1-4)
   B. God-centered praying (108:5-6)
II. **Confidence through Scripture and Prayer (108:7-13)**
   A. God's promises (108:7-9)
   B. Prayer for help against the foes (108:10-13)

Psalm 108 combines Psalms 57:7-11 and 60:5-12. The former is an individual lament, and the latter is a communal lament. Psalm 57 is in the context of danger; David was fleeing from Saul in a cave. Psalm 60 is in the context of David and his troops having been defeated. Both psalms end with notes of praise and confidence. This tone of God-centered confidence and praise comes at the beginning of Psalm 108, and then the conflict is mentioned later. Despite this change in flow, Psalm 108 also includes praise and prayer in the midst of conflict.

Due to the repeated nature of the psalm, many commentators refer readers back to their previous notes on these texts. I will keep my exposition brief, but I don't want to skip it completely. I like what Spurgeon said about the repetition of these verses:

> We cannot find it in our heart to dismiss this psalm by merely referring the reader first to Ps 57:7-11 and then to Ps 60:5-12, though it will be at once seen that those two portions of Scripture are almost identical with the verses before us. It is true that most of the commentators have done so, and we are not so presumptuous as to dispute their wisdom; but we hold for ourselves that the words would not have been repeated if there had not been an object for so doing, and that this object could not have been answered if every hearer of it had said, "Ah, we had that before, and therefore we need not meditate upon it again." The Holy Spirit is not so short of expressions

that he needs to repeat himself, and the repetition cannot be meant merely to fill the book: there must be some intention in the arrangement of two former divine utterances in a new connection; whether we can discover that intent is another matter. It is at least ours to endeavor to do so, and we may expect divine assistance therein.

We have before us The Warrior's Morning Song, with which he adores his God and strengthens his heart before entering upon the conflicts of the day. (Spurgeon, *Treasury*, vol. 2, 425)

Let us hear these verses of the "Warrior's Morning Song" afresh, for the Holy Spirit has included these words again for our strength and edification. We need to hear them again because we have new battles every day. We need to hear every day, "With God we will perform valiantly" (v. 13).

David provides us with a daily battle plan for cultivating God-centered confidence for new faith ventures. Let's study it in two simple parts.

Confidence through Songs and Prayer
PSALM 108:1-6

These opening verses begin with a note of confidence and commitment to praise God. In the midst of a stressful time, the psalmist draws the congregation's attention to the need for wholehearted praise and God-glorifying, relationally oriented prayer.

God-Centered Singing (108:1-4)

The psalmist begins with an expression of confident hope in God as he offers thanksgiving to the Lord. The psalmist, though facing trials, focuses his attention on "God" (v. 1). David's confidence doesn't emanate from himself but from his Creator and Redeemer (cf. 27:1-3).

Because of God's faithfulness and love, David not only has confidence in the midst of adversity but also can sing in the midst of it (cf. Exod 15:1). He's not into half-hearted praise but praise that includes "the whole of [his] being" (cf. Pss 57:8; 16:9). This seems odd to people who only praise God when things are going well. The challenge is to praise God in the midst of the fight, or when you know trouble is soon coming.

It's indeed important that we worship in the midst of conflict and confusion. Singing praises to God, especially in the corporate assembly, will help you fight the good fight. It will encourage your spirit and empower you to press on. Keller says of this psalm, "There is aggressive joy here" (*Songs of Jesus*, 284). Without having all the answers, the psalmist courageously commits to sing praise to God and therein finds great joy to strengthen himself. Dear Christian, don't neglect worshiping in the midst of the war. Praise your way out of despair and doubt and into God-centered confidence and strength. Resolve to praise him today and always. Lawson says, "A steady heart is a singing heart" (*Psalms 76–150*, 181).

In verse 2 the psalmist commits to offer morning praise to God. He can't wait to praise God, for he wants his instruments, the harp and lyre, to awaken for praise (cf. 71:22-23). What a beautiful picture of praise (cf. 113:3). The dawn is supposed to wake people up, but David wants to wake the dawn with praise. Someone said you can wake up each day and say, "Good morning, Lord!" or, "Good Lord, it's morning." Don't start the day defeated but with confident hope in the sovereign Lord.

Next, David mentions the act of praising God "among the peoples" (v. 3; Ps 96). This would include the people who make up the present threat. David's praise will serve as a testimony to the nations about the greatness and faithfulness of his God. David wants the Gentiles to know of God's glory. In Romans 15:9-12 Paul quotes passages like this one to describe the gospel going to the Gentiles. God has a passion for the nations, and we should share in this reality. He's a global God with a global mission.

In verse 4 David mentions God's greatness and faithfulness as the motivation for his praise. His confidence isn't naïve optimism. It's rooted in truth. It's rooted in the character of God. Regardless of the battle, David knows something of the height of God's love and the expansive nature of God's faithfulness. Our times and circumstances change, but God never changes. He will always be with his people. You can also trust in his love and faithfulness. For that reason we should constantly give him praise.

God-Centered Praying (108:5-6)

David now prays for God to be exalted and to grant deliverance. I (Tony) love the rhythm of Psalm 108. David praises and then prays. He considers God's promises (vv. 7-9) and then prays (vv. 10-12). This psalm shows us the nature of the fight of faith. Sing. Pray. Read. Pray. Sing. Pray. Read. Pray. Repeat.

Having begun with a commitment to praise God, David asks God to make his glory known throughout the earth. He takes his mind to the transcendence of God and the sovereignty of God over the nations. He wants this God, against whom the nations rage, to be exalted.

This is a God-centered prayer. Our prayers should center on the glory of God. Jesus gave us a model of such praying (Matt 6:9-13), teaching us to begin our prayer, "[May] your name be honored as holy." We should long for God's glory to be known throughout the whole earth.

David's prayer is also specific. He prays for the Lord to rescue him. The exact trial in Psalm 108 isn't clear (though it seems to be some type of military battle), but the nature of the appeal is certain. David asks God to extend mercy to those whom the Lord loves. It's an intimate appeal. It's the way one may speak to a spouse, best friend, or a child (Goldingay, *Psalms*, 267). This prayer is relationally oriented. In times of trial, you may appeal to your Father, who loves his children. Ask him to strengthen, help, and deliver you in times of need. He is your Abba, and you can rest in him. Our God has all authority, and you can trust in him.

Confidence through Scripture and Prayer
PSALM 108:7-13

Another chief discipline to strengthen our faith is meditation on Scripture. David now speaks of God's promises, which for us come in the form of the Bible. We need to meditate on it daily in order to wage the good war with holy confidence.

God's Promises (108:7-9)

David begins, "God has spoken in his sanctuary." God is making a promise by his own holiness, that is, by his own character. There's nothing he could swear by that would be bigger than himself (Goldingay, *Psalms*, 268). His holy Word is totally trustworthy. When you doubt, go to God's totally sufficient and reliable Word.

As in Psalm 60:6-8, verses 108:7b-9 recall when a word about God's plan for Israel was given. The places mentioned in verses 7-8 were all parts of the land God promised Israel (Shechem, Succoth, Gilead, Manasseh, Ephraim, and Judah). Judah is important in the story of the Bible. Starting in Genesis, we read of how the coming Messiah would be born from the tribe of Judah (Gen 49:10; Mic 5:2). Moab, Edom, and Philistia were neighboring lands that also belonged to Yahweh (Exod 19:5). One of the ways Israel blessed the nations of the earth in David's time was by putting these pagan nations under Israelite sovereignty (Collins, "Psalms"). An aspect of mission in the Old Testament involved military campaign, but not just for the sake of increasing territory. Rather, it was to make God's glory and grace known to the Gentiles.

Our mission today is different in various ways, but we are similarly tasked with making God's glory known among the nations, and we still need to take God at his Word. Fight fear by trusting in God's promises recorded in Scripture. Ask the Spirit of God to strengthen you as you meditate on God's Word and as you seek to make disciples among all nations—until the nations are gathered to sing praises to the Lion of the tribe of Judah (Rev 5:5,11-14)!

Prayer for Help against the Foes (108:10-13)

The fight of faith involves a variety of emotions and questions. As a real struggler, David asks some questions in prayer (v. 10). In other words, he's asking, "Who will grant me the victory? Who will help me?" Some people had the impression that God wasn't for them. They're in the middle of a military conflict (v. 11). They realize their weakness and their need for the divine Warrior's aid.

Knowing that apart from God, they can do nothing, David prays (v. 12). What a wonderful little prayer! Who will give us the victory in the midst of trials? Who will enable us to triumph? Not human help ultimately, but God himself! In all of our battles, we need God's power in order to overcome (cf. John 15:5; Eph 6:10-18).

David ends on a powerful note of confidence (v. 13). Ligon Duncan helps us apply this verse to various situations:

> We're called to do valiantly, but to remember all along that it will not be our valiant deeds that win the day; it will be God and God alone who wins the day. That's a life motto. We will do valiantly, but God will tread down our foes.
>
> That's a motto for your marriages. If you find yourself in a perplexing situation in your marriage—"God, by Your grace, I will do valiantly, but You will be the One who gives victory in this marriage."

That's a good place for you if you're perplexed in your relationship with children or parents—"I will do valiantly, Lord, by Your grace, but You will win the victory."

Shouldn't that be our posture as well in our community, as we look at the plight, not just the physical, but the spiritual plight of our city? Do you not want to say with the psalmist that you want God to be exalted in your own community? If that is going to happen, we will do valiantly, but it will have to be Him that gives the victory.

This could be a life motto. And aren't you glad that David, under the inspiration of the Holy Spirit, put those two parts of the psalms, 57 and 60, together like he did, in order to equip us for the perplexing moments and the daunting challenges that will face us in the day ahead? And by God's grace, we'll wake up in the morning and we'll awaken the dawn, trusting in Him, ready for our own challenges. (Duncan, "Determined to Worship")

Amen! Let's press on with verse 13 in our minds and hearts!

Looking back over the entire psalm, we see several important truths about Scripture that we need to remember in order to fight the good fight of faith.

First of all, see the importance of *biblical repetition*. God's Word was repeated here in Psalm 108. We need to hear God's truth over and over again (1 Cor 15:1; Phil 3:1; 2 Tim 2:14). God is happy to repeat himself, and we shouldn't grow weary of hearing the gospel over and over again—or of preaching and teaching it over and over again—because we need it over and over again.

Second, see the importance of *biblical application*. Psalm 108 comes from two texts, but it's applied in a different situation. Remember to study the text not just for information but also for personal application. After discerning the meaning of a text, allow the text to change your heart and life.

Third, see the importance of *biblical exaltation*. God's people are gathering together to sing about God's promises and God's character. Singing the Bible will encourage and strengthen the saints. Remember that songs provide take-home theology. With God-centered, Christ-exalting songs, one can be reminded of the gospel all day long.

Finally, see the importance of *biblical supplication*. David ponders the character of God and the word of God, and then he prays. We should follow this example of Word-driven, God-centered prayer.

Psalm 108 is indeed a "Warrior's Morning Song." It teaches us how to prepare for and endure the battle. It reminds us that we can overcome opposition, not because we are strong but because with God we shall perform valiantly!

And who makes this relationship with God possible? It's none other than David's greater Son, King Jesus. He conquered our greatest enemies through his death and resurrection. Because of him, we can engage our mission with confidence. See him in the Scriptures. Apply his Word to your situation. Sing about him wholeheartedly. Draw near to God through him. Praise God that "we are more than conquerors through him who loved us" (Rom 8:37).

Reflect and Discuss

1. Read Psalms 57 and 60. Notice how they appear in Psalm 108 again. Note the similarities and differences.
2. Why is it important to be reminded of the same biblical truths? What are some ways Scripture repeats certain truths?
3. Why is it important to sing in the midst of opposition? Do you find this to be a challenge presently?
4. What does this text teach us about God's love and faithfulness?
5. What does this text teach us about the nature of prayer?
6. Why do we need to meditate on God's promises in times of adversity? How should one do this?
7. What does this psalm teach us about God's plan for the nations?
8. What's your reaction to Psalm 108:13?
9. How does this psalm point us to Jesus?
10. Take a few moments to pray through this psalm.

Character Assassination

PSALM 109

Main Idea: David pours out his heart to God during a time in which he suffered a vicious attack from evil accusers.

I. **Understanding Imprecatory Psalms**
II. **Understanding Psalm 109**
III. **Applying Psalm 109**
   A. Pour out your heart to God (109:1-5).
   B. Give your enemies to God (109:6-20).
   C. Appeal to, and rest in, the character of God (109:21-29).
   D. Keep praising God (109:30-31).

Over the holiday season, I (Tony) made the mistake of watching the Netflix documentary titled *Making a Murderer*. It was a mistake to start this ten-part program because I couldn't stop watching it! Plus, it kept me from sleeping at night! If you prefer shows that don't arouse your emotions, stay away from it. It's a story about crime, corruption, innocence, guilt, and the justice system. It has attracted millions of viewers. News programs have carried additional pieces related to the story. The early episodes tell of how a Wisconsin man, Steven Avery, spent eighteen years in jail for a violent crime he didn't commit. It's enough to infuriate you. The rest of the episodes explore what happened after he was released. Was he guilty of a second violent crime, for which he is now in prison? I'll leave you to draw your own conclusions about the second arrest.

My point in referencing this show is that the popularity of it says something about what it means to be human. It speaks to some of our most fundamental beliefs and instincts. People sympathize with innocent sufferers. They long for justice. They witness and experience evil. They care about reputation and honor. In short, I think this documentary shows us that we long for the coming kingdom of God, where peace, truth, righteousness, and justice reign. We long for a place where Jesus Christ, the ultimate innocent sufferer, who took the punishment for sinners, will reign forever. Our longing for justice is ultimately a longing for Jesus.

Psalm 109 speaks about sin, justice, evil, an innocent sufferer, and the need for the coming King. It does so in a most attention-grabbing way. This psalm shocks a lot of modern readers. David's outburst against his enemies causes some to wonder how this psalm could be part of Scripture. Some even view it as "sub-Christian." It reflects lament qualities, but it is best known for being an "imprecatory psalm." Imprecatory psalms call down curses ("imprecations") and express hatred toward God's enemies. There are about one hundred verses with imprecations in the Psalms. Many Christians wonder, *Do we have permission to pray these imprecatory psalms?* Well, probably not *exactly* like the psalmists, who were inspired writers of Scripture, but these prayers should inform the way we pray when faced with similar situations. But we need to understand them first.

Understanding Imprecatory Psalms

While imprecations are found throughout the Psalter (Pss 5:10; 10:15; 28:4; 31:17-18; 35:4-6; 40:14-15; 58:6-11; 69:22-28; 109:6-15; 139:19-22; 140:9-10), C. S. Lewis stated that Psalm 109 is "perhaps the worst" (*Reflections*, 12). This psalm contains about 24 curses! Lewis and others throughout the centuries have struggled with these psalms. Lewis said, "In some of the Psalms the spirit of hatred which strikes us in the face is like heat from a furnace mouth" (ibid.).

The problem, of course, lies with the seeming contradiction with the New Testament call to love our enemies and pray for those who persecute us (Matt 5:43-48), which is a distinguishing mark of Christian love (Luke 23:34; Acts 7:6; 1 Pet 2:19-23). If we only love those who love us, we're no different than pagans. So how could it be possible for God's people to pray with a seemingly vindictive and harsh spirit?

One approach is simply to scrap the imprecatory psalms. Some have done this. But for those who believe in the inspiration of Scripture and the profitableness of all Scripture, this isn't an option. In the Old Testament we find imprecatory prayers in other books, like Jeremiah (11:18-20; 15:15-18; 17:18; 18:19-23; 20:11-12) and Nehemiah (6:14; 13:29). Further, neither Jesus nor Paul avoided them. Psalm 69 seems to have been a favorite of Jesus, for he cited it several times to express aspects of his own life and ministry (John 15:25 = Ps 69:4; John 2:17 = Ps 69:9; Matt 27:24 = Ps 69:21). Paul quoted Psalm 69:22-23 in Romans

11:9-10 as having biblical authority. Both Jesus and Paul found these psalms divinely inspired and profitable.

Others want to argue that this is an area of Old Testament ethics that the New Testament improves on. But that won't work either. The New Testament writers believed themselves to be heirs of Old Testament ethics (Matt 22:34-40), and strikingly, the New Testament contains some curses of its own, either explicitly (1 Cor 16:22; Gal 1:8) or implicitly (Matt 10:11-15; 2 Tim 4:14; Rev 6:9-10).

Still others assert that we should only apply these prayers today as prayers of judgment against Satan and his demons. They assert that these prayers only apply to spiritual warfare with our ultimate enemy. There's definitely some helpful truth to this idea, but this position doesn't take into account other important matters.

None of these options are fully satisfying. We must be careful with them, but these psalms are not sub-Christian. They're inspired Scripture (2 Tim 3:16-17). I agree with Kidner that we should see them mainly for our *instruction*, not precise *imitation* (*Psalms 73–150*, 389). They have much to teach us about God, our enemies, salvation, and prayer. But we should be extremely cautious in making one-to-one correlations with the psalmists' imprecations.

Each of the imprecatory psalms must be read in its own context and interpreted individually. However, there are some general principles to keep in mind.

First, the people being cursed aren't enemies over minor matters. These enemies are wicked. These bloodthirsty liars hate God and God's people. They participate in gross and vicious evil (Pss 5:4-6,9-10; 10:15; 42:3; 94:2-7). These aren't people who cut you off in traffic or referee basketball games!

Second, we must remember the covenantal context of the Old Testament. In Deuteronomy 27–28 we see that obedience would bring Israel blessing, while disobedience would bring curses. Israel invited curses on themselves should they fail to honor God. These prayers are in many ways the simple asking of God to do what he promised in his word, which Israel agreed to follow. We see the promise of divine vengeance expressed in the Song of Moses (Deut 32:1-43), the principle of divine justice outlined in the *lex talionis* (Deut 19:16-21), and the assurance of divine cursing as well as blessing in the Abrahamic covenant (Gen 12:2-3).

Third, both the Old and New Testaments hold in tension the requirement of love and the hatred of evil (VanGemeren, "Psalms," 831). Loving one's enemies isn't just a New Testament idea (Lev 19:17-18; Prov 25:21). And the notion that people are accountable to God isn't merely an Old Testament idea (Acts 17:30-31). The New Testament clearly teaches that, apart from Jesus, we're under the righteous wrath of God. Jesus and Paul both rebuked unbelief strongly (Matt 7:23; 11:21-24; Luke 10:13-15; 1 Cor 5:5; Gal 1:8-9; 5:12). The Christian life involves both love of neighbor and hatred of evil, celebration and trembling, happiness and holy awe. It involves both love (1 Cor 13) and discipline (1 Cor 5:5; 1 Tim 1:20).

Fourth, the curses are poetic; therefore, we should see the blend of rhetorical hyperbole and righteous anger (Kidner, *Psalms 73–150*, 389). Kidner states that sometimes the speaker piles up horror upon horror more to convey his sense of outrage rather than to spell out the penalties he literally intends (ibid., 27). They're comparable to the outbursts in Job and Jeremiah (ibid., 389). How these curses are executed is left to God (cf. Ps 10).

Fifth, these curses express moral indignation, not personal vengeance. We should appreciate this. We shouldn't want those who persecute the faithful and turn people away from God not to be punished. Remember, punishment isn't sinful. It's not evil, so long as it's carried out properly.

Sixth, these prayers are fueled by zeal for the honor of God's name and for the triumph of God's kingdom. They're God centered, not selfish, evil, or childish. The ultimate character assassination is happening against God's character. That bothers the psalmists. We should also have a zeal for God's holy name.

Seventh, we must remember that there's a prophetic element to the imprecatory psalms. We can see this in various ways, one of which can be observed in Romans 15:3. There Paul quotes David's words regarding Psalm 69:9 (an imprecatory psalm) as the words of *Christ*: "For even Christ did not please himself. On the contrary, as it is written, 'The insults of those who insult you have fallen on *me*'" (emphasis added). David spoke in these psalms as the king who prefigured King Jesus. The latter has the right to pronounce final judgment on his enemies and will do so (Piper, "Do I Not Hate Those"). In light of this fact, we should see the Christ emphasis in these psalms and be slow to make a one-to-one correlation between the supplicant and ourselves.

Eighth, most of the imprecatory psalms (Psalm 109 included) assume these persecutors will not repent. They have resisted the love of the godly (Ps 109:4-5). We, on the other hand, are called to love and seek the salvation of the wicked. We don't have perfect knowledge of the possibility of someone's repenting. We're not biblical writers. We're not prophets and apostles. While we pray for God to execute judgment and establish peace, our prayer for our enemies should focus on God's bringing people to repentance. Further, in Psalm 83:17-18 the prayer sees punishment as a means of grace leading the wicked to repentance. You can see in Psalm 109 that this is a *song*. Imagine that! Why sing about God's judgment? One reason is to strike fear in the ungodly in hopes that they may repent. Our deepest desire for our enemies, even those who persecute us and inflict abuse on the church, is that they may be saved. Our hope for ISIS ultimately is that these wicked men may experience the undeserved grace of Jesus (Luke 23:34; Rom 9:1-3; 10:1; 1 Tim 2:4; 2 Pet 3:9). We should trust God to execute justice on those who refuse to believe and persist in wickedness.

Ninth, Christians should remember that any prayer for Jesus to return implies the destruction of the wicked; thus, these imprecations aren't that unusual. Paul says that when Jesus returns he will inflict vengeance on those who don't know God (2 Thess 1:7). We want Jesus to crush our enemies and destroy the chief of all accusers, Satan.

Finally, remember that we know more about the afterlife than Old Testament saints. Old Testament saints focused mainly on the temporal, but people on this side of the cross have an eternal perspective; we wait for an eschatological day of judgment (Allen, *Psalms 101–150*, 77). We can leave ultimate judgment to God, as the psalmist does in praying this prayer. Psalm 109 challenges us to be patient; final judgment will come.

Understanding Psalm 109

Psalm 109 has been outlined in various ways. One may study it in four parts: *lamentation* (vv. 1-5); *imprecation* (vv. 6-20); *desperation* (vv. 21-29); and *adoration* (vv. 30-31). I will offer four applications based on this structure in the next section. Let me mention a few high-level ideas first.

Psalm 109 is similar in content and tone to Psalm 69, both of these assert Davidic authorship. The main difference is that in Psalm 69 David acknowledges that his wrongdoing has played a role in his suffering, whereas in Psalm 109 the psalmist professes innocence. This helps us see the application to Jesus and Judas in verse 8. When we look at Jesus's words to Judas, we find Jesus (the true innocent sufferer) condemning Judas harshly (Matt 26:24; Mark 14:21). The Gospels contain harsh condemnations of Pilate and the Jewish leaders as well (John 19:11). With this in mind, I think we are wise to read this psalm with Christ in view.

In both psalms (69 and 109) it seems that the "enemies" are influential Israelites who are unfaithful to the covenant (Collins, "Psalms"). God's people knew the consequences of not obeying the covenant. David is essentially asking God to do what he already said he would do, namely, curse the wicked.

Further, we should remember that to assault God's chosen king was an assault against God himself. This psalm is about the honor of God's name (v. 21), not personal vengeance. With this in mind, we should see that this opposition to David's kingship foreshadows opposition to Jesus's kingship. We should long for Jesus to reign and make his enemies a footstool and for God to magnify his name.

David doesn't administer these curses personally. Beginning in verse 6, he asks God to act. He doesn't take matters into his own hands.

Additionally, these curses picture a deserved judgment, not a judgment against the innocent (vv. 8-20). It's right to desire that God execute just judgment on the earth (Matt 23:35; Luke 18:8). We should appreciate the cry of the martyrs (Rev 6:10). If you've seen dark wickedness, you should long for Jesus to return and establish peace and righteousness.

Next, we should tremble at God's holiness and thank God for the Savior. Jesus took the judgment we deserved. This psalm should cause us to adore the Substitute.

Finally, see how David's enemies won't repent. They resist his sustained love (v. 5). We must remember that as we desire justice for the wicked, we should also long for them to repent (1 Cor 5:5).

So then, can you hold all of this in balance as we read Psalm 109? Do you believe God is holy and that his name should be honored? Do you believe the wicked should be punished? Do you see Jesus as the righteous Sufferer, who gave you salvation when you deserved judgment? Do you believe we should also long for the wicked to be saved? Are you OK with leaving vengeance to God? Let's seek to hold these things in balance by the grace of God.

Applying Psalm 109

Like other laments Psalm 109 teaches us to *pray* through our anger and frustrations. It teaches us to submit our hearts and lives to God's will with a gospel-centered, eschatological perspective. This aspect of Psalm

109 we can certainly imitate. We will have enemies in this life. We will face character assassinations. Let's learn from this psalm how to pray when it happens, with the previous principles in mind.

Pour Out Your Heart to God (109:1-5)

In verse 1 David calls on God to speak. He doesn't want people to think God is indifferent toward evil. He wants God to act and, indeed, is confident the Lord will act. David had a close and bold relationship with God.

David speaks of *praising God* in both the beginning and end of this psalm. He's going to vent to God in the verses in between and arrive back at this place of praise. When you express your burden to God, it's amazing how you end your prayer with praise.

Why does David want God to act? His character is being attacked. The nature of this character assassination is pretty clear in verse 2. This isn't a secret campaign but something that's out in the open. David is surrounded "with hateful words" and is attacked "without cause" (v. 3). David is the object of a cruel attack by "wicked and deceitful" liars. It reminds us of Jesus being the object of trumped-up charges. Interestingly, the word *accuse* or *accuser(s)* appears in verses 4, 6, 20, and 29; this is derived from a Hebrew word from which we get the name *Satan.*

The remainder of the psalm shows more of the depth of these wounds. Verses 4-5 reveal the sadness of these attacks. David has done everything to befriend these opponents. He has shown love to them. He has prayed for them (v. 4; see Kidner, *Psalms 73–150,* 388n2). He has sought their good (v. 5). But they have repaid him with evil and hatred. It was a betrayal "almost worthy of Judas" (ibid., 388).

What should you do when someone turns on you? How do you respond when people say wicked things about you? Before doing anything or talking to anyone, learn to pour out your heart to God in prayer first.

Give Your Enemies to God (109:6-20)

Next we see David specifically pouring out his heart by leaving his enemies with God. While this section may be hard to stomach, learn from David. We see him here submitting to God's will, not seeking to retaliate personally. He's not *plotting;* he's *praying.* This is an important application. His refusal to take matters into his own hands, and instead leaving the problem to God, reflects the biblical emphasis of loving one's enemies and seeking to overcome evil with good (Rom 12:14-21).

While it's good and right to expect evil men to face consequences on this earth, we must avoid repaying evil with evil. Because we believe in the supernatural and the life to come, we can take the long view, leaving the matter to God. Moreover, on this side of the cross we have a better eternal perspective than Old Testament saints.

John Calvin said, "No greater injury can be inflicted upon men than to wound their reputation" (in Lawson, *Psalms 76–150*, 184). What will you do when you're the object of a character assassination? It's certainly wise and good at times to give a defense, but that's another sermon! Psalm 109 is teaching us to commit such a matter to prayer and entrust ourselves to our God. Character assassinations are painful, but God's presence is medicinal. Bring your wounds to Jesus, the one who was wounded for you. Lawson says, "The best way to get rid of an enemy is to leave him or her with the Lord" (ibid., 185). Amen.

In verses 6-20 David pronounces specific judgments that he wants God to carry out. This is his list of how he would like God to bring about judgment on the apparent ringleader of the opposition ("him," vv. 6-19) and the rest of the accusers (v. 20). We may consider the curses in two broad categories (Lawson, *Psalms 76–150*, 188).

Appoint a wicked man against him (vv. 6-7). In some type of court of law, David asks for his accuser to be accused and indicted. In light of his enemy's wickedness, David asks for a wicked man to oppose this wicked enemy. "Give him some of his own medicine!" he pleads. Since David's enemy is evil, he wants his enemy to be found "guilty," with no "prayer" for help.

Appoint a painful future for him (vv. 8-20). Next David expresses his desires for the enemy's future. He asks for his enemy's days to be few and then for someone else to take over his office. Apparently this enemy had some official position. The apostles refer to this text in the replacement of Judas (Acts 1:20).

In verses 9-10 David asks God to deal with his enemy's children and wife. The main concern here seems to be public disgrace and for future sins not to continue. He adds that he wishes his enemy's children to be beggars and for his offspring to be homeless. Then he wants all his possessions seized and his children to be neglected (vv. 11-12). In verse 13 he asks God to cut off his enemy's descendants. Here's the ultimate disaster: the cutting off of the family line. There was nothing more precious to the Israelite than the generations to come (Williams, *Psalms 73–150*, Kindle). In short, David asks God to execute judgment on the whole family.

Such a disastrous judgment is even pronounced against the evil man's predecessors (vv. 14-15). He doesn't want anyone even to remember them.

Why such harsh punishment? David tells us in verse 16. His enemy didn't show covenant love; he didn't do justice and love mercy and walk humbly with God (Mic 6:8). He deserves punishment (cf. Ps 10).

The thought of this man's sinfulness triggers more curses in verses 17-20. To summarize them, David asks the Lord to give this man what he deserves. In verse 20 David concludes by addressing the whole group of accusers, not merely the ringleader.

While it's hard to imagine praying things against someone's family, remember that David's prayer is based on Old Testament principles and practices. For example, God said that the sins of the fathers would be visited on the children to the third and fourth generations of *those who hate him* (Exod 20:5; Deut 5:9; cf. Prov 3:33; 17:13). God warned that the unrepentant would be punished. Since God gave such promises, his people weren't wrong in petitioning him to fulfill them.

Further, we should remember that in verse 9, "Let his children be fatherless and his wife a widow," the psalmist is looking back to God's word in Exodus 22:22-24 (cf. Deut. 27:19):

> *You must not mistreat any widow or fatherless child. If you do mistreat them, they will no doubt cry to me, and I will certainly hear their cry. My anger will burn, and I will kill you with the sword; then your wives will be widows and your children fatherless.*

David was reminding God to be true to his promise.

Moreover, the execution of the wicked was also for Israel's protection. God would not let his people—in particular, the lineage of David—be exterminated by wicked men. In God's love, he protected his people, from whom the Messiah would eventually come.

More practically, notice David's example of presenting this matter to God instead of inflicting personal vengeance. We should learn to ask God to act. We should ask God to execute justice on the wicked or to change their hard hearts and convert them. The apostle Paul was present at Stephen's martyrdom, approving of an innocent man's death, but the Lord changed Paul's heart. It's right to pray for justice to be executed against terrorist groups, and it's also right to pray for God to convert such Paul-like individuals. Further, this mention of the chief of all accusers should also make us long for Christ, the better David, to return and cast Satan into the lake of fire forever (Rev 20:10). Right now the accuser is deceiving many, and he deserves every curse we could imagine.

Believe it or not, you will have enemies in this life! How will you respond? Pray for God to execute justice or change them by his mercy. Pray for God to act. Leave your enemies to God in prayer. Be patient, for Christ will bring total justice in the future.

Appeal to, and Rest in, the Character of God (109:21-29)

When falsely accused, meditate on God's character. In these verses we find David appealing to and resting in God's justice and faithful love as he confesses his own weakness.

In the context of judgment, David asks the Lord to "rescue" him and "help" him (vv. 21,26). He turns his attention to the character of God with an emphatic contrast: "But you, LORD, my Lord" (v. 21a). David considers the greatness of God's sovereignty, the righteousness of God's judgment, and the steadfastness of God's love in order to find strength in time of need. If we find ourselves wrongly accused or persecuted, we too would do well to meditate on the character of our God. Keller helps us apply this prayer:

> Lord, I thank you that your reality changes everything. I am weak—O, but you . . . I deserve nothing—O, but you . . . I don't see any way out of this—O, but you . . . My life seems to be derailed—O, but you . . . I don't know how to pray. Ah, but you will help me. Amen. (*Songs of Jesus*, 289)

Pondering who God is changes everything! It allows us to rest. It gives us confidence. It gives us strength.

After shifting his attention to God's character, David goes on to seek God's help for his own good and ultimately for God's glory (v. 21). This spirit is at the heart of our prayers for the Lord's return, that his people may have peace and blessing and that Christ may receive the glory he is due.

After praying for the Lord to deliver him, David asks the Lord to consider his broken condition, which gives the reason for his desperate plea for deliverance. He tells the Lord that his heart is wounded (v. 22), that his life is fading (v. 23), that his knees are collapsing (v. 24a), that his body is emaciated (v. 24b), and that his accusers are scornful (v. 25; Lawson, *Psalms 76–150*, 189). He casts his insufficiency on God's self-sufficiency. Out of his weakness, he turns to God for strength. And he finds strength by meditating on the character and purposes of God. David then offers a petition to God. Verse 26 is another desperate plea for God *to save him.* Verses 27-29 are pleas for God *to shame them.* Again, he desires for God's name to be honored. This must be at the heart of our prayers.

When you feel weak and defeated, discouraged and beaten, broken and wounded, follow David's lead and say, "But you, my Lord." He is our unchanging rock. He is our refuge. He protects and he delivers. He strengthens the weak.

Keep Praising God (109:30-31)

In the final section David finishes with a confession of faith and vow to praise God. So David ends where he began: with praise to the God of justice and mercy. He commits to praise God *passionately* (v. 30a). David's not speaking about routine, mindless praise, but heartfelt thanksgiving. He also commits to give God praise *publicly* (v. 30b). Everyone will know he loves his God.

Don't let false accusations and enemies keep you from magnifying the Creator and Redeemer. Praise God through the affliction, like Paul and Silas did in the Philippian prison.

Verse 31 contains two reasons to praise God that point us ahead in the biblical narrative to the Savior. David says God is worthy of passionate and public praise because he stands with the needy, and he saves the condemned.

This phrase "at the right hand" (v. 31a) appeared in verse 6, referring to his enemy's accuser. Now *God* is pictured standing at David's right hand, in a position of support. In the New Testament we read how the Spirit (the *parakletos*) comes alongside to help us (John 16:7), and how Jesus advocates and intercedes for us (Rom 8:34; 1 John 2:1). What wonderful support the Christian has! Jesus is at our Father's right hand, praying for us. The Spirit is with us to counsel and help us. I'm reminded of Stephen's martyrdom, where an innocent man suffered. Luke tells us that before Stephen breathed his last breath, he saw Jesus standing at the Father's right hand (Acts 7:56). Jesus was in the position of intercession. Let's remember we're not alone when we're afflicted and persecuted.

Jesus's path to this position came through the cross. At the cross Jesus took the curses that we deserved (Gal 3:13-14). We deserved God's wrath, but that wrath fell on the greater David, Jesus. Through no fault of his own, Jesus was betrayed, mocked, made the object of lies, and crucified shamefully on a cross. He took the punishment that was due us. In Christ we are saved. The wrath of God will not fall on us. Psalm 109 should help us see how much we need a Substitute. And because we know the Savior, and we have the Savior interceding for us, we also have the strength we need to love our enemies and the strength we need to leave vengeance to God. Maranatha!

Reflect and Discuss

1. How have you seen people reflect the human desire for justice?
2. What was your first reaction upon reading Psalm 109? Why?
3. Explain David's trials. Why is he so troubled?
4. What does this psalm teach us about pouring out our hearts to God?
5. How does Judas's relationship to Jesus relate to this psalm?
6. How should we pray for our enemies?
7. In verse 21 David shifts his attention to the character of God. Why is this important?
8. How does David express his weakness to God?
9. Why does David desire to continue praising God (vv. 30-31)?
10. Take a few moments to pray in light of this psalm and in light of Jesus's work on the cross.

The Great King-Priest of Psalm 110

Main Idea: Jesus is the better and perfect King-Priest sent by God.

I. **Messiah Jesus Is Our Great King (110:1-3).**
   A. He is enthroned by the Lord (110:1).
   B. He is empowered by the Lord (110:2-3).
II. **Messiah Jesus Is Our Great High Priest (110:4-7).**
   A. His priesthood is irrevocable (110:4).
   B. His power is invincible (110:5-7).

Psalm 110 is the psalm most quoted in the New Testament. Verse 1 appears at least 25 times, and verse 4 appears at least five times. It shines Christologically as bright as the noonday sun. Here King David plays the role of poetic prophet portraying the coming Messiah, joining company with Psalm 22 and Isaiah 53. No wonder Allen Ross says, "Psalm 110 is one of the most fascinating psalms in the entire collection" (*Psalms 90–150*, 339).

In Matthew 22:42-46 our Lord, in a confrontation with the Pharisees, turned the tables on them by citing this psalm when he asked,

> *"What do you think about the Messiah? Whose son is he?"*
> *They replied, "David's."*
> *He asked them, "How is it then that David, inspired by the Spirit, calls him 'Lord': The Lord declared to my Lord, 'Sit at my right hand until I put your enemies under your feet'? If David calls him 'Lord,' how then can he be his son?" No one was able to answer him at all, and from that day no one dared to question him anymore.*

With unmistakable clarity, Jesus affirms Davidic authorship of Psalm 110 (something some liberal scholars reject), affirms the inspiration of the Holy Spirit in Scripture, and makes clear that the Messiah, a human descendant of David, would be more than just a man. This event was so crucial in the life of Jesus that all three Synoptic Gospels record it (Matt 22:41-46; Mark 12:35-37; Luke 20:41-44).

Psalm 110 is a purely messianic, prophetic psalm with Yahweh as the speaker. The language and themes are so exalted and magnificent they cannot apply appropriately to any mere human. Luther was so taken by it he wrote 120 pages of commentary on it (Boice, *Psalms 107–150*, 896).

This "Lord" (*adonai*) is a King-Priest. This Lord sits at Yahweh's right hand, watches Yahweh strike down all his enemies, and is an eternal high priest after the order of Melchizedek (Gen 14:18-20). He is human because he descends from David, but he is also God because he has co-authority with "the LORD" and his priesthood is of eternal duration. The psalm brims with eschatological overtones as God's people look forward to the great and climactic victory of their King-Priest.

Even the Jews of Jesus' day believed Psalm 110 was messianic. They did not know, however, how awesome the Messiah would truly be, both in his person and in his work. James Boice captures beautifully this psalm's message when he says,

> Psalm 110 is entirely about a divine King who has been installed at the right hand of God in heaven and who is presently engaged in extending his spiritual rule throughout the whole earth. It tells us that this divine Messiah is also a priest, performing priestly functions, and that additionally he is a judge who at the end of time will execute a final judgment on the nations and rulers of this earth. (*Psalms 107–150*, 892–93)

The psalm naturally and easily divides into two stanzas, with each stanza functioning as a divine oracle. The pattern in both is the same: there is a promise and a result. Stanza one rejoices, in a manner like Psalm 2, in the Messiah as a great king. Stanza two exalts the Messiah as the great priest after the order of the mysterious Melchizedek. He is crowned as king in verses 1-3 and consecrated as priest in verses 4-7.

Messiah Jesus Is Our Great King
PSALM 110:1-3

Stanza one sings of Yahweh and his chosen king. David overhears a heavenly conversation between "the LORD" (Yahweh) and David's Lord (*adonai*), between the Father and his Messiah-Son. Here the Father makes three promises to his Messiah-Son: I will defeat your enemies (v. 1), I will extend your kingdom (v. 2), and I will give you a great army (v. 3).

Verse 1 in particular plays a significant role in the New Testament. It makes plain Jesus's identity as the Messiah. As noted, Jesus cited this verse to prove that the Messiah is more than a mere physical descendant of David. Peter also quotes Psalm 110:1 on the day of Pentecost to demonstrate that Jesus is the Messiah-Lord (Acts 2:34-36). The writer of Hebrews, likewise, quotes this verse to argue that the Messiah (who is Jesus) is greater than the angels (Heb 1:13). The writers of the New Testament cite the verse in order to show that since Jesus's crucifixion, resurrection, and ascension (Acts 2:33-34; Heb 6:20), he is seated at the right hand of God the Father in heaven. The New Testament writers also state that God the Father places his enemies under his Son Jesus' feet (1 Cor 15:25-28; Eph 1:22; Heb 10:13). In this psalm God clarifies and makes plain just how he will fulfill his great promise to David in 2 Samuel 7 that he would "establish the throne of his kingdom forever" through David's son (vv. 13,16).

He Is Enthroned by the Lord (110:1)

Of this opening phrase Patrick Reardon asks, "In all the Psalter, is there a line more precious and beloved than this?" (*Christ in the Psalms*, 217). This statement contains a divine oracle or word of revelation. Yahweh and *adonai* stand as one against those who are enemies (twice in vv. 1-2) of both! To oppose God's King-Priest is to oppose God as well.

The "right hand" points to the place of honor, authority, and power. God grants the Messiah-King his power and authority by virtue of who he is (king) and what he does (priest). This King-Priest fully participates in divine royal dignity and power. Echoes of this statement ring in Philippians 2:9-11:

> *For this reason God highly exalted him and gave him the name that is above every name, so that at the name of Jesus every knee will bow—in heaven and on earth and under the earth—and every tongue will confess that Jesus Christ is Lord, to the glory of God the Father.*

"Footstool" is a symbol of complete and total victory. God's chosen king will place his feet on the necks of his defeated enemies, and all of this is the work of Yahweh. The New Testament writers apply this promise to the risen Christ no less than seven times (Acts 2:32-36; 1 Cor 15:25; Eph 1:20-21; Col 3:1; Heb 1:13; 8:1; 10:12-13). What a difference there is between God's evaluation of his Son and those on earth who mock, ridicule, and diminish him. How much more wonderful it is to sit with him on his throne than to be crushed under his feet.

He Is Empowered by the Lord (110:2-3)

Verses 2-3 proclaim a great reversal. The world's evaluation of this King-Priest is turned on its head by heaven. Men may reject Jesus as Lord, but in so doing they oppose God himself.

The phrase "your mighty scepter" is placed at the beginning of verse 2 for emphasis. The scepter is a symbol of the king's domination, strength, power, and authority. Once again, this is Yahweh's doing! This strong scepter extends from Zion, but it does not stop until all his enemies are his footstool and he rules in their midst! The verb "rule over" is imperative. The Messiah will sit with his feet on his enemies' necks, and he will rule as King.

Verse 3 affirms that Messiah Jesus will have volunteers who freely join him in the day of battle. Cheerfully and promptly, they obey the Messiah's commands, consecrating themselves in "holy splendor" (NASB, "holy array"; ESV, "holy garments"). These volunteers have realized his greatness and acknowledged his superiority. They gladly surrender everything to do anything he would ask. Nothing is too great for them to do or to give for this King. They are prepared, strong, and ready!

The phrase "holy splendor" may suggest that his servants are to be holy as their priestly king is holy. Exodus 19:6 and Revelation 5:10 both identify the Messiah's followers as a "kingdom of priests." They will share in his reign, and they share in his service.

The last phrase of verse 3 is challenging; its exact meaning is unclear.[2] It could describe the freshness and enthusiasm of his large army of volunteers. It may even refer to their beauty, brilliance, and attractiveness as it relates to their holy garments. However, it is also possible that our eternal King-Priest is the focus. Our King-Priest is portrayed as clothed in royal, priestly apparel and perpetually preserved in his youth and vigor. This King-Priest does not grow old, tire, or faint. He does not need a break, timeout, or midday nap. He is perpetually and forever empowered by the life of God in him. He goes forth in youthful vigor, holiness, and glory as the head of a great host who willingly follow him everywhere he goes and deploy anywhere he sends them. Kidner's summation is certainly helpful: "This verse (as I see it) pictures the Messiah going forth in primal vigor, holiness and glory, as the head of a host. . . . The Christian can identify such an army with the overcomer portrayed in Revelation 12:11" (*Psalms 73–150*, 394–95).

---

[2] The CSB translates it "from the womb of the dawn, the dew of your youth belongs to you." The ESV reads in a similar fashion.

Walter Chantry captures well how we should respond to the King of verses 1-3:

> Anyone who has caught a glimpse of the heavenly splendor and sovereign might of Christ would do well to imitate the saints of ages past. It is only appropriate to worship him with deep reverence. You may pour out great love in recognition of your personal relationship with him. He is your Lord. You are his and he is yours. However, you are not pals. He is Lord and Master. You are servant and disciple. He is infinitely above you in the scale of being. His throne holds sway over you for your present life and for assigning your eternal reward. A king is to be honored, confessed, obeyed and worshiped. (*Praises for the King of Kings*, 59)

Messiah Jesus Is Our Great High Priest
PSALM 110:4-7

The union of the offices of king and priest never actualizes in the Old Testament era. Yet it is prophesied and anticipated not only in Psalm 110 but also in Zechariah 6:12-13 (HCSB):

> *You are to tell him: This is what the LORD of Armies says: Here is a man whose name is Branch; He will branch out from His place and build the LORD's temple. Yes, He will build the LORD's temple; He will be clothed in splendor and will sit on His throne and rule. There will be a priest on His throne, and there will be peaceful counsel between the two of them.*

The office of king and priest were separate roles in the Old Testament. But the coming Messiah will have both of these roles. The one who rules God's people and the one who intercedes between God and man will be the same person!

Here in Psalm 110, the text takes an unexpected turn. To unite the office of king and priest was not on the Hebrew radar screen. However, back in Genesis 14:18-20 there was a King-Priest from Salem (Jerusalem before it was Jerusalem) by the name of Melchizedek. He appears out of nowhere and then is gone in a flash. He is only mentioned three times in the Bible: Genesis 14; Psalm 110; and the book of Hebrews. In Hebrews he is mentioned no less than eight times. Now, in this central verse of

Psalm 110, this King-Priest of peace and righteousness is revealed. A more perfect type of Christ is found nowhere else in all of the Bible. Like verse 1, verse 4 is crucial in developing the Christology of the New Testament. Here Jesus receives the title of high priest (only expressly stated in Hebrews), a title after which he did not grasp but one the author of Hebrews clearly says belongs to him (Heb 4:14-15; 5:10; 6:20; 7:26; 8:1; 10:21). By being a high priest after the order of Melchizedek, Jesus is the mediator and source of salvation for all who believe in him (Heb 5:9-10). Jesus, having become a Melchizedekian priest, entered the presence of God to show the way for believers to enter heaven (Heb 6:20). By becoming a priest after the order of Melchizedek, Jesus initiated a new order (Heb 7:17). Jesus' priesthood, after the order of Melchizedek, is a greater priesthood than that of the Levitical order arising from Aaron (Heb 7:15-21). It is eternal in him and will never end.

His Priesthood Is Irrevocable (110:4)

Verse 4 is the heart of the psalm. It sends a seismic shock throughout our spiritual system with its beginning. Here is a solemn divine promise. The sense is, "May I die if I break my word or renege on my promise." If anything is stronger than a divine oracle (v. 1), it is a divine oath.

To reinforce the binding nature of the oath, the Lord adds, "[I] will not take it back" (i.e., I will not change my mind). The Lord promises eternal priesthood to the Messiah. You and no other, says the Lord, are the great priest. As Melchizedek—a name that means "King of Righteousness"—was a king-priest in his day, you shall be a King-Priest forever, he promises. No one will ever succeed you.

The Messiah would be a priest like Melchizedek. He would be a priest for all nations, not just Israel. He would be a King-Priest, combining two offices. His reign will be without beginning and without end much like Melchizedek's, whose origin and destiny are not told in Scripture. And as Abram saw Melchizedek to be associated with the victory God had given him, so Messiah will be victorious in battle against his foes, a matter described in verses 5-7.

His Priesthood Is Invincible (110:5-7)

The last three verses of Psalm 110 transition us from the book of Hebrews to the book of Revelation. Our great high priest is not a wimpy or weak priest. He is a Warrior Lamb! The playground bullies of the world, both spiritual and physical, meet more than their match in this "divine warrior." His sitting at God's right hand (v. 5) should strike terror in his enemies and bring joy to his people.

The "day of [his] battle" or "power" (v. 3 ESV) is now identified as "the day of his anger" (v. 5). There is a fixed day and time when he will make himself known for who he truly is. Revelation 6:16-17 calls it the great day of the wrath of the Lamb. Five bold affirmations are declared concerning what this King-Priest will do to his enemies. While this King-Priest is an advocate for all who follow him, he is a deadly adversary to all who oppose him. First, "he will crush kings in the day of his anger" (v. 5). Second, according to verse 6, "he will judge the nations" (note Ps 2:8, which also emphasizes this theme). Third, he will fill the places [the nations] with dead bodies ("corpses"; v. 6). This language anticipates the Armageddon judgment of Revelation 19:17-21. Fourth, "he will crush leaders over the entire world," literally "the head [Hb *rosh*] over many lands." Genesis 3:15 and the protoevangelium are in the shadows of verse 6. The head of the old serpent and all who follow in his lying, deceitful, and evil path will be crushed by the thorn-crowned head of a risen King-Priest (see Ross, *Psalms 90–150*, 357). Fifth, and finally, "he will drink from the brook by the road." Following his great victory, he is refreshed as he returns to his throne (v. 7). Therefore, "he will lift up his head" (Hb *rosh*).

Conclusion

In verse 6 a head is cut down, executed, and "crushed," recalling the language of Genesis 3:15, a promise proclaimed in Romans 16:20. Now another head, the head of a crucified and risen King-Priest, is lifted up and exalted. The book of Hebrews paints an extraordinary picture of this King-Priest and his works. He is the author of eternal salvation (Heb 5:9). He is the hope we have as an anchor of the soul (Heb 6:19). He has the power of an endless life (Heb 7:16). He is the guarantee of a better covenant (Heb 7:22). He is able to save completely those who come to God through him since he always lives to make intercession for them (Heb 7:25; cf. Rom 8:34). He is holy, innocent, undefiled, and separate from sinners, and he has become higher than the heavens (Heb 7:26). He offered himself without blemish to God to cleanse your conscience from dead works to serve the living God (Heb 9:14). He appeared in order to put away sin by the sacrifice of himself, which was offered once to bear the sins of many (Heb 9:26-27). After he had offered one sacrifice for sins forever, he sat down at the right hand of God and is waiting until his enemies are made his footstool (Heb 10:12). He makes it possible for us to have boldness to enter the most holy place by his blood (Heb 10:19). A perfect kingdom needs a perfect king. A perfect temple needs a perfect priest. Jesus is our perfect King-Priest.

Reflect and Discuss

1. What are some reasons Jesus's connection with the expected Messiah is so important?
2. Can Christians have Jesus as their Savior but not as their King? Why or why not? Have you emphasized Jesus's kingship in your Christian life? If yes, how so?
3. If the Messiah was to subdue his enemies, why did Jesus focus on loving his enemies in the New Testament? How does the redemptive story of the Bible help you answer this question?
4. What parts of Psalm 110 are connected with Jesus's first coming? Which will occur at his second coming? In what ways is it good that Jesus will fulfill all of Psalm 110 at two separate times?
5. How do the Christian's relationship to God as Father and Jesus as King relate to and affect one another?
6. Why is it necessary that Jesus be both a king and a priest? What does each role contribute to Christ's work?
7. The offices of king and priest are less common today than during David's time. How might you explain Jesus's role as King-Priest to someone who is not familiar with the Bible?
8. Using the pattern of Hebrews, how will Jesus's future kingdom be better since he is a perfect King-Priest?
9. Verse 5 mentions that the Lord will "crush kings on the day of his anger." How does this verse relate to the teaching that "God is love" (1 John 4:8)?
10. Compare Philippians 3:20-21; Colossians 1:13; and 1 Peter 2:11-15. How can you describe your identity in light of Jesus's role as King?

God and Godliness at Work

PSALMS 111–112

Main Idea: The person who fears the Lord and submits to his Word will reflect God's own character.

I. **God at Work (111)**
   A. Praise the Lord (111:1).
   B. Consider the works of the Lord (111:2-7a).
   C. Consider the instructions of the Lord (111:7b-9).
   D. Fear the Lord (111:10).
II. **Godliness at Work (112)**
   A. Individual and family (112:1-2)
   B. Fortune and misfortune (112:3-4)
   C. Generosity and security (112:5-6)
   D. Threat and trust (112:7-8)
   E. Compassion and consequences (112:9-10)

Psalms 111–112, like peanut butter and jelly, are best enjoyed together. VanGemeren says, "[These] form a unit and may have been written by the same author or originated from within the same general approach to piety" ("Psalms," 700). Kidner agrees:

> There is an especially close bond between 111 and 112.
> These two are acrostics, each having 22 lines beginning
> with successive letters of the Hebrew alphabet. But they are
> also matched in subject matter, which tells us of God in this
> Psalm [111], and of the man of God in the next [112], even
> sharing the same or similar phrases in one or two verses.
> (*Psalms 73–150*, 396)

Virtually all commentators point out the alphabetic acrostic pattern in these psalms, which makes for good poetry and memorability but not for the most logical development. Nevertheless, these psalms, like the Proverbs, are rich with wisdom. Both contain a call to praise, but they are concerned with communicating wisdom, particularly wisdom about the wonders of God's providence and redemption and the practice of godliness.

These psalms set me thinking about biblical manhood since this subject appears here (112:2-9). How would you go about training a young man in the practice of godliness? We definitely need such training! We may start in various places, but these two psalms are instructive. Men (and women too!) need to know *who God is*, and they need to know *what a godly life looks like.* One could build an entire curriculum around this simple two-part structure.

Regarding the former, it's imperative that we give young men a proper vision of God. For if we teach them about godliness apart from God, they will lack the necessary worldview, power, and motivation for godliness. I would venture to say that we lack a culture of biblical manhood because we lack a culture of *theology.* A godly life flows from knowing God personally and deeply. It involves reflecting the character of God. So let's begin and infuse all of our training with a faithful and passionate explanation of the nature and work of the Triune God.

In Psalm 111 we see "God at work," and in Psalm 112 we see "godliness at work" (both Kidner and Allen use these titles). As we celebrate the great works of the Lord, and as we consider godliness in everyday life, may we all grow in God-centered wisdom.

God at Work

PSALM 111

The psalmist begins by celebrating the works of God in creation/providence, and especially his works in redemption, accomplished on behalf of his "covenant" people (vv. 5,9). The author's purpose is to remind the congregation of their astonishing privileges as God's people and their responsibility of walking in the fear of their Lord. Indeed, the Lord is the focus of the psalm, for we read of his character as being great, splendid, majestic, righteous, gracious, compassionate, faithful, just, trustworthy, steadfast, holy, and awe-inspiring. The only proper response to this God is to stand in awe before him and order our lives according to his holy Word.

Praise the Lord (111:1)

The psalmist opens and closes with a call to praise (vv. 1,10). He begins with "Hallelujah!" We are created and redeemed to do this: to give praise to God. But how? The psalmist tells us in verse 1. The call is both *personal* and *corporate*. We're reminded here that our faith is intimate but not individualistic. Godliness involves *heartfelt* worship (Deut 6:5; Ps 100:1-2), and it involves *public participation* in worship.

This verse corrects two common problems: private mysticism and religious hypocrisy. The mystics are all about worship, but they never unite with a local assembly in public worship and practical ministry. They live isolated lives. This is not biblical Christianity. The religious hypocrites are physically present in public worship, but their worship is heartless and insincere. This type of worship doesn't honor the Lord (Matt 15:8). Psalm 111 provides needed corrective for these two problems. Let's worship with other believers, and let's worship from the heart.

Consider the Works of the Lord (111:2-7a)

Now for the theme of the psalm (v. 2). "The Lord's works" could refer to his redemptive works (v. 6), but here the psalmist is probably speaking of the things God has made, the things of heaven and earth (cf. Pss 8:3; 19:1; 102:25; 104:24; Kidner, *Psalms 73–150*, 397). These works reveal God's wisdom (cf. 104:24). We should study God's creative works and "delight in them" (111:2b), just as God delights in his creation (cf. 104:26,31).

This verse gives us added support to the need to study God's general revelation with childlike wonder and amazement. But we must resist the urge to worship created things rather than Creator God (Rom 1:24-25). These wonders should lead us to the awe-inspired worship of our Creator and Sustainer (Ps 111:10).

God's work is then described as "splendid and majestic" (v. 3). If the psalmist is referring to God's providence, we can understand him calling God's providences "majestic" (cf. 8:1-2; 19:1-4a; 104:1,31). But if he's thinking more specifically about God's works in redemption, these terms apply as well (cf. 106:21-22; Exod 15:11). We probably shouldn't draw too sharp a distinction here. Everything the Lord does is splendid and majestic (Isa 45:9-13), and such work flows from his righteous character, which "endures forever" (111:3; cf. 103:6; Rev 15:4).

In verse 4 the psalmist draws attention to God's "wondrous works," which the Lord caused to be "remembered." Here the psalmist almost certainly has in mind God's works in redemption, of salvation history in general, and perhaps of the Passover in particular (Exod 12). Such redeeming works flow from the Lord's being "gracious and compassionate" (cf. 103:8; Exod 34:6). The redeeming works of God reveal the Lord's character, and we must not forget who he is and what he has done. In Jesus Christ we have experienced a greater Passover (1 Cor 5:7) and greater exodus (Col 1:13-14). This salvation is clearly the result of God's being gracious and compassionate to us and not a result of our morality or goodness.

The psalmist gets more specific in verse 5. God's provision involves more than his general provision for creation. The psalmist probably has God's miraculous feeding of Israel in the wilderness in mind (Exod 16). This covenant-keeping God protects and blesses his people with needed provisions. Whatever his people needed during the exodus, God provided for them. Throughout generations, God's people have been able to give testimony of the Lord's provision and grace. Consequently, we should trust in him who works out all things according to the counsel of his will and whose love endures forever (Rom 8:28-39).

God provided for his people not only in the wilderness but also when bringing them into the promised land (v. 6). Food and land are visible displays of God's power and his faithfulness to his covenant. God has revealed his power to Christians by sending his Son to be our Savior. Jesus has broken the powers of sin, Satan, death, and judgment through his substitutionary death and victorious resurrection. And he has given us an inheritance that is altogether glorious (Eph 1:3-14)!

The psalmist strikes the theme of the psalm again (v. 7a), before transitioning to the nature of the Lord's instructions (v. 7b). Blended with God's mercy and grace is his truthfulness and justice. These aspects of the Lord's character help us understand redemption in that they remind us of God's promises and his covenant. God does what he says. God does what is right. Godliness involves imitating God in these ways (cf. 112:5).

Consider the Instructions of the Lord (111:7b-9)

Moving from God's works to God's words, we should see the connection between the two. The psalmist speaks of "all his instructions" (ESV, "precepts") as being "trustworthy" (v. 7b; cf. 119:4). Everything God says—his blessings, warnings, encouragements, threats, instructions, and promises—are true! God's words reflect his true and trustworthy character, so they endure "forever and ever" (v. 8a; cf. Matt 24:35). Therefore, we should seek God's Word diligently and endeavor to enact his instructions in a true and trustworthy manner.

God's Word also brings life and redemption (v. 9). Again we hear echoes of the exodus (cf. Exod 15:13). God brought his people out of slavery and then gave them his instructions at Sinai. God redeemed his people that they would walk in holiness before him by living under his word humbly and happily. Such redemption magnifies his holy and awesome character. The Lord's works and the Lord's instructions reveal his holy and awesome nature. Until we stand in awe of him, we will neither understand godliness nor desire to walk in it.

Fear the Lord (111:10)

What should our response to this awesome God be? Fear him, the one whose "praise endures forever" (v. 10; cf. Rev 5:13b; 7:12).

A wise and godly life *starts* with a proper fear of the Lord (Prov 1:7; 9:10; Eccl 12:13). And a wise and godly life is *sustained* by maintaining a proper fear of the Lord. So let us stand in awe of him daily. Let us remember that holy reverence will lead to humble and faithful obedience. And let us remember that we cannot know this God rightly if we do not give ourselves to "his instructions" (v. 10b). We need biblical "insight" (v. 10b) in order to know our Redeemer and Provider and to walk in his ways. Psalm 112 picks up this essential application of fearing God for Christian discipleship.

Godliness at Work
PSALM 112

In this wisdom psalm the psalmist uses the "happy person" language (v. 1), which opens the Psalter (1:1). As in Psalm 1, the psalmist contrasts the happy person (112:1-9) with the "wicked" (v. 10). We should also observe that Psalm 112 not only spotlights the honor of the happy person but also reminds us of the reality of times of darkness (v. 4), bad news (v. 7), and adversaries (v. 8). Thus, the truly happy life isn't an easy life. The psalmist teaches us how to live a godly and happy life in the midst of a broken world. Let's consider five categories of practical godliness (adapted from Wilcock, *Message*, 171–72).

Individual and Family (112:1-2)

The psalmist opens with a call to praise and then makes the overarching statement about the godly. The godly person has been so transformed by God's grace that he's marked by God-centered holiness and biblical happiness.

Specifically, the godly person here delights in God's commands. In Psalm 111 the godly delight in the study of God's works in creation, and here in Psalm 112 the godly delight in God's words in Scripture (cf. 1:2; 119:24,77,92,143,174). Real, abiding, durable, and deep delight comes through meditating on the wonders of God in creation and the wonders of God's words in Scripture. Do you delight in meditating on God's words?

Ligon Duncan comments on the importance of delighting in God's commands from this passage:

> Have you ever had the privilege of working with or for someone who, in the course of working with and for that person, you develop such an admiration for that person's character, such an appreciation for their vision and their integrity that you would do anything for that person? It delights you to work for them. It's been my joy in life to be a number-two man, a right-hand man, a junior assistant to several truly great men from the time I was a teenager through my thirties[.] I got to be the person who stood behind someone else and sort of held their luggage and sort of helped them along and watched them do their ministry. And I so admired those godly men that the Lord put in my life that I would have chewed through steel bars for them. And that's what true piety is like in relation to God. When you realize what a loving heavenly Father He is, how generous He has been, when you realize the marvel of His character, you love Him so that you long, you desire, you delight to do His will. Your attitude is not, "Oh, do I have to?" it's "You mean I get to do that? I delight to do His will!" Why? Because you love to please Him. It's not a burden to please Him. You love the encouragement; you love the blessing of doing that which is pleasing in His sight. And this is piety to delight in duty, to delight in doing what God commands.

> William Plummer, the great southern Presbyterian commentator on the Psalms says, "The greatest want in

the world is a want of true piety." And it's certainly one of the greatest wants in the church. If our congregation was characterized by a true delight in God and a true delight in His commands and a true reverence and fear of Him, what a witness there would be to the world around us, what a witness. (Duncan, "Living in the Right Kind of Fear")

So then, holiness and happiness are not at odds. Jesus said, "Blessed are the pure in heart, for they will see God" (Matt 5:8). You are blessed with real happiness, real delight, when you follow God's commands. The reason there's so little happiness in our world today is there's so little holiness in our world. Let's delight in doing our heavenly Father's will. Such delightful obedience will have great impact on the world around us.

Verse 2 reminds us that the godly life isn't a private matter. The blessing of a godly person extends to his descendants. The psalmist says children enjoy the blessings of living in a godly home (cf. 2 Tim 1:5). While bodily exercise has some value, godliness is profitable in many ways, extending to the family and to the next life (1 Tim 4:8).

While children must make the faith personal, there's no denying that kids of believing parents enjoy certain privileges that children of unbelieving parents don't enjoy. They get to hear the gospel. They get to hear the Scriptures taught in the home. They get to be led in prayer by their parents. They get godly counsel for living. They get to see a just and kind life modeled before them. Again, this doesn't ensure their conversion, but it does mean they should see privileges they enjoy. And we parents should see our responsibility to train them up in the gospel that they may find life and blessing.

Further, we should seek to reach kids of unbelieving parents that they may become part of the family of God. We should consider the needs of children around us. We should consider adoption. We should be involved in foster care. We should reach out to the functionally fatherless in our schools and neighborhoods. We should volunteer in various community programs—all to the end that kids may hear the good news and be drawn into a relationship with the Redeemer.

Fortune and Misfortune (112:3-4)

The psalmist continues talking about the blessing of the home (v. 3). He is speaking of the overall stability of the home. The godly often enjoy seasons of fortune in which they're blessed with many material blessings.

But we should avoid two readings of this verse. First, we shouldn't adopt a "let go and let God" philosophy of work. That is, we shouldn't think human work isn't involved in the acquisition of provision. Rather, godly men are hard-working, "mighty" men (v. 2 ESV). They work the land (Prov 12:11,27), and God provides the rain and blessing.

Second, we shouldn't read this verse as a proof text for the prosperity gospel—that is, the idea that if you have enough faith, then you will have plenty of health, wealth, and prosperity. The psalmist emphasizes the enduring nature of "righteousness" (v. 3), not the fleeting nature of riches. Jesus later teaches us that many will actually be *persecuted* for righteousness (Matt 5:10-12), not have prosperity. Yet the righteous will have a reward that far surpasses earthly treasures.

What about seasons of misfortune? The godly sometimes experience loss and poverty (Phil 4:12). "Darkness" in verse 4 is a metaphor for adversity (VanGemeren, "Psalms," 709). Light is a metaphor of redemption and the joy of life (ibid.; cf. Pss 27:1; 36:9; 56:13; Isa 9:2; 10:17). In the midst of adversity, in the midst of misfortune, the light of God shines on the godly. The godly person doesn't succumb to the darkness, but instead, by the power of God, the godly shine in the darkness (cf. 1 John 1:5-6).

This blessing of shining in the darkness is the result of God's being "gracious, compassionate," and full of righteousness (v. 4b). These character qualities of God are then put on display by the godly in the midst of a corrupt and dark world (cf. Phil 2:15), and others are blessed by such grace, compassion, and righteousness.

Generosity and Security (112:5-6)

Psalm 111:5-6 teaches us about God's generosity, and these verses (along with v. 9) show us about the corresponding generosity of a godly person. God is generous. God gave us his Son, and God's people follow his model of grace-enabled, grace-oriented generosity (2 Cor 8:9).

A godly person is concerned with the needs of others. He or she lends money and resources compassionately (v. 5; cf. Luke 6:30). Greedy men aren't godly men. The godly person also shows himself to be a person of justice, who conducts all of his business fairly. In the words of righteous Job, the godly person "wears justice" (cf. 29:14 NLT). In other words, he lives with a commitment to honesty and integrity. He lives with a social conscience. Administering justice isn't merely something one does on a mission trip; it's a way of life for the godly.

Thus, the godly person avoids two common problems with wealth: *greed* and *abuse*. Instead of greed, he chooses generosity. Instead of abusing the power that money gives, he chooses justice. Generosity and justice mark the godly person. These characteristics are traits of the Messiah, who is gracious and just (Isa 11:1-5). The Spirit of God is working in believers to make them more like Jesus. What would happen in our world if we had a revival of generosity and justice?

Because the instructions of the Lord endure forever, and the just person lives by the instructions of the Lord, it makes sense for the psalmist to use words like "never" and "forever" (v. 6). The godly live with an unshakable confidence in God. The godly person perseveres in the midst of trial (cf. Jas 1:6-8). He's dependable. He's remembered forever (cf. Prov 10:7). Every person should ask the question, "Would these things be said about me?"

Threat and Trust (112:7-8)

Because the godly person is stable, bad news will not bring him fear (v. 7). Godliness doesn't insulate us from bad things and bad news. What distinguishes the godly is his or her perspective of, and response to, the bad news.

How can the godly be unshakable in the midst of calamity? Once again, the answer revolves around God's Word. Because God's Word is sure, and because God's Word contains the good news, the godly can endure hard times. The godly may feel the pain of bad news, but they can persevere and not freak out when they hear it. They can remain "assured" and "will not fear" (v. 8). They can know that their "foes" (v. 8b) will not have the last word.

These verses point us ahead to the gospel. Since our greatest problem has already been solved through the atoning death of Jesus, we can endure bad news. For the believer, this life is as bad as it's ever going to be. We can trust in the Lord in the hard times because we know the best is yet to come. Our ultimate adversaries have already been defeated. The challenge for us is to believe the good news, to delight in it, and to use it as the means of enduring the bad news.

Compassion and Consequences (112:9-10)

The psalmist returns to the theme of compassionate generosity. We must underline the relationship between godliness and generosity. Generosity isn't the only characteristic of a godly person, but this characteristic certainly fills the mind of the psalmist. He comments on the results of compassion (v. 9). Generous living has enduring reward.

Paul restates this verse in 2 Corinthians 9:9 as he teaches the church that the one who "sows generously" will also "reap generously" (2 Cor 9:6; cf. Gal 5:22-23; 6:8-10; Jas 3:17-18). The godly practice compassionate generosity with joy, laying up treasures in heaven (Matt 6:19-21; 1 Tim 6:18-19). They will experience the enduring exaltation that comes from a life of generosity (112:9).

Throughout the Scriptures we read that God takes note of our compassion for and involvement with the poor. God identifies with the poor. We read in Proverbs, "The one who oppresses the poor person insults his Maker, but one who is kind to the needy honors him" (Prov 14:31); "The one who mocks the poor insults his Maker" (Prov 17:5a); "Kindness to the poor is a loan to the LORD, and he will give a reward to the lender" (Prov 19:17). The psalmist in Psalm 112 is carrying on this concept. Generosity to the poor gets God's attention. God is honored by compassion. So let's pursue a life of compassion for those in need (Jas 1:27).

Not only does generosity care for the poor and honor God, but it also impacts the wicked (v. 10). When the wicked person sees God's blessing on the godly, he will melt away (VanGemeren, "Psalms," 712). The wicked person will be filled with bitterness, jealousy, and anger. All of his successes will be short-lived. How much better to follow the model of the blessed person in verse 1 than the way of the wicked in verse 10!

The good news of the gospel is that Jesus died for the wicked so that they may enjoy everlasting blessing. He transforms wicked people. The call, then, is for every sinful person to look to Jesus—the ultimate blessed person, who bore the curse that sinners deserved. He kept God's commands perfectly and died on behalf of those who broke them. At the cross, he put on display God's grace and compassion, along with God's righteousness and justice. Let us bow before this Savior in repentance and faith. Let us follow his example of godliness by the power that he provides to us. Every spiritual blessing comes through our union with him (Eph 1:3-14). And let us stand in awe of him, knowing that as we behold him, we will be transformed more into his image (2 Cor 3:18).

Reflect and Discuss

1. How are these two psalms linked together?
2. Why are these psalms useful for teaching biblical manhood?
3. How does Psalm 111:1 help us understand true worship?

4. In Psalms 111 and 112 the happy or blessed person delights in God's works and God's words. How can we do this practically?

5. What does Psalm 111 teach us about God's works of redemption?

6. What does it look like to fear the Lord in day-to-day life?

7. What kind of blessings do children of believing parents receive?

8. What does Psalm 112 teach us about the godly person's response to bad news?

9. What does Psalm 112 teach us about generosity? How can you live a more generous life?

10. What characteristics of God in Psalm 111 are reflected in the godly in Psalm 112? Take a moment to ask the Lord to work these character qualities into your own life.

There's No One like Our God

PSALMS 113–114

Main Idea: The psalmist calls us to praise our incomparable God for his majesty, grace, and redeeming power.

I. **God Is High Above Yet Reaches Far Down (113).**
   A. The call to praise (113:1-3)
   B. The reasons for praise (113:4-9)
      1. The Lord is exalted (113:4-6).
      2. The Lord reaches down (113:7-9).
II. **God Redeems with Earth-Shaking Power (114).**
   A. Rejoice at God's power to redeem (114:1-2).
   B. Rejoice at God's power over nature (114:3-6).
   C. Rejoice at God's power to provide (114:7-8).

Recently, some friends and I (Tony) visited the famous Cameron Indoor Stadium at Duke University to watch Syracuse vs. Duke. These two legendary basketball programs also have legendary coaches. Our seats were located on the other side of their benches, so I got to pay particular attention to each coach. While I observed many interesting features about the way coaches Boeheim and Krzyzewski led their teams, I was struck by how often they repeated basic fundamentals. For instance, each coach said, "Block out!"—accompanied with arm motions—multiple times. Why? Do their players not already know they need to block out? Do they not know that rebounding is important? You know (or can guess) the answer. Good coaches know that you have to keep reminding players of the fundamentals.

So it is in the Christian faith. As you read the Psalms, one of the fundamental practices of our faith that's repeated over and over again is the call to praise the Lord. We should be thankful that the Lord keeps reminding us of this basic practice since all of life flows from the heart. God keeps repeating it because it's so important.

Psalm 113 begins what is commonly known as the "Egyptian Hallel" (Pss 113–118). *Hallel* means "praise." These psalms were used in the Passover liturgy as Israel reflected on their God-granted freedom from

Egyptian captivity. It seems that Psalms 113 and 114 were sung before the meal, and the following psalms were sung after the meal. At our local church, after we take the Lord's Supper, we often recite either Matthew 26:30 or Mark 14:26, which mentions the singing of a psalm (or hymn) after Jesus ate the Supper with the disciples. Matthew says, "After singing a hymn, they went out to the Mount of Olives."

Stop and think about this. It's highly likely that Jesus and his disciples sang these psalms (Pss 113–118) during the opening event of our Lord's passion. These psalms were likely in the mind and heart of Jesus at this crucial time period. They were on his lips. This gives particular significance to these psalms. We're reading the hymnbook of Jesus. Knowing what was on his mind and heart should greatly affect our minds and hearts and, by God's grace, make us more like him.

Derek Kidner summarizes the Egyptian Hallel:

> Only the second of them (114) speaks directly of the Exodus, but the theme of raising the downtrodden (113) and the note of corporate praise (115), personal thanksgiving (116), world vision (117) and festal procession (118) make it an appropriate series to mark the salvation which began in Egypt and will spread to the nations. . . . There was more relevance in these psalms to the Exodus—the greater Exodus—than could be guessed in Old Testament times. (*Psalms 73–150*, 401)

So then, with the exodus in mind, and with the greater exodus in view (i.e., the salvation we have in Christ Jesus), we are ready to consider the wonder of these "before the meal" psalms. Both of these psalms highlight the fact that there's no one like our God.

God Is High Above Yet Reaches Far Down
PSALM 113

The outline of Psalm 113 is simple. The psalmist first calls us to praise the Redeemer (vv. 1-3). Then he gives reasons to praise God: he is exalted (vv. 4-6), and he stoops to care for the lowly (vv. 7-9).

The Call to Praise (113:1-3)

The psalmist begins with an explosive call to praise. He focuses our attention on the object of praise: "the LORD." The exhortation

"Hallelujah!"—praise Yahweh—begins and ends the psalm. The psalmist also reminds worshipers of their identity: "servants." Yahweh has redeemed these servants. He has made them his people. Consequently, these servants of God should be known for their praise of God (cf. Exod 19:6; Heb 13:15). They serve God out of the overflow of a heart of worship to their Redeemer.

In verse 2 the exhortation is repeated again for more emphasis. This time God's "name" is emphasized. Notice the threefold repetition of the "name of the LORD" in verses 1-3. God's name expresses his nature (Exod 3:14-15; 34:6-7). We are called to praise the "I AM." Praise the One who is "a compassionate and gracious God, slow to anger and abounding in faithful love and truth" (Exod 34:6). In the New Testament, Peter says that salvation is found only through the "name" of Jesus (Acts 4:12). Whoever calls on the name of the Lord in repentance and faith will be saved (Rom 10:13; Phil 2:10-11). If you have experienced this great salvation, praise the Lord!

How often should we praise? The psalmist says, "Both now and forever" (v. 2b). When you praise the Lord now, you are participating in something eternal. Revelation indicates that the redeemed will praise the Redeemer forever.

Further, the psalmist builds on the call to praise the Lord "now" by adding a beautiful word picture (v. 3). When you wake up, praise the Lord! When you lie down to sleep, praise the Lord! At all times in between, praise him. Let the sun lead you to worship the Son.

The Reasons for Praise (113:4-9)

The psalmist now gives us fuel for praise. Why praise the Lord? He gives two powerful reasons.

First, we should praise the Lord because "the Lord is exalted" (vv. 4-6). The psalmist says our God is exalted higher than anything we can imagine. He transcends everything. This reality speaks of God's sovereignty. He's sovereign over "the nations" (v. 4a). Isaiah says, "The nations are like a drop in a bucket" (Isa 40:15). God is also sovereign over "the heavens" (v. 4b). Solomon confessed, "Even heaven, the highest heaven, cannot contain you" (1 Kgs 8:27). God is above all and worthy of all praise.

In verses 5-6 we read about the uniqueness of our God. The psalmist raises a question: "Who is like the LORD our God?" Answer? There's no one like our God! The psalmist says, "Show me someone like God! Who compares to him? There's no one!" God is incomparable. He alone is the Judge of all the earth. Micah raises this question as well and comes to the same conclusion (Mic 7:18-20).

While God is absolutely sovereign, he also observes and governs the things of heaven and earth, but he has to stoop to do so! Spurgeon says,

> He dwells so far on high that even to observe heavenly things he must humble himself. He must stoop to view the skies, and bow to see what angels do. What, then, must be his condescension, seeing that he observes the humblest of his servants upon earth, and makes them sing for joy like Mary when she said, "Thou hast regarded the low estate of thine handmaiden." (*Treasury*, vol. 3, 30)

Isaiah put it like this:

> For the High and Exalted One, who lives forever, whose name is holy, says this: "I live in a high and holy place, and with the oppressed and lowly of spirit, to revive the spirit of the lowly and revive the heart of the oppressed." (Isa 57:15)

What a God! He's high and holy, yet he dwells with the meek and lowly!

Remarkably, this great God condescends to us. He loves us. He cares about our lives. Such divine humility expressed in these Old Testament texts prepares us for the coming of Christ, whose humility causes us to worship him with awe and wonder (Phil 2:5-11). The Lord's condescension leads to more commentary on the Lord's compassion in the following verses, which takes us to the psalmist's second reason to praise.

Second, we should praise the Lord because *the Lord reaches down (vv. 7-9)*. Our God cares for the humble. He not only knows what's going on in the world but also intervenes in it as an act of divine grace. The CSB translates 7b as "trash heap." "Garbage pile" conveys the idea vividly. The poor around the world often live around the garbage piles of their cities. One can see the poorest of the poor dwelling in such filth. It's a picture of desperation. Here, the psalmist says that God is there in the dump. God is there to rescue them (cf. 1 Cor 1:26-31).

Tim Keller describes God's transcendence and rescuing grace:

> Praise God because there is nothing too great for him. He is over all time (verse 2), all places (verse 3), and all human

power and authority (verse 4). But also praise him because there is no one too small for God (verses 7-9). He enthrones the poor (verse 7). . . . God's greatness is seen in his regard for the ungreat. In Jesus he proved to be great enough to become small himself. (*Songs of Jesus*, 294)

The Lord's care for the poor was expressed when Jesus began his earthly ministry in Luke 4. Jesus said, "The Spirit of the Lord is on me, because he has anointed me to preach good news to the poor" (Luke 4:18a). Jesus not only ministered to the physically poor but also granted eternal riches to "the poor in spirit" (Matt 5:3). Every spiritual beggar who comes to Jesus in repentance and faith finds eternal riches. God will raise him up and give him a glorious inheritance (Eph 1–2).

God's exaltation of the poor is mentioned in Psalm 113:8. The Lord will make the poor sit with "nobles"! God gives dignity and privilege to the poor. Such a picture of God's grace prepares the way for the New Testament's announcement that we believers will be joint heirs with Jesus Christ. We will reign with him (Rom 8:17)!

How great is God's concern for his people? Verse 9 says he cares for the "childless woman." He is able to reverse her fortune. To be unable to bear children was miserable for Israelite women. Many women today know that pain. Does this verse mean all barren women will be able to have children? No. We live with the effects of a fallen world. But this text does mean that God cares for the barren with divine tenderness. We cannot fathom all of God's ways. They're higher than our thoughts. But God isn't distant and remote. He's near to those who grieve and suffer. And one day the curse will be reversed, and all his redeemed will experience the fullness of joy in his presence.

The story of Hannah illustrates God's care for such barren women (1 Sam 1:2-17), a situation that is repeated in Scripture. In fact, verses 7-8 are a quote from 1 Samuel 2:8. Kidner says, "Hannah's joy became all of Israel's; Sarah's became the world's. And the song of Hannah was to be outshone one day by the *Magnificat*" (*Psalms 73–150*, 402).

It's true. God is mindful of the poor. We should rest in this fact. We should pour our hearts out to him with our needs. And we should imitate his concern for the poor and needy.

Most of all, the psalm is teaching us to praise God for his sovereign grace. Verse 9b reminds us of the end of it all: "Hallelujah!" God is above all, so praise him! God reaches down to bless us, so praise him!

God Redeems with Earth-Shaking Power
PSALM 114

This psalm celebrates the grace of God. God's people enjoy a special relationship with him. This God, who governs all of nature, has blessed his people. This God, who has mountains quaking before them, has redeemed his people.

The psalmist reflects on God's redeeming work by mentioning the exodus from Egypt, the covenant at Sinai, the crossing of the Jordan River, and God's provision for his people in the wilderness. The writer uses exuberant personification to highlight these events, events that should encourage God's people regardless of their present conditions. Spurgeon says, "True poetry here has reached its climax: no human mind has ever been able to equal, much less to excel, the grandeur of this Psalm" (*Treasury*, vol. 3, 41). The reason for the dramatic language is simple. The psalmist wants to draw attention to the Lord's awesome power.

Indeed, the Passover celebration reminded God's people of the Redeemer's power. They were to stand amazed by it and rejoice in it. They were never to forget God's freeing them from Egypt.

We too should mark particular moments in our lives when we experience God's power and grace. When we consider God's intervention in our lives, it can lift us from present despair. It can give us God-centered hope now.

Rejoice at God's Power to Redeem (114:1-2)

The opening verse begins with the exodus event. God brought the "house of Jacob" ("Israel" in v. 1a, and "Judah" in v. 2) out from a strange land (cf. 105:23), from a people with a strange language (Isa 28:11; Jer 5:15). He intervened. God rescued Israel from their oppressed state in Egypt (Exod 20:2). What a powerful picture of the gospel!

At the heart of God's redeeming work is his purpose to redeem a people in order that he may dwell with them (v. 2). Israel was unique because the presence of God was with them (Exod 33:15-16). Further, God purposed to display his rule and reign ("his dominion") in the midst of his people. The same holds true today for believers in the Lord Jesus Christ. In an even greater way, by the work of the Spirit, God dwells in us and with us, and he reveals his kingly reign through us (Eph 2:19-21; 3:16-17; 1 Pet 2:5).

Praise God for his intervention! Where would we be without God's rescuing work? We needed Jesus to come and live the life we couldn't live and die the death we should have died in order to be in right relationship with God. Jesus Christ has brought us believers out of an even greater bondage than slavery in Egypt: bondage to sin and death. And he has transferred us out of the kingdom of darkness into his loving, eternal, glorious kingdom (Col 1:13-14).

Rejoice at God's Power over Nature (114:3-6)

The psalmist next describes nature's response to Israel's journey from Egypt to the promised land. The seas flee and the mountains skip like rams! What a scene! Keller says,

> God's love for us shakes the world, because nothing can come between us and God's love (Rom 8:38). At both Jesus's death (Matt 27:51) and his resurrection (Matt 28:2) the earth shook, indicating God's power to save. (*Songs*, 295)

The reference to the sea (v. 3a) refers to the parting of the Red Sea (Exod 14). The phrase "the Jordan turned back" (v. 3b) recalls the parting of the Jordan River when Israel entered into the promised land (Josh 3). God's power was displayed through these events.

God's power is so tremendous that the psalmist says it caused "the solid mountains to leap in the air like startled lambs" (Allen, *Psalms 101–150*, 105). Again the scene is one of awe. The water parts at the sound of God's voice, and the mountains skip when he speaks (cf. Ps 29). Allen says, "With gleeful triumph the psalmist re-enacts the ancient scenario for the contemporary generation of God's people" (ibid.).

This thought of creation responding in such a dramatic way continues in verses 5-6. The psalmist does a bit of trash talking. He taunts the sea and the mountains! "Why did you respond that way?" he asks. He makes the worshipers feel as if they were there in this past experience (ibid.). Of course, he knows the answer. The sea turned tail and the mountains skipped because of Yahweh's power. When Yahweh appeared to Israel and established his kingdom in Israel, nature responded with joy and fear (VanGemeren, "Psalms," 717). Spurgeon says, "Men fear the mountains, but the mountains tremble before the Lord" (*Treasury*, vol. 3, 42).

We who know Jesus Christ should remember the great power that is ours (Eph 1:15-23). If God is with us, in us, and for us, we should not fear. Look at his power! It's easy to despair in this life. It's easy to become anxious in this life. It's easy to be intimidated when given an opportunity to speak the gospel. But we need not cave in to these feelings. Allow this psalm to confront you and change you. Allow it to comfort you. If you are the Lord's, you can rest. You can trust. You can hope.

Rejoice at God's Power to Provide (114:7-8)

The psalmist continues speaking of God's earthshaking power in verse 7 but then pivots in verse 8 to talk about how this all-powerful God graciously provides for his people. By pointing out God's provision of water for Israel (Exod 17:6-7; Num 20:8-11; Isa 41:18), the psalmist picks up the idea from the ending of the previous psalm; that is, God is mindful of the needs of his people. He cares for them.

The power of Yahweh to make the earth shake stirs up fear and trembling. In fact, the psalmist orders the mountains to tremble (v. 7; cf. 97:4-5).

Whatever God pleases to do, he can do. Yet this mighty God is also good. Verse 8 shows how his power is displayed in a wonderful action of provision. He not only has the ability to provide but also has the love to do so. Therefore, let us trust him for all that we need. One writer says, "He who made water flow from the rock at Rephadim and the cliff at Kadesh . . . can still provide streams of blessing for His people" (Kirkpatrick in VanGemeren, "Psalms," 718). Yes, he can!

So let's remember that God's displays of power weren't for shock-and-awe purposes. He wasn't trying to put on a show. His mighty acts were done for the sake of his people and the glory of his name. May God be pleased to work powerfully in our lives, our churches, and our land today! Let us pray for God to pour out streams of blessing on us today!

After reflecting on the nature of God's grace and power in Psalms 113–114, one can imagine singing these psalms with Jesus before his crucifixion. Jesus, the ultimate Passover Lamb (1 Cor 5:8), would provide sinners with full redemption. His earthshaking resurrection gave us the ultimate victory over our enemies. All who are in him enjoy spiritual blessing (Eph 1:3).

Who is like the Lord Jesus Christ? Who is like this King of glory, who looks down with mercy and saves poor sinners? Who raises up spiritual beggars and makes them royalty forever? Answer? No one else. There's no one like the Lord Jesus. He's in a category by himself. Praise him. Just as coaches need to remind their players to block out, so we need to be reminded of the redeeming work of Jesus and of the praise we should give him because of it.

> Lord Jesus, I praise you that one infinitely greater than the universe with all its galaxies would become a tiny infant who needed to be fed and carried and changed. And you did it for me. That humbles my heart and yet lifts it to the stars as well. Thank you, Lord. Amen. (Keller, *Songs*, 294)

Reflect and Discuss

1. Why do we need to be reminded of the fundamental practices of the faith?
2. What does Psalm 113 teach us about the Lord's transcendence?
3. What does Psalm 113 teach us about the Lord's grace?
4. Why should Psalm 113 encourage troubled saints?
5. How does Psalm 113 point us ahead to the ministry of the Lord Jesus?
6. Read 1 Samuel 2:1-11. How does it compare to Psalm 113?
7. How is God's power described in Psalm 114?
8. Why should Psalm 114 encourage us?
9. Think about Jesus and the disciples singing these psalms before the Passover meal. Does that image move you? If yes, how so?
10. Take a few moments to join the psalmist, giving praise to God and asking God to provide for your physical and spiritual needs.

Trust in the Lord; He Is Our Help and Shield

PSALM 115

Main Idea: The psalmist exalts the superiority of God over man-made idols, exhorting God's people to worship and trust in God alone.

I. **To His Name Be the Glory; the Living Praise Him (115:1-3,16-18).**
   A. Not to us, but to his name (115:1-3)
   B. Not the dead, but we the living (115:16-18)
II. **What Idols Can't Do; What God Does (115:4-8,12-15)**
   A. Idols are worthless (115:4-8).
   B. God blesses his people (115:12-15).
III. **Trust in the Lord, Our Help and Shield (115:9-11).**

Various leaders have cited this popular first verse at pivotal points in history (Duncan, "Non Nobis Domine"). My favorite of these occasions involves the resilient William Wilberforce. This famous British statesman fought to abolish slavery for 46 years. Wilberforce loved the Psalms. He was known for reciting Psalm 119 by heart. But he cherished Psalm 115, too. After Parliament finally passed a bill to abolish slave trade, this little, five-foot, three-inch warrior went home to mediate on Psalm 115:1 (Kidner, *Psalms 73–150*, 404). What an appropriate response to a major victory! We should follow Wilberforce's example. If the Lord ever accomplishes anything through us, let us be quick to give him all the glory.

On a personal level, my bride and I (Tony) had some friends sing a modern version of Psalm 115 at our wedding. Our prayer was for the Lord to be glorified in our marriage. In addition, one of my favorite Christian rap songs is Shai Linne's "The Glory of God." The song begins with the words of verse 1 of this psalm repeated 12 times. Then the artist proceeds to exalt the greatness of God with many edifying lines.

Psalm 115:1 is a prayer for all Christians at all times. We are meant to live for God's glory, not our own. In whatever we do—in word, action, or thought—we should long to bring glory to God (1 Cor 10:31). Does this verse reflect your heart's desire?

While verse 1 is the most popular verse in the psalm, the central exhortation appears in the middle of the psalm. The psalmist encourages Israel to *trust the Lord* in a particularly stressful season. Allen says this complex psalm is a "communal complaint" (*Psalms 101–150*, 108). The specific context is unclear. It actually reflects various points in Israel's history. (Allen believes it to be postexilic given that verse 14 reflects a small population of postexilic Judah; ibid., 109.) It clearly reflects Israel's trying to survive in the midst of a hostile environment (ibid., 111). So if you find yourself in a season of distress and weakness, a time when it's difficult to worship and trust in the Lord, you can identify with Psalm 115. The psalmist is trying to lift the spirits of the saints by extolling the greatness of God over against the worthless idols of the nations in order for God's people to worship and trust him.

I have chosen to follow the chiastic structure of Wilcock to help us see the psalm as a whole and to emphasize this need to trust in the Lord. You will see below how parts one and five correspond to each other (vv. 1-3 and 16-18); how parts two and four correspond to each other (vv. 4-8 and 12-15); and how verses 9-11 stand as the central section (Wilcock, *Message*, 182). Below is the proposed structure:

Not to us but to his name be the glory (vv. 1-3).
What idols can't do (vv. 4-8)
Trust in the Lord; he is their help and shield (vv. 9-11).
What God does (vv. 12-15)
Not the dead but the living praise God (vv. 16-18).

Based on this structure, we will begin our exposition at the two ends and work toward the middle of the psalm.

To His Name Be the Glory; the Living Praise Him
PSALM 115:1-3,16-18

Not to Us but to His Name (115:1-3)

The psalmist opens with the declaration that God, not men, should receive glory. At the center of the universe is not self but God. Ever since the garden humanity has tried to compete with God's glory (Rom 3:23). Because of sin we want to be our own kings. We want praise. We don't want to submit to God's authority. But God will not share his glory with another (Isa 48:11). And our greatest good and highest joy will come when we live for God's glory, not our own. Our problems in life come when we fail to live for God's glory. In our "selfie" culture today, we desperately need the message of verse 1. Self-absorption doesn't satisfy. It turns off others, and it dishonors God. Tim Keller states, "There's nothing that makes you more miserable (or less interesting) than self-absorption" (*King's Cross*, 16). The cure for this is to become "God absorbed." We need a dynamic encounter with God that makes us long for him and his glory rather than our own glory and selfish desires. We need to live by the lines from A. B. Simpson's hymn:

Not I, but Christ, be honored, loved, exalted;
Not I, but Christ, be seen, be known, be heard;
Not I, but Christ, in every look and action,
Not I, but Christ, in every thought and word. ("Not I, but Christ")

The second part of verse 1 tells us why God should receive glory. God's faithful love and truth are two attributes identified with God's covenant faithfulness to his people (Exod 34:6). His loyal love and truthfulness are sufficient reasons for us to live for God's glory.

In verse 2 the psalmist cites the taunt of Israel's enemies. Then he provides a retort to the taunt in verse 3. You can imagine the mighty nations looking at weak Israel at various points in her history and mocking the people. "Where is your God? Look at your condition! You talk about God's power and love, and yet look at your family! Look at your nation! Where is your God?"

Concern for the Lord's reputation among the nations appears throughout the Old Testament (Exod 32:12; Num 14:13-14). Israel was called not simply to defend their religion but to make God's fame known among the nations (Josh 4:24; 1 Kgs 8:41-43). So, Israel must give an answer to this taunt, not merely to look sensible in the eyes of culture but to commend this God to unbelieving Gentiles.

The retort in verse 3 says it all. The psalmist confesses that God is sovereign. God is "in heaven" (v. 3a; cf. Ps 113:4-5; Eph 1:20-23), and this God "does whatever he pleases" (v. 3b; cf. Ps 135:6; Isa 46:10), meaning that he's working out his sovereign will despite what one may think. Did God accomplish his purposes in Israel's trials in the exodus and exile? Yes. Did these enslavements somehow stop his redemptive mission? No. Did the Messiah come? Yes! In Daniel 4:35 and Jonah 1:14 the Gentiles confessed that God works according to his own will and pleasure, once they realized who the real Lord is.

Speaking of the Messiah, you can hear this sort of taunt at the crucifixion, as the enemies mockingly said things like, "If you are the Messiah, why are you on a cross? Why don't you save yourself!" Yet, in the midst of the agony of Golgotha, our God was redeeming lost humanity. Today we have the same responsibility of commending our God, who is mocked by many but stands as the hope of the world.

The fact is, God's sovereign purposes are higher than many want to accept. The unbeliever's vision is shortsighted. If one can't affirm God's absolute sovereignty, one is left only with what the human eye can see and comprehend. The result of human wisdom alone is skepticism, agnosticism, or atheism. We must remember that God doesn't promise to stop all tragedies and sicknesses or resolve all evils until the coming of Christ. He is free to act and free to delay, but one thing we must confess is that he reigns over all, and he does all that he pleases. For some this answer won't do, but for believers, it brings hope and comfort. Our God is reigning in the heavens, and one day he will correct all wrongs and reverse the curse.

These three verses remind us that the wicked don't ultimately prosper. Psalm 73 is correct: They may prosper for a season, but we must take the long view. God is still sovereign, and God will work out all things according to the counsel of his will (Eph 1:11). So trust him.

Not the Dead, but We the Living (115:16-18)

At the end of the psalm, the psalmist reiterates God's heavenly position in verse 16. This time the writer says the heavens belong to the Lord. God reigns over all the earth, but he has delegated responsibility to humans to work the earth as stewards of his creation as he reigns from heaven.

In light of man's privileged position as steward/worshiper, the psalmist presents an important contrast in verses 17-18. The psalmist doesn't have the complete understanding of the eternal state, but he knows that the spiritually dead won't praise God after death (v. 17; cf. Pss 6:5; 88:10-12); moreover, those who belong to God will praise the Lord now and *forever* (v. 18; cf. Rev 5:8-14).

So, what's the point of verses 17-18? It's simple. Praise God while you have breath, and you will praise him after your breath is gone! Don't waste your life on substitute gods.

Therefore, at the beginning and ending of Psalm 115, the psalmist urges us to worship only God. This high, God-centered, heavenly minded, kingdom-oriented vision reminds us of the opening of the Lord's Prayer: "Our Father in heaven, your name be honored as holy. Your kingdom come. Your will be done on earth as it is in heaven" (Matt 6:9-10). Jesus says, "Pray like this." Pray with a desire for God's glory and God's name to be regarded as holy, for God's kingdom to come, and for God's heavenly will to be done. In the words of the psalmist, pray, "Not to us, Lord, not to us, but to your name give glory." The Lord's Prayer and Psalm 115:1 sound strange in a self-centered world, but they are the foundation of the Christian life. As Jesus instructed us, let's pray sincerely in our prayer closets, and not with empty pharisaical phrases (Matt 6:5-9), for God's glory to be known through us. Then, when God does some work through us, let's assign all glory to him.

What Idols Can't Do; What God Does
PSALM 115:4-8,12-15

In these verses the psalmist exalts the superiority of Yahweh over the idols of the nations. He deconstructs idols in verses 4-8, and then he describes the nature of the covenant-keeping God of Israel in verses 12-15.

Idols Are Worthless (115:4-8)

After stating that God does whatever he pleases (v. 3), the psalmist tells us what pagan gods can't do. The psalmist's description here resembles several Old Testament texts, like Isaiah 44 and 46 where the prophet expounds on the folly of god making and on how to transport a god (Isa 44:9-20; 46:6-7; cf. Ps 135:15-18; Jer 10:1-9; Hab 2:18-19). The prophets and the psalmist describe the foolishness of bowing down to handmade metal images (v. 4) instead of worshiping the Maker of heaven and earth (v. 15). These images have no power. Jeremiah said that idols are like scarecrows in a cucumber patch (Jer 10:5). They can't walk, talk, or do anything. Idols are the product of the sinful imaginations of people. Why worship man-made things instead of the Maker of all things?

The psalmist highlights the worthlessness of idols by showing how human they look and how lifeless they actually are. In short, they're nothing and can do nothing. They're made, and then they rot. So why worship and trust in them?

Idols were attractive to Israel because the surrounding nations worshiped idols. They were also attractive because idols don't speak like Yahweh speaks (vv. 5,7). It was much easier to submit to a silent god than to a talking God who calls individuals to holiness. People today may not reject God in theory, but they don't want a talking God who makes demands on their lives either. They want a silent God.

Idols are still attractive today because, like Israel, our hearts are wicked. We want to love, trust, worship, and find satisfaction in things other than the God of the Bible. Idols don't merely include idolatrous images in false religions. Idolatry is a heart problem. One can make a substitute god out of anything.

Tim Keller's book *Counterfeit Gods* is helpful for discerning the common idols of today, such as money, sex, and power. Idolatry has a "mental aspect" and a "heart aspect." Mentally, we indulge in idolatry when we have thoughts about God that are unworthy of him. It consists of embracing false teaching about God. John ends his first letter, after talking about false teaching, by saying, "Little children, guard yourselves from idols" (1 John 5:21; cf. John 4:24). Heart idolatry involves trusting in anything other than Christ to give us meaning, significance, joy, and salvation. This could involve a house, a car, an investment, a relationship, sexual pleasure, peer approval, and much more. What excites you? What do you spend time, energy, and resources on? For what do you make sacrifices? Whatever this is, it's likely an idol, and there can be no spiritual growth without the detection and destruction of idols.

So how do you destroy an idol? Take note of this psalm. What is the psalmist doing? The psalmist is deconstructing idols. He's showing us the stupidity of loving and trusting in anything other than God. You may need to verbally repudiate your idol, too. You may need to pray and ask the Lord to show you that money, sex, power, peer approval, entertainment, comfort, Xbox, sports, or alcohol cannot satisfy, will not save, and will not bring you meaning. Deconstruct your idols. See them for what they are, and then elevate your vision of God, based on Scripture, that you may adore God rather than idols.

If you don't destroy your idols and replace them with the worship of God, verse 8 will be the result (cf. Ps 135:18). Here's a super-important principle regarding worship: *You become like that which you worship* (see G. K. Beale, *We Become*). The psalmist says both the idol makers and the idol worshipers become like the worthless idols they worship. In 2 Kings the writer says that Israel "followed worthless idols and became worthless themselves" (2 Kgs 17:15; cf. Rom 1:21-32). When people worship worthless idols, they will live spiritually worthless lives. In contrast, those who worship the living God will grow into his image. Paul says, "We all, with unveiled faces, are looking as in a mirror at the glory of the Lord and are being transformed into the same image from glory to glory; this is from the Lord who is the Spirit" (2 Cor 3:18). By constantly beholding the glory of Christ, we become more like him. This is how transformation works. Beholding leads to becoming. The Spirit does this work in our hearts.

So, what are you doing to look at the Savior? Are you looking at him daily in Scripture? Are you looking at him in corporate worship? Are you looking at him in your heart throughout the day?

God Blesses His People (115:12-15)

After giving the central exhortation to trust in the Lord in verses 9-11 (which we will cover next), the psalmist describes God's grace toward his people. You can't miss the emphasis on how God blesses his people. Five times the writer mentions God's blessing. The threefold call to trust in the Lord in verses 9-11 is complemented by a threefold assurance of God's blessing on each group of people in verses 12-13: "Israel" (vv. 9,12b), "the house of Aaron" (vv. 10,12c), and those who "fear the LORD" (vv. 11,13). The psalmist is assuring all of God's people—both "small and great"—that blessing rests on those who trust in the Lord. Even though the people may experience affliction, God "remembers" his covenant (v. 12). To deliver and bless them fulfills his promises (VanGemeren, "Psalms," 722). This blessing is indiscriminate. The religious leaders ("great") and the social outcasts ("small") may experience God's blessing when they trust in him. Both Jew and Gentile—all who fear him—may enjoy this blessing.

God is the giver of all blessings, both material and spiritual. Our daily bread is a gift from God. In Jesus Christ we have received every spiritual blessing in the heavenly places (Eph 1:3). All who have faith in the Son enjoy the blessings of forgiveness, adoption, inheritance, and everlasting peace in a new heavens and new earth. And these blessings are granted to every person on the planet—whether small or great—who repents and trusts in Christ.

Next the psalmist prays for God to grant increase to small Israel with the blessing of children, both in the present generation and in the generations to come (v. 14). The psalmist is praying for the people to once again become fruitful and multiply. The psalmist asks for God's blessing with confidence because he knows the nature of God's covenant love and also because God is the "Maker of heaven and earth" (v. 15).

What a contrast between the living God and lifeless idols! The living God blesses, fulfills promises, and dispenses grace on both the small and the great. His blessing, fulfilled promises, and abundant grace have been experienced by all who have trusted in the redeeming work of his Son, our Savior. Lifeless idols, in contrast, never provide what they promise. They only leave you longing for more. They never bless, only deaden. They never grant grace, only condemnation. The only logical response is to trust in the Lord, not in created things. That leads us to this middle section, the central exhortation.

Trust in the Lord, Our Help and Shield
PSALM 115:9-11

Instead of trusting in created things, the people are urged by the psalmist to trust in Yahweh. The psalmist speaks to the worshipers in the beginning of each verse, and then someone speaks about the worshipers in the second part of each verse.

It's a threefold call to trust in the Lord, to three groups of people (Israel, Aaron's house, and God fearers), and it contains a promise of protection to those who trust in the Lord ("He is their help and shield"). This psalm seems to have arisen out of a liturgical setting in which one group called for trust in the Lord, and the antiphonal group sang in response about God's being the help of his people (VanGemeren, "Psalms," 721). Thus, we see the community of faith reminding one another of the blessings they enjoy. This is one of the blessings of the church today. We need brothers and sisters to encourage us to find our help in the Lord.

This repeated phrase could be said of everyone who places faith in the Lord Jesus Christ today. He is our ultimate help and our ultimate shield. Not that he will shield us from earthly affliction but that we will ultimately be shielded from our greatest enemies—death, Satan, and the wrath of God—because Jesus took our punishment for us. And we know that anything that does befall his saints in this life is not purposeless. He is with us always, and we have nothing to fear (Heb 13:5). So until we see Christ face-to-face, our call is to trust in the Lord. Put your confidence in him, not in idols. If you're trusting in the Lord, you can know the peace and joy of the Lord. Then you can say with the psalmist, "Our hearts rejoice in him because we trust in his holy name" (Ps 33:21).

In a lecture given in one of my (Tony's) classes, my friend Steve Timmis argued that there are three ways to read the whole Bible coherently, that is, three ways to understand the "story line of the Bible." These really aren't three different ways but three different emphases or applications, and they have significant overlap. They include: (1) a formal summary of the Bible, (2) a dynamic summary of the Bible, and (3) an existential summary of the Bible. I like to call these categories (1) a *theological* reading of the Bible, (2) a *communal* reading of the Bible, and (3) a *personal* reading of the Bible. The first involves the categories of *creation, de-creation, re-creation,* and *new creation.* This form emphasizes important theological progression in the biblical story line. The second reading can be summarized in this idea: *God has always planned to have a people for himself—a people he reveals his glory to and displays his glory through.* One can see the communal/relational dimension of the biblical story, that is, God and his people. But the third reading, the existential summary, involves a two-word personal application: "Trust me." This reading emphasizes *our personal response* to creation, de-creation, re-creation, and new creation. It emphasizes our personal response to the fact that we are made for community. We enter the Christian life by *faith,* and we continue in the Christian life by *faith.* God's command and invitation to sinners is, "Trust me." These words are at the heart of the biblical narrative, at the heart of Psalm 115, and at the heart of the Christian faith.

So let us trust the Lord. Trust him in hard times and good times. When you are perplexed by what he is doing, you can trust that he is in control and that he is good. How do we know this? Calvary. The cross is all the proof we need that we can trust in the Lord. Does God keep his promises? Yes! Remember, Psalms 113–118 were sung at the Passover celebration. Psalm 115 would have been sung after the meal. In his steadfast love, Jesus went to the cross to be our Passover Lamb, and now he says to everyone, "Trust me."

So in the words of Proverbs,

> *Trust in the Lord with all your heart, and do not rely on your own understanding; in all your ways know him, and he will make your paths straight.* (Prov 3:5-6)

In what are you trusting? Trust in the Lord. He is our help and shield.

Reflect and Discuss

1. Why is verse 1 central to the Christian life? How can you live a more God-absorbed, less self-absorbed life?
2. In light of verse 2, how do unbelievers mock the Christian faith today? How should we respond?
3. What does verse 3 teach us about our response to the taunts of unbelievers, and what does it teach us about God's sovereignty?
4. What do verses 4-7 teach us about idols? What are common idols today? What idols do you struggle with?
5. What does verse 8 teach us about the relationship between worship and our character?
6. In light of this whole psalm, how does the exhortation to trust in the Lord encourage and challenge you?
7. Explain the relationship between trusting the Lord and the blessing of the Lord in verses 9-15.
8. What do verses 17-18 teach us about making our lives count here on earth?
9. How should this psalm affect how we pray? How should it affect our desires?
10. Take a few moments to pray through this psalm.

Precious in the Sight of the Lord Is the Death of His Saints

PSALM 116

Main Idea: Faithful servants pray to and trust in the Lord during distress because he cares for them.

I. Faithful Servants Have a Passionate Love for the Lord (116:1).
II. Faithful Servants Continually Call on the Lord for Help (116:2-4).
III. Faithful Servants Know the Character of the Lord They Serve (116:5-7).
IV. Faithful Servants Trust in the Lord Even in Terrible Suffering (116:8-11).
V. Faithful Servants Keep Their Word and Serve the Lord out of Gratitude for Their Salvation (116:12-14).
VI. Faithful Servants Believe That in Life and Death They Are Valued by the Lord (116:15).
VII. Faithful Servants Offer a Sacrifice of Praise and Thanksgiving to the Lord for All to Hear (116:16-19).

In her book *A Path through Suffering*, Elisabeth Elliot asks, "Did the earthly life of our Lord appear to be a thundering success? Would the statistics of souls won, crowds made into faithful disciples, sermons heeded, commands obeyed, be impressive? Hardly" (*A Path through Suffering*, 39). These words not only apply to our Savior but also to one of his choice servants, a precious young lady who would die at the tender age of 19 on the way to a mission field she would never see: Harriet Atwood Newell. And like our Lord's, her death would not be in vain. Rather, as was said at her memorial service, her death "will certainly turn to the advantage of missions" (Newell, *Delighting in Her Heavenly Bridegroom*, 238).

In so many ways the life and death of Harriet Newell is a marvelous reflection of Psalm 116, the fourth of the Egyptian Hallel psalms (Pss 113–118). Jews sang these psalms at Passover to celebrate how the Lord rescued the Hebrews from Egyptian slavery. Our Lord would have sung this song with his disciples on the night his passion began. It is a personal psalm of gratitude and thanksgiving for the Lord's deliverance from trouble—trouble so great that it nearly led to death. Several features make this psalm appropriate for this use:

- Four times the psalmist speaks of calling on the Lord (vv. 2,4,13,17).
- Three times allusions are made to death (vv. 3,8,15).
- Two times the author promises to fulfill his vows to the Lord "in the presence of all his people" (vv. 14,18).
- The personal pronouns *I, me,* and *my* occur in every verse of the psalm but two (vv. 5,19).

The psalm is deeply personal, reflecting on what God has done and continues to do for us and what is our rightful response. This biblical truth could have enabled Harriet to write in her journal at the age of 18—a little more than a year before she would die on the Isle of France (Mauritius)—these powerful words:

> O that I had a thousand pious relatives well-calculated for the important station of missionaries. . . . I would say to them, "Go and let the destitute millions of Asia and Africa know there is compassion in the hearts of Christians. Tell them of the love of Jesus and the road to bliss on high." (Newell, *Delighting in Her Heavenly Bridegroom,* 124)

Seven truths from this wonderful psalm are beautifully reflected in the life story of Harriet Newell.

Faithful Servants Have a Passionate Love for the Lord
PSALM 116:1

The psalmist begins by proclaiming his love for the Lord. You can feel his emotion and excitement as he declares, "I love the LORD" (Yahweh). Why does he love the Lord? He loves the God who hears and answers prayers, unlike the dumb idols of Psalm 115:6 that "have ears but cannot hear."

Like the psalmist, Harriet also loved the Lord who heard her prayers. Harriet was born on October 10, 1793, in Haverhill, Massachusetts. She had a deep and passionate love for her Lord. She took great delight in referring to him as her "Immanuel." This intimate love is not surprising, as she lost her earthly father on May 8, 1808, when she was 14 years old. Dying of tuberculosis, he left behind a wife and nine children. Harriet believed with the psalmist that God her Father heard her voice and pleas for mercy. A few entries from her writing exemplify her love for and prayers to her heavenly Father:

> **Praying for a lost friend:** "I have just formed a solemn resolution of devoting one part of every day to fervent cries to God for a near and dear friend. Who knows but my Father in heaven will lend a listening ear to the voice of my supplications and touch her heart with conviction and converting grace!" (Newell, *Delighting in Her Heavenly Bridegroom*, 75)

> **Confident in his disciplining hand:** "I think I am willing to bear whatever God sees fit to lay upon me. Let my dear Heavenly Father inflict the keenest anguish, I will submit, for He is infinitely excellent, and can do nothing wrong." (Ibid., 86)

> **Captivated by his love:** "How condescending is God to permit hell-deserving sinners to commune with Him at His table! What on earth can equal the love of Jehovah! He treats those who are by nature His *enemies*, like *children*." (Ibid., 96; emphasis in original)

Such love moved Harriet to love her Immanuel passionately in return.

Faithful Servants Continually Call on the Lord for Help
PSALM 116:2-4

Verse 2 naturally flows from verse 1 and then moves into one of the main themes of the psalm: death. Because the Lord hears our voices and cries for mercy, we can be confident that we have his ear (v. 2). So we call on him as long as we live; the length of life is not specified (v. 2; cf. v. 4).

The psalmist then recalls a specific time when he especially needed the Lord's help. *The Message* paraphrases it this way: "Death stared me in the face, hell was hard on my heels. Up against it, I didn't know which way to turn." So, like Jonah sinking in a sea that was about to drown him, the psalmist "called on the name of the LORD" (v. 4). Flat on his back, he could only look up! At the end of his rope, he looked to the One who held the rope and cried, "LORD, save me!"

Harriet stared death in the face more than once. In 1810, at the age of 17, she took fever and nearly died. Yet she called on and trusted in the Lord, drawing strength from the hymn by Isaac Watts entitled "God of My Life." Often she would repeat the verse,

> God of my life, look gently down,
> Behold the pains I feel;
> But I am [silent] before Thy throne,
> Nor dare dispute Thy will.

God used this time of sickness to strengthen Harriet's faith and prepare her to answer his call to go to the nations. In a series of journal entries dating February 10–25, 1810, she would write,

> What great reason have I for thankfulness to God that I am still in the land of the living and have another opportunity of recording with my pen His tender mercy and loving kindness! . . .
>
> Jesus has undertaken to be my physician. He has graciously restored me to health . . . and brought me to resign my soul into His arms and to willingly wait the event of His Providence, whether life or death. Oh, that this sickness might be for my eternal good! . . .
>
> He has again laid His chastising rod upon me by afflicting me with sickness and pain. But "I will bear the indignation of the Lord, because I have sinned against Him." I have a renewed opportunity of examining my submission to God. And I do now, as in His presence, resolve to devote myself a living sacrifice to Him. I think I can say that afflictions are good for me. . . .
>
> But I fall infinitely short of the honor due to His glorious name. When, oh when, shall I arrive at the destined port of rest and with blood-washed millions who praise the Lamb of God for His redeeming love? Hasten, blessed Immanuel, that glorious period when all Thy exiled children shall arrive at their eternal home and celebrate Thy praises when time and nature fail. O for a tongue to sound aloud the honors and glories of the dear, matchless Saviour! (Newell, *Delighting in Her Heavenly Bridegroom*, 85–87)

Faithful Servants Know the Character of the Lord They Serve
PSALM 116:5-7

Those who know God best will serve him best. A knowledge of his character and his ways promotes gratitude, and it provides a motivation to trust him and serve him in a way that comes by no other means. In verse 5 we learn three things about our Lord's character: he is gracious, righteous, and compassionate. In verse 6 we learn of his ways: "The LORD guards the inexperienced," the one who in childlike faith depends on him. Indeed, when "I was helpless, . . . he saved me." In verse 7 we see our proper response: serene "rest" and gratitude.

Even as a tender teenage girl, Harriet Newell captured a glimpse of this important truth:

> **Nov. 20, 1810, a letter to Sarah Hills:** "I still find the promises precious and Jesus unchangeable. Though I am worthless and undeserving, yet the blessed Immanuel is lovely and worthy of the united praises of saints and angels." (Newell, *Delighting in Her Heavenly Bridegroom*, 98)

> **Feb. 24, 1811 (journal):** "I was remarkably favored with the presence of Immanuel. Never before did I gain such access to the mercy seat and entertain such glorious views of the character of God and such humiliating ideas of my situation as a sinner." (Ibid., 100)

> **March 25, 1811 (journal):** "God has not left Himself without witness in the earth. No—He is still manifesting the riches of His grace in bringing home His chosen ones. . . . I cannot but stand amazed to see the salvation of God! 'Come, behold the works of the Lord' [Ps. 46:8]." (Ibid., 105)

Faithful Servants Trust in the Lord Even in Terrible Suffering
PSALM 116:8-11

Those who love the Lord and serve him well are not immune to hardship and suffering. They should expect it as they walk in the footsteps of their suffering servant Savior. The psalmist could rejoice in God's deliverance (v. 8) and in the truth that he walks "before the LORD in the land of the living" (v. 9). But how did he get here? He had traveled a road that brought his soul to the edge of death, filled his eyes with tears, and saw his feet stumbling to maintain his walk with the Lord. It was not an easy path. Still, as verse 10 testifies, he believed even as he said, "I am severely oppressed." In contrast to the God he could trust in his suffering, he also saw another truth more clearly than ever and could shout in his alarm, "Everyone is a liar." In their depravity and sinfulness, people are perpetually unreliable. God, however, is not. Men may lie, but God only tells the truth.

Perhaps no event in the life of Harriett and her husband, Samuel Newell, illustrates this truth so well as the tragic death of their newborn baby girl. She would live only five days and be buried at sea. Harriet became pregnant soon after her marriage to Samuel. Their little daughter was a honeymoon baby conceived as they traveled almost eighteen thousand miles to India. Interestingly, she never once mentions her pregnancy in her letters or journal, never using the morning sickness and fatigue that hit her at sea as an excuse to complain or question God. In the last letter she would ever pen, she shared these words with her mother:

> Port Louis, Isle of France, Nov. 3, 1812. My ever dear Mother, since I wrote you last, I have been called by God to rejoice and weep, for afflictions and mercies have both alternately fallen to my lot. I address you now from a bed of great weakness—perhaps for the last time. Yes, my dear Mama, I feel this mud-walled cottage shake, and expect ere long to become an inhabitant of the world of spirits. Eternity, I feel, is just at hand. But let me give you some account of God's dealings with me, which I shall do at intervals, as strength will admit.
>
> On the cabin floor, with no other attendant but my dear husband, we could weep for joy and call ourselves the happiest of the happy. [She had just given birth to a baby girl, also named Harriet.] But alas! On the evening of the 5th day, the dear object of our love was snatched from us by death, and on the day following committed to its watery grave. Heart-rending stroke to a parental heart! Mine almost bled with deep anguish. (Newell, *Delighting in Her Heavenly Bridegroom*, 214)

She was never able to finish the letter.

Faithful Servants Keep Their Word and Serve the Lord out of Gratitude for Their Salvation

PSALM 116:12-14

One of the great dangers to those who have been saved for many years is losing the wonder of their salvation. We can take for granted what Jesus did for us on the cross, how he bore in his body the wrath of God in our place. It becomes a common thing. The psalmist was acutely aware of this danger, and he provides a helpful remedy to avoid this debilitating spiritual disease.

Never lose sight of God's benefits or his blessings (v. 12). In other words, day by day ask yourself the question, What might I do for my Lord given all he has done and will continue to do for me? Reflect on past, present, and future grace. In his book *Future Grace: The Purifying Power of the Promises of God,* John Piper puts it this way:

> The gospel events of history have an ever-present impact on the believer. Romans 5:8 says it best with its verb tenses. "God *shows* [present tense] his love for us in that while we were still sinners, Christ died [past tense] for us." This means that the past gospel events mediate the present experience of the love of God. We feel loved *now* by God because of the effect of those *past* gospel events. This profound sense of being loved by God *now* is the way that past grace becomes the foundation for our faith in future grace—that God will fulfill every promise for our good. (*Future Grace*, xiv; emphasis and brackets in original)

Reflecting on God's past benevolence, I will come to him to ask and receive even more from him (vv. 12-13)! Charles Spurgeon said it like this:

> The best return for one like me,
> So wretched and so poor,
> Is from his gifts to draw a plea,
> And ask him still for more. (*Treasury*, vol. 3a, 70)

We avoid spiritual lethargy and complacency by asking God for more of what he has already given us, is giving us, and will give us—a "cup of salvation" full and overflowing. Jesus took the cup of God's wrath and, in its place, gives us a cup of salvation! No wonder the psalmist now, and only now, says in verse 14, "I will fulfill my vows to the LORD in the presence of all his people" (cf. v. 18). Out of hearts overflowing with gratitude, we must declare to "all his people" how great is our God. Reflecting on his benefits in saving us, we cannot keep this good news to ourselves.

Converted at age 12, Harriet would write,

> I was brought to cast my soul on the Saviour of sinners and rely on Him alone for salvation. . . . I was filled with a sweet peace and a heavenly calmness which I never can describe. The honors, applauses, and titles of this vain world appeared like trifles light as air. The character of Jesus appeared infinitely lovely, and I could say with the psalmist, "Whom have I in heaven but Thee, and there is none on earth I desire besides Thee!" [Ps 73:25]. (Newell, *Delighting in Her Heavenly Bridegroom*, 64–65)

The following journal entries give evidence of her growing passion to make known this salvation to all peoples:

July 16, 1809: "What am I, that I should be blessed with the gospel's joyful sound, while so many are now perishing in heathen darkness for lack of knowledge of Christ?" (ibid., 68)

July 26, 1809: "But I think I could say that it was good for me to be afflicted [v. 10]. God was graciously pleased to assist me in calling upon His name, and permitted me to wrestle with Him in prayer . . . for the conversion of sinners." (ibid., 69)

August 7, 1811: "Providence now gives me an opportunity to go myself to the heathen. Shall I refuse the offer? Shall I love the glittering toys of this dying world so well that I cannot relinquish them for God? Forbid it heaven! Yes, I will go. However weak and unqualified I am, there is an all-sufficient Saviour ready to support me. In God alone is my hope. I will trust His promises and consider it one of the highest privileges that could be conferred upon me to be permitted to engage in His glorious service among the wretched inhabitants of India." (ibid., 124)

Faithful Servants Believe That in Life and Death They Are Valued by the Lord

PSALM 116:15

In Oswald Chambers's *My Utmost for His Highest*, the February 5 devotion reads,

> It is one thing to follow God's way of service if you are regarded as a hero, but quite another thing if the road marked out for you by God requires becoming a "doormat" under other people's feet. God's purpose may be to teach you to say, "I know how to be abased" (Philippians 4:12). Are you ready to be sacrifice like that? Are you ready to be less than a mere drop in the bucket—to be so totally insignificant that no one remembers you even if they think of those you served? Are you willing to give and be poured out until you are all used up and exhausted—not seeking to be ministered to, but to minister?

Verse 15 comes out of nowhere. In a psalm rejoicing in God's deliverance from death, it does not seem to fit. Yet it does. The same God who delivers us *from* death delivers us *through* death. And the death of even one of God's saints is a precious thing, a "valuable" thing, to him. He values highly one's death and sees it as a costly thing. The NLT translates verse 15, "The Lord cares deeply when his loved ones die."

It is hard for me to imagine that the death of any saint was more precious to King Jesus than that of Harriet Newell. As a teenager newly married, she left her widowed mother and eight brothers and sisters, knowing and accepting that she would never see them again. She was pregnant for most of the four-month journey to India, where she and Samuel would be denied permanent residence. On the way to the Isle of France, with only her husband at her side, she would deliver a baby girl they named Harriet, only to watch her die five days later. Less than a month later, taken with both tuberculosis and pneumonia, baby Harriet's mother would also die. And yet as the hour of her death approached, she could write to Ann Judson,

> How dark and mysterious are the ways of Providence. . . . But "it is well." Everything that God does must be right, for He is a being of infinite wisdom as well as power. . . . I think I have enjoyed the light of Immanuel's countenance and have

known joys too great to be expressed. (Newell, *Delighting in Her Heavenly Bridegroom*, 203)

In describing Harriet's death to her mother, Samuel would write,

She was by no means alarmed at the idea of death, nor was she melancholy. She was calm, patient, and resigned. During the last week of our voyage she read through the whole book of Job, and, as she afterwards told me, she "found sweet relief from every fear in submitting to a sovereign God, and could not refrain from shedding tears of joy that God should give her such comfortable views of death and eternity." . . . The enjoyment of God was what she expected and longed to find in heaven. Her mind seemed to repose with comfort and delight on the glorious perfections of Jehovah, her covenant God. She spoke repeatedly of the pleasure she took in dwelling on the character of God. . . . When I asked her if she was not willing to live longer she replied "Yes, if I could live better than I have ever yet done. But I have had so much experience of the wickedness of my heart that if I should recover, I should expect the remainder of my life to be much like the past, and I long to get rid of this wicked heart and go where I shall sin no more." This thought, that death would be a complete deliverance from sin, she repeated many times with great delight. . . . The day, I think, before her death, I asked her how her past life appeared to her. She replied, "Bad enough—but that only makes the grace of Christ appear the more glorious." She then repeated these favorite lines:

"Jesus, Thy blood and righteousness
My beauty are, my heavenly dress;
'Midst flaming worlds in these arrayed,
With joy shall I lift up my head."

On the Sabbath of the 29th of November, the day before her death. . . . Dr. Wallich, a friend of ours from Serampore, who had lately arrived in the Isle of France, called to see us. After looking at Harriet, he took me aside and told me he thought she could not live through the next day. When I told Harriet what the doctor said, she raised both hands,

clasping them with eagerness, and with an expressive smile on
her countenance, exclaimed—"Oh! Blessed news!" (Newell,
Delighting in Her Heavenly Bridegroom, 203)

Yes, precious in the sight of the Lord is the death of his saints!

Faithful Servants Offer a Sacrifice of Praise and Thanksgiving to the Lord for All to Hear

PSALM 116:16-19

Our psalm concludes with the psalmist tangibly expressing his love for
the Lord (v. 1). In verse 16 he gladly identifies himself as the Lord's
servant out of gratitude for the Lord's deliverance from the chains of
his afflictions (v. 10). In verse 17 he will offer sacrifices and praises of
thanksgiving as he again (for the fourth time) calls on the name of the
Lord. In verse 18, for a second time, he pledges to publicly fulfill his
vows to the Lord. Finally, in verse 19 he specifies the place of his declaration and offering as the temple courts in Jerusalem, concluding with
an outburst of worship: "Praise the Lord!" (NLT; CSB, "Hallelujah!").
Kidner says the flame of the psalmist's love for his God "is not with-
drawn to burn alone. Placed in the *midst* [of God's people], it will kindle
others, and blaze all the longer and better for it" (*Psalms 73–150*, 411;
emphasis in original).

Commenting on his wife's death to a friend in Boston, Samuel
Newell wrote,

> Tell [Harriet's mother] that her dear Harriet never repented
> of any sacrifice she had made for Christ and that on her dying
> bed she was "comforted by the thought of having had it in her
> heart to do something for the heathen, though God had seen
> fit to take her away before we entered on our work." (Newell,
> *Delighting in Her Heavenly Bridegroom*, 216)

I (Danny) cannot help but wonder if she somehow knew her sacrifice of
praise and thanksgiving would resound for all to hear in her death. Her
memorial preacher was right when he said,

> Henceforth, every one who remembers Harriet Newell will
> remember the Foreign Mission from America. And every
> one, who reads the history of *this* Mission, will be sure to read
> the faithful record of her exemplary life and triumphant

death. . . . Her life measured by months and years was *short*, but far otherwise when measured by what she achieved. She was the happy instrument of much good to the holy kingdom of Christ. She died in a glorious cause. Nor did she pray and weep and die in vain. Other causes may miscarry, but this will certainly triumph. The LORD God of Israel has pledged His perfections for its success. The time is at hand when the various tribes of India, and all the nations and kindreds of the earth, shall fall down before the KING of ZION and submit cheerfully to His reign. A glorious work is to be done among the nations. Christ is to see the travail of His soul. (Newell, *Delighting in Her Heavenly Bridegroom*, 238–39; emphasis in original)

Conclusion

Harriet Atwood Newell died in the arms of her missionary-husband Samuel on November 30, 1812. She was only 19 and had been married for less than a year. He would carry her to her grave and bury her alone. On her deathbed she had pled with her husband to relay to her family a final message: "Tell them—*assure* them, that I approve on my dying bed the course I have taken. *I have never repented leaving all for Christ*" (Newell, *Delighting in Her Heavenly Bridegroom*, 209; emphasis in original).

How could Harriet die with such an attitude? Listen well to the heart of an 18-year-old girl poured out to her Immanuel just eight months before her transition into heaven:

March 26: The sacrifices which I have made are great indeed, but the light of Immanuel's countenance can enliven every dreary scene and make the path of duty pleasant. Should I, at some future period, be destitute of *one* sympathizing friend in a foreign, sickly clime, I shall have nothing to fear. When earthly friends forsake me, "the Lord will take me up." No anticipated trials ought to make me anxious, for I know that I can do and suffer all things "through Christ who strengthens me." In His hands I leave the direction of every event, knowing that He who is infinitely wise and good can do me no wrong. (Ibid., 159–60; emphasis in original)

Harriet was buried on the Isle of France. A marble monument would be erected over her grave with the following inscription:

Early devoted to Christ, her heart burned for the heathen; for them, she left her kindred and her native land, and welcomed danger and sufferings. Of excellent understanding, rich in accomplishments and virtues, she was the delight of her friends, a crown to her husband, and an ornament to the missionary cause. Her short life was bright, her death full of glory. Her name lives and in all Christian lands is pleading with irresistible eloquence for the heathen. This humble monument to her memory is erected by the American Board of Commissioners for Foreign Missions. (Newell, *Delighting in Her Heavenly Bridegroom*, 222)

Biographer Jennifer Adams notes that back in America there was an explosion of little girls being named Harriet Newell in honor of this brave and godly teenage missionary (ibid., 13). At her memorial service, she was called "the first martyr to the missionary cause from the American world" (ibid., 237), and the preacher drove home the significance of her passing: "The death of Harriet, instead of overcasting our prospects, will certainly turn to the advantage of missions" (ibid., 238). He was right. By 1840 many from America had visited her grave. Her memoirs, which she was burning as she was about to leave for the mission field but which were spared by her mother's request, were published and widely distributed with a new edition being printed annually for the next 25 years. These memoirs resulted in many conversions and many people answering the call to go to the nations.

Her husband Samuel would go on to serve for seven years in a successful mission in Ceylon. On May 30, 1821, his life would end from cholera before his thirtieth birthday. Once more the truth was claimed: precious in the sight of the Lord is the death of his saints!

Reflect and Discuss

1. If success in ministry does not always appear visibly, how can you know if you are following God faithfully?
2. Would you describe your relationship to God as one of "passionate love"? Why or why not? Can passionate love be expressed in multiple ways? If so, how?
3. When your life is in distress, is your first inclination to run to or away from God? How can Christians help one another run to God first?

4. This section teaches that "those who know God best will serve him best." What effect does knowing God have on one's ability to serve God?

5. Why does God allow those who follow him faithfully to experience suffering?

6. What are some ways to keep your salvation from becoming a common thing? How can Christians help one another keep the wonder of their salvation?

7. How is the psalmist able to be committed to the Lord even when the "ropes of death" encompass him? What promises does Scripture give for hope during grim times?

8. Harriet Newell's life has positively impacted the Great Commission even though she never made it to the mission field. How does knowing this shape how you view your own life and desire to serve God?

9. What part of Harriet Newell's life would you most like to emulate? What steps can you take toward that?

10. What about Harriet Newell's life encourages you and challenges you the most?

A Little Psalm with a Big Message

PSALM 117

Main Idea: The nations should worship the Lord because of his eternal covenant love.

I. **The Lord Is to Be Magnified among the Nations (117:1).**
   A. God desires that all the nations praise him.
   B. God desires that all the nations extol him.
II. **The Lord Is to Be Magnified Because of His Nature (117:2).**
   A. Our God is a God of love.
   B. Our God is a God of faithfulness.

In his classic work on missions, *Let the Nations Be Glad!*, John Piper notes, "Missions is not the ultimate goal of the church. Worship is. Missions exists because worship doesn't. Worship is ultimate, not missions, because God is ultimate, not man" (35). These words capture what Psalm 117 is all about: missions to the nations who do not worship God in order that they may worship him.

Psalm 117 is both the shortest psalm in the Psalter and the shortest chapter in the Bible. Spurgeon, however, is right:

> This psalm, which is very little in its letter, is exceedingly large
> in its spirit; for, bursting all bounds of race or nationality,
> it calls upon all mankind to praise the name of the Lord.
> (*Treasury*, vol. 3a, 97)

Luther loved it and wrote a thirty-six-page commentary on it—that is 18 pages per verse!

Psalm 117 is also a part of a sextet of songs, Psalms 113–118, known as the Egyptian Hallel (VanGemeren, *Psalms*, 831). Built around the emphasis of Psalm 114, a celebration of the exodus, these six songs were sung as the Hebrews gathered to celebrate the Passover, God's great act of salvation on their behalf. They sang Psalms 113 and 114 before the memorial meal and Psalms 115–118 afterward. Jesus and his disciples would have sung these psalms on the night they celebrated the Passover before his betrayal and arrest (Matt 26:30; Mark 14:26). Interestingly, two other sections of the Psalms are known as Hallel ("praise") Psalms. Psalms 120–136 are called the "Great Hallel," and Psalms 146–150 conclude the Psalter with "Hallelujah," which means "Praise the Lord."

Psalm 117, the fifth of the Egyptian Hallels, is anonymous. Cosmic and international in scope, it reveals the heart of God toward the nations. He loves them (v. 2) and desires that they worship him (v. 1). Paul quotes this little jewel in Romans 15:11 as evidence that God's redemptive love and purpose have always included the nations, just as he promised Abraham in Genesis 12:1-3. In two short verses Psalm 117 brings the whole world before our eyes, revealing where and why the Lord is to be magnified.

The Lord Is to Be Magnified among the Nations
PSALM 117:1

The psalm follows a command-reason pattern. Verse 1 tells us what to do, and verse 2 tells us why we do it. One can see classic Hebrew parallelism in both verses since the second line in each verse reinforces the truth in the first. Further, the psalm opens and closes with "Praise the Lord!" or "Hallelujah!" Psalm 117 is a universal invitation to people everywhere to praise and brag on Yahweh because of his merciful love and faithfulness. No god is like our God!

God Desires That All the Nations Praise Him

The psalm begins with a call to praise (Hb *hallelu*) the Lord (Yahweh). However, what follows is a surprise. Normally it is the people of God, the covenant community, who are called to praise the Lord, but here it is all the *goyim*, the "nations."

"Nations" does not refer to political states. It refers to people groups, different ethnic and linguistic groups. As of January 2020, the Joshua Project lists more than seventeen thousand different people groups in the world, with more than seven thousand still unreached (joshuaproject.net). The percentage of unreached people groups is approximately 41 percent, totaling more than three billion people. According to Wycliffe Bible Translators, of the estimated seven thousand total languages in the world, more than three thousand have some portions of the Bible in their language. But there are still more than thirty-nine hundred languages (covering 252 million people) without a single verse of the Bible translated ("Latest Bible Translation Figures Show Progress"). At this moment these language groups have no hope of praising King Jesus as Lord of the universe. They are perishing and headed toward hell, and yet our great God desires that they would praise him and be saved.

God Desires That All the Nations Extol Him

The word "glorify" means to boast, laud, or praise. It has the idea of bragging on someone. It means to make much of someone. Our God is great, good, and awesome. We are to gossip, in a good way, about the great God we know, love, worship, and serve.

The word "peoples," like "nations," refers to ethnic, linguistic, and cultural groupings of people. "Tribes" captures the meaning well. "Peoples" occurs in the plural 203 times in the CSB. Tribes live around the world and down the street. They are individuals who share a common language, culture, interests, ideals, and values. Whether a mile away or ten thousand miles away, they need to be confronted with Yahweh, the only God worthy of praise and glory. And they need to hear the message in a way they will understand.

Missions is a cross-cultural strategy and lifestyle that aims to help people stop making much of themselves and to start making much of Jesus. It aims to show them that no one else is worthy of such worship and devotion. It aims to show them that our maximum joy and pleasure are found only in praising and adoring this God. As John Piper says,

> The reason God seeks our praise is not because he won't be complete until he gets it. He is seeking our praise because we won't be happy until we give it. . . . Missions is calling the world [to] do what they were created to do, namely, to enjoy making much of God forever. ("Everlasting Truth for the Joy of All Peoples")

The Lord Is to Be Magnified Because of His Nature
PSALM 117:2

There is a reason the psalmist calls for the nations to magnify God's name. It is not arbitrary, whimsical, or misplaced. It is not the "because I said so" of a celestial bully or capricious deity on a cosmic ego trip. No, it is a call rooted in the loving and faithful character of God that causes us to rise up and worship him. He is great in his love for us, and he will be faithful to love us forever.

Verse 2 is grounded in one of the greatest Old Testament verses in the Bible: Exodus 34:6. It says,

> The LORD passed in front of [Moses] and proclaimed: "The LORD— the LORD is a compassionate and gracious God, slow to anger and abounding in faithful love and truth."

Our God Is a God of Love

Once more the beautiful and rich Hebrew word *chesed* appears in our text. The various ways English translations attempt to capture its meaning is instructive:

NKJV: merciful kindness	NIV: love
NASB: lovingkindness	ESV: steadfast love
CSB: faithful love	NLT: unfailing love

And his faithful love is "great." This is a strong and vigorous word used of the stronger side in a battle or overflowing floodwaters. Ideas like "mighty" or "prevailing" capture something of the significance of the word (Kidner, *Psalms 73–150*, 411). It is fronted in the Hebrew text for emphasis. God floods his children with his love. Our God is a God of love. He loves you. He loves me. He loves the world (John 3:16). First John 4:8 and 16 tell us love is the essence of his nature and character.

Our God Is a God of Faithfulness

If our Lord's faithful love is great, his faithfulness endures forever. God made a promise to Abraham in Genesis 12 that all the earth, all the peoples, would be blessed by his descendants. From Abraham came Israel. From Israel came Jesus. God kept his word.

What God has promised to do for us in Christ is as certain today as on the days he made Abraham and Israel. And it will always be this way, now and forever. God's character cannot change, and his promises cannot be broken. Ross says it well: "God's faithful loyal love is eternal—he fulfills all his covenant promises" (*Psalms 90–150*, 436). Call on him and you will be saved. But to call on him, you must know about him. This is God's heart. This is our mission. Praise the Lord! Hallelujah!

Conclusion

Derek Kidner is right when he says, "This tiny psalm is great in faith, and its reach is enormous" (*Psalms 73–150*, 411). He is also correct when he argues that it finds its prophetic fulfillment in Revelation 7:9-10 where we read,

> *After this I looked, and there was a vast multitude from every nation, tribe, people, and language, which no one could number, standing before the throne and before the Lamb. They were clothed in white robes with palm branches in their hands. And they cried out in a loud voice, "Salvation belongs to our God, who is seated on the throne, and to the Lamb!"*

John Piper is right, too: "Missions exists because worship doesn't." Let's get to work for Jesus and see Psalm 117 fulfilled so that all the nations might sing "Hallelujah" to our God and to the Lamb.

Reflect and Discuss

1. Why do you think Piper felt it necessary to say, "Missions is not the ultimate goal of the church. Worship is"? How should this goal change how the church engages in missions?
2. What implications are there for the church if God wants all peoples to praise him? Is God's praise from all peoples a part of your church's mission? If not, how might you begin to incorporate it?
3. In what ways does praise from all peoples glorify God better than praise from only one people group?
4. Do you know what people groups are living near you? What steps can you take to discover and engage them?
5. This section connects joy and pleasure to cross-cultural missions. Why is it important to pursue missions with joy? What happens when Christians pursue missions without joy?
6. Describe some ways God has shown his faithful character to you.
7. Is worship of God difficult or easy for you right now? Why? How can verse 2 help you praise God when it is not easy to praise him?
8. What does this psalm imply you can do to motivate your worship?
9. Should you praise God when you do not feel the desire to praise him? Or should you wait until your feelings move you to praise? Why?
10. Read Romans 15:7-13. How is this psalm used there? What is Paul's point?

The Lord's Faithful Love Will Never End

PSALM 118

Main Idea: God's faithful love is sufficient for our most desperate needs, and his awesome salvation is worthy of our deepest praise.

I.   Give Thanks to the Lord for His Steadfast Love (118:1-4).
II. Trust in the Lord Who Is on Your Side (118:5-9).
III. Be Strong in the Name of the Lord Who Gives You Victory (118:10-12).
IV. Sing for Joy to the Lord of Your Salvation (118:13-18).
V.   Praise the Lord That He Answers Your Prayers (118:19-21).
VI. Rejoice at How the Lord Works in Marvelous Ways (118:22-24).
VII. Bless the Lord for the Savior He Sends (118:25-29).

Psalm 118 was almost certainly the last hymn Jesus and his disciples sang at the Last Supper (Matt 26:30) on the night he was betrayed. Allen Ross notes,

> Tradition tells us that for a Passover meal Psalms 113–116 were sung before the meal, and Psalms 117 and 118 closed the evening. This psalm, then, was the hymn that Jesus and the disciples sang in the upper room after the last supper (Matt 26:30). After the evening concluded with the line "Bind the sacrifice with cords to the horns of the altar," Jesus and his disciples went out into the Garden of Gethsemane to watch and pray—and await the fulfillment of their hymn. (*Psalms 90–150*, 457)

Psalm 118 is the last of the Egyptian Hallel psalms celebrating the Lord's deliverance of the Hebrews from Egyptian bondage (Pss 113–118). It rightly looks back to that great event of redemption, but it also looks forward to the greater redemption provided by Jesus Christ in his death and resurrection. The psalm is quoted or alluded to 23 times in the New Testament (Greidanus, *Preaching Christ from Psalms*, 390). It is a psalm of thanksgiving, celebrating the victory of the king and his people in battle, accompanied by a parade or procession to the temple to praise the Lord for his never-ending love and deliverance. Its long shadow finds its climactic meaning and fulfillment in the passion of the Christ. As Sidney Greidanus writes,

> As the king was in distress and called on the LORD (Ps 118:5), so Jesus was in even greater distress in Gethsemane and on the cross and called on the LORD. As the king was surrounded by enemies who wanted to kill him (Ps 118:10-12), so Jesus on the cross was surrounded by enemies who were in the process of killing him. As the king testified, "The LORD has punished me severely, but he did not give me over to death" (Ps 118:18), so King Jesus was being punished for "the sins of the whole world" (1 John 2:2) but was not given over to ultimate death: he rose again. As the king was rejected by his enemies but became the chief cornerstone (Ps 118:22), so Jesus was rejected by all, sentenced to death, and became the chief cornerstone (Mark 12:10). (*Preaching Christ from Psalms*, 391)

We will examine this magnificent psalm in seven movements. It begins and ends by highlighting the character of our God and his faithful love that endures forever.

Give Thanks to the Lord for His Steadfast Love
PSALM 118:1-4

We can thank God for many things, but this psalm begins by pointing out two: "he is good" and "his faithful love endures forever." The theme of his "faithful love"—also translated as his "steadfast love" (ESV), his "lov-ingkindness" (NASB), and "his love [that] never quits" (*The Message*)—is stated four times. Israel, in particular, should thank him for this never-ending love. But everyone who fears and reveres him should do the same. There is to be a universal recognition of the inherent goodness and eternal love that characterizes this God! Yahweh ("the LORD") is the essence of *chesed* ("faithful love"). Of no one else can this be said. The first lines of the hymn "He Lifted Me" proclaim this truth well: "In loving-kindness Jesus came, my soul in mercy to reclaim, and from the depths of sin and shame, through grace he lifted me."

Trust in the Lord Who Is on Your Side
PSALM 118:5-9

Romans 8:31 says, "If God is for us, who is against us?" If God is on our side, it does not matter who is on the other. This simple phrase summarizes most of Psalm 118, especially verses 5-9. The psalmist was "in distress" (NIV, "hard pressed"; *The Message,* "pushed to the wall"). We might say, "His back was against the wall." What did he do? He called on the Lord who is "good" and whose "faithful love endures forever." What was the Lord's response? "The LORD answered me and set me free" (ESV). Divine intervention arrived from the "LORD [who] is for me" (in the Hebrew in both 6 and 7). He is "my helper" (v. 7) and "refuge" (vv. 8-9). This good, loving, rescuing God is on the psalmist's side because he praises him and he trusts him. He is delivered (v. 5), and fear is vanquished (v. 6). In hope he says, "I will look in triumph on those who hate me" (v. 7). That is why he fled to the Lord for safety and security rather than to mere mortals. No matter what their station in life may be (even "nobles"), it is better to trust the Lord (vv. 8-9). How true these words are of our Lord Jesus throughout his life and especially in his passion. How true they should be for us who celebrate the truths of this psalm with him (see Heb 13:6). The God who was on the side of his people thousands of years ago is still on their side today.

Be Strong in the Name of the Lord Who Gives You Victory
PSALM 118:10-12

Verses 10-12 build on and continue the theme of verses 5-9. The phrase "in the name of the LORD I destroyed them" (ESV, "I cut them off") appears three times, and the phrase "they surrounded me" appears four times. What seems to be a hopeless situation experiences an amazing reversal and victory because of "the name of the LORD." The nations came against him (v. 10), but the Lord cut them down—a phrase that could be translated "circumcised" (Ross, *Psalms 90–150,* 450). He was "surrounded" on every side (v. 11), but the Lord cut them down. Like swarming bees with their venomous stings, they attacked him (v. 12), but the Lord cut them down. Their defeat was quick and complete. They were "extinguished like a fire among thorns." The power of the Lord gave him the victory over those who would harm and even destroy him. He may have been no match for them, but they were no match for his God! Romans 8:37-39 aligns with these truths well:

No, in all these things we are more than conquerors through him who loved us. For I am persuaded that neither death nor life, nor angels nor rulers, nor things present nor things to come, nor powers, nor height nor depth, nor any other created thing will be able to separate us from the love of God that is in Christ Jesus our Lord.

We can say with Paul, "But thanks be to God, who gives us the victory through our Lord Jesus Christ!" (1 Cor 15:57).

Sing for Joy to the Lord of Your Salvation
PSALM 118:13-18

As Psalm 118 progresses, the momentum builds to a crescendo. Motyer says, "The king turns suddenly to address his unsuccessful enemies directly—and why not?" (*Psalms by the Day*, 328). The king's enemies pushed hard to take him down and make him fall, but they failed. Why? Because the Lord who is his strength, song, and salvation helped him (vv. 13-14). Once more, this work was all God's doing. His powerful right hand performed valiantly and was exalted in victory (vv. 15-16). No wonder "there are shouts of joy and victory in the tents of the righteous" (v. 15).

Verses 17-18 make clear how desperate and dire the situation was. Death was close, but the Lord delivered the king. His response? He will joyfully "proclaim what the LORD has done" (v. 17). None of this happened by accident and without purpose. The Lord was in it all. The king wisely exclaims, "The LORD disciplined me severely but did not give me over to death." Derek Kidner points out that verses 15-17 contain another echo of the Song of Moses found in Exodus 15 (cf. vv. 14,28). He writes, "The Exodus events stamp out their likeness on God's acts of redemption throughout history . . . consummated in the work of Christ" (*Psalms 73–150*, 414). Victory was won through the delivering and disciplining hand of the heavenly Father. It was severe, but it was also healing. Shout for joy to the Lord of our salvation.

Praise the Lord That He Answers Your Prayers
PSALM 118:19-21

God's salvation is now celebrated in a victory parade through the "gates of righteousness," "the LORD's gate," which only the righteous may enter. The goal of the righteous is to thank the Lord for his salvation

(vv. 14-15) and for how he answered the king's prayer (vv. 21). Verse 21 concludes with the declaration that God has "become my salvation." Kidner makes a vital observation here: "The battle was single-handed; the victory is shared" (*Psalms 73–150*, 414).

Our Lord God is a prayer-answering God. He heard the prayers of Israel in the past. He heard the prayer of the king as reflected in this psalm. He heard the prayer of Jesus in Gethsemane and on the cross in ultimate fulfillment of this psalm. And he hears the prayers of his righteous children today—righteous because of the imputed righteousness of King Jesus that is theirs by faith in his perfect atoning work and glorious resurrection. Call on the Lord today for salvation. He will hear and answer your prayer.

Rejoice at How the Lord Works in Marvelous Ways
PSALM 118:22-24

The righteous now proclaim why they are thankful to God for his salvation. It is because of a great reversal concerning the king. Michael Wilcock notes that what was true of Israel so many times in her history (rejection by men but vindication by God) was about to happen to the king.

> He was himself the Stone, the true Israel. He was the
> Righteous one, entering the gate (v. 20). Once he had
> suffered for their sins, he and all his people would *not die but
> live* (v. 17). Once he had risen, he would claim authority over
> *all the nations* (vv. 10-12). His love endures forever (vv. 1, 29).
> (*Message: Songs*, 192)

The discarded stone has become the most important stone, "the cornerstone." And "this came from the LORD" (v. 23). Isaiah 28:16 promised that "the Lord would lay in Zion a stone for the foundation when he restored the people. And other passages identified the Messiah and his kingdom as a stone (see Isaiah 8:14; Daniel 2:34 and 45; and Zechariah 3:9)" (Ross, *Psalms 90–150*, 453). In Matthew 21:42-44 Jesus declares publicly, "I am that stone! I am the Messiah King sent by the Lord. The nations, the religious leaders, and the Romans may reject me, but the Lord will establish me and build his kingdom on me. All of this comes from the Lord and it is wonderful in his people's eyes" (cf. Ps 117:23). This day of salvation is "the day the LORD has made; let's rejoice and be glad in it" (v. 24). James Boice makes a wonderful application on this verse: "You must not stumble at God's grace in Jesus Christ, as many have, tripping over that stone. You should come to Jesus instead and build your life on that secure foundation" (*Psalms 107–150*, 961).

Bless the Lord for the Savior He Sends
PSALM 118:25-29

The psalm closes as it began with a note of thanksgiving. Verse 25 has a familiar ring considering its New Testament use. "Save us" is the Hebrew equivalent of the Aramaic word *Hosanna*, shouted by the people on the occasion of Jesus's triumphal entry at the beginning of Passover/Passion Week (Matt 21:9; Mark 11:9-10; John 12:13). Little did they know how true their words were. In context it is a prayer for God's blessing and has a beautiful parallelism:

> LORD, save us!
> LORD, please grant us success!

Salvation and continued blessings come only through the Lord's constant care and involvement. Salvation and blessing are rightly tied to the one "who comes in the name of the LORD" (v. 26). Its blessing includes the Lord as our God and the light of his presence (cf. Num 6:25; Isa 9:2), the light of his salvation (v. 27).

The latter part of verse 27 is striking: "Bind the festival sacrifice with cords to the horns of the altar." As Ross remarks,

> Although there is no mention of such a practice in the Old
> Testament, the existence of the horns and the need for
> securing the sacrifices in place makes perfectly good sense. . . .
> This interpretation would fit well the New Testament
> correlation with the arrest of Jesus to be taken to his sacrificial
> death. (*Psalms 90–150*, 455)

Such a great and glorious salvation, such a great and glorious Savior, rightly deserves both praise and thanksgiving. This is how our psalm ends. "You are my God," says the psalmist, and I am your servant. Therefore, he says, "I will give you thanks" and "I will exalt [praise] you" (v. 28). The repetition of "my God" is intentionally emphatic. The psalm then concludes as it began, repeating verse 1 (an example of *inclusio*).

Whatever happens, whatever our God does, we thank him now and forever because we know two things are forever true: "he is good" and "his faithful love endures forever" (vv. 1,29).

Conclusion

Alec Motyer captures what Psalm 118, indeed what the whole Bible, is about when he writes,

> When the New Testament finds Jesus in something from the Old Testament it is always worthwhile going back to look at the Old Testament context, where we will discover how exactly the Scriptures are being quoted and what a fuller portrait of the coming Messiah emerges. This is richly true, for example, of the list of quotations from the Psalms in Hebrews 1, and notably true of Psalm 118. . . . When we look at everything Psalm 118 says about the Davidic king, we see what was then "writ small" of him was finally written in cosmic and eternal letters by the King himself. Follow this nine-fold portrayal through into the New Testament: the king prayed under extreme pressure and was answered (verse 5; Hebrews 5:7); he was confident against all comers (verses 10-14; John 18:3-6); he overcame through the Name (verse 12; John 10:25; 17:12); faced one particular, individual foe (verse 13; John 12:21; 14:30); found Yahweh's help, strength and salvation (verses 14-16; John 6:57; 8:29); came through deadly danger alive (verse 17; Matthew 28:5-7); endured Yahweh's "chastening" (verse 18; Isaiah 53:10; John 18:11; Hebrews 5:8); was qualified to enter the gates of righteousness (verses 19-21; John 16:8-10; Hebrews 5:5; 6:19; 9:24; 10:20); was rejected by human judgment (verse 22a; Matthew 21:42; 1 Peter 2:7); became the chief cornerstone (verse 22b; Matthew 21:42; Acts 4:11; Ephesians 2:20). Was the earlier king aware that his experiences were predictive and anticipatory? Probably not, but we speak, do we not, of "coming events casting their shadow before them" and this is what happened right through the Old Testament. Historical events and significant persons all took the shape they did within the shadow of the One to come. The whole Bible is about Jesus. (Motyer, *Psalms by the Day*, 330)

Reflect and Discuss

1. How would you explain God's *chesed* (his faithful love) in your own words?

2. How does the beginning refrain ("His faithful love endures forever") provide the foundation for the whole psalm? How might this refrain also serve as the foundation for all of Scripture?

3. Can Christians claim to be conquerors and victorious when they experience persecution? Why or why not?

4. Why does the Lord discipline his people? What does a lack of discipline reveal about God's relationship to us? (See Heb 12:5-13.)

5. When are you tempted to avoid praying for help? How can the gospel give you confidence to pray?

6. How is the psalmist able to pray as he does in verse 6? What other passages of Scripture echo this same idea?

7. Describe a time when God answered your prayers for help. Can you see evidence of the truth from verses 8-9 in this circumstance? If so, how?

8. What can difficult circumstances teach us about God and ourselves that easy ones cannot? How can you keep a desperate need for God when life is easy?

9. Where is this passage quoted in the New Testament? How do Jesus's life and death exemplify the truth of this psalm?

10. What does verse 22 teach us about how God works out his plan of salvation? How can it give you hope during challenging times?

The Incomparable Word of God

PSALM 119

Main Idea: The Word of God is our incomparable guide to a blessed and God-honoring life.

I.   Stanza Aleph: Those Who Walk in the Law of the Lord Are Blameless and Blessed (119:1-8).

II. Stanza Beth: Those Who Treasure God's Word in Their Heart Will Live a Life That Pleases the Lord (119:9-16).

III. Stanza Gimel: Those Who Look Carefully into the Word of God Will See Wonderful Things (119:17-24).

IV. Stanza Daleth: Those Who Are Experiencing Troubles Will Find Life and Strength in the Word of God (119:25-32).

V.   Stanza He: Those Who Allow the Lord to Teach Them His Word Will Obey Him, Live Well, and Finish Well (119:33-40).

VI. Stanza Waw: Those Who Rest in The Lord's Faithful Love and Keep His Law Will Be Ready to Answer Those Who Challenge Them (119:41-48).

VII. Stanza Zayin: Those Who Remember God's Word Will Be Comforted by It (119:49-56).

VIII. Stanza Cheth: Those Who Run after the Lord Will Befriend All Who Also Fear Him (119:57-64).

IX. Stanza Teth: Those Who Are Afflicted by the Discipline of the Lord Will Learn How Good His Instruction Is (119:65-72).

X.   Stanza Yod: Those Who Receive Comfort from the Lord's Faithful Love Will Delight in His Word (119:73-80).

XI. Stanza Kaph: Those Who Grow Weary and Discouraged Should Put Their Hope in the Lord's Salvation and His Word (119:81-88).

XII. Stanza Lamed: Those Who Trust in the Lord's Perfect and Powerful Word Delight in His Teachings (119:89-96).

XIII. Stanza Mem: Those Who Love the Lord's Instruction Meditate on It All Day Long (119:97-104).

XIV.   Stanza Nun: Those Who Keep the Lord's Righteous Judgment
        Find It to Be a Lamp for Their Feet and a Light for Their Path
        (119:105-112).
XV.   Stanza Samek: Those Who Reject the Wicked Trust in the Lord
        and Love His Word (119:113-120).
XVI.   Stanza Ayin: Those Who Are Servants of the Lord Are
        Marked by Justice, Righteousness, and a Love for God's Word
        (119:121-128).
XVII.   Stanza Pe: Those Who Find God's Word Wonderful Weep over
        Those Who Don't (119:129-136).
XVIII. Stanza Tsade: Those Who Are Zealous for the Righteous
        God Acknowledge That His Righteousness Is Everlasting
        (119:137-144).
XIX.   Stanza Qoph: Those Who Call on the Lord to Save Them Will
        Call on Him Early and Know He Is Near (119:145-152).
XX.   Stanza Resh: Those Who Need to Be Rescued by the Lord
        Will Ask Him to Be Their Champion as They Love His Word
        (119:153-160)
XXI.   Stanza Sin/Shin: Those Who Are Persecuted Will Fear, Rejoice
        in, Love, and Praise the Lord for His Word That Gives Them
        Abundant Peace (119:161-168).
XXII.   Stanza Taw: Those Who Cry Out to the Lord as Their Shepherd
        Can Ask Him to Help Them According to His Promise
        (119:169-176).

Psalm 119 is the longest chapter in the Bible, consisting of 22 stanzas and 176 verses. It is an alphabetic acrostic. As Allen Ross explains, "In each paragraph (strophe) of eight verses each line begins with the same letter of the Hebrew alphabet. (The 22 strophes correspond to the 22 letters of the alphabet.)" ("Psalms," 879). From verse 1 to verse 176, the anonymous psalmist meditates and reflects on the incomparable Word of God. Interestingly, it is the last psalm out of the 150 psalms that Augustine expounded. Why? Augustine said, "Because as often as I began to reflect upon it, it always exceeded the utmost stretch of my powers. . . . I cannot show how deep it is" (Augustin [*sic*], *Expositions on the Psalms*, 560). Anyone who mines the treasure of this psalm can readily identify with the great church father.

Stanza Aleph: Those Who Walk in the Law of the Lord Are Blameless and Blessed
PSALM 119:1-8

Psalm 119 begins like Psalm 1 with the theme of the "happy" or "blessed" (ESV) life. Blessed people are also "blameless" because they "walk according to the LORD's instruction" (v. 1). What is the key to this kind of life? They "seek [the LORD] with all their heart" (v. 2) and "praise [him] with an upright heart" (v. 7). Who we are on the inside inevitably reveals itself on the outside. Jesus teaches us, "What comes out of a person is what defiles him. For from within, out of people's hearts, come evil thoughts, . . . evil actions" (Mark 7:20-22). Spurgeon is right: "God is not truly sought by the cold researches of the brain: we must seek him with the heart" (*Treasury*, vol. 3a, 142). If we seek him with our hearts and obey his Word, we will enjoy the happy and blameless life.

Stanza Beth: Those Who Treasure God's Word in Their Heart Will Live a Life That Pleases the Lord
PSALM 119:9-16

Verse 11 is one of the most loved and memorized verses in the Bible. It teaches us that those who have "treasured" God's Word in their heart will not live a life dominated by and enslaved to sin. Their lives will be characterized by purity as they seek the Lord with all their hearts (vv. 1-2). And as they are taught by the Lord through his Word (v. 12), they will testify (v. 13) to the greatness of his Word and "rejoice" in it "as much as in all riches" (v. 14). They will "delight" in the Lord's Word and never forget it (v. 16). Luther says of verse 11, "I have purposed to serve You with my whole heart. Therefore, I have imprinted Your words on my heart, so that I may no longer sin against them" (*First Lectures on the Psalms II*, 419). Here is not a person who is *sinless*. It is, however, a person who *sins less*.

Stanza Gimel: Those Who Look Carefully into the Word of God Will See Wonderful Things
PSALM 119:17-24

That which is a treasure to the psalmist (v. 11) now becomes "wondrous" (v. 18). Franz Delitzsch says,

The Tôra beneath the surface of its letter contains an abundance of such "wondrous things," into which only eyes from which God has removed the covering of natural short-sightedness penetrates; hence the prayer in v. 18. (Keil and Delitzsch, *Psalms*, 738)

The psalmist needs this wondrous Word because he is under attack from persons of influence ("princes," v. 23). However, he is the Lord's "servant" (vv. 17,23). What his Master commands, he will obey because the Lord's "decrees are [his] delight and [his] counselors" (v. 24). He will not seek advice from princes who "wander" from the Lord's commands (v. 21). He will not listen to the "arrogant" who are under God's "curse" (v. 21). No, he will "think about [the Lord's] statutes" (v. 23) and be "continually overcome with longing for [his] judgments" (v. 20). He is following the path of the wise person of Psalm 1, and he will stay on this path.

Stanza Daleth: Those Who Are Experiencing Troubles Will Find Life and Strength in the Word of God
PSALM 119:25-32

The arrogant who insult and hold the psalmist in contempt (vv. 21-22) are wearing him down. He feels like his "life is down in the dust" (v. 25). He is "weary from grief" (v. 28) and susceptible to "the way of deceit" (v. 29). Still, he is convinced that there is life through God's Word and help as he meditates on its "wonders" (v. 27). Therefore, the writer will choose "the way of truth" (v. 30) and "cling" to the Lord's decrees (v. 31). His soul may "cling" (ESV) to the dust (v. 25), but he will "cling" to the Word of God (v. 31), trusting that his Lord will strengthen him (v. 28) and not "put [him] to shame" (v. 31). God is faithful. He will minister to his heart (v. 32). The psalmist knows no matter what, the Lord is all he needs.

Stanza He: Those Who Allow the Lord to Teach Them His Word Will Obey Him, Live Well, and Finish Well
PSALM 119:33-40

Verses 33-40 contain eight petitions or prayer requests. Each is related to the Lord as the divine teacher. The psalmist wants to end well. Concerning the Lord's Word, he pledges, "I will always keep [it]" (v. 33).

Therefore, he says to the Lord, "Teach me" (v. 33), "Help me understand" (v. 34), "Help me stay on the path" (v. 35), "Turn my heart to your decrees" (v. 36), "Turn my eyes from looking at what is worthless" (v. 37), "Confirm" (v. 38), "Turn away the disgrace" (v. 39), and "Give me life" (v. 40). The psalmist could ask for no better teacher (God) and no better book (Scripture). We would be wise to follow his example so that we too can live and finish well.

Stanza Waw: Those Who Rest in The Lord's Faithful Love and Keep His Law Will Be Ready to Answer Those Who Challenge Them
PSALM 119:41-48

First Peter 3:15 reminds us to be "ready at any time to give a defense to anyone who asks [us] for a reason for the hope that is in [us]." The psalmist wants to be ready to "answer the one who taunts [him]" (v. 42). To do this he must rest in the Lord's "faithful love" and "salvation" (v. 41). He must "trust" the Word and "hope" only in it (vv. 42-43). He must be a faithful witness in deed (v. 44) and word (v. 46). Because he is loved by God (v. 41), he will love God's Word (vv. 47-48). Warren Wiersbe is right: "Our lives speak for the Lord (vv. 44-45) if our 'walk' agrees with our 'talk'" (*Bible Exposition Commentary*, 316).

Stanza Zayin: Those Who Remember God's Word Will Be Comforted by It
PSALM 119:49-56

The psalmist is once again being harassed and hounded by his enemies. Even though he is the Lord's servant (v. 49), "the arrogant constantly ridicule" him (v. 51). What is his course of action? "Remember!" He asks the Lord to "remember your word to your servant," which gives him "hope" and "comfort" (vv. 49-50). In turn the psalmist says, "I remember your judgments from long ago and find [more] comfort" (v. 52). Further, he says, "Lord, I remember your name in the night" (v. 55), which is perhaps a poetic way of speaking of those dark nights of discouragement in the soul, "a time of dread and anxiety" (Anderson, *Psalms 73–150*, 824). Drawing near to his Lord for comfort (v. 50,52), he will sing to the Lord (v. 54) and obey the Lord (vv. 55-56). Prayer, singing, and obedience to the Word will sustain him throughout his "earthly life" (v. 54). Willem VanGemeren is right: "This section is full of confidence in God and comfort to those who are waiting for his deliverance. Difficult as life may be, God's Word can help the suffering sing, even at night" (v. 55) (*Psalms*, 869).

Stanza Cheth: Those Who Run after the Lord Will Befriend All Who Also Fear Him

PSALM 119:57-64

Trouble continues. The psalmist feels like "the ropes of the wicked [are] wrapped around" him (v. 61). Still, even though he is experiencing difficulty, he will trust the Lord who is his "portion" (v. 57), his inheritance. He will keep the Lord's Word as he seeks God's favor with all his heart (vv. 57-58). He will reflect on his life and repent if he needs to (v. 59). He will be quick to keep the Lord's commands (v. 60), maintain a thankful heart (v. 62), and make friends with the right people (v. 63). The Lord's "faithful love" is his, but it is such a great love that it fills the whole earth (v. 64). The psalmist longs for such a God to be his instructor and teacher (v. 64). Spurgeon is right: "Those who have God for their Portion long to have him for their Teacher. Moreover, those who have resolved to obey are the most eager to be taught" (*Treasury*, vol. 3a, 258).

Stanza Teth: Those Who Are Afflicted by the Discipline of the Lord Will Learn How Good His Instruction Is

PSALM 119:65-72

The Hebrew word "good" dominates this stanza. It occurs six times in the Hebrew text and is translated "well" (v. 65), "good" (vv. 66,68,71), and "better" (v. 72). Amazingly, the psalmist says, "It was good for me to be afflicted" (v. 71). Why? It kept him from an arrogant, hard, and insensitive heart (vv. 69-70), and it prepared him to learn from the Lord and receive his instruction (vv. 70-72). Such teaching is once more described as priceless. It is better "than thousands of gold and silver pieces" (v. 72). God's Word is more valuable than anything this world can offer. This servant knows this truth. So did the quintessential Servant of the Lord, the Lord Jesus Christ. What a Savior! What an example!

Stanza Yod: Those Who Receive Comfort from the Lord's Faithful Love Will Delight in His Word

PSALM 119:73-80

The psalmist draws from the language of Psalm 139:13-15, acknowledging that the Lord "made [him] and formed [him]" (v. 73). Even as he is "afflicted" by the Lord who created him (v. 75), he can ask the Lord to do several things for him. Lord, he says, "May your faithful love comfort me" (v. 76). He wants to experience the Lord's "compassion" in order that he may live (v. 77). He continues, "Let the arrogant be put to shame for slandering me with lies" (v. 78). In that light, he says, "May my heart be blameless . . . so that I will not be put to shame" (v. 80). All of this comes to pass as the Lord gives him understanding (v. 73), and as he hopes in the Lord's Word (v. 74), delights in the Lord's instruction (v. 77), meditates on his precepts (v. 78), and gives proper regard to his statutes (v. 80). Once again we see the intimate relationship of the Lord's love, comfort, and Word for the life of the believer.

Stanza Kaph: Those Who Grow Weary and Discouraged Should Put Their Hope in the Lord's Salvation and His Word

PSALM 119:81-88

The psalmist has been discouraged before, but in stanza *Kaph* his discouragement plunges to a whole new depth. He longs for salvation (v. 81). His eyes are "weary" and look for God to keep his promise and comfort him (v. 82). He feels as if his life is of little or no value (v. 83) and as if God is never going to answer his prayer (v. 84). His arrogant enemies have set traps for him (v. 85) and have persecuted him with lies (vv. 85-86). Indeed, they have almost killed him (v. 87). Still, he will put his hope in the Lord's Word (v. 81), never forget his statutes (v. 83), and never abandon his precepts (v. 87). Because he is certain of God's *chesed,* his "faithful love," the psalmist will obey all that God has spoken (v. 88). The psalmist knows, as Robert Ketchum says, "Your Father in heaven loves you too much to harm you, and He is too wise to make a mistake" (quoted in Wiersbe, *Bible Exposition Commentary,* 322).

Stanza Lamed: Those Who Trust in the Lord's Perfect and Powerful Word Delight in His Teachings
PSALM 119:89-96

Nothing compares to the Word of God. It is eternal and "firmly fixed in heaven" (v. 89). It gives life (v. 93) and "is without limit" (v. 96). It is given by a faithful God (v. 90) for whom all things are his servants (v. 91). Therefore, the songwriter will delight in this Word (v. 92) and never forget it (v. 93). He will continually seek to know this Word (v. 94) and contemplate (carefully consider) it (v. 95). He knows "the wicked hope to destroy" him (v. 95), but the life-giving Word will save him (v. 94). I like what Thomas Manton says of this stanza:

> Let us be much in hearing, reading, studying, and obeying this Word, that makes us everlastingly happy! If the commandment be [without limits], why do we make no more use of it? (*Psalm 119*, 308)

Stanza Mem: Those Who Love the Lord's Instruction Meditate on It All Day Long
PSALM 119:97-104

Followers of Jesus must do more than read the Bible. They must meditate on it (vv. 97,99). They must love it (v. 97), keep it close by (v. 98), and obey it (v. 100). It will make them wiser than their enemies (v. 98) and more insightful than their teachers (v. 99), and it will give them understanding that surpasses that of their elders (v. 100). They will find that it will keep them from evil (vv. 101,104) and that it is "sweeter than honey" (v. 103). We should ask God to give us an appetite for his Word! Meditate on it, and you will find it to be the sweetest thing you have ever tasted.

Stanza Nun: Those Who Keep the Lord's Righteous Judgment Find It to Be a Lamp for Their Feet and a Light for Their Path
PSALM 119:105-112

Verse 105 is one of the best-known verses in the Bible: "Your word is a lamp for my feet and a light on my path." God's Word guides us and directs us. It shows us where to walk and how to avoid danger. The wicked may set a trap (v. 110) and afflict us (v. 107), but the Bible will give us life (v. 107), lead us to praise (v. 108), teach us (v. 108), and give us joy (v. 111). Such a Word should give us a resolve to obey it "to the very end" (v. 112). Leupold is right: "He that uses [the Word] faithfully learns where to set his foot as he walks along the slippery paths of this life. He need not stumble or fall" (*Exposition of the Psalms*, 846).

Stanza Samek: Those Who Reject the Wicked Trust in the Lord and Love His Word

PSALM 119:113-120

The psalmist has some harsh words for his enemies in this stanza. He says he hates those he calls "double-minded" (v. 113), "evil ones" (v. 115), and "the wicked on earth" (v. 119). Loving our enemies as Jesus teaches us in Matthew 5:43-44 does not mean we accept their cruelty, evil, treachery, and wickedness. It is a delicate balance, to be sure. That is why we must love the Lord's instruction and flee to him as our shelter and shield (vv. 113-114). We must put our hope in his Word, run from evil, and obey his commands (vv. 114-115). We must look for sustaining strength only from God and his Word (vv. 116-117). We love his decrees, tremble in awe of him, and fear his judgments (vv. 119-120), knowing he "rejects all who stray" from his statutes because they are liars (v. 118). How important it is for us to love the right things but also hate the right things. Both are essential to our spiritual health.

Stanza Ayin: Those Who Are Servants of the Lord Are Marked by Justice, Righteousness, and a Love for God's Word

PSALM 119:121-128

Three times in stanza *Ayin* the songwriter is called the Lord's servant (vv. 122,124,125). The word "servant" appears 14 times in Psalm 119. Being a servant is a wonderful reality when you consider that our Master is Jesus. And because we have such a wonderful Master, we do "what is just and right" (v. 121). We look long and hard for the Lord's salvation and righteous promise (v. 123). We can ask the Lord to deal with us based on his faithful love, teach us his statutes, and give us understanding

(vv. 124-125). In response we will trust the Lord to act against those who violate his instruction (v. 126), we should love his Word more than the purest gold, follow his every precept, and "hate every false way" (vv. 127-128). Spurgeon is correct: "We who rejoice that we are sons of God are by no means the less delighted to be his servants" (*Treasury*, vol. 3a, 369).

Stanza Pe: Those Who Find God's Word Wonderful Weep over Those Who Don't
PSALM 119:129-136

This stanza draws attention to the believer's mouth, feet, and eyes. With his *mouth*, he pants; he wants more of something (v. 131). That something is the wonderful decrees of God (v. 129), a revelation that brings light and gives understanding (v. 130). With his *feet*, the psalmist wants his steps to be steady so that sin cannot "dominate" him (v. 133). To accomplish this task he asks God to "redeem [him] from human oppression" (v. 134), to show him favor as the Lord's servant, and to teach him his statutes (v. 135). Finally, with his *eyes*, he weeps because people do not love and obey God's Word (v. 136). Some things should break our hearts and cause us to weep. Disregard for God's Word is one of those things.

Stanza Tsade: Those Who Are Zealous for the Righteous God Acknowledge That His Righteousness Is Everlasting
PSALM 119:137-144

"Righteousness" is the dominant word of stanza *Tsade*; some form of it occurs six times in the Hebrew text. The CSB renders the Hebrew word *tsedeq* as "righteous," "righteousness," and "just." God always does what is right, correct, and in harmony with his own holiness and justice. Because we are servants of this righteous God, we must love his pure Word (v. 140). We should not forget it (v. 141). Indeed, we should delight in it (v. 143) and know that it is essential to our lives (v. 144). It will minister to us when our enemies come against us and overtake us with trouble and distress (v. 143). Alec Motyer gives two helpful responses to this verse: "Life's adversities should drive us all the more to our Bibles," and "Troubles should increase our delight in the Word whose life-giving power makes up for our inadequacies" (*Psalms by the Day*, 357).

Stanza Qoph: Those Who Call on the Lord to Save Them Will Call on Him Early and Know He Is Near
PSALM 119:145-152

Once more the psalmist addresses the value of early morning prayers to the God who is near (v. 151). He will call on the Lord with all his heart and ask the Lord to save him even as he obeys (vv. 145-146). And when will he go to God in prayer? "Before dawn" (v. 147) and "through each watch of the night" (v. 148). He knows that the God who is near is a God of faithful love, a life giver, and just (v. 149). Evil people may draw near to harm the psalmist, but the Lord is also near, so he will be just fine! God has given his Word, and his Word is true, having been established forever (v. 152). Spurgeon puts it perfectly when he says, "God is near and God is true, therefore his people are safe" (*Treasury*, vol. 3a, 403).

Stanza Resh: Those Who Need to Be Rescued by the Lord Will Ask Him to Be Their Champion as They Love His Word
PSALM 119:153-160

The psalmist again needs to be delivered. Three times he asks the Lord to "give [him] life" (vv. 154,156,159). He makes these requests because he is being afflicted (v. 153), and his "persecutors and foes are many" (v. 157). God, therefore, must "consider" and "rescue" (v. 153), "champion" and "redeem" (v. 154). Everything he asks from the Lord is tied to his actions: he has "not forgotten" the Lord's instruction (v. 153), he has not turned from them (v. 157), and he loves the Lord's Word (v. 159). The wicked may not seek God or obey his Word (vv. 155,158), but our songwriter will because "the entirety of [God's] word is truth, each of [his] righteous judgments endures forever" (v. 160). Leupold notes, "The Word is one of the few things that continues unshaken and immovable through the ages. Happy the man whose life is built on that foundation!" (*Exposition of the Psalms*, 857).

Stanza Sin/Shin: Those Who Are Persecuted Will Fear, Rejoice in, Love, and Praise the Lord for His Word That Gives Them Abundant Peace
PSALM 119:161-168

The psalmist praises the Lord for the "abundant peace" (v. 165) he enjoys despite being persecuted by princes (leaders in the land) without a cause (v. 161). He can praise the Lord "seven times a day" (v. 164) because his heart only fears God's Word (v. 161). He loves the Word, something he declares three times in this stanza (vv. 163,165,167). The Lord's Word is like a "vast treasure" (v. 162) with "righteous judgments" (v. 164). This Word will keep him from stumbling, and it will give him salvation (vv. 165-166). He will gladly obey the Word, knowing the Lord sees everything he does (vv. 166-168). Trust and obey. Love and obey. These are beautiful companions as we walk with the Lord in the light of his Word.

Stanza Taw: Those Who Cry Out to the Lord as Their Shepherd Can Ask Him to Help Them According to His Promise
PSALM 119:169-176

The idea of the shepherd is present in the final stanza of Psalm 119 even though the word does not appear. In verse 176 the songwriter wanders "like a lost sheep" that will not find its way home without the help of its shepherd. This stanza is intensely personal. The psalmist is desperate: "Let my cry reach you" (v. 169); "Let my plea reach you" (v. 170); "May your hand be ready to help me" (v. 173); "I long for your salvation, LORD" (v. 174); "Let me live" (v. 175); "Seek your servant," the lost wandering sheep (v. 176). In all his desperation, our songwriter is confident that God will come through for him. His rescue will come according to the Lord's promise. What could be more certain than that?

Conclusion

Psalm 119 is the Word-of-God psalm. Like a table displaying an abundant and elaborate banquet meal, this psalm's 22 stanzas and 176 verses show how excellent, desirable, and satisfying God's Word is. They exalt and extol the beauty, perfection, and power of Holy Scripture. It is a golden alphabet that ends with what Motyer calls the "Wandering Sheep's Charter" (*Psalms by the Day*, 364). Wandering sheep need a shepherd. The Bible again and again points us to one. He is the Lord our Shepherd (Ps 23), the good Shepherd (John 10), the great Shepherd (Heb 13), and the chief Shepherd (1 Pet 5). This Shepherd will feed us and will sustain us by his powerful and potent Word. Delve into Psalm 119, and let the feast begin!

Reflect and Discuss

1. What types of requests does the songwriter make to the Lord throughout this psalm? What are his primary concerns? Which of these do you also want to pray?

2. What images and metaphors does the psalmist use to describe God's Word? What do these teach us about the Word of God? Do you view God's Word in these ways?

3. Why is God's Word valuable? What does the psalmist achieve or receive by prioritizing the Word?

4. What do the psalmist's encounters with the wicked (e.g., vv. 61,69,110) teach you about his view of God and God's Word?

5. How does the psalmist describe a happy or blessed life? How does this compare with what the world says it means to be "happy" or "blessed"?

6. What does this psalm teach about the relationship between our emotions and our actions concerning how we relate to God's Word?

7. In what ways does God's character shape his Word?

8. The psalm uses the entire Hebrew alphabet to praise God's Word. Why is it important to care about *how* we talk about God in addition to *what* we say about him? What other poetic and artistic ways have you seen people use to praise God and his Word? Are there any skills you have that you could use to artistically show how great God is? If yes, explain how you might use them.

9. How would you describe the psalmist's level of commitment to God's Word? How does this compare to your own? What must happen in our hearts before we can obey and love God's Word like the psalmist?

10. What promises does this psalm give for those who commit to obeying God and enjoying him?

Songs of Ascents (Tracks 1–3)

PSALMS 120–122

Main Idea: As Christian pilgrims we have much to learn from these first three "Songs of Ascents," which were likely sung as Jewish pilgrims ascended to Jerusalem for worship during one of three major festivals.

I. **The Pilgrims' Mess (120)**
   A. Assurance (120:1)
   B. Plea (120:2)
   C. Submission (120:3-4)
   D. Desperation (120:5-7)
II. **The Pilgrims' Help (121)**
   A. A timid pilgrim's question: Where is my help (121:1-2)?
   B. A seasoned pilgrim's counsel: Trust in the Lord's watchcare (121:3-8).
III. **The Pilgrims' Worship (122)**
   A. Gladness (122:1-2)
   B. Unity (122:3-5)
   C. Longing (122:6-9)

If you look at the beginning of Psalms 120–134 you will notice that they share the same inscription: "A Song of Ascents" (the inscription is part of the Hebrew Bible). Some of these psalms (often referred to as "Pilgrim Songs") are familiar to many Christians, but others are less familiar. They appear to have been sung during the three annual festival processions as Jewish pilgrims ascended to Jerusalem ("ascents," plural, indicating multiple journeys; i.e., Passover in the spring, Pentecost in early summer, and Tabernacles in the fall). They begin with a pilgrim in an alien setting (Ps 120) and end with praise given to God in the temple (Ps 134).

Today we sometimes see churches or musical groups make a collection of songs for Christmas or some other season or occasion. That's comparable to what we have here. The Songs of Ascents were a miniature song book, a "pilgrim hymnbook," used for the journey to

Jerusalem. They were probably written at different times but grouped together later to form this collection.

Christians can relate to the pilgrim nature of the Christian life. The author of Hebrews says, "For we do not have an enduring city here; instead, we seek the one to come" (Heb 13:14). In his book on the Songs of Ascents, entitled *A Long Obedience in the Same Direction*, Eugene Peterson points out the importance of the pilgrim imagery: "There are two biblical designations for the people of faith that are extremely useful: *disciple* and *pilgrim*" (p. 17). The former emphasizes our apprenticed relationship to Jesus, and the latter emphasizes the "not home" nature of our faith, with Abraham serving as our "archetype" (Heb 11:8-11) and Jesus showing us the way home (John 14:5-6).

Further, like the ascending pilgrims, we should be advancing in spiritual maturity, growing in this Godward life. This growth happens as our hearts ascend in regular praise and prayer to our Creator and Redeemer. The Songs of Ascents assist us in this growth process.

Indeed, one of the reasons we need the whole book of Psalms is to strengthen our interior lives. Dietrich Bonhoeffer commented on the spiritual value of the Psalms, reflecting on Luther's words:

> But whoever has begun to pray the Psalter seriously and regularly will soon give a vacation to other little devotional prayers and say: "Ah, there is not the juice, the strength, the passion, the fire which I find in the Psalter. It tastes too cold and too hard" (Luther). (Bonhoeffer, *Psalms*, 25)

Couldn't you use some more "juice" to revitalize your worship life? Couldn't you use some more strength to your prayer life?

Bonhoeffer continues his argument for the church to return to the "Prayer Book of the Bible":

> In the ancient church it was not unusual to memorize "the entire David." In one of the eastern churches this was a prerequisite for the pastoral office. The church father St. Jerome says that one heard the Psalms being sung in the field and gardens in his time. The Psalter impregnated the life of early Christianity. Yet more important than all of this is the fact that Jesus died on the cross with the Psalter on his lips.
>
> Whenever the Psalter is abandoned, an incomparable treasure vanishes from the Christian church. With its recovery will come unsuspected power. (Ibid., 26)

I'm not trying to argue for us to sing *only* straight from the Psalms in corporate worship, but I agree with Bonhoeffer that Christians would benefit greatly, and would grow in Christlikeness, by growing deeply familiar with the Psalter. The Songs of Ascents are great places to start! They are all short psalms, easy to memorize and use in personal and corporate worship. My plan is to look at three psalms in each exposition.[3]

The Pilgrims' Mess
PSALM 120

The first song begins rather darkly. The songwriter explains the day-to-day struggle of life in a broken world. We can identify with feelings of "distress" (v. 1) and "misery" (v. 5) and "war" (v. 7). In this context, the psalmist brings his trouble to the Lord, which is where we should take our troubles as well.

Assurance (120:1)

The pilgrim says, "In my distress I called to the Lord, and he answered me." From this declaration he goes on to offer a plea to the Lord for deliverance (v. 2) and then to explain his dreadful situation in more detail (vv. 3-7). The language resembles laments in Psalms 3:4; 18:6; 22:21; 66:14; and 118:21.

There are at least three ways to read this declaration in verse 1. First, the pilgrim could be giving a *past testimony* of answered prayer(s), which then fuels his present plea in verse 2 (Goldingay, *Psalms,* 448; as in Pss 34:4,6; 118:5). Second, he could be testifying to how God *already* answered this particular prayer in verse 2. Or he could be *anticipating* God answering his plea, and even hinting at how God already assured him of the answer (VanGemeren, "Psalms," 769). I lean toward the first option. It seems most natural to see the psalmist remembering a time of distress in the past in which the Lord answered him, giving him encouragement to now seek the Lord in the present crisis.

This much is clear: the psalm begins with the confident note of *assurance.* The Lord answers prayer! By "answering," the Lord both "hears" and "acts" (cf. Pss 86:1,7; 102:2; 108:6). Throughout the Psalter we see

---

[3] At our local church, I (Tony) originally preached three Songs of Ascents per week. These "mini-sermons" lasted about 15 minutes each and were spaced out between various songs and prayers.

that the Lord answers us! He may sometimes say yes, sometimes no, and sometimes not now. But the Lord answers. This assurance should give us confidence to continue calling out to him!

With cell phones today, we have access to people. I remember in the '80s and '90s we would have to make sure we were home at a certain time. You would say, "I have to be home at 8:00 pm. I'm expecting a call." Or if you missed the guys at the meeting spot at 3:00 pm, you were on your own! You couldn't call and say, "Where are you guys?" But now we can reach one another all day with cell phones. Yet some people never pick up the phone! Have you ever found yourself asking, "Why do you even have a phone if you never answer?" Maybe someone has said that to you! Be encouraged today; the Lord answers his people. You can and should call on him.

Plea (120:2)

The pilgrim is in an oppressive situation. Foes are speaking falsely about him, and he cries for help because the lies wound.

While you may not have people specifically lying *about* you, many in the culture are lying *to* you. Many tell you about the origins of life without reference to God; they tell you about love without reference to God-centered covenant love; they speak of meaning and fulfillment, joy and peace, without God. We can identify with the frustrated pilgrim who constantly hears the voices of the godless.

So in light of this mess, the pilgrim opens up like a child who pours out suppressed feelings, pouring forth tears and pent-up emotion. Take a cue from the psalmist here and cry out for deliverance! Sometimes the Lord brings us to places where all we can do is cry out to him. Sometimes we can act, but sometimes we can merely cry out; sometimes all we can do is groan (Rom 8:26). But we pray.

Submission (120:3-4)

What's the psalmist doing? He's submitting the problem to God. He says to his attackers that Yahweh will shoot burning arrows at them.

In the Scriptures words are likened to sharp arrows (Pss 57:4; 64:3-4) and fire (Prov 16:27; 26:18; Jas 3:6). While the attackers shoot their arrows at the psalmist, the believer says God will have the last shot. The ESV (along with other translations) mentions "glowing coals of the broom tree," whose charcoal was apparently the best. The judgment of God will not only kill but also consume. Ultimately, God will have the last word for the wicked. We can leave our oppressors to God's judgment. We must take this eternal perspective.

Desperation (120:5-7)

The pilgrim speaks about his misery as his alien status comes to light. He's dwelling in "Meshech" (modern-day Turkey) and in the tents of "Kedar" (the Arabian desert). These statements in verse 5 may be taken in different ways, but I take them metaphorically to express how the psalmist is living *among the godless.* He's a pilgrim. He doesn't feel at home.

In verses 6-7 the psalmist expresses his tiredness. Israel was told to seek the peace (*shalom*) of the city when in exile (Jer 29:7). The pilgrim has done so, yet he is frustrated with the lack of peace.

Paul's words to the Roman Christians, living as sojourners on earth, come to mind here:

> *If possible, as far as it depends on you, live at peace with everyone.*
> *Friends, do not avenge yourselves; instead, leave room for God's wrath,*
> *because it is written, Vengeance belongs to me; I will repay, says the*
> *Lord.* (Rom 12:18-19; cf. Matt 5:43-48)

We're called to seek peace and to love our enemies. And as this psalm teaches, we should trust in God's final judgment of evildoers.

So, what happens when you don't experience peace in your sojourning? This psalm encourages us to pray. These closing words are essentially an *implied prayer* that the Lord would establish peace. The entire psalm is really a prayer for peace or *shalom* (VanGemeren, "Psalms," 771).

Take your mess to the Lord. Perhaps you have lost your job. Perhaps you have lost your dignity over something. Perhaps people are saying evil things to you or about you. Whatever the reason for your darkness, take it to the Lord. He answers our pleas. We can express our grief and desperation to him, and we can trust in his sovereignty to bring ultimate peace, even though we may only see a glimmer of it in this life.

Let's also remember that the Lord Jesus embodied this psalm. He surely knew it, and he definitely experienced it. He experienced great distress, most dramatically in Gethsemane (Mark 14:33) and at Golgotha (Mark 15:34). He was the object of evil words; his reputation was smeared; he was a stranger on earth. Through him, because of his atoning work in Jerusalem, we can have peace with God by the enablement of the Spirit, and we will one day live in a new creation filled with total *shalom*. Look to Jesus today. He understands your grief, and he grants grace to distressed pilgrims.

The Pilgrims' Help

PSALM 121

In Psalm 121 the serious hazards of travel are noted, as an interesting dialogue takes place. The anonymous pilgrim (perhaps a young man?) raises a question in verse 1 and then answers his own question generally in verse 2. But then another voice speaks in verses 3-8. This other voice could simply be an inner dialogue, with the pilgrim speaking to himself, like we read about in Psalms 42–43. Or (more likely) the second voice represents a more seasoned pilgrim, perhaps a minister, who offers godly counsel. We may also envision multiple people speaking or singing these reassuring words to the worried pilgrim.

A Timid Pilgrim's Question: Where Is My Help? (121:1-2)

As the pilgrim considers his journey, he looks at the mountains and wonders about hope. The "mountains" are enigmatic. Do they represent *refuge, danger,* and/or *anticipation of arrival* in Jerusalem? Regarding *refuge*, the mountains surrounding Jerusalem conveyed a peaceful image of the Lord's protection of Israel (125:2; cf. Goldingay, *Psalms*, 456). The mountains may have also stirred up a sense of peace since the Lord made the mountains. Others see the pilgrim as looking with *anticipation* at arriving in Jerusalem, which is set among the mountains. But I think it's best to read the hills conveying the *danger* that exists along the journey. While he may have indeed had a mixture of emotions in his heart, I think his primary thought was that the hills were part of *the problem.*

The hills sheltered bandits. And, significantly, they were home to pagan gods who "lived" among the high places (cf. Jer 3:23). Later in the psalm the pilgrim highlights the Lord's character, seemingly alluding to the Lord's transcendence and supremacy over pagan gods. Unlike the pagan gods, the Lord doesn't sleep or take a vacation (vv. 3-8; cf. 1 Kgs 18:27). The Lord is always watching over his people. The references to the moon and sun may also be allusions to the gods.

The hazards of travel today may look different. We might imagine walking through a rough part of a major city at night or, if you're from the hills, a particular back road that one shouldn't enter at night. We might imagine our missionary friends praying Psalm 121 in regions where there are hostile terrorists. Other hazards of life include madmen with guns, diseases, weather-related disasters, and automobile dangers. Like this pilgrim, we need protection from the threats of this life.

This much our pilgrim friend knows: his help will come from the "Maker of heaven and earth" (v. 2; cf. 115:15; 134:3). One can hear this verse in the opening line of the Apostles' Creed, which Christians have recited for hundreds of years. God is Creator and therefore reigns over all things, including pagan deities. The pilgrim's help won't come from Baal, Asherah, or the moon priestess.

Yet the pilgrim needs something more. He needs to know of the personal, intimate nature of the covenant-keeping God of the Bible. He needs to know God not just as Creator but as Companion and Guardian. He needs to know what precedes the affirmation of God as Creator in the Apostles' Creed: "We believe in God, *the Father* Almighty, Maker of heaven and earth" (emphasis added). That's what everyone needs. They need a relationship with God, which of course comes through Jesus.

Many non-Christians believe in a Creator God but have no relationship with him. You might even hear them say "God help me" in a moment of panic and desperation. I believe this instinctive cry is saying something about human nature: we're made to know this God. We sense that God exists (Rom 1), but many fail to know him as Savior and Shepherd.

At the same time, many Christians will affirm that they know God both as Creator and Redeemer through Jesus Christ but functionally live worried lives. We are prone to fear, aren't we? In moments of crisis, we need to experience our theology. We need to work our theology of God into our hearts. We know the Father, through the Son, by the Spirit (Eph 2:18), and this should bring us peace. That's what the timid pilgrim needs. So another voice reassures him of the personal nature of the Lord.

A Seasoned Pilgrim's Counsel: Trust in the Lord's Watch Care (121:3-8)

The reassuring speaker has a dominant theme: *trust the Lord's watch care.* He encourages the anxious traveler to remember that God is always looking out for his followers. In verses 3-8 the verb *protect* appears six times, also translated as "watch over" (NIV) or "keep" (ESV). This Lord doesn't watch from a distance. He watches like a father looking over his children while they sleep.

This protection doesn't mean, however, that the traveler may never stub his toe, get injured, suffer, or even die. It means that God's purposes can't be thwarted. Nothing can separate us from the love of God in Christ Jesus (Rom 8:18-39). He will watch over us throughout this whole life, and ultimately he will take us to glory.

We learn three truths about the Lord's personal, intimate, fatherly, shepherd-like watch care.

First, the Lord's watch care is constant (vv. 3-4). Our Lord's protection involves him holding us up. He will keep us from falling. Asaph wrote in Psalm 73, "But as for me, my feet almost slipped; my steps nearly went astray" (73:2), but the Lord was there to uphold him and bring him peace by granting the wobbly worshiper an eternal, God-centered perspective (73:23-28). We too may feel like our faith is weakening and our hope decreasing, but the Lord has his grip on his people (John 10:29). We need to cast our burdens on him and trust him (cf. Ps 55:22).

Our pilgrim friend also reminds us that the Lord's protection never ceases. Unlike the pagan gods, the Lord never sleeps. That's the first qualification of a good watchman: you have to stay awake! It's hard to guard anything when you're asleep! In our humanness we get tired. We get weary. We need sleep. But our God never gets tired. He's never weary. He never needs a timeout. Oh, we may think he's asleep sometimes, but he's always watching over us as our gracious Shepherd.

As we look to the New Testament, we find Jude saying these amazing words about the Lord's preserving grace:

> Now to him who is able to protect you from stumbling and to make you stand in the presence of his glory, without blemish and with great joy. (Jude 24)

What hope! The Lord will keep us from stumbling and get us to our final destination.

Second, the Lord's watch care is comforting (vv. 5-6). He shades us and protects us. The counselor says that the Lord stands between every threat and us—whether the scorching heat of the Middle East or the dangers and cold temperatures of the moonlit night—as he is at our "right hand" (v. 5 ESV; cf. 16:8). Indeed, the Lord's presence is like "shade" (v. 5 ESV) or "shelter," bringing us refreshment as well as safety (cf. 91:1). And his presence overcomes our nighttime problems.

We need this sort of comfort. Have you ever been worried because of your surroundings? Have you ever been asleep at night and woken up, only to then toss and turn with fears entering your mind and heart? Psalm 121 would be a good one to memorize and recite during these moments (along with Ps 127). May you trust in the Lord's watchcare over you as he deals with the dragons of the night. And may his presence refresh you as you deal with the intense pressures of the day.

Finally, the Lord's watchcare is comprehensive (vv. 7-8). The psalmist offers these encouraging words by pointing to the future. All harm, your whole life, your coming and your going, now and forever—this is comprehensive protection!

So "even when [we] go through the darkest valley," we can fear no evil because our Shepherd is with us (Ps 23), and he will see to it that we arrive at our heavenly destination. The Lord will hold our hands in this life, and afterwards he will receive us into glory (73:24).

The Pilgrims' Worship
PSALM 122

If you have ever traveled to a lovely city, you can identify with the pilgrim as he reflects on arrival into Jerusalem, except that his joy is greater because he wasn't visiting Jerusalem as a tourist but as a *worshiper*. His joy is expressed in three snapshots, like postcards or Instagram pictures, with little captions (or #hashtags!) to go along with them. The worshiper's first caption may say "gladness" (vv. 1-2), the second, "unity" (vv. 3-5), and the third, "longing" (vv. 6-9).

Gladness (122:1-2)

After the frustration of living among the godless (Ps 120) and enduring the dangers of travel (Ps 121), the pilgrim's trouble has been replaced with joy (Ps 122, originally penned by David). You can feel his joy. What a contrast between 122:1-2 and 120:5! The pilgrim is no longer in a far country but is now in the holy city (122:2). He's no longer in the company of liars, but of brothers who encourage him to worship (122:8; cf. 120:2,7). His companions said, "Let's go," and he happily joined the worshiping party.

As we ponder the pilgrim's happy arrival into the city, Derek Kidner helps Christians, who are living on this side of the cross, apply this psalm. He says, "There is a miniature of this gladness in any meeting for true worship" (*Psalms 73–150*, 433; cf. Ps 92; Heb 12:22-24). While we aren't making a pilgrimage to Jerusalem, we do share the joy of worshiping corporately with brothers and sisters in Christ.

Do you share the pilgrim's excitement about gathering with the redeemed in your local assembly? We should desire this tremendous blessing. In corporate worship, we bring our tired, broken, desperate selves before God, thanking him for redemption and provision and asking him for his help. Corporate worship is an unspeakable blessing to traveling pilgrims.

Kidner then adds a second application: "The Christian's equivalent to this progress and arrival is finely expressed in the doxology of Jude" (ibid.). We referenced Jude in Psalm 121, and we may also consider it with Psalm 122 in view. The Lord will "protect [us] from stumbling" until we arrive "in the presence of his glory, without blemish and with great joy" (Jude 24). In other words, our ultimate arrival—our ultimate worship experience—is yet to come. We are seeking a better city (Heb 11:10; 13:14). We're anticipating a great garden-city of the redeemed.

Unity (122:3-5)

The pilgrim now takes the city tour of Jerusalem, and he marvels at the unity of the city. He may have inserted a #i❤Jerusalem after posting his picture! He notes the essence of this city is its unity. The shape of the city speaks of its *togetherness* (v. 3). Kidner says, "Such was the blueprint; such will be the ultimate reality (Rev 21:10ff)" (*Psalms 73–150*, 433). Peter draws out the unity that exists between God's people, as living stones, who together worship God through Jesus (1 Pet 2:4-5).

The happy pilgrim then states that his brothers from different tribes gather united as "the LORD's tribes" (v. 4). They are one people.

Being with other pilgrims increases our joy in worship. Calvin said,

> Our joy, in like manner, *should be doubled* when God by his Holy Spirit not only frames each of us to the obedience of his word, but also produces the same effect upon others, so that we may be united together in the same faith. (*Psalms*, 4:70; emphasis added)

Personal worship brings joy; corporate worship brings double joy!

Further, the people united to express gratitude (v. 4c; cf. Exod 23:14-17; Deut 16:16-17). They celebrated what Yahweh did in making the crops grow, and they also remembered the stages of redemptive history, in which the Lord freed his people from slavery and brought them into the land (Goldingay, *Psalms*, 465).

Finally, they come to a place where, ideally, under God's appointed king, justice is executed (v. 5). Kidner notes that a ruler's first duty and best gift is the establishment of justice (*Psalms 73–150*, 434). As we consider the concept of justice broadly, we're reminded that it characterizes the messianic era (Isa 9:7; 11:35). Ultimately, the just King (Ps 72) will fulfill this duty and give us this best gift: a place of total peace and justice.

Longing (122:6-9)

The final picture of the city may have a caption that reads something like, "Pray for the peace." The pilgrim longs for *shalom*, peace in the city. Jerusalem, "the city of peace," didn't always experience peace. So the song moves from joy to longing. And it moves from joy to commitment to seek the good of the city. We too should long for peace within the community of faith, our "brothers and friends," and seek to do good to everyone, especially those of the household of faith (Gal 6:10; Heb 13:1-3).

When Jesus, the great Pilgrim, entered the city, he "wept over it" (Luke 19:41-44 ESV). He lamented Jerusalem's rejection of him and the upcoming destruction of the city. Then near Jerusalem, Jesus, the perfectly obedient Pilgrim, died for sinners and rose on their behalf. He ascended into heaven and poured out his Spirit among his people in Jerusalem. These pilgrims went out from Jerusalem to tell the whole world where they could find real peace: in Jesus Christ, who "is our peace" (Eph 2:14). You don't need to go to a temple to find peace. You need to go to a person, Jesus Christ. That's how you find peace. That's how you find peace with one another (Eph 2:14-22). And ultimately, we will know the fulfillment of this peace when the Prince of Peace comes in glory. While it's good to pray for peace in the Middle East (1 Tim 2:1-3), the Christian's ultimate prayer is, "Come quickly, Lord Jesus!"— #maranatha!

Reflect and Discuss

1. Do you believe God answers prayer? Why or why not?
2. What mess are you experiencing right now? Stop and take your burden to the Lord.

3. Do you feel like a pilgrim in this life? Explain.
4. What kinds of lies are distressing you? Explain.
5. What kinds of threats are worrying you? Explain.
6. How does Psalm 121 encourage you? Explain.
7. Does the Lord's *protection* of his people (Ps 121) mean that believers will never suffer? What does it mean that the Lord is watching over us?
8. Do you look forward to corporate worship? Why should we?
9. Stop and give thanks to the Lord for his redemption, protection, and daily provision, both personally and with others.
10. How does Psalm 122 point us to Jesus? Reflect on and rest in his person and work, and in his kingdom.

Songs of Ascents (Tracks 4–6)

PSALMS 123–125

Main Idea: These three Songs of Ascents express various desires of the community of faith, helping us express our pleas and praise to God together.

I. **The Pilgrims' Longing Look (123)**
   A. The problem: Enduring contempt (123:3b-4)
   B. The solution: Looking in the right direction (123:1-3)
      1. Let's lift our eyes to the majestic One (123:1).
      2. Let's look to the hand of the merciful One (123:2-3).
II. **The Pilgrims' Empowering History (124)**
   A. Marvel at what God has done (124:1-5).
   B. Praise God for what he has done (124:6-7).
   C. Apply what God has done (124:8).
III. **The Pilgrims' God-Centered Confidence (125)**
   A. Those who trust in God know his stability (125:1).
   B. Those who trust in God know his security (125:2-3).
   C. Those who trust in God know his goodness (125:4).
   D. Those who trust in God know his holiness (125:5).

In these three psalms we continue pondering the pilgrim nature of the faith. While "we seek the city that is to come" (Heb 13:14 ESV), we live out our pilgrim days in song and prayer to God. These psalms help give expression to our cries to God as we journey.

One finds practically every human emotion in the book of Psalms—it covers highs and lows, joys and sorrows, laments and celebrations, and more. We find both individual and communal emotions. John Calvin called the Psalms, "An Anatomy of All the Parts of the Soul" (*Psalms*, 1: xxxvii). That's a terrific description. He continues, "The Holy Spirit has here drawn to the life all the griefs, sorrows, fears, doubts, hopes, cares, perplexities, in short, all the distracting emotions with which the minds of men are wont to be agitated" (ibid.). Saints love the Psalms because they can identify with these various issues.

We shouldn't read the Psalms merely to study doctrine. The Psalms are poems or songs. They help us express our hearts to God. In the words of Eugene Peterson, paraphrasing Athanasius from the fourth century, "Most of Scripture speaks *to* us; the Psalms speak *for* us" (in Peterson, *Working*, 55; emphasis in original). What a gift this book is to us, helping us cry out to God.

In Psalms 123–125 we find various pleas, with an emphasis on the community of faith. Psalm 123 is mainly a *communal lament* (verse 1 begins with an individual lament but moves to a communal prayer in verses 2-4). Psalm 124 is a *communal thanksgiving song.* Psalm 125 is a *communal psalm of confidence* (VanGemeren, "Psalms," 787; some call 125 a *communal lament*). Here, then, we're reminded of the importance of the *community.* As believers in Jesus, we should lament *together,* give thanks *together,* and express our confidence in the Lord *together.* Let's learn from our pilgrim family about looking to God for mercy, about the need to remember what God has done, and about resting in the Lord's protection.

The Pilgrims' Longing Look
PSALM 123

The psalm begins with an anonymous individual expressing his personal dependence on God (v. 1), before shifting to plural, expressing a corporate dependence on God (vv. 2-4). The shift from "I" to "we" may indicate that a king or a leader, such as Nehemiah, or a worship leader, like a Levite, could have originally written this psalm (Goldingay, *Psalms*, 470). It also fits various times of Israel's history, such as Hezekiah's reign (ibid.). Regardless, it's clearly a prayer of the community of faith.

Because we aren't given specifics, we can easily apply it. We're not told about the context of this scorn and contempt (vv. 3-4) that creates the lament. We don't know when it happened or how it happened. Contempt may have been coming from unfaithful Israel, unbelieving Gentiles, or a combination of both. All we know is that this pilgrim and his fellow pilgrims are suffering contempt and are in need of mercy. Christians can identify with this struggle.

The psalmist's solution comes in verse 1, though the problem isn't mentioned until the psalm's end (vv. 3b-4). So let's begin with the problem first and then consider the solution in 1-3a in order to better understand and identify with the community's prayer.

The Problem: Enduring Contempt (123:3b-4)

Throughout history God's people have been the object of contempt, oppression, and persecution. The psalmist is weary of this experience. You can feel the psalmist's frustration. Contempt is irritation directed at a person you feel is at a lower status. It involves disrespect. It usually includes cutting words (e.g., condescending words, name-calling, damaging words) that can break a person's spirit. It could involve an attitude of disgust or an attitude of cool dismissal to go along with those words. Jesus had strong words about those who have contempt for their neighbor, ranking it as "more murderous than anger" (Kidner, *Psalms 73–150*, 435-36; Matt 5:22).

To be looked on with contempt means to be the object of ridicule, to become a laughingstock. Bratcher and Reyburn comment, "'Treated with contempt' may be rendered sometimes as 'treated us as if we were nothing' or 'treated us as if we were not people'" (*Translator's Handbook*, 1,060). Eugene Peterson translates these verses even more descriptively: "We've been kicked around long enough, Kicked in the teeth by complacent rich men, kicked when we're down by arrogant brutes" (123:3b-4 *The Message*). Indeed, throughout history God's people have been kicked around, ridiculed, disrespected, mocked, and treated as nothing by proud and powerful oppressors.

In the New Testament we find many texts that highlight the reality of such opposition. In the early chapters of Acts, the church faced intimidation (Acts 4:1-4), threats (4:17-22), physical suffering (5:40), and eventually martyrdom (7:54-60). How did they endure it? They endured with prayer (Acts 4:29-31) and, remarkably, *with Spirit-enabled joy*. Luke writes, "Then they went out from the presence of the Sanhedrin, *rejoicing* that they were counted worthy to be treated shamefully on behalf of the Name" (Acts 5:41; emphasis added; cf. 1 Pet 5:12-19; John 15:18-25).

Ridicule and expressions of contempt for God's people are present today. This stems from pride, as this text indicates (v. 4). Let me mention three groups of arrogant people who may dislike you, mock you, speak condescendingly to you, and/or persecute you.

For starters, the "intellectually superior" ridicule the church for our view on certain issues, like marriage. This attitude is manifested daily in the media and in universities. They see the church as primitive, uncultured, and naive. Consequently, they often dismiss the Christian's point of view without serious consideration. They may mock believers and, in some places, physically assault them.

Next, contempt may come from the "immorally comfortable." Many are at ease (v. 4 ESV) in their ungodly lifestyles and hate the idea of a moral standard, so they mock Christians for presenting one. Often students in middle school and high school are mocked for not going along with the crowd, for being unwilling to cave in to the pressure of doing ungodly things. Later in life, adults who don't want to be confronted for their rebellion will reject the counsel of caring Christians because they prefer to stay in their sin. When pressed, they may speak disrespectfully and show aggression toward the believer.

A final group that comes to mind involves the "spiritually hostile" crowd. For various reasons, many people hate the gospel and Christians. In rage they slander, assault, and kill believers. They may be hostile for some of the previous reasons just mentioned; they may be hostile because they're convicted by their own need for Christ; they may be hostile because they're under the attack of the evil one; or they may be hostile because they embrace a different god or believe in no god at all. The fact is that many would like to wipe the Christian religion off the face of the earth.

So *let's not be surprised* when we aren't part of the majority culture. God's people have faced the assault of unbelievers for years.

Further, *let's not be intimidated* by the culture's attitude toward Christians. While we should live with respect and gentleness before a watching world, we must not shrink back from engaging the world boldly. The author of Hebrews exhorted the saints, "Let us, then, go to him outside the camp, *bearing his disgrace*. For we do not have an enduring city here; instead, we seek the one to come" (Heb 13:13-14; emphasis added). Jesus is outside the camp; the mission is outside the camp. Engage! Remember, we aren't at home on this earth. We're headed to another city. Until we arrive, we will face opposition. That's the normal Christian life.

The Solution: Looking in the Right Direction (123:1-3)

How do we endure contempt and persecution? The psalmist gives us the solution (v. 1). In Hebrew "to you" is emphasized. The solution involves looking to the Lord! In Psalm 121 the psalmist essentially did the same thing. He started with the hills but continued lifting his eyes to the Lord. In 123 the psalmist begins with a look in the right direction. He also tells us about our God and proposes two actions we should take.

First, let's lift our eyes to the majestic One (123:1). The psalmist reminds us that the Lord is not just enthroned on earth, but he's enthroned in heaven. You can't get higher than this! This verse speaks of God's absolute reign over all things. Even though it may not look like he's reigning, especially when you are enduring contempt, he is still exalted over all (115:3). Sometimes the Lord allows us to bear contempt in order to sanctify us (Lam 3:25-33; 1 Pet 1:6-7).

This prayer in 123:1 is similar to how Jesus taught us to pray: "Our Father *in heaven*" (Matt 6:9; emphasis added). In our daily struggles as pilgrims, we need to lift our eyes to our enthroned God. When Stephen was persecuted, he lifted up his eyes and saw the risen, reigning Jesus standing (Acts 7:56)! Just one lift of the head makes all the difference. Look up when others look down on you! When you do, you may be able not merely to tolerate your enemies, but like Stephen and our Lord Jesus, even show mercy to them (Luke 23:34; Acts 7:60, also Matt 5:43-44).

Second, let's look to the hand of the merciful One (123:2-3). In verses 2-3 the psalmist continues to look, but this time to the hand of God. We see that God is not only majestic but also merciful. The community expresses its need for the Lord's mercy.

We have a servant-Master relationship with God. God is in the position of exaltation and power, and we're in the position of submission and need. However, we should not read this text in an oppressive light. God isn't an abusive Master. Our Master, the Lord Jesus, had his hands nailed to the cross for sinners.

Our Master does give us directions, and he is in charge, but we look to his hand for directions because they're for our good. His directions are acts of mercy.

Further, we look to the hand of our Master because in his mercy he also *provides for* and *protects* us. His hand keeps us from harm, so we should look to God in times of fear. Like a father who opens up his hand to give his children some money, our merciful God gives to us wisdom, strength, and provision in times of suffering. In case you doubt that he can or will, look again to the cross, where God's mercy was put on full display (Rom 8:32).

The psalm further instructs God's people to look to the hand of the merciful One *patiently* (v. 2). How long must we look? The text says, "until he shows us favor." In other words, we must persist in prayer. We must keep asking God for mercy. Keep asking for his wisdom and grace for your trials.

In verse 3 the psalmist repeats his need for mercy, this time expressing it in a direct prayer: "Show us favor, LORD, show us favor," or as the ESV renders it, "Have mercy upon us, O LORD, have mercy upon us." So look to God for mercy in patient *prayer*.

We can have confidence that the Lord hears our prayers for mercy. In Luke 18 Jesus taught on prayer. He said that the Pharisee who sounded self-righteous in his praying didn't understand himself, God, or prayer. But the lowly tax collector who prayed, "God, have mercy on me, a sinner!" (Luke 18:13 ESV) truly understood God's mercy and grace and the nature of salvation. The desperate cry for mercy is the type of prayer God hears. If you're not a Christian, realize your need for mercy and the provision made by Jesus Christ, our sin-bearing Substitute. Cry out, "God have mercy on me, a sinner," as you look to Jesus for the forgiveness of your sins. He forgives rebels who cry out to him for mercy. Richard Sibbes once said, "There's more mercy in Christ than sin in us" (*Bruised Reed*, 13). Claim that hope and cry out to the Lord for salvation. If you are a Christian and are in great need today—perhaps enduring contempt or some other weight—you too should cry out to the God who is "compassionate and gracious, slow to anger and abounding in faithful love" (Ps 103:8). In and through Jesus Christ, we have access to the Father. Take advantage of it personally. May we take advantage of this access corporately. O Lord, have mercy on us.

The Pilgrims' Empowering History
PSALM 124

In C. S. Lewis's *Reflections on the Psalms*, he writes, "A man can't be always defending the truth; there must be time to feed on it" (*Reflections*, 5). Indeed, the psalms nourish our inner persons. In Psalm 124 we have the opportunity to feast on the Lord's salvation. Often we find ourselves defending and proclaiming his salvation, but here we should delight in it and praise him for it.

We see that as the community of faith reflects on the Lord's deliverance in history, they burst forth with thanksgiving. In order to provide strength for present trials, the singers articulate how God delivered his people in the past.

David originally penned this psalm, but the context is vague. This fact makes the psalm easily applicable for saints across the ages. Kidner points to the attacks of the Philistines in David's day as a possible context (*Psalms 73–150*, 436; cf. 2 Sam 5:17-25). This makes good sense. Goldingay says one can see this psalm being sung during Hezekiah's day, during exile, or during Nehemiah's day (*Psalms*, 478). Again, we aren't given specifics, and it's therefore a relevant psalm for God's people who suffer in any situation in any age. The Lord delivers; we declare his praise (cf. Exod 15).

The psalmist includes word pictures for the Lord's deliverance, characterizing the forces that vainly sought to destroy Israel: a devouring beast (v. 3), a torrential flood (v. 4), another devouring beast (v. 6), and a hunter's net (v. 7). These images should stimulate gratitude and praise for our salvation.

As believers in Jesus Christ, we have been delivered from the threat of death and hell. We have come to know this great salvation in an even fuller sense. We have also enjoyed "smaller deliverances" throughout our Christian pilgrimages. We should, therefore, reflect on what God has done for us and then apply the past to present experiences. In fact, one of the ways you get through your present trials is by reflecting on the fact that your greatest problem has already been solved through the death and resurrection of Jesus.

Marvel at What God Has Done (124:1-5)

David begins by acknowledging the people's absolute need for the Lord's deliverance in redemptive history. He doesn't want the people to misinterpret the events. The victory wasn't owing to the people's strength and strategy but to the Lord's salvation. The people couldn't save themselves. Observe the focus on "the LORD." The psalm begins with repetition for emphasis. He's leading the community, saying, "Come on, say it with me! The LORD was on our side!" One can hear an echo of this type of declaration in Paul's words to the Romans: "What, then, are we to say about these things? If God is for us, who is against us?" (Rom 8:31). We need to remind one another of the Lord's grace.

Notice also the "if/then" pattern throughout the psalm. The writer wants the people to know how desperate they are for the Lord's deliverance. So he says,

> If *it had not been the* LORD *who was on our side* . . . then *they would have swallowed us up alive,* . . . then *the flood would have swept us away,* . . . then *over us would have gone the raging waters.* (ESV; emphasis added)

Clearly the psalmist knows that apart from the Lord's gracious activity, the people would have been destroyed. The Lord protected them from all sorts of dangers and enemies. The "anger" (v. 3) of these enemies posed a real threat, but the Lord protected his people from devouring beasts and the torrential flood.

Historians have pointed to a powerful moment when a group of saints sang Psalm 124. In 1582 a Scottish minister named John Durie was imprisoned for preaching the gospel. When he was later released from prison, a few hundred of his congregants met him at the gates of the prison and began walking up the street in Edinburgh. That group of people began singing Psalm 124. Soon, about two thousand people joined in the song. One of his persecutors witnessed this moment and said he was more alarmed by that sight and song than anything he had ever witnessed in Scotland (in Ligon Duncan, "Our Help"). This song has given strength to saints for years. It should give us strength as well. It's our story. The Lord has delivered us from our greatest imprisonment, and he also delivers through other smaller trials on this earth. Marvel at what he has done. Let the marvel lead you to praise.

Praise God for What He Has Done (124:6-7)

Verse 6 transitions into praise for the Lord's deliverance, as the writer magnifies the danger. When the psalmist ponders the Lord's rescuing work, he bursts forth into praise and confesses his confidence in the Lord. Apart from the Lord's grace, the people would have drowned, been devoured, and been trapped. And the snare has also been *torn apart*!

It's fitting to move from marveling at God's saving work in Christ to praising him. We should give expression to our delight and awe at God's grace. C. S. Lewis said, "The most valuable thing the Psalms do for me is to express that same delight in God which made David dance" (*Reflections*, 23). Yes! Deliverance should make us dance with joy! Allow this psalm to feed your delight in the Redeemer.

To help us feel this joy, the writer mentions how the Lord kept the people from being devoured by wild beasts (v. 6b). The writer also twice mentions escaping (v. 7). The Lord didn't let them get caught like a bird by a hunter. Verse 7 also includes a note of triumph: "The net is torn, and we have escaped!" Because they have escaped, they should praise the Lord!

Are you aware of particular events in which the Lord delivered you—from dangers, concerns, fears? What do you make of these deliverances? They should feed your faith. They should build your trust. They should stimulate great joy. They should give us confidence for today's trials. Do you need to be delivered from some danger, threat, or problem? Seek the Lord's deliverance now.

Apply What God Has Done (124:8)

Finally, the writer applies the Lord's past work to present experience. He summarizes Israel's experience: "Our help is in the name of the LORD, the Maker of heaven and earth." This declaration was also made in Psalm 121:1-2. It has been said that Calvin used this verse to open the worship services in Geneva (Duncan, "Our Help"). Like Calvin, we can see its simple, timeless relevance to the people of God.

Because God is fighting for us (Rom 8:31), and indeed has already won the ultimate victory for us through the death and resurrection of Jesus Christ, we can trust in God in present trials. David said in a previous psalm, "Some trust in chariots and some in horses, but we trust in the name of the LORD our God" (20:7 ESV). Life is war. Each battle is the Lord's. Trust in him, for that's where our ultimate help comes from. He has been faithful in the past, and you can trust him in the present.

The Pilgrims' God-Centered Confidence
PSALM 125

This psalm is all about trusting in God, a central mark of God's people. It's a psalm of confidence highlighting God's trustworthiness. The chief image of this Song of Ascents once again is "the mountains" (cf. 121:1). The holy city is in view, and the stability and security of God's people are described with this image. Kidner notes the basic nature of the psalm, saying, "True religion starts at the center, the Lord in whom all things—Mount Zion included—hold together" (*Psalms 73–150*, 437). This psalm helps us remember who is at the center of all things, including our lives—namely, the Lord.

The Scriptures emphasize trusting God. Abraham, our pilgrim father, "believed the LORD, and he credited it to him as righteousness" (Gen 15:6; Rom 4:3; cf. 4:22). Likewise, the Christian faith begins here, with faith in Christ alone (Rom 5:1; Eph 2:8-9). But then our Christian lives continue in a pattern of trusting in God (Heb 11). This involves a series of steps of trusting in God as the Lord sanctifies us. We must learn to trust in God in all sorts of difficulties and trials (Prov 3:5-6).

Trusting God implies that we believe God is trustworthy. So, for what do you need to trust God? What challenge are you facing? What fear do you have? What hardship are you experiencing? What frustration are you enduring? This is an opportunity for you to trust God and for your relationship with God to deepen.

The psalmist teaches us that those who trust God know his *stability*, *security*, *goodness*, and *holiness*.

Those Who Trust in God Know His Stability (125:1)

The psalmist says we will be like God's rock-solid, holy mountain: unshakable (cf. Pss 46; 48:2). When trials come, he says you will be immovable. You will be anchored. You will not collapse and panic in hardships. You won't sink.

Specifically, build your life on Jesus Christ and you can be stable in the storms of life (cf. Matt 7:24-27). Beware of a false faith. James says even the demons believe and tremble (Jas 2:19). Trust in the Savior alone for life and salvation. And also commit your life to him. Cling to him. Have confidence in him. All other ground is sinking sand.

Stability doesn't mean we don't grieve. It doesn't mean we don't weep. It means we don't freak out in the midst of trials; we trust in the Lord.

Those Who Trust in God Know His Security (125:2-3)

The figure of speech changes in this verse. Now God is pictured as the hills that surround Jerusalem. Mountains are not only stable but also protective. In a world concerned with security, this psalm helps us remember where our ultimate security rests—namely, in the Lord.

Mount Zion wasn't the highest peak of the mountain range around Jerusalem. The surrounding mountains protected the city. Invading armies would have to march up the mountains or through the mountain passes (leaving them vulnerable). Jerusalem was thus defensible. The hills served as a great wall. The psalmist is saying that God similarly surrounds his people (cf. Ps 34:7). Nothing will come into our lives that isn't permitted by God, for the good of the person trusting in him, and for the glory of God. He will protect you. The prayer of Saint Patrick comes to mind:

Christ be with me, Christ within me,
Christ behind me, Christ before me,
Christ beside me, Christ to win me,
Christ to comfort and restore me.
Christ beneath me, Christ above me,
Christ in quiet, Christ in danger,
Christ in hearts of all that love me,
Christ in mouth of friend and stranger. ("St. Patrick's
    Breastplate")

When the King of kings is with you and is protecting you like this, you're secure! Peterson says, "Being a Christian is like sitting in the middle of Jerusalem, fortified and secure" (*Long Obedience*, 91).

Further, the psalmist says in verse 3 that if the people will trust in God, they will be protected from wicked leaders. "The scepter of the wicked" represents an evil king (e.g., Sennacherib). The psalm is saying that no evil power will be allowed to come against Jerusalem if the people will trust in God. But if they put their trust in horses and chariots, destruction will result, which is what you read about in Israel's history. Many would "apply their hands to injustice." It proved to be disastrous.

While Israel did have to endure godless rulers, the psalmist is instilling the ideal principle. God will not allow the unrighteous to rule his people forever. From the New Testament we know that the King of kings has come, and he will come again to set up his eternal kingdom. With that hope we are secure. And the New Testament also teaches that we should pray for leaders in churches and nations, that their leadership would exemplify righteousness.

Those Who Trust in God Know His Goodness (125:4)

The psalmist says that those who trust in the Lord learn of God's goodness and seek his provision for all their needs. The psalm shifts to a prayer. Those who do good and those who are upright are those who "trust in the LORD" (v. 1). Trusting precedes doing good works and practicing righteousness (Eph 2:8-10). Having said that, let's not minimize the implied call to godliness here. God's people should reflect God's character.

The psalmist is asking God to bless those who walk in God's ways. He knows God is good, so he asks for God's blessing and favor. James says, "God resists the proud but gives grace to the humble" (Jas 4:6). So humble yourself before him, walk in holiness, and seek him for his grace, for the Lord is good and does good (Ps 34:8).

Those Who Trust in God Know His Holiness (125:5)

Those who refuse to humble themselves before God and walk in his ways will suffer dreadful consequences, as the psalmist explains in one frightening verse. If people turn away from God, he will give them a "push in that direction" (Lawson, "Trusting God").

So the option in this psalm is either *blessing* or *banishment*. Trust in God and receive blessing (especially eternal blessing), or reject God and perish. Those who trust God know that he is holy and must not be trifled with.

The writer concludes fittingly with this word: "Peace be with Israel." This is really the theme of the psalm. If you trust God, you can know his peace. If you don't trust him, you will freak out and worry. You will be restless. But you can rest when you rest in him. As believers, we rest in God until we experience total *shalom*, total well-being. In the New Testament Paul says,

> Don't worry about anything, but in everything, through prayer and petition with thanksgiving, present your requests to God. And the peace of God, which surpasses all understanding, will guard your hearts and minds in Christ Jesus. (Phil 4:6-7)

Take your petitions to God! Don't worry about anything, but pray about everything, and you can know the peace of God that will guard your heart.

How does one come to know this supernatural peace of God? It comes through Jesus Christ, the Prince of Peace. Paul writes to the Romans, "Therefore, since we have been declared righteous by faith, we have peace with God through our Lord Jesus Christ" (Rom 5:1 HCSB). You can have *peace with God* through Jesus, who forgives sins and grants eternal life. And you can know the *peace of God* through daily resting in him.

Let's trust God and experience his stability in the midst of chaos. Let's trust God and experience his security in the midst of fear. Let's trust God and experience his goodness in time of need. As we trust him, we can know his peace even in times of anxiety.

Reflect and Discuss

1. Why is it important to recognize the communal nature of these three psalms?
2. Have you ever been looked down on or disrespected (even been physically persecuted) for being a Christian? Explain how Psalm 123 applies to such experiences.
3. What does Psalm 123 teach us about persistent prayer?
4. What does Psalm 123 teach us about the Lord's sovereignty? How does this attribute of God encourage you?
5. In light of Psalm 124, explain how looking back on God's grace can encourage us for present-day trials.
6. Do you need to be delivered from some danger, threat, or problem? If so, explain. Seek the Lord's help.
7. In what ways do you need the Lord's help (Ps 124:8)? Explain.
8. What does Psalm 125 teach us about the believer's stability and security?
9. What does Psalm 125 teach us about the Lord's goodness and justice?
10. Since each of these psalms emphasize community, take some time to pray through these psalms with other believers or perhaps sing some songs in community—expressing your need for mercy, expressing thanksgiving, and expressing confidence.

Songs of Ascents (Tracks 7–9)

PSALMS 126–128

Main Idea: These three Songs of Ascents speak of our great need for God's blessing on our personal, corporate, and family lives.

I. **The Pilgrims' Joy (126)**
   A. The memory of renewal (126:1-3)
   B. The means of renewal (126:4-6)
      1. Praying for renewal (126:4)
      2. Sowing for renewal (126:5-6)
II. **The Pilgrims' Dependence (127)**
   A. Depend on the Lord in your working and watching (127:1).
   B. Depend on the Lord instead of worrying and overworking (127:2).
   C. Depend on the Lord for blessing on your family (127:3-5).
III. **The Pilgrims' Family (128)**
   A. The blessing of a godly family (128:1-4)
   B. A prayer for God's blessing (128:5-6)

Psalm 126 is a communal psalm of thanksgiving that turns to a prayer for God's continued blessing. Psalms 127 and 128 are wisdom psalms. Together, these psalms teach us about our need for God in all areas of our lives. We need his favor, his blessing, and his grace in our personal lives, in our corporate life with God's people, and in our families.

The Pilgrims' Joy
PSALM 126

You can't miss the emphasis on joy in Psalm 126. The writer associates God-given *renewal* or *revival* (I use these terms interchangeably) with great joy. He reflects back on God's past work of renewal in verses 1-3 and then prays for God to do it again in verses 4-6. The psalm resembles Psalm 85. Observe a similar pattern of remembering the past and seeking God for a new work of revival:

*L*ORD, *you were favorable to your land;*
you restored the fortunes of Jacob.
You forgave the iniquity of your people;
you covered all their sin. Selah
You withdrew all your wrath;
you turned from your hot anger.
Restore us again, *O God of our salvation,*
and put away your indignation toward us!
Will you be angry with us forever?
Will you prolong your anger to all generations?
Will you not revive us again,
that your people may rejoice in you? (Ps 85:1-6 ESV; emphasis
added)

As believers in Jesus Christ, we too have an amazing history of God's work in the world. But we shouldn't simply read history as admirers; we should read it as prayer warriors and passionate missionaries. We should long for God to do it again!

Our (Tony's) church is currently supporting a German church planter named Stephan. He's planting a gospel-believing church in the heart of Frankfurt, Germany. Many consider this area an unreached people group because it's less than 1 percent evangelical. He told our congregation that his prayer is that the Lord would send another reformation to Germany, as in the days of Martin Luther. He said, "God has done it in the past; He knows how to do it in Germany!" He added, "Sometimes I pray, 'God get the file out that says "Revival in Germany" and do a copy/ paste!'" Then Stephan humbly said, "You know, there's no button we can push for God to send an awakening. We can just focus on the gospel (like Luther did), and pray for God to do it again. That's what we're doing."

Like Stephan, we can appreciate the former days of the Lord's work, but we shouldn't stop there. We should seek a gospel renewal in the present through prayer and gospel-centered labor. This psalm points us in this direction.

The Memory of Renewal (126:1-3)

Many Bible teachers associate this psalm with Israel's release from the Babylonian exile (compare various translations for verse 1). This may be the context for the psalm. Release from exile would have been like a dream come true for God's people.

However, the term "fortunes" in verses 1 and 4 doesn't have to be limited to captivity and release (cf. Job 42:10; Pss 14:7; 85:1). Furthermore, at the end of the psalm, we read of toil and blessing, *not merely a homecoming* (Kidner, *Psalms 73–150*, 439). I don't think we can be so certain about the original context. The particular mercy that God displayed isn't mentioned, and the language fits a variety of situations. Whatever the context, the joyful restoration described was God given (v. 1a), remarkable (vv. 1b-2), and widely talked about (v. 2b).

The psalmist says, "*The* LORD restored the fortunes of Zion" (v. 1; emphasis added). God's people couldn't manufacture renewal and restoration. The Lord sent it. He delivers. He blesses. He restores.

The restoration was remarkable. The writer says the people were so filled with joy and blessing that they had to pinch themselves to make sure it was real, like the disciples who were "in disbelief because of their joy" when seeing the resurrected Christ (Luke 24:41). The psalmist says that this blessing was like a dream, but it was indeed a reality. It was a radical restoration; they were laughing and shouting for joy (v. 2b; cf. Isa 44:23; 48:20; 49:13).

The unexpectedness of the Lord's grace produces joy and laughter. This was the case in the book of Acts. After Jesus rose from the dead and poured out his Spirit, many in Jerusalem who previously denied Jesus became his followers and were filled with great joy (cf. Acts 2:46). No one expected the resurrection, it seems. But when the Christ events unfolded, it produced a dynamic sense of gladness. The seed, Christ, went into the ground and died, but that produced great fruit (John 12:24; cf. Ps 126:5-6). That fruit involved a group of glad followers, who could have sung, "The Lord has done great things for us, and we are joyful."

I can't help but think of some of the videos I've seen of tribal peoples who watch the Jesus film. They often weep when Christ dies, but then after the resurrection they explode with joy and with mouths filled with laughter. Resurrection joy is the best joy.

One of the fruits of a revival is renewed joy (Jer 31:4), even laughter. This shouldn't be news to us since the fruit of the Spirit involves joy (Gal 5:22). However, some straight-laced religious people insist, "Christianity is no laughing matter." It's true that being a Christian is a serious matter. But as Sinclair Ferguson says, "Sometimes it jolly-well ought to be a laughing matter. If Christians have nothing to laugh about, then nobody has anything to laugh about" ("Do Dreams Come

True?"). When the Lord restores a person, or a people, such experiences of joy are good and right. When you realize what God has done for you, you will sometimes feel deep humility and sometimes feel great happiness, and oftentimes a blending of both. The gospel both humbles us and cheers us.

The writer adds a third note, saying that the Lord's gracious activity was talked about "among the nations" (v. 2). The Lord's activity served as a witness to the nations (cf. Exod 15:14-15). We read of this dynamic elsewhere in Scripture, such as in Psalm 98:

> *Sing a new song to the Lord,*
> *for he has performed wonders;*
> *his right hand and holy arm have won him victory.*
> *The Lord has made his victory known;*
> he has revealed his righteousness in the sight of the nations.
> *He has remembered his love and faithfulness to the house of Israel;*
> all the ends of the earth have seen our God's victory. (Ps 98:1-3;
>   emphasis added)

May we long for the Lord's grace to be made known among the nations through our ministries today (Ps 96:3; Isa 52:7-10). One of the ways we will impact the nations is by displaying a satisfaction and delight in God as we minister the gospel. Our joy in the Savior impacts our neighbors.

Verse 3 is still reflecting on the past and could be rendered, "The Lord did great things for us; we were overjoyed" (Kidner, *Psalms 73–150*, 439). This memory of renewal provides hope for the present.

The Means of Renewal (126:4-6)

A reflection on the past inspires hope for new mercies today. The writer calls our attention to two means of renewal: praying and sowing.

Praying for renewal (126:4). The writer turns the past work of God in verse 1 into a prayer in verse 4. The writer uses a word picture to express the people's need for God to send renewal. Streams in the Negev would have been a dramatic transformation. This area was usually dry, but on rare occasions when it rained, the water would gush down the streambeds (VanGemeren, "Psalms," 791). That's a great picture of God's blessing. We may indeed want to pray something like this: "We're dry, Lord, like a desert; please send the rain and cause us to flourish again!" If the Lord sends the rain, the desert can be transformed into a place of grass, flowers, and fruit overnight (Kidner, *Psalms 73–150*, 440).

We can't cause the rain, and we can't manufacture revival. God sends it. This is the first lesson for spiritual renewal: we are desperate for the Lord's blessing.

Sowing for renewal (126:5-6). The next picture involves sowing and complements prayer. While we can't manufacture revival, we can labor. If we are applying this picture to the Christian mission, we must sow the gospel seeds as we do good works with heartfelt passion and persistence, and then we must pray for God to send the rain. Unlike the unpredictable nature of literal farming, here the psalmist promises a spiritual harvest to faithful sowers.

The farming metaphor is used throughout Scripture. Christ used it of his death and resurrection (John 12:24). It's also used to illustrate Christian ministry. Like farming, most ministry joys are experienced through much toil and faithful, persistent, brokenhearted labor (2 Cor 9:6; Gal 6:7-10; Jas 5:7-11). I often tell seminary students, "When you think church planter, don't think rock star; think farmer." Most of ministry isn't glamorous. Like farming it's laborious. Over time, by God's grace, we can see fruit and experience renewed joy. But tears and labor precede the joy.

Tim Keller points out that the recovery of the gospel itself (along with prayer) is present in seasons of revival, illustrated by the ministries of Jonathan Edwards and George Whitefield's preaching of salvation by grace, not human effort. Keller adds that gospel application and gospel innovation are the ways the true gospel is brought home to people. Gospel application involves preaching, personal evangelism, small groups, informal conversations about the gospel, and pastoral counseling. Gospel innovation involves the creative and missionally appropriate ways we do gospel application (Keller, *Center Church,* 73–76). In other words, in seasons of revival the gospel seed is sown faithfully, widely, constantly, and effectively.

We should never imagine a revival apart from desperate prayer. And we should never imagine a revival apart from faithful sowing of the gospel seed. Throughout history both of these dynamics were present in seasons of renewal: a recovery and proclamation of the gospel seed and dependent prayer (look at the book of Acts for this combination of prayer and gospel proclamation). Different tribes of believers seem to favor one of these means of renewal over the other. One group prays but never labors. That's laziness and presumption. Another group labors but never prays. That's pride and self-righteousness. Let's do both: pray and sow. God has sent renewal in the past; he can do it again!

The Pilgrims' Dependence

PSALM 127

Psalm 127 speaks about three basic interests of people: creating, conserving, and raising a family. King Solomon—a builder, a king, and a father—penned this particular psalm, as the inscription indicates (sadly, Solomon often wrote better than he lived!). The psalm is closely tied to Psalm 128, which also focuses on the family.

In these pilgrimages to Jerusalem, a person normally didn't travel alone; his family went with him. So these psalms reflecting on the family are fitting. In Jewish tradition, Psalm 127 is recited as part of the thanksgiving service after childbirth (VanGemeren, "Psalms," 793).

While building, securing, and raising a family are the main topics of the psalm, a dominant theme running through the entire psalm (esp. v. 1) is the idea of *dependence on God*. Clearly the key to building a house and securing a city is having the Lord build it and watch over it (v. 1). Solomon then touches on the Lord's provision of sleep in verse 2 and the Lord's blessing on the family in verses 3-5. On the whole, he says that a godly home and significant work cannot occur apart from God's blessing. Consider three important lessons from this wisdom psalm.

Depend on the Lord in Your Working and Watching (127:1)

Verse 1 is straightforward and contains a simple Hebrew parallelism. Unless the Lord builds, we labor in vain; unless the Lord guards, we stay awake in vain. The psalm, then, warns against the danger of overconfidence. In the words of Jesus, "You can do nothing without me" (John 15:5).

Solomon himself serves as a warning to us. He ruined the kingdom through his pride, self-reliance, and rebellion. We must be on guard against such sins.

The psalm isn't teaching that those who fail to depend on the Lord will fail to put bread on the table (millions of godless workers testify that one can work and provide without depending on God). The emphasis isn't on temporal results but on the eternal kingdom value of one's labor. If you don't depend on the Lord and order your life around his

Word, you can live an insignificant life. Kidner asks, "The house and the
city may survive, but were they worth building?" (*Psalms 73–150*, 441).
You may build "a monument of futility" (Piper, "Don't Eat"). You play
the fool if you try to build a home or guard a city apart from the Lord.

So what are you building, and what are you protecting? In these
efforts, realize your need for the Lord in order for your work to be significant and fruitful. We may apply this idea in a variety of ways:

- Unless the Lord adds to the church, we evangelize in vain.
- Unless the Lord teaches the class, we prepare in vain.
- Unless the Lord guides the ministry, we serve in vain.
- Unless the Lord restores the family, we counsel in vain.
- Unless the Lord blesses the writing project, we compose in vain.
- Unless the Lord expands the business, we market in vain.
- Unless the Lord protects us on the mission field, we travel in
  vain.
- Unless the Lord guards us in the urban centers, we secure our-
  selves vain.
- Unless the Lord watches over our children, we care for them
  in vain.
- Unless the Lord looks after the church, we pastor in vain.

Don't live an overconfident life. It will prove disastrous. Instead,
live with constant reliance on the Father. And enjoy the fact that he's
with you. Every day we believers get to live like a kid with his father on
take-your-kid-to-work day! Every day we get to labor in view of God, by
the power of God, for the glory of God. That's what makes our work
meaningful and significant.

Depend on the Lord instead of Worrying and Overworking (127:2)

While verse 1 warns against overconfidence, verse 2 warns against
overwork—that is, working without resting physically and spiritually in
the Lord. One way we can express a failure to depend on the Lord is
by working in our own strength and working slavishly, with anguish and
anxiety. The psalmist is teaching us to find a healthy rhythm between
hard work and grateful rest.

Some people play the sluggard—failing to work hard. That's unac-
ceptable. The psalmist isn't speaking against getting up early and working hard. He's addressing the problem of being enslaved to one's work

and working without a proper trust in the Lord and a proper goal of glorifying the Lord.

The person who never sleeps, but is a slave to work, is a candidate for great anxiety, ulcers, and panic attacks. These are some of the many results of a failure to rest in God. Worry involves a lack of faith, a lack of dependence on God. So remember this: every night when you have an opportunity to rest (after a good day's work), you have the opportunity to express your trust in God. He continues to work while we rest.

Believers should remind themselves of three truths when they go to bed: (1) we aren't God (cf. Ps 121:4); (2) we need God; and (3) we are loved by God. Regarding the third lesson, the text tells us, "He gives sleep to the one he loves." Every day you have the opportunity of laboring for God's glory by God's power and then resting in God's love when the day is done—all of this through Jesus Christ.

Or, as verses 1-2 together teach, you can play the fool, build futile monuments, become a slave to work and wealth, experience constant unrest, and end up saying like Solomon, "Absolute futility. Everything is futile" (Eccl 1:2). The words of Ecclesiastes 5 remind us that working for God's glory and resting in God's love is better: "The sleep of the worker is sweet, whether he eats little or much, but the abundance of the rich permits him no sleep" (Eccl 5:12).

Depend on the Lord for Blessing on Your Family (127:3-5)

Solomon goes on to affirm that children are gifts ("heritage") from God. So we should *see children as a blessing (v. 3)*. God graciously gives children, and they should be viewed as a blessing, not a burden. The text is clear that children come "from the LORD." They are expressions of favor, "a reward." While we must not make idols out of our children, we most certainly should treasure them and thank God for them. They are visible reminders of God's love and mercy toward us.

Our culture doesn't have a high view of children, so this psalm is important. It reminds us of God's perspective on kids.

See children as a source of protection (vv. 4-5). Solomon goes on to say that children also protect the family (especially "sons" in this context). Like "arrows" (weapons), they defend the family. Solomon essentially says, "Godly sons will watch your back when you get older." This is especially true if the kids are born when the parents are young. When the parents reach middle age, the kids will be old enough to provide support.

Therefore, parents are "happy" or blessed if they have a "quiver" full of children (v. 5). The more kids, the more likely the practical protection. Children may also provide parents emotional protection from the threats of loneliness and abandonment (VanGemeren, "Psalms," 795). Further, in verse 5 Solomon adds that because there is strength in numbers, the father will also be able to confront his "enemies at the city gate," where justice is carried out. He can triumph without shame. The once-small boys will grow up to become strong men and will provide legal or social protection. Having children to bless you in these ways is certainly a great gift from the Lord.

Older people around the world are often vulnerable. Violent men prey on widows regularly in impoverished, unjust societies. They physically assault the defenseless widow and seize her property. Other aging men and women suffer from loneliness and abandonment, having no children to visit them. One of the responsibilities given to the church is to care for widows (and more generally, for all the vulnerable of society), especially those in our local churches. We must honor the elderly as if they were our mothers and fathers and ourselves their sons and daughters, providing the protection and care they need (1 Tim 5:1-16).

The Pilgrims' Family
PSALM 128

Like Psalm 127, this wisdom psalm emphasizes the family. It begins with a *blessing*, reflecting an application of the priestly blessing (cf. Num 6:24-26; VanGemeren, "Psalms," 795), and ends with a *benediction*. It's a psalm about being blessed. The writer begins with the word "happy" or "blessed" (ESV), denoting a sense of satisfaction and fullness. To know true happiness is an important goal in the Psalter (see 1:1; 94:12; 112:1; 119:1-2).

The Blessing of a Godly Family (128:1-4)

The writer describes the secret to being blessed. Notice the condition for blessing and the context of blessing on the family.

The condition for blessing (128:1). How does one come to know this happiness? The psalmist says reverence and obedience lead to happiness. One must fear the Lord (v. 1a) in order to experience this wellness and blessing. Throughout the Scriptures we see this central command (Ps 112:1; Prov 1:7; 9:10; Eccl 12:13). To fear the Lord means to revere him. It means to hold him in the highest esteem. It means to submit to him or to live according to his instruction. It means to live a life of integrity before God (cf. Prov 19:1).

Those who fear the Lord will learn wisdom and experience blessing. Those who refuse to fear God will live in folly and experience heartache. Fearing God and obeying him lead to happiness.

The context for blessing (128:2-4). The writer adds that the godly man will be blessed in all of his endeavors and in his family. Regarding the former, God's favor will rest on the God-fearing man as he labors. This man will enjoy his work and find satisfaction in his work (v. 2a).

The psalmist then adds a general statement assuring the godly man that fearing God always involves reward and blessing (v. 2b). Kidner's words about the whole psalm are appropriate here: "Here is simple piety with its proper fruit of stability and peace" (*Psalms 73–150*, 443). Indeed, to know stability and peace, fear the Lord, ordering your life according to his Word.

Next the writer says that God's blessing will rest on the godly man's family. He begins with the wife. The vine represented fruitfulness (in Ps 128 explicitly), sexual charm (Song 7:7-8), peace (1 Kgs 4:25), and festivity (Judg 9:13; ibid.). A godly wife certainly blesses the husband in many ways. She stands in contrast to the rebellious woman in Proverbs 7, who only destroys others and dishonors God. The godly wife, though, blesses the husband in many ways (Prov 31:10-31) and honors God.

Regarding the children, the writer uses another word picture common in David's time to convey blessing (it's also associated with the messianic era; cf. Mic 4:4; Zech 3:10): the olive tree (v. 3b). Children are like olive shoots, representing hope and promise for the future. The olive tree is a symbol of longevity and productivity. Children who have been nurtured and cultivated patiently will flourish and bring joy and honor to the family eventually (Ps 52:8; Jer 11:16; Hos 14:6). The blessedness of a godly man extends beyond his lifetime. Here, many children are viewed as a rich blessing, giving emotional satisfaction and protection (cf. Ps 127).

In verse 4 the writer summarizes the godly person's blessedness. He reemphasizes the fact that the person who reveres the Lord will experience God's blessing. God restores the most basic aspects of life that were damaged by the fall: work, marriage, sexuality, and family. In the new covenant in Christ, we find creation restored even more fully. New Testament writers affirm this same type of blessing on our work, marriage, sexuality, and family (e.g., Eph 4–5; Donald Williams, *Psalms 73–150*, Kindle). Therefore, to fear the Lord and experience God's blessing in these realms of life, look to Jesus. He redeems and restores our lives and heals broken relationships.

A Prayer for God's Blessing (128:5-6)

The psalmist now pronounces a blessing on God's people. Since a fruitful and fulfilled life comes from God, the psalmist asks God to bless his people. By implication, he also asks God to bless the nation and one's family line. The prayer is then concluded with a prayer for "peace" (*shalom*) or total wholeness on God's people.

It's good for us to pray in the same spirit today. We should pray for God to bless parents, children, cities, churches, nations, kingdom work around the world, and the coming generations.

As we look at the whole psalm, we see again the value of both *Godfearing labor* and *God-centered prayer*. We should seek to serve faithfully in our homes, in our churches, and in our world. And, as we serve, we should pray for God to bless our efforts and the efforts of others in these particular areas of life. In seeking his blessing, let's remember that our God delights to bless his people. One could study the story line of the Bible with the idea of "blessing" in mind (e.g., Gen 12:1-3; Matt 26:26-27; Luke 24:50-51). In Christ Jesus we have "every spiritual blessing in the heavens" (Eph 1:3). Let's keep asking for God's blessing here.

Finally, as we look at the whole psalm, we're also reminded of God's amazing grace. If you have learned to fear God, this is evidence of God's grace in your life. Marvel at this grace. Walk in this grace-enabled fear of God until you arrive at your final destination. In the words of John Newton, "'Twas grace that taught my heart to fear. . . . And grace will lead me home."

Reflect and Discuss

1. How should we reflect back on what God has done in history based on Psalm 126?
2. Explain the relationship between spiritual *joy* and spiritual *renewal*.
3. How does Psalm 126 instruct us about seeking spiritual renewal?
4. How often will you pray for the Lord to "do it again" (bring renewal) in your life and church?
5. What does Psalm 127 teach us about our dependence on God?

6. Why are we overconfident at times? How does Psalm 127:1 rebuke us for overconfidence?
7. What does Psalm 127:2 say about being overworked and worried?
8. What does Psalm 127:2 teach us about sleep? How does this verse challenge you or encourage you?
9. What does Psalm 127:3-5 teach us about children?
10. How would you summarize Psalm 128? How does this psalm challenge or encourage you?

Songs of Ascents (Tracks 10–12)

PSALMS 129–131

Main Idea: These three Songs of Ascents should elevate our concept of God and increase our love for God, as we consider three important experiences of the people of God: affliction, confession, and humility.

I. **The Pilgrims' Affliction (129)**
    A. The persecution of God's people (129:1-3)
    B. The preserver of God's people (129:4)
    C. A prayer of God's people (129:5-8)
II. **The Pilgrims' Confession (130)**
    A. A cry for attentiveness (130:1-2)
    B. A confession of confidence (130:3-4)
    C. A cry of patience (130:5-6)
    D. A call to the audience (130:7-8)
III. **The Pilgrims' Humility (131)**
    A. Learn to humble yourself before God (131:1).
    B. Learn to hush before God (131:2).
    C. Learn to hope in God (131:3).

We come to three more soul-strengthening Songs of Ascents. Psalm 129 is a communal song of confidence. Psalm 130 is often classified as a penitential psalm. Psalm 131 is an individual psalm of confidence. Read together, they teach important lessons related to persecution, the forgiveness of sins, and personal humility. These three psalms should elevate our concept of God and increase our love for God as we consider these three experiences of the people of God.

The Pilgrims' Affliction

PSALM 129

An overcoming perseverance marked the 2015 World Series champion, the Kansas City Royals. In game five they had yet another come-from-behind win to close out the series. They came from behind in each of their four wins against the Mets to win the championship (including three wins in which they were trailing in the eighth inning or later). No team has ever won postseason games in such comeback fashion as the Royals had that year. In a total of eleven postseason wins, eight of them were come-from-behind victories! Their incredible resilience caused some baseball fans to dub them "the kings of improbability." Here in Psalm 129, the psalmist reminds us of another resilient group of people. Throughout history God's people have been knocked down but not knocked out.

This psalm reminds us of the need to stick to it, to persevere in the midst of persecution (cf. Heb 12:1-3) but not in our own power. The message here isn't reflecting "Tubthumping" by Chumbawamba—for a variety of reasons! We can only get up again because the Lord is with us. All boasting goes only to him, who is on the side of his people. We can persevere by his grace.

Some of the features in Psalms 124 and 125 are reflected in Psalm 129. We may divide this psalm into three parts: (1) the persecution of God's people (vv. 1-3), (2) the preserver of God's people (v. 4), and (3) a prayer of God's people (vv. 5-8) (Lawson, *Psalms 76–150*, 295).

The Persecution of God's People (129:1-3)

The psalmist begins with a statement followed by an invitation for others to join in liturgically. The phrase "let Israel say" is identical to Psalm 124:1-2. Corporately then, the people should respond with verse 2.

The statement in verse 1 looks back to the events in the book of Exodus, in which God's people were brought into existence in the midst of suffering (Exod 1:12-14; 2:23-25; cf. Hos 11:1). Despite the suffering, the enemies never "prevailed" against the people; they couldn't eliminate them.

Paul wrote about believers, "We are afflicted in every way but not crushed; perplexed but not in despair" (2 Cor 4:8). The sixteenth-century French Reformer Theodore Beza told King Henry of Navarre, "Sire, it is the lot of the Church of God to endure blows and not to inflict them. But may it please you to remember that the church is an anvil that has worn out many hammers" (in Wilcock, *Message*, 237). The people of God persevere by grace.

I find it interesting that the people *sing* about affliction. The Lord doesn't want them to forget their history nor to despair and quit when faced with present affliction.

The Christian church was also born in affliction and must continue to endure it with hope and joy (Acts 5:41-42). We must also remember the persecuted church around the world, praying for her to persevere faithfully.

My (Tony's) friend C. J. Mahaney says, "In your darkest moments, you will need your best theology." This psalm addresses a powerful theological concept that can indeed strengthen us in dark moments; that is, it points us to the Suffering Servant, Jesus. For instance, Psalm 129 actually provides us with a key for understanding Matthew's quotation of Hosea 11:1. Hosea writes, "When Israel was a child, I loved him, and out of Egypt I called my son." Hosea sees Egypt as the childhood of the nation. In Matthew's Gospel, Jesus and his parents leave Bethlehem because of the persecution of Herod and head to Egypt (Matt 2:13-14). They stay there until Herod dies. Then Matthew says that the reason the angel told Joseph to flee Bethlehem and to go to Egypt was to fulfill what Hosea said: "Out of Egypt I called my Son" (Matt 2:15). Some critical scholars think Matthew wrongly applied this verse to Jesus, but I disagree. I concur with Ligon Duncan, who says that as Israel was born into suffering in Egypt, so God's one true Son went into Egypt in suffering also. He would then leave Egypt, return to his people, live in suffering, and then die in suffering. Why? Because Jesus is the fulfillment of all the Suffering Servant songs of the Old Testament (Duncan, "Greatly Afflicted"). Matthew ties together this whole Old Testament theme. We see this theme in Psalm 129. Israel was born into suffering; Jesus was born into suffering. Jesus would live a perfectly obedient life (unlike Israel) and create a new people who are united in him.

Here's the hope for dark moments: we can endure affliction with great hope because Jesus Christ has already suffered the ultimate affliction on our behalf. Isaiah says that Jesus was "struck down by God, and afflicted" (53:4); he "was oppressed and afflicted" (Isa 53:7) as he offered up his body and blood on behalf of sinners (Isa 53:4-6). Because of Jesus's atoning death and glorious resurrection, any suffering we face on this earth is short-lived. We will prevail over the grave because Jesus has prevailed. And any suffering we face in this short life, we can find grace through Christ to endure it. Therefore, let's labor with humble, Christ-centered confidence.

In verse 3 the psalmist likens the enemies of God to a farmer who plows the fields with long rows—with the field being the "back" of Israel. They inflicted great gashes on the backs of God's people (cf. Exod 5:14).

Moreover, the furrows were "long," meaning that the suffering occurred over a long period of time. The powers of darkness often try to wear God's people down until they give up.

One can hear the Servant Songs of Isaiah here again: "I gave my back to those who beat me" (Isa 50:6) and "we are healed by his wounds" (Isa 53:5). And now, though not for atonement but for gospel advancement, we must "follow in his steps" (1 Pet 2:21). Jesus identifies with us in such suffering and enables us to endure it (Phil 1:29).

The Preserver of God's People (129:4)

The psalmist reminds the people of the Lord's character in verse 4. Kidner says, "Many of the later ordeals of Israel, unlike the Egyptian bondage, were punishments; but God's character as righteous . . . and as rescuer (4b) shines through them all" (*Psalms 73–150*, 444). Despite the affliction, the psalmist says that the Lord, the righteous One, has intervened. He has preserved his people. He is faithful to his promises (cf. Gen 12:1-3). He hears the cries of his people in distress (cf. Exod 2:24-25).

In pointing the people to the character of God, the psalmist teaches us a great lesson. In seasons of trials, ponder the Lord's attributes. Ponder his work in history. Ponder his promises. He is righteous. He is a rescuer. Let hope arise as you ponder his ways. You will need good theology in dark moments.

The particular context in view here may be Israel's release from Babylonian captivity, in which the Lord "cut the ropes of the wicked" (v. 4), but we can't be certain. The fact is, the Lord set Israel free from a host of enemies, including Egypt, Amalek, and Assyria, just to name a few. Indeed, the Lord's specialty is cutting ropes! He breaks the bonds of oppression, addiction, and affliction. Ultimately, he has cut the ropes of the great enemy, death, through the resurrection of Jesus! Look to the rope-cutting Lord in times of hardship and temptation.

A Prayer of God's People (129:5-8)

As they say, "Haters gonna hate." In verses 5-8 the psalmist reminds us that though God's people will be hated (John 15:18-25), their haters will eventually lose.

These verses are to be read either as a prayer or as a declaration of confidence (Goldingay, *Psalms*, 519). Wilcock says, "Vv. 5-8 may be a prayer, but they are also in effect a prophecy" (*Message*, 237). The psalmist prays with confidence for none of the plans of the enemies to prevail. These enemies have no regard for the Lord's presence among his people, his covenant and blessing, and the hope of a victorious kingdom to come (VanGemeren, "Psalms," 798–99).

In view of the seriousness of opposing God's people, the people call down destruction on the enemies of God with three curses. First, they plead for those who "hate Zion" (i.e., those who hate God's people) to be shamed by defeat and turned back in retreat (v. 5). Israel will be victorious.

Second, they plead for those who afflict God's people to be useless, "like grass on the rooftops" (v. 6). Roofs were flat during this time, and the grass might sprout for a season in the shallow dirt. But it would soon wither because of the beating sun. The grass would grow but would be useless. The reaper wouldn't even have to cut it down or bind it into sheaves (v. 7). The psalmist, then, is praying for the enemies to be scorched and fruitless—for the enemies to harm God's people no longer.

Finally, they plead for the enemies to remain unblessed (v. 8). When Israel passes by the territory of her enemies, they're not to bless them in a neighborly way (v. 8; cf. Ruth 2:4). They are to be held under the curse. The blessing of Psalm 128 is contrasted with the lack of blessing in Psalm 129 (Goldingay, *Psalms*, 519).

We must also remember that the Lord is just, and he is right to condemn the wicked. He cannot sweep sin under the rug and remain holy. So you are wise to fear him. The writer of Hebrews says, "It is a terrifying thing to fall into the hands of the living God" (Heb 10:31).

Further, praying against one's enemies in this context is an expression of concern for God's kingdom. We share this concern today. We share the psalmist's desire for the kingdom of God to prevail against the kingdom of darkness. Sometimes that may mean our enemies are brought to justice, other times that they're converted (Matt 5:44).

This psalm reminds us that everyone is either under a curse or under God's blessing (cf. Gen 12:1-3; Deut 28; Ps 1). There's no third option. The way one goes from curse to blessing is by looking to the afflicted Christ, who bore our curse on the cross and poured out blessings on repentant sinners who turn to him in faith (Gal 3:13-14).

Further, as we survey the whole story line of the Bible, we must remember that this prayer is, in the grand scheme of things, a prayer of *love*. *God's preservation of his afflicted people led to the coming of Jesus Christ*, who inaugurated the kingdom of God. For God so loved the world that he preserved his people so that, through Jesus, all the ends of the earth may be saved. That's love. God graciously invites everyone to bow the knee to Jesus and confess him as Lord, so that they will not perish like grass on the roof but have everlasting life (John 3:16).

In sum, how do believers in Jesus Christ endure affliction? We endure with prayer. We remember that affliction is part of our faith. We remember that Jesus identifies with us in suffering. We take comfort in knowing that the Lord stands with us in suffering (cf. 2 Tim 4:17-18). We live with the assurance that Christ will never leave us or forsake us (Heb 13:5). We remember that through Christ we are more than conquerors (Rom 8:37). And we live with confidence, knowing that we will have the ultimate victory over the grave because "the greatest comeback ever" has occurred with the resurrection of the Suffering Servant, Jesus, the real "King of Improbability!"

The Pilgrims' Confession
PSALM 130

Many people are familiar with John Wesley's conversion story. It happened one May evening in 1738 in a London meetinghouse as he listened to a reading from Martin Luther's preface to his commentary on Romans. But few are familiar with the events that preceded this historical moment. Earlier that same day, in St. Paul's Cathedral, Wesley was deeply moved by the singing of Psalm 130. Wilcock says, "The cry of the psalmist was his cry; the word of the apostle [from Romans] was God's answer" (*Message*, 238). Wesley deeply desired to be right with God, and by God's grace he found it in Christ.

This psalm is part of the wider biblical theme of sin and forgiveness. In fact, Luther called this psalm, along with the other penitential psalms (i.e., psalms of confession), "Pauline Psalms" because they emphasize confession of sin and guilt and express the need for divine forgiveness (VanGemeren, "Psalms," 799). In this psalm the supplicant is overwhelmed with trouble of some kind, but the context presupposes that this trouble resulted from his own wrongdoing (Goldingay, *Psalms*, 522). That's why he needs forgiveness. In the last verse he calls on the community to follow him in looking to God for redemption.

So the pilgrim cries out, looks, longs, and waits for God's mercy as a result of his guilt. He never asks God to do anything but be "attentive" (v. 1). However, the psalmist's confidence in God's willingness to forgive repentant sinners runs through this prayer, and he believes that "if one can get [Yahweh's] attention, action will follow" (Goldingay, *Psalms*, 523). The context is unknown. The psalm falls into four parts: (1) a cry for attentiveness, (2) a confession of confidence, (3) a commitment to patience, and (4) a call to the audience. The first three parts involve an individual seeking God, and the last part calls on the community to have confidence in God's love.

A Cry for Attentiveness (130:1-2)

The phrase "out of the depths" implies having been cast into the depths of the sea, a place of trouble and despair (cf. Ps 69). The psalmist uses the expression to describe the anguish of a godly person who has fallen into sin and guilt, as he mentions in verse 3, "iniquities."

The biblical character that comes to mind immediately here is Jonah. His prayer in the belly of the great fish expresses this anguish (see Jonah 2). Like the psalmist and Jonah realized, our sin alienates us from God. The good news, however, is that God hears sinners' desperate pleas, even from "the depths" or the belly of a fish!

Another Old Testament character comes to mind here. In verse 2 the psalmist asks God to "be attentive" to his cry (v. 2). The word *attentive* hardly appears anywhere else, except for Nehemiah, as he pleaded for God to hear his prayers of confession and of need for himself and the people (cf. Neh 1:6,11). Later in the book, Nehemiah and the people confess their sin and express a similar confidence to that of the psalmist: "But you are a forgiving God" (Neh 9:17). How hopeful this truth is! God is more ready to forgive than we are to confess.

So, where do you turn when you're in the depths? Drugs? Alcohol? The pits of depression? Learn from the psalmist, and cry out to the God who hears desperate pleas.

A Confession of Confidence (130:3-4)

The psalmist goes on to make a statement of confidence about God's ability and willingness to forgive; it's similar to Nehemiah's statement. Can you imagine your "sin score" right now? If God was keeping a record of sin, or "acts of waywardness" (Goldingay, *Psalms*, 526), we could not remain in his presence. Even the best of men would have no hope. The good news is that he forgives (Exod 34:7; Pss 86:5; 103:3; Mic 7:18-20). In his kindness he leads us to repentance (Rom 2:4).

How should one deal with guilt? This is an important question because every human being tries to deal with it. Some people choose *denial*. They refuse to believe that they're guilty of anything. Others choose *rationalization*. They may admit they're guilty, but they blame it on something or someone—parents, teachers, government, culture, or genes. Another wrong option is *relativization*. Those who choose this response point out that others are guilty also and that their guilt thus isn't so bad (Williams, *Psalms 73–150*, Kindle). Have you ever played these games?

Instead of denying, blame shifting, or relativizing our guilt, the psalmist gives us the way to deal with the root of guilt: admit it and confess it to God in order to receive forgiveness. If you choose this way, you won't have to carry your guilt anymore. The faulty options will not remove your guilt. If you confess your sin to God, you can experience God's healing. So the question is, Are you confessing sin to him? You will never find liberty, joy, and renewal in hiding sin. Richard Sibbes remarked, "The way to cover our sin is to uncover it by confession" (in Lawson, *Psalms 76–150*, 297). God does cover our sin, but we must confess it (cf. 1 John 1:9).

We know something more than even the psalmist knew here. We know that in Jesus Christ you can find the type of forgiveness John Wesley found in the gospel: complete pardon for your sins. While this psalm doesn't mention the cross, we see two fundamental concepts that are expressed in the atoning work of Jesus: God's hatred of sin and God's willingness to forgive. The cross displays how God punished sin and how he forgives sinners at the same time, through the wrath-absorbing, sin-covering death of his Son (Rom 3:25-26; 1 John 2:1-2). In great love Jesus endured the floodwaters of judgment for us. If you look to Jesus Christ, you hear the words of Paul: "Therefore, there is now no condemnation for those in Christ Jesus" (Rom 8:1).

Praise God he can and does forgive desperate sinners! Paul told the Corinthians about how anyone who looks to Jesus can find such full forgiveness, saying, "In Christ, God was reconciling the world to himself, not counting their trespasses against them" (2 Cor 5:19a). God has now entrusted to us this ministry of reconciliation, giving us the privilege of sharing this good news with the world (2 Cor 5:19b-21).

Further, for those who have been justified by God through Jesus Christ (Rom 5:1), we have the responsibility of maintaining healthy fellowship with God by daily repenting of sin in the process of sanctification.

There's one more important note related to forgiveness in Psalm 130:4. The psalmist tells us the natural response of one who has been forgiven such debt: *reverence.* When we understand God's forgiveness, we will rightly fear God. Spurgeon said, "None fear the Lord like those who have experienced his forgiving love" (in Wilcock, *Message,* 239). Indeed, forgiven sinners will stand in awe of him (Deut 5:29; Mark 2:12; Rom 6:1; 1 Pet 1:17). Our respect for him will increase. And this awe will inspire us to seek this daily renewal.

A Cry of Patience (130:5-6)

The psalmist continues by expressing his commitment to wait for the Lord. Here we find the supplicant's present position. He knows God is merciful (vv. 3-4), so he waits for him.

What does this waiting involve? According to Psalm 62:5, this type of waiting may involve *silence*; that is, being still before God and experiencing his grace. Psalm 40:1 adds that it involves a sense of waiting in *expectation* before God; that is, waiting for him to act. Here in Psalm 130 it involves *hoping* in God's Word; that is, his promises. In each of these three verses about waiting for God, one thing is common: the psalmists are looking to *the Lord*. They are longing for God himself to work, not simply for an escape from punishment (Kidner, *Psalms 73–150,* 446). And in Jesus Christ the final work has come. We needed something more than a mere priest and a goat (Lev 16:8-9); we needed the blood of Jesus, the spotless Lamb of God.

What is this waiting for God like? In verse 6 the pilgrim says that he waits like a watchman waits for the sun to rise in the morning. He waits eagerly for the Lord and with the assurance of God's new mercies every morning (cf. Lam 3:22-23).

Practically speaking, based on this text, one of the ways we should express a deep longing for the mercies of God is by seeking him in his Word. In his Word he meets with us and speaks to us. In his Word we hear the gospel afresh, his assurance of pardon every day (Ps 119:147-48). In our busy world we must fight to find time to sit patiently before the Lord and in his Word. Our spiritual lives will be shallow if we refuse to wait for the Lord, if we refuse to be long in the prayer closet. The Puritans used to say, "Pray until you've prayed." Don't get in a hurry. Seek God in the quiet place. Protect your daily communion with God, and long to see the risen Son, like the watchmen long to see the rising sun.

A Call to the Audience (130:7-8)

The psalmist's hope causes him to call the whole nation to renew its hope in the Lord. Kidner says of the whole psalm, "There is a steady climb towards assurance, and at the end there is encouragement for the many from the experience of the one" (*Psalms 73–150*, 446). The psalmist has put his personal hope in the Lord (v. 5), and now he tells the people to do the same.

In verse 7 the supplicant mentions three wonderful concepts: "faithful love" and "redemption." When you think about the God of the Bible, these terms should come to mind. Because God is ready to forgive, faithful to his promise, and the great Redeemer, we should put our "hope in the Lord" (v. 7). We have reason to hope in him. We have reason to look to him.

God's unfailing love and abundant redemption are bestowed on people sovereignly and mercifully. His mercy is so great that in verse 8 the psalmist says he can redeem people from "all [their] iniquities." In the words of Paul, "Where sin multiplied, grace multiplied even more" (Rom 5:20).

So then, the picture is that God forgives sinners who repent. What sort of forgiveness do you need? Do you need salvation that comes only through Christ? Do you need restored fellowship with God? Does the community of faith need forgiveness? Let's seek him in these ways with the confidence that with him there is forgiveness (v. 4).

The Pilgrims' Humility
PSALM 131

Spurgeon said of this individual psalm of confidence, "It is one of the shortest psalms to read, but one of the longest to learn" (*Treasury*, vol. 3, 136). Why would he say that? It's because humility is not something we ever fully live out. To assume you have arrived at humility proves otherwise!

David expresses a childlike, humble trust in the Lord. He shares his experience (vv. 1-2) as an encouragement to the whole community of faith (v. 3). David's childlike trust and contentment have much to teach us.

Learn to Humble Yourself before God (131:1)

David begins by confessing his spiritual condition with three denials. He claims that his heart is not lifted up ("proud"). His eyes are not raised too high ("haughty"). He doesn't occupy himself with things that are too great or difficult. These denials suggest that this condition hasn't always been the case (Lawson, *Psalms 76–150*, 301). David, like us, knew the temptation of spiritual pride and selfish ambition. His pride caused him to look down on others with his haughty eyes. VanGemeren summarizes pride powerfully: "The proud person looks, compares, competes, and is never content" ("Psalms," 803).

Pause for a moment and take an inventory of your heart. Are you constantly comparing yourself to others? Are you constantly competing with others? Are you seeking to outdo and outperform others? Are you discontented? These are manifestations of sinful pride that need to be killed.

What does David mean by things "too great or too wondrous"? David may be thinking about great theological mysteries. The intellectually arrogant lack theological humility. But I think David has in mind great *plans and accomplishments* (cf. Deut 17:8; 30:11). Goldingay puts it well:

> The line is concerned with more than seeking to understand things that are too great for human comprehension. Rather the supplicant has avoided trying to go about doing great wonders, like God, rather than walking in faithfulness (Prov 8:20). This psalm testifies to having escaped "vain ambition." (*Psalms*, 536)

David is giving up trying to do things beyond his control and things for his own glory. His selfish ambition and actions were expressions of arrogance, not humility. This new path that he expresses, however, involves a commitment to simple faithfulness.

Today we try—often with good intentions—to do the wonders of God. But let's stop trying to be God. Let's learn to be faithful. Let's learn to rest in God, like a child (v. 2). The attitude that God expects from us is conveyed in this psalm. We need to admit our frailty. We need to admit our own limitations. We need to avoid rating others lower than ourselves. We need to be aware of the destructive nature of pride (2 Chr 26:16; cf. 32:25). We need to remember that God hates pride (Pss 18:27; 101:5; Prov 6:16-19; 16:5; 30:13). We need to remember that competition and comparison, discontentment, and selfish ambitions are forms of pride. We need to remember, "God resists the proud but gives grace to the humble" (Jas 4:6). We need to remember that God calls us "to act justly, to love faithfulness, and to walk humbly with [our] God" (Mic 6:8). Like David, let us look to God as we seek to grow in humility (Prov 18:12). We need the message of Philippians 2:1-11 to work deeply in our hearts.

Learn to Hush before God (131:2)

Richard Foster writes, "In contemporary society our Adversary majors in three things: noise, hurry, and crowds" (*Celebration*, 15). So then, we should pay close attention to verse 2, as David talks about being quiet and calm before the Lord.

David says that he is like a "child" in the presence of God. This child-like spirit creates peace and contentment instead of restlessness and discontentment. By trusting God and listening to God, he has found contentment. While believers should not be *childish*, they are called to be *childlike* in faith (Matt 18:3). We should have a simple, dependent, confident trust in the Father, in whose presence we find all we need. So let us learn to be still before him (Ps 46:10).

One of the reasons we experience contentment through silence before God is because, like a child, we experience the love of the Father. As believers, we don't have to run around competing with others and promoting ourselves. We have already been accepted through Jesus Christ. The Father loves us with an everlasting love. So let's stop and be quiet and receive his love in the quiet places. Let's trust him for daily bread, and let's find contentment in knowing him and being known by him.

Learn to Hope in God (131:3)

Based on David's relationship with God, he calls the people to hope in God. Childlike faith leads to hope in God. This hope isn't wishful thinking, but a deeply settled confidence in God. When believers are confident in God, they find contentment and peace. David tells Israel to hope in the Lord "forever," that is, to never stop hoping in him. Let's never stop hoping in him until our faith ends in sight.

Corrie ten Boom said, "Never be afraid to trust an unknown future to a known God" (in Lawson, *Psalms 76–150*, 302). How true! If you know him, humble yourself before him, quietly rest in his love, and keep hoping in him.

Reflect and Discuss

1. Why are the people told to sing about *affliction*?
2. Why is it important for us to remember the nature of affliction in the Christian life?
3. What does Psalm 129 teach us about the character of God? How should we respond to this?
4. Regarding Psalm 130, what are some common ways people try to (wrongly) deal with their guilt? How does this psalm teach us to deal with guilt?
5. What does Psalm 130 teach us about the character of God? How should this encourage us to respond?
6. What does it look like to wait for the Lord?
7. How does Psalm 130 point us to the work of Jesus?
8. What is your reaction to Psalm 131? How does Psalm 131 teach us about pride and humility?
9. What does Psalm 131 teach us about contentment and resting in God?
10. Take a few moments to pray through these psalms.

Songs of Ascents (Tracks 13–15)

PSALMS 132–134

Main Idea: These final three Songs of Ascents magnify the glory of the presence of God and highlight the blessing of unity among the people of God.

I. **The Pilgrims' King (132)**
   A. David's passion for God's glory (132:1-5)
   B. David's pursuit of God's presence (132:6-10)
   C. God's oath to David (132:11-12)
   D. God's presence in Zion (132:13-18)
II. **The Pilgrims' Brothers (133)**
   A. The goodness of unity (133:1)
   B. Pictures of unity (133:2-3a)
   C. The blessing of unity (133:3b)
III. **The Pilgrims' Blessing (134)**
   A. The call to bless the Lord (134:1-2)
   B. A prayer of blessing (134:3)

Eugene Peterson calls the Songs of Ascents a "dog-eared songbook" (*Long Obedience*, 18). It's a fitting title as you think about this collection of songs the pilgrims used year after year in moments of reflection, worship, and prayer. These songs continue to instruct and inspire Christian pilgrims as they continue their Christian journeys.

Scholars classify Psalm 132 as either a royal psalm or a song of Zion. Psalm 133 is called either a liturgical song of blessing or a wisdom psalm. Psalm 134 is known as a liturgical hymn.

The Pilgrims' King

PSALM 132

Our God is King over all things, and here we read about his relationship with his anointed earthly king, David. This special relationship would bless not only Israel but also the whole world, eventually.

Goldingay entitles this psalm, "The Reciprocity of Prayer" (*Psalms*, 542). We see a prayer offered to God related to David in the first half of the psalm (vv. 1-10) and then a promise by God related to David in the second half (vv. 11-18). Each half has ten lines, with each half beginning and ending with references to David (ibid.). The poem has some beautiful stylistic features, such as balance, symmetry, and repetition. Goldingay adds, "One can imagine that the psalm might be a liturgy in which the people or the choir say vv 1-10 and a priest says vv 11-18" (ibid., 544).

This idea of prayer and promise has great application for us. Psalm 130 reminded us that God hears us; Psalm 132 reminds us that God is faithful to fulfill his promises. Be reminded of the importance and power of having a holy conversation with God through prayer and praise.

This psalm is different from the other Songs of Ascents in a variety of ways, with the most obvious difference being its length. It's at least twice the size of the others. This fact says something about its significance. It not only highlights God's relationship to David but also magnifies God's special presence symbolized in the ark (Exod 25; 37).

The ark of the covenant had accompanied the people from Sinai to Israel through the wilderness journey and had been kept at Shiloh from the time of conquest. In a battle the ark had been captured by the Philistines and was a war trophy until they experienced shame and disaster as a result of possessing it (see 1 Sam 4–7). It was eventually returned to Israel, to Kiriath-jearim (1 Sam 7:1-2), where it rested for some 20 years until David retrieved it and brought it to Jerusalem (2 Sam 6–7). This momentous occasion serves as the background to Psalm 132 (cf. Pss 24; 68).

In a broken world it's good to know that God is with us and that God is faithful to his promises. We should seek him in prayer and praise him for these basic and glorious truths.

David's Passion for God's Glory (132:1-5)

Verses 1 and 10 both state a prayer for "David." The people ask the Lord to "remember" all of David's acts of devotion to the Lord. The request for remembering expresses covenantal language (cf. Exod 6:5; 32:13; Lev 26:42; Deut 9:27). In this case the reference is probably to God's promise made to David earlier regarding the establishment of his house and throne (2 Sam 7:10-16). Later, in verse 10, the people ask God to continue treating David's royal descendants with kindness.

"Hardships" in verse 1 could refer to David's whole life, but it probably refers to the immediate context of 2 Samuel 5–6, where we read of David's conquest of Jerusalem (2 Sam 5:6-9) and his relocation of the ark to Jerusalem (2 Sam 6). In the latter case his hardship involved what Kidner calls "heart-searchings" (*Psalms 73–150*, 449), including the shock and distress David felt at the death of Uzzah (2 Sam 6:6-10). In joyful relief, David eventually danced before the Lord when the ark arrived in its dwelling place (2 Sam 6:14). His joy demonstrated a sense of acceptance and favor with God.

The psalmist begins to recount David's motive for getting the ark (see 2 Sam 6; 1 Chr 13–16). When he heard that God blessed Obed-Edom, the guardian of the ark (2 Sam 6:12), David immediately sought to bring the ark to Jerusalem. David didn't retrieve and relocate the ark for political reasons but for God's glory. Verse 2 highlights David's God-centered resolve. The phrase "Mighty One of Jacob" is derived from Genesis 49:24 and speaks about the Lord's protection, guidance, and blessing of Jacob (VanGemeren, "Psalms," 805). It connotes the Lord's divine strength that makes victories possible for God's people. David certainly knew the power of the Mighty One in battle (cf. 2 Sam 5:12).

Verses 3-5 show how David resolved to complete this task quickly. If a doctor were to ask him, "How well are you sleeping?" he would have to say, "I haven't been sleeping much." The writer says that David vowed not to lie down or sleep until he found a dwelling place for God (vv. 3-5; cf. Prov 6:4). This figure of speech illustrates David's zeal for God's glory.

David made a temporary dwelling for the tabernacle and then later desired to build a more permanent structure. He accomplished the former, but his son Solomon would accomplish the latter. God promised to "tabernacle" among his people (cf. Exod 25:8-9), and David desired this blessing in his own day.

We're reminded here of the wonder of God's dwelling with us and the logical response of living passionately for his glory. In Jesus Christ, God "tabernacled with us" (John 1:14 literal translation), not in a building but in the flesh. Because of Jesus's saving work, we now have the promise of dwelling with God forever (Rev 21:3). Until we enjoy this ultimate dwelling with God, we live by the power of the indwelling Holy Spirit (Rom 8:9; John 14:16-18). Find comfort in God's dwelling with us and in us (John 14:17). By the Spirit's power, passionately live for God's glory, and don't chase lesser glories.

David's Pursuit of God's Presence (132:6-10)

The psalmist says that David and his men heard about the ark's location while in Ephrathah and soon found it in Kiriath-jearim (1 Sam 6:21–7:2), which is alluded to here as "the fields of Jaar." The ark resided in obscurity. *Jaar* means "thicket" (Kidner, *Psalms 73–150*, 450). They basically found it out in the woods!

Think about this context for a moment. Kidner comments, "The search for the ark in verse 6, as for something almost *totally forgotten*, brings out the fact that as David put it, 'we neglected it [or "him," CSB] in the days of Saul (1 Chr 13:3)'" (*Psalms 73–150*, 449; emphasis added). Totally forgot the ark? Neglected it? Eugene Peterson paraphrases 1 Chronicles 13:3 like this: "the Chest that was out of sight, out of mind during the days of Saul" (*The Message*). It's amazing what people will live without! In this case the people were living without the ark until David led them in pursuit of it.

Many knew that God was everywhere, as Psalm 139 teaches us. But the ark symbolized God's *special* presence. It manifested God's power and glory. And it was the place where sacrifice for sin was made on the Day of Atonement. The mercy seat or the atonement cover served as a lid on the ark. It had cherubim of gold facing each other with their faces bowed, symbolizing God's holy presence (Pss 99:1; 80:1). Here the high priest would make a great sacrifice for all the people once a year on the Day of Atonement, as he sprinkled blood on the mercy seat (Rom 3:25; Heb 2:17; 1 John 4:10). But in David's day no one seemed to miss the ark, this most vital item for worship! No one seemed to care that it was somewhere out there in the woods. No one seemed to miss the special presence of God. No one seemed to miss this work of atonement. They didn't seem to miss the ark because they didn't miss God.

Consider the problem of spiritual *neglect*. Many people don't seem to care about the special presence of God, nor do they seem to care about Jesus's full atonement at Golgotha. Many in the church go through the motions, doing the "work of God" apart from a yearning for the mighty working of the Spirit of God. Many teach and minister in the name of Christianity but fail to point people to the sacrificial Lamb who takes away the sin of the world. If God's special presence was removed from our gatherings and no one exalted the work of Jesus, how many people would care?

I pray that we will see here the necessity of preserving first things. If we don't have God's special presence, and if we don't have a Substitute to exalt in word and ordinance, we're a mere religious club administrating activities. No presence? No power. No cross? No hope. The return of the ark reminds us of our need to stay committed to what matters most.

I read recently where a couple from Northern California found over thirteen million dollars in gold buried in their yard next to a tree. A treasure was right in their grasp. How wonderful is it to know that in the words of Paul, "He is not far from each one of us" (Acts 17:27)? Don't neglect the opportunity to know Jesus. If you know him, don't neglect time in his Word, enjoying his presence. Don't neglect fellowship with God's people. His grace surpasses all earthly treasures.

In verses 7-8 the worshipers set their faces to Jerusalem for worship. The language conveys great passion for worship. The Lord's "footstool" refers to the ark (99:5,9; 122:1), which symbolized the earthly rule of God (VanGemeren, "Psalms," 807; Ps 99:1-2).

So the people are joining in the procession as the ark travels from Obed-Edom's house to the dwelling place of Jerusalem, referred to in verse 8 as God's "resting place." The people pray that God would visit them again. The might of God is magnified here. The ark had been a symbol of God's power during the wilderness journey, and there's an echo of Moses's words here: "Arise, LORD" (Num 10:35-36; cf. Ps 68). The people are praying for the Lord to bless them and go to battle on their behalf.

VanGemeren underscores the significance of this event: "The placement of the ark in Jerusalem ushered in a new era in God's rule over Israel: the Davidic era" ("Psalms," 807).

The people also pray for the priests. Fittingly, they pray for the priests to be "clothed with righteousness" (v. 9); that is, that they do their work faithfully, dispensing blessing. In response, the godly are to "shout for joy" (v. 9).

In verse 10 the writer returns to the original plea in verse 1. He desires a favorable hearing "for the sake of your servant David" (v. 10). The supplicant asks God not to "reject" the contemporary king, "your anointed one" (v. 10), in David's line.

Let's likewise share this passion for God's glory and this pursuit of God's presence as we bow before the King of kings, Jesus Christ. We hear whispers of this King, the greater David, in the next two verses.

God's Oath to David (132:11-12)

After reading of David's oath in verse 2, we now read of God's promises in verses 11-12. God's promise to David in 2 Samuel 7:12-16 is condensed and restated poetically here. God's promise is certain (cf. Ps 89:3,35). It's a "sure oath" (v. 11 ESV), just as his word is trustworthy (2 Sam 7:28). God assures the people that David's sons would rule forever (cf. Gen 17:6). However, there was also a conditional dimension to this promise (v. 12). The king and his heirs must keep the covenant. They must live according to God's Word. How is this tension resolved—an unconditional yet conditional promise?

This tension gets resolved finally in Jesus. We know from history that the later monarchy displayed the need for a better king. And in Jesus Christ, the better King came! Jesus is the fulfillment of the unconditional promise: the Son of David reigns forever. And he is the fulfillment of this conditional promise: only he kept God's law perfectly. In Peter's Pentecost sermon, he proclaimed Jesus as the fulfillment of God's promise to David (Acts 2:30; cf. 7:46). This risen King now reigns at the Father's right hand as the exalted Messiah (Eph 1:20), and he calls everyone to confess him as Lord.

God's Presence in Zion (132:13-18)

Now we read about God's promise regarding Zion. This response answers the previous longings of verses 1-10. Consider the promises God makes and notice the "I" statements. Because the Lord has chosen Zion, the people can rest secure in God's provisions (vv. 13-14). They can delight in the Lord.

These verses should encourage us to seek God in prayer. Verse 16 contains a specific answer to the prayer in verse 9. Verses 17-18 contain the answer to the prayer of verses 1 and 10. The Lord will make a "horn grow for David" (v. 17). Here's an interesting expression. Try that out today as you greet a friend: "May a horn grow for you!" The people understood this horn to symbolize *strength;* the horn was the embodiment of an animal's strength (Goldingay, *Psalms,* 557). In the future the Lord will raise up a strong, saving King. This brings to mind God's promise to raise up a "Righteous Branch" (Jer 23:5), that is, the messianic King.

God also promised a "lamp" for Israel, that is, to preserve the dynasty (132:17b; 2 Sam 21:17; 1 Kgs 11:35). Finally, the Lord promised that the king's "crown" will shine (cf. Ps 89:39), symbolizing a glorious rule.

If you know what happened later in Israel's history, you might wonder about how to take these claims. The answer comes in reading this prophetically and messianically. God will dwell in Zion forever—in the heavenly city of the redeemed (Rev 21:3). Jesus Christ, the ideal King of Psalm 72, will bring perfect justice and abundant provision (Rev 21:26; 22:2). The new creation will be filled with joyous worship from those who fall facedown before the throne (Rev 7:9-17).

By establishing his rule in Jerusalem and enthroning David, God prepared the way for the day when that rule would be consummated in his Son (Williams, *Psalms 73–150*, Kindle). Psalm 132 points us to the majestic rule and dominion of Jesus, our strong King, who will make all his enemies a footstool (1 Cor 15:25-28; Rev 19:17-21). His glorious rule will have no end. Crown him Lord of all!

The Pilgrims' Brothers
PSALM 133

In this little psalm David encourages unity among the saints as they journey to Jerusalem for worship. He uses two illustrations to magnify the blessedness of unity, one from local geography and the other from religious ceremony.

The Goodness of Unity (133:1)

The psalmist pronounces a blessing on those who "live together in harmony." One can imagine the scene as pilgrims ascend to Jerusalem. They would have traveled from various places. They would have been from various tribes. They would have had different backgrounds and interests. Yet they all assembled for the common purpose of praising God. Together, God's people expressed a common heritage and faith. The writer testifies to the sweetness of this unity.

The longer people follow Jesus faithfully, the more they value unity among God's people. That's because mature believers value what Jesus values, and Jesus values (among other things) unity (John 17:20-21). Mature believers will grow concerned when unity is threatened. They will be eager to maintain the unity of the Spirit (Eph 4:3). The Spirit of God creates a longing for unity and empowers our pursuit of unity. Unity is both gift and effort. When it's enjoyed, it's good and pleasant.

Oftentimes today you hear people say things like this: "The church is not good for people." While it's true that the church has its flaws, when the church gathers in worship—under the Word, before the Table, with one another in prayer and praise—it most definitely is good for people.

The sweetest times in this short life involve gathering in worship with God's people with a united desire to exalt the Son.

Thinking back to Genesis 1, when God calls his creation "good," he is saying in a sense that this is how it is meant to be. So it is with God's people when dwelling in unity. We can say in the midst of pleasant unity, "This is how it was meant to be." We won't know this unity completely in this life; but in the new creation, when we gather with the redeemed, we will truly be able to say, "This is how it was meant to be."

Pictures of Unity (133:2-3a)

The psalmist proceeds to compare the goodness of unity to fine oil and the dew of Hermon. These two descriptions of a gathering of God's people may sound strange to modern ears. Imagine someone asking you what your Sunday worship gatherings are like, and you respond, "It's like oil on a pastor's beard, and like wet grass!" That's essentially what the psalmist says.

As a man who appreciates good beard oil, I (Tony) find this verse striking! Aaron must have had an impressive beard since the writer says it extended to his robes. One writer commented, "Indeed, the Holy Scripture is very strict on the point. The priest may not shave his beard, and the man who can't grow a beard cannot be a priest" (Reardon, *Christ in the Psalms*, 266). Amen!

Regardless of your bias regarding facial hair, the analogy is important. What is the psalmist saying about this oil running down Aaron's beard? Simply put, the unity that exists among the brethren is like the aromatic and holy priestly oil. This image calls attention to the sacredness of worship enjoyed in the tabernacle, as people from various tribes united in giving honor to God. In Exodus we read that special oil was used for anointing the tent of meeting and for the priests; the ingredients for this oil were not to be used for ordinary purposes (Exod 30:22-33). Aaron is mentioned here as the head of the priestly clan. His name represents the other priests (VanGemeren, "Psalms," 816).

The analogy is pressed further as the writer says that the unity of the worshiping saints is like a plentiful amount of oil, like oil that runs down Aaron's beard, onto his robes. This image conveys a spirit of joy that exists among God's people who dwell in unity. To live together in spiritual oneness—in fellowship, worship, and mission—is a rich blessing.

It's refreshing and energizing to the people, and it's a pleasing aroma to God. Unity blesses the entire body. It has a pervasive effect.

In the New Testament, through Jesus Christ, our great high priest, we share in the priesthood of all believers. What a blessing it is to enjoy the unity Christ has established! As believers in Jesus, we don't create unity; he created it. We simply maintain it (Eph 4:3). And when our established unity (in the gospel) becomes an experienced unity (in our cultivating and maintaining it), it's sweet, pleasant, and refreshing. This passage has me praying for unity in our congregation each day I put on lotion and beard oil! Perhaps you can make a point to pray for unity in your church as you smell sweet perfumes and the wonderful scents that exist in God's beautiful creation.

The next illustration concerns local geography (v. 3a). Mount Hermon is a majestic mountain that rises over nine thousand feet above sea level; it's located about 120 miles north of Jerusalem. Snow covers the mountain peaks throughout the year, causing dews to nourish the region. The melting ice is a major source of the Jordan River. The psalmist says the unity of God's people is nourishing and life-giving.

If we may modernize this illustration a bit, consider the highlands you've visited. Have you ever been up in the mountains and breathed that cool, refreshing air? It's so calming to stressed-out, busy people, especially those who live in bustling cities. It's that sort of refreshment God's people experience as they worship together. Each week we bring our busy, stressed-out lives to the assembly, and the Spirit of God blesses us with refreshment. We leave renewed, encouraged, and ready to engage the world again.

Don't underestimate the importance of your corporate gatherings! You need this "Hermon encouragement." In seasons of dryness and anxiety, don't distance yourself from the community. Pursue fellowship with God's people.

The Blessing of Unity (133:3b)

The psalmist concludes by testifying that the Lord blesses those who dwell in unity. When brothers dwell in unity, life is enjoyed forever.

This blessing reminds us that fellowship with God and fellowship with one another go together. To be in right relationship with God means you're in right relationship with God's people. The closer we draw to other believers, the closer we draw to God. Great blessings await those who make every effort to dwell in unity!

The Pilgrims' Blessing
PSALM 134

This little psalm is the last of 15 Songs of Ascents. Kidner says, "The Songs of Ascents, which begin in the alien surroundings of Meshech and Kedar (Ps 120), end fittingly on the note of serving God 'day and night in the temple'" (*Psalms 73–150*, 453). It focuses on blessing, for the idea appears in each verse. The servants are called to bless the Lord, and then the priest pronounces a blessing on the people.

Part of the reason this psalm is so lovely is its simplicity. The worship called for in this psalm isn't showy. That's because worship isn't about entertainment; it's about exalting God in Spirit and in truth.

The Call to Bless the Lord (134:1-2)

The psalmist summons all the servants of the Lord to bless the Lord. True worship is God centered. You can't miss the emphasis on "the LORD" (vv. 1-3). Worship isn't about our work, our performance, or our goodness; it's about God's work, God's grace, and God's goodness. He is worthy of praise.

The psalmist summons the "servants of the LORD" (v. 1). These individuals were either the priests who ministered in the temple (the likely reference) or simply all who stand before God in the temple precincts. Either way, the call to keep first things first is clear: worship the Lord. To "stand" means to be "present, alert, and ready to do whatever the master wants done" (Goldingay, *Psalms*, 572).

Recently, our church hosted a church-planting partner who is serving in Germany. After a full day of worship, I (Tony) commented, "It was so good to have you worshiping with us. As partners, we shouldn't underestimate the value of being together for corporate worship."

He said, "Yes, this is the end for which we exist." Indeed. We exist to glorify God and enjoy him forever.

While this psalm speaks of the priestly servants, we understand that every believer in Jesus has access to God and also is called to worship him (1 Pet 2:4-5,9-10). What a privilege we have to commune with God!

These servants are called to worship the Lord "at night" (v. 1). This reference could refer to guards waiting for the morning (cf. Ps 130:6) or to other worshipers showing up at the temple before dawn (cf. 119:14). The writer of 1 Chronicles 9:27,33 speaks of the Levitical singers being on duty day and night. Allen points to a worship service held at night during the Feast of Tabernacles as the context (*Psalms 101–150*, 218). Regardless of the specific reference, it reminds us today of the ongoing nature of worship. Day and night the Lord is worthy of praise.

In verse 2 the psalmist summons everyone to add another physical activity to their worship experience: the lifting up of their hands in worship (cf. Ps 28:2). This symbol represents adoration, dependence, and submission (1 Tim 2:8). It's also a symbol of blessing, which leads into verse 3 (Lev 9:22; Goldingay, *Psalms*, 572). Since the worshipers are standing in the "holy place," the earthly sanctuary, they are perhaps being called to direct their worship either to the heavenly sanctuary (cf. Ps 150:1) or to the most holy place in the temple (1 Kgs 8:6; Ps 132:7).

So then, this little psalm provides some good reminders for worship. Worship should be God centered, it should happen day and night, and it involves the whole person.

A Prayer of Blessing (134:3)

Verse 3 concludes with a blessing. This might be a prayer offered by the priests and Levites as the people leave God's house in Jerusalem for their homes throughout the region (Lawson, *Psalms 76–150*, 313). The first words sound much like the priestly blessing of Numbers 6:24.

The blessing involves a desire for the Lord to bless the people from "Zion." This place was blessed because it contained the earthly symbol of the heavenly sanctuary. This exalted God is the "Maker of heaven and earth." He has all power, and he delights in blessing his people.

We are reminded that the Lord has blessed us from Jerusalem, as well. Through the cross and the resurrection of Jesus Christ some two thousand years ago, blessing has flowed to the nations. Hebrews 12:22-24 speaks about a true Mount Zion, where Jesus is the mediator of a new covenant and reigns in the midst of his people. What a privilege to join in this assembly of the redeemed to worship the living God!

Kidner puts both parts of Psalm 134 together: "To bless God is to acknowledge gratefully what He is; but to bless man, God must make of him what he is not, and give him what he has not" (*Psalms 73–150*, 454). Yes, let's bless God, "who has blessed us with every spiritual blessing in the heavens in Christ" (Eph 1:3). And let's ask him to grant us what we need and to make us what we should be.

Reflect and Discuss

1. Read 1 Samuel 4–7. What strikes you the most about this drama surrounding the ark?
2. Read 2 Samuel 6:1-15. What strikes you the most about David's retrieval of the ark?
3. What does Psalm 132 teach us about God's promises?
4. How does the covenant in Psalm 132:11-12 point us ahead to the coming of Christ?
5. What does Psalm 132 teach us about prayer?
6. Why should we value unity among God's people?
7. What can we do to cultivate unity among God's people?
8. What do the illustrations of unity in Psalm 133 teach us?
9. What does Psalm 134 teach us about worship?
10. Take a few moments to pray through these psalms, focusing on the prayer for unity.

No God Is Like Our God!

PSALM 135

Main Idea: Only the covenant-keeping Lord who acts for his people is worthy of praise.

I. **Praise the Lord because He Is Good (135:1-4).**
II. **Honor the Lord because He Is the Creator (135:5-7).**
III. **Thank the Lord because He Fights for His People (135:8-14).**
IV. **Worship the Lord because He Is the One True God (135:15-18).**
V. **Bless the Lord because He Lives among His People (135:19-21).**

In Psalm 103:2 David, the gifted songwriter and king of Israel, reminds us, "Let all that I am praise the LORD; may I never forget the good things he does for me" (NLT). Forgetfulness is all too common for the people of God, people who have been blessed with grace upon grace from the Lord who is good (103:3; 136:1). Psalm 135 is a hymn of descriptive praise about God the Creator (vv. 5-7), the Lord of history (vv. 8-12). Willem VanGemeren notes, "The reader will be struck by the many allusions as well as direct citations to other passages of Scripture" (VanGemeren, *Psalms*, 940). Alec Motyer points to the psalm's close relationship to Psalm 136 and writes,

> The two psalms are "orphans" in that no authorship or other
> attribution is made. The only reason for attaching them to
> the songs of the Great Ascent is suitability; both psalms sketch
> the great pilgrimage of Yahweh's people from Egypt to the
> promised land (135:8-14; 136:10-22), and it is easy to imagine
> their use by festival pilgrims. (*Psalms by the Day*, 390)

As the people of God marched up to Jerusalem, Psalms 135 and 136 would help them remember who had delivered them and from what he had delivered them. They would recall the abundant reasons they had for praising and blessing "the name of the LORD" (v. 1).

Before proceeding further, it is worth observing the beautiful structure of the psalm. Its chiastic structure highlights certain truths and can also aid memorization. Michael Wilcock's design is helpful:

247

Praise to our electing Lord (vv. 1-4),
   the "making" God who gives life (vv. 5-7)!
      Pharaoh's servants have been vanquished (vv. 8-9);
         with the gift of the land (vv. 10-12),
      Yahweh's servants have been vindicated (vv. 13-14).
   The "made" gods bring death (vv. 15-18);
praise to our indwelling Lord (vv. 19-21)! (*Message: Songs*, 247)

Wilcock's outline will influence our study of this psalm.

Praise the Lord because He Is Good
PSALM 135:1-4

As in Psalm 134, the worship of God's people is led by, but not restricted to, the priests "who stand in the LORD's house at night!" (134:1; see also 113:1). In Psalms 134 and 135 they are called "servants of the LORD" (134:1; 135:1). Repeatedly they are told to "praise the LORD" in verses 1-4. Why? Because "the LORD is good," his name "is delightful" (v. 3), and he "has chosen Jacob for himself, Israel as his treasured possession" (v. 4). Our God, the Lord, is good and delightful (ESV, "pleasant") in general but also in particular. Evidence of his particular goodness is his sovereign and gracious choosing of Israel (see Exod 19:5; Deut 7:6; 14:2; Ps 114:2; Mal 3:17). Commenting on this truth, Calvin writes,

> The mercy was surely one of incomparable value, and which
> might well stir them up to fervent gratitude and praise,
> adopted as they were into favor with God, while the whole
> Gentile world was passed by. . . . [God] bound the posterity of
> Abraham to him by a closer tie, such as that by which he now
> adopts men generally into his Church and unites them with
> the body of his only-begotten Son. (*Psalms 93–150*, 172)

The God we serve is good! He is worthy of our praise. He sets his electing pleasure on undeserving sinners like Jacob, sinners like you and me.

Honor the Lord because He Is the Creator
PSALM 135:5-7

Not only is the Lord good (v. 3), but also he is "great, . . . greater than all gods" (v. 5). God's greatness is something the psalmist "knows" beyond a shadow of a doubt. Allen Ross informs us:

These are words that Jethro used in Exodus 18:11 when he
met Moses and Israel after the great deliverance from Egypt. It
is the kind of confession of faith that any believer could make.
(*Psalms 90–150*, 766–67)

The pagan nations worship false gods who can do nothing. In complete contrast we worship a God, "the Lord [who] does whatever he
pleases" (v. 6). The Lord is the sovereign Creator "in heaven and on
earth, in the seas and all the depths." He controls the clouds, lightning, rain, and wind (v. 7). He has absolute and total control and
authority over what he has made. Nature responds to his every command, and so should we! John Piper provides helpful theological
insight on these verses:

> Whenever God acts, he acts in a way that pleases him. God
> is never constrained to do a thing that he despises. He is
> never backed into a corner where his only recourse is to
> do something he hates to do. He does whatever he pleases.
> And therefore, in some sense, he has pleasure in all that he
> does. . . . [Therefore] we should bow before God and praise
> his sovereign freedom—that in some sense at least he always
> acts in freedom, according to his own "good pleasure,"
> following the dictates of his own delights. He never becomes
> the victim of circumstance. He is never forced into a situation
> where he must do something in which he cannot rejoice.
> ("The Pleasure of God in All That He Does")

Our God is the Creator. And he is a sovereign Creator with absolute and
complete authority over all that he has made.

Thank God because He Fights for His People
PSALM 135:8-14

The Lord is good (vv. 1-4) and he is great (vv. 5-7). He is also gracious
(vv. 8-14). His graciousness is made abundantly clear in his deliverance
of the Hebrews from Egypt in the exodus (vv. 8-9) and in his empowering them to conquer the promised land (vv. 10-12). In summary fashion,
the psalmist describes God's victories over Pharaoh and the Egyptians,
particularly in the tenth plague (vv. 8-9; cf. Exod 12:29-36), and over
"many nations" as he "slaughtered mighty kings" (v. 10), specifically
"Sihon king of the Amorites, Og king of Bashan, and all the kings of

Canaan" (v. 11; cf. Num 21:21-26,33-35; Deut 2:30-33; 3:1-6; Josh 12:1-
24). Having fought for his people and defeated their enemies, the Lord
"gave their land as an inheritance, an inheritance to his people Israel"
(v. 12). They did not deserve it, and they did not earn it. It was a sovereign act of his goodness and grace.

In response to this recounting and remembrance of God's gracious
acts, the psalmist breaks forth in praise of the Lord's name that "endures
forever" and the Lord's reputation, which will endure "through all generations" (v. 13). Once again we are reminded that no God is like our
God. His mighty name will never be forgotten. And "the LORD will vin-
dicate his people and have compassion on his servants" (v. 14). Derek
Kidner's comments fit so well:

> These verses allude to Exodus 3:15 and Deuteronomy 32:36.
> The latter (from the Song of Moses) makes it clear that the
> rescue of God's people will be wholly undeserved: the saving
> of fools and apostates from the predicament they deserve to
> find themselves in. (*Psalms 73–150*, 456)

This salvation shows compassion for the undeserving. This salvation
is pure grace showered on the Lord's servants. And it is important not to
miss that verses 13-14 "look to the future as the previous verses looked to
the past" (Boice, *Psalms 107–150*, 1177). As James Boice also says,

> The God who has been gracious in past days will continue to
> vindicate his people and have compassion on them in days yet
> to come (v. 14). God's love will indeed endure forever (Psalm
> 136, refrain). . . . God does not change. (Ibid.)

God is forever good, he is forever great, and he is forever gracious.
No God is like our God. Never forget that!

Worship the Lord because He Is the One True God
PSALM 135:15-18

The psalmist now wishes to compare the one true God with the false
idols that this world ("the nations") so foolishly constructs and worships.
Spiritual insanity could not be more evident. Drawing from Psalm 115:4-
8, the songwriter is clear and concise in his polemic against the false
gods. First, they are "made by human hands" (v. 15)—even the most
valuable gods ("silver and gold"). They are creations, not the Creator.

Second, they are mutes (v. 16). Third, they are blind (v. 16). Fourth, they are deaf (v. 17). Fifth, they are dead. That is, they have no life (v. 17). Those who foolishly bow down to them and put their "trust" and hopes "in them" are destined to be "just like them" (v. 18). Commenting on this truth, Spurgeon writes, "Idolaters are spiritually dead, they are the mere images of men, their best being is gone. . . . Their mouths do not really pray, their eyes see not the truth, their ears hear not the voice of the Lord, and the life of God is not in them" (*Treasury*, vol. 3b, 188). How absurd and foolish to abandon the worship of the one true God.

Bless the Lord because He lives among His People
PSALM 135:19-21

Psalm 135 concludes with a fivefold call to praise ("bless") the Lord. Each occurrence of the word "bless" is imperative, and the verses draw from Psalms 115:9-11 and 118:2-4. By piling up the names of Israel, Aaron, and Levi (vv. 19-20), the psalmist "makes it clearer that the people who revere Yhwh are the people as a whole" (Goldingay, *Psalms*, 585). The concluding phrase of verse 20 supports this observation: "You who revere the LORD, bless the LORD!" Respect and reverence are natural and appropriate responses in recognition of this good, great, and gracious God who is like no other gods! The psalm ends with a personal and comforting word. The God of Israel, Aaron, Levi, and Jacob (v. 4) is a God who is intimate with his people. He is the Lord we bless "from Zion; he dwells in Jerusalem" (v. 21). The God who can localize his omnipresence chose as an act of grace to live among his people Israel as their God. He is here with us. He is near, not far away. No wonder God's people shout with praise, "Hallelujah!" "Praise the . . . LORD" (cf. vv. 1-3). We have come full circle. We end as we began.

Conclusion

The words of the wonderful expositor Warren Wiersbe provide a fitting conclusion to the psalm that teaches us that no god is like our God:

> Israel could praise the Lord because He was present with His people. No other nation could claim that distinction. His glory led Israel through the wilderness, and that glory resided in the sanctuary until God had to depart because of the nation's sins (Ezek. 7–11). What other nation had the glory of God

dwelling in their midst (63:2; Rom. 9:4)? The Lord is not a distant God; He is a "very present help in trouble" (46:1). Jesus is "Immanuel—God with us" (Matt. 1:20-25; 28:20). "I will never leave you nor forsake you" (Heb. 13:5; Gen. 28:15; Josh. 1:5; Isa. 41:10, 17). Praise the Lord! (*Bible Exposition Commentary*, 361)

Reflect and Discuss

1. Why is forgetfulness common for God's people? In what ways do you forget God's grace and goodness? How does forgetting God's grace and goodness affect what you believe and how you live?
2. How can praising God help you combat forgetfulness? What else can Christians do to help them remember God's goodness and grace?
3. How would you describe your joy in the Lord when you first understood the gospel and during the time you were baptized? How often do you think about these moments? In what ways could thinking about these moments help you remember God's goodness?
4. God does what he pleases. Why is that good for people?
5. Describe a time where you have seen God's grace and goodness in your life.
6. How can remembering God's past goodness help you during seasons of difficulty and mourning?
7. Why does the psalmist take time to describe the worthlessness of idols while he praises the Lord? What are some idols in your life that you give praise to instead of to the Lord?
8. What does it mean that those who worship idols become like them? In what ways does one become like what one worships?
9. How does becoming like what you worship challenge you to think about what you spend your time doing?
10. How does sin affect your worship of God? How can praise to God help you fight sin?

Be Thankful to the Lord! His Faithful Love Endures Forever!

PSALM 136

Main Idea: God's mighty acts of creation and salvation reveal his enduring and faithful love for his people.

I. **Praise the Lord for His Faithful and Everlasting Love because of Who He Is (136:1-3).**
   A. He is good (136:1).
   B. He is sovereign (136:2-3).

II. **Praise the Lord for His Faithful and Everlasting Love because of What He Has Done (136:4-25).**
   A. The Lord made everything (136:4-9).
   B. The Lord saves his people (136:10-16).
   C. The Lord blesses his people (136:17-22).
   D. The Lord remembers and rescues his people (136:23-24).
   E. The Lord provides for everyone (136:25).

III. **Praise the Lord for His Faithful and Everlasting Love because of Where He Is (136:26).**
   A. Remember our posture.
   B. Remember his position.

One of the most precious phrases and promises in the whole Bible appears in Psalm 136. Actually, it appears 26 times in Psalm 136. Patrick Reardon notes, "The litany-like refrain makes it one of the easiest psalms to memorize and sing spontaneously on every occasion" (*Christ in the Psalms*, 271). Its depth of meaning is revealed, at least in part, in how various English translations render the original Hebrew:

CSB: "His faithful love endures forever."

ESV: "His steadfast love endures forever."

NIV: "His love endures forever."

NASB: "His lovingkindness is everlasting."

AMP: "His lovingkindness endures forever."

CEB: "God's faithful love lasts forever."

GNT: "His love is eternal."

KJV: "His mercy endureth forever."

The Message: "His love never quits."

If we put these translations together, we might grasp the depth and breadth of what the psalmist is saying by wording it like this: The LORD (Yahweh), our God (*Elohim*), is faithful in his everlasting covenant love toward his people. It is a love that will endure forever, never coming to an end. This attribute of faithful love is at the essence of who our God is. He is "faithful love." He is everlasting lovingkindness. How do we know? The psalmist takes us on a magnificent 26-verse tour to make an irrefutable case. Derek Kidner points out, "Every verse of this psalm either echoes, quotes or is quoted by some other part of Scripture" (*Psalms 73–150*, 455). What an appropriate conclusion it is to the Great Hallel psalms (Pss 120–136).

Praise the Lord for His Faithful and Everlasting Love because of Who He Is
PSALM 136:1-3

A theology of God (theology proper) should always begin with who God is—his character and attributes. This powerful psalm on the Lord's faithful, forever love does exactly this. Although our God possesses many marvelous attributes, the psalmist highlights two in verses 1-3 (cf. Ps 135:3-5). He does so using the phrase "Give thanks" in each verse (cf. v. 26).

He Is Good (136:1)

We should praise or "give thanks to the LORD [Yahweh]" because "he is good." The word translated "good" (*tov*) occurs more than seven hundred times in the Old Testament. Allen Ross writes,

> This word embraces everything that is beneficial for life, pleasing to life, and harmonious with life. . . . [God] is good because what he creates and what he gives is all good. (*Psalms 1–41*, 753)

He Is Sovereign (136:2-3)

The Lord is good, and he is also sovereign. He is the "God of gods" (v. 2) and the "Lord of lords" (v. 3). These verses echo Deuteronomy

10:17, which says, "For the LORD your God is the God of gods and Lord of lords, the great, mighty, and awe-inspiring God, showing no partiality and taking no bribe." They also anticipate the second-coming description of Jesus in Revelation 19:16: "And he has a name written on his robe and on his thigh: KING OF KINGS AND LORD OF LORDS." Our God alone is Lord!

Praise the Lord for His Faithful and Everlasting Love because of What He Has Done
PSALM 136:4-25

The psalmist now moves from who God is to what God has done. Verses 4-25 focus on the mighty acts of our mighty God. They are the heart of the hymn, and they focus on the twin themes of creation and redemption (cf. Rev 4–5). Nancy deClaissé-Walford helpfully explains the psalm's use of these two themes:

> As the singers of Psalm 136 enunciated the words of the psalm, they brought the past powerfully into the present. God who created is creating. God who delivered is delivering. God who sustained is sustaining. (*Book of Psalms*, 952)

The Lord Made Everything (136:4-9)

Verses 4-9 are a creation hymn within the larger hymn of Psalm 136. Our God does "great wonders" (NLT, "mighty miracles"). By means of his supernatural power, our God "made the heavens skillfully" (ESV, "by understanding"; cf. Prov. 3:18; 8). "He spread the land on the waters" (v. 6; cf. Psalm 24:2). "He made the great lights" (v. 7), "the sun to rule by day" (v. 8), and "the moon and stars to rule by night" (v. 9). Our God is the Creator God of Genesis 1–2 who brought into existence all that is. This creation gives witness to God's power and wisdom. It gives evidence to his faithful covenant love that endures forever. From the original creation to the new creation (Rev 21–22), God's steadfast love sustains all that he has created.

The Lord Saves His People (136:10-16)

Verses 10-24 rehearse the great redemptive acts of God on behalf of his people. Verses 10-22 parallel Psalm 135:8-12, recounting the exodus and conquest. The psalmist begins in verse 10 with God's signal act of redemption in Israel's history and then moves forward. The Lord "struck the firstborn of the Egyptians" (v. 10) in the tenth plague (Exod 11–12). He then "brought Israel out from among" the Egyptians (v. 11). He did this "with a strong hand and outstretched arm" (v. 12). This deliverance was an act of divine power. But that was not all! God "divided the Red Sea" (v. 13). He "led Israel through" (v. 14) and "hurled Pharaoh and his army into the Red Sea" (v. 15; see Exod 14–15). The Lord then "led his people in the wilderness" (v. 16). God saved and sustained his people because "his faithful love endures forever."

The Lord Blesses His People (136:17-22)

Verses 17-22 continue the redemptive theme of verses 10-16, drawing attention to specific kings the Lord conquered and the inheritance of land he gave to his people. Our Lord defeated and "struck down great kings" (v. 17). He "slaughtered famous kings" (v. 18). Two examples are given: "Sihon king of the Amorites" (v. 19) and "Og king of Bashan" (v. 20). Their defeat is recorded in Numbers 21:21-35. Having beaten Israel's enemies, God "gave their land as an inheritance" (v. 21), "an inheritance to Israel his servant" (v. 22). This was an inheritance given out of a faithful love that endures forever. It was also an inheritance with responsibilities for Israel as the Lord's servant.

The Lord Remembers and Rescues His People (136:23-24)

Our God with his faithful, ever enduring love is especially precious when we are humble and humiliated. It is good to know God "remembers" us at those times (v. 23). Allen Ross notes that this verse may refer to the time of the judges, or "it could simply be a general reference covering from the time of the settlement in the land until the restoration from the exile" (*Psalms 90–150*, 782). Regardless of the time or times, we can be sure our God has not forgotten us "in our low estate" (v. 23 ESV). He remembers, and he rescues "us from our foes" (v. 24). Regardless of our situations, the Lord's faithful and enduring love marches forward on behalf of his people.

The Lord Provides for Everyone (136:25)

As the psalm moves toward its close, "the hymn returns to a reflection on God's goodness as the Creator. His 'love' to all creation is evident in that he continually cares for his creatures" (VanGemeren, *Psalms*, 948). God is committed in covenant love to his creation. Therefore, he provides and "gives food to every creature." Israel and the nations! Humans and animals. His faithful, enduring, forever love extends to all!

Praise the Lord for His Faithful and Everlasting Love because of Where He Is

PSALM 136:26

Michael Wilcock summarizes well this psalm:

> From the beginning of creation to the climax of redemption, from the first making of the heavens to the final inheritance of the saints, all is to be seen against the background of the love of God. That love is both indestructible, because it is covenant love, and boundless, because it endures forever. As you look around at all that he has made, and follow through all that he has done, at every point the psalm is saying "*Covenant love did this.*" (*Message: Songs,* 251; emphasis in original)

In light of this remarkable truth, what is our proper response?

Remember Our Posture

Thankfulness! This is our proper response and posture before such a great and awesome God. He is good (v. 1). He is the God of gods (v. 2). He is the Lord of lords (v. 3). Verses 1 and 26 anticipate the directive of Paul in 1 Thessalonians 5:18: "Give thanks in everything; for this is God's will for you in Christ Jesus."

Remember His Position

The God we worship and to whom we give thanks is "the God of heaven." This is the only time "God of heaven" appears in the psalms. The phrase does appear in Ezra 1:2; Nehemiah 1:4; and Jonah 1:9, among other places. It emphasizes God's sovereignty as the Creator and ruler over all things. Nothing is outside his lordship. As Abraham Kuyper so eloquently put it, "There is not a square inch in the whole domain of our human existence over which Christ, who is Sovereign over *all,* does not cry: 'Mine!'" (*Abraham Kuyper: A Centennial Reader,* 488; emphasis in original).

Conclusion

It takes many words to describe God's *chesed,* as Psalm 136 makes clear. But God's *chesed* is captured best in a person, the Word (John 1:1), the Lord Jesus Christ. Scripture ascribes to him absolute lordship (Phil 2:9-11; Rev 19:16). It tells us he is the Creator (John 1; Col 1; Heb 1), the Redeemer (Rom 3; Rev 5), and the Sustainer of the whole creation

(Col 1). It all flows fully and freely from the One who in his being and essence is love (1 John 4:8,16). To such a God, we ought to give thanks. Such a Savior we ought to worship now and forever. After all, his faithful, steadfast, enduring, never-ending love is forever!

Reflect and Discuss

1. How is God's love different from the ways we love? What are some ways you are able to emulate God's love to others?
2. Which of the three reasons for praising the Lord (who he is, what he has done, and where he is) do you praise him for most often? Which do you praise him for the least? In what ways does each reason uniquely inspire you to praise God?
3. The psalmist praises God because he is good and because he is sovereign. What would be different if God was only good but not sovereign? What if he was only sovereign but not good?
4. In what ways does God's character (his goodness and sovereignty) affect how he acts? What has God done in your life that reveals parts of his character?
5. How can God's identity as the Creator give you hope during difficulty?
6. Describe a time when God rescued you from a difficult situation. Do you regularly take time to remember and praise God for his past work? How might this practice help you in future difficult situations?
7. In what ways can thankfulness and praise help you combat fear and complaining?
8. What does God's position in heaven teach us? How would failing to remember God's position affect you?
9. Why do you think the psalmist praises God for giving food to every creature? How does this action relate to Israel's salvation in the exodus?
10. How does the New Testament describe God's love? Is God's love in the New Testament similar to or different from God's love in the Old Testament?

Down but Not Out!

PSALM 137

Main Idea: During loss God's people should lament over sin and destruction then hope in God's justice.

I. **A Time for the Lord's People to Mourn (137:1-4)**
   A. We mourn when we experience loss (137:1).
   B. We mourn when taunted by the wicked (137:2-4).
II. **A Time for the Lord's People to Renew Their Faith in God (137:5-6)**
   A. Remember what God has done (137:5).
   B. Rejoice in where God dwells (137:6).
III. **A Time for the Lord's People to Commit Final Judgment to God (137:7-9)**
   A. Commit to God those who want your total destruction (137:7).
   B. Commit to God those who have treated you with great evil (137:8-9).

Psalm 137:9 is one of the most difficult verses in the whole Bible to read and understand. It sounds so unchristian and foreign to the spirit of Jesus, who told us to love our enemies and pray for them (Matt 5:44). And yet there it is, plain as day: "Happy is he who takes your little ones and dashes them against the rocks." What are we supposed to do with this verse? How do we make sense of it?

In a psalm composed of lament (vv. 1-4) and commitment (vv. 5-6), Psalm 137 ends in what is called a psalm (or at least a stanza) of imprecation (vv. 7-9). Psalms in which God's people call on God to bring devastating judgment on their enemies are not rare. Pastor Sam Storms lists the following that could legitimately fall under the category of "imprecatory psalms": Pss 5:10; 6:10; 7:6; 9:19-20; 10:2,15; 17:13; 28:4; 31:17-18; 35:1,4-8,19,24-26; 40:14-15; 41:10; 54:5; 55:9,15; 56:7; 58:6-10; 59:5,11-14; 63:9-10; 68:1-2; 69:22-28; 70:2-3; 71:13; 79:6,10-12; 83:9-18 (cf. Judg 4:15-21; 5:25-27); 94:1-4; 97:7; 104:35; 109:6-19,29; 119:84; 129:5-7; 137:7-9; 139:19-22; 140:8-11; 141:10; 143:12 ("10 Things You Should Know about the Imprecatory Psalms"). Furthermore, we must recognize that words of imprecation are not found only in Old Testament Scripture. They also appear in texts like Luke 10:10-16; 1 Corinthians 16:21-22; Galatians 1:8; 5:12; 2 Thessalonians 1:6-10; 2 Timothy 4:14; and Revelation 6:10; 19:1-2. Even our Lord Jesus used imprecatory language in Matthew 23 (cf. his use of Ps 41:8-10 in Matt 26:23-24). And Peter cites the imprecations of Psalm 69 and 109 in reference to Judas in Acts 1:20 (Storms, "10 Things"). Keeping in mind that the psalms use poetic and emotive language expressing the heartfelt fervor of the writer offers some help, but more needs to be said to make sense of all of these words in light of our view of the Bible as inspired, inerrant, and infallible. Again, Sam Storms is helpful here. He gives 10 principles on imprecatory psalms:

> **1.** What we read in these OT Psalms are not emotionally uncontrolled outbursts by otherwise sane and compassionate people. . . . [They] are the product of reasoned meditation (not to mention divine inspiration!). . . .
>
> **2.** We should remember that in Deuteronomy 27–28 the Levites pronounce imprecations against Israel if she proves unfaithful to the covenant. Israel, in accepting the law, brought herself under its sanctions. She in essence pronounced curses upon herself should she break the covenant, and God looked on their response with favor. . . .
>
> **3.** These prayers are not expressions of personal vengeance. . . . There is a vast difference between *vindication* and *vindictiveness.* David's passion was for the triumph of divine justice, not the satisfaction of personal malice. The OT was as much opposed to seeking personal vengeance against one's personal enemies as is the NT (see Exod. 23:4-5; Lev. 19:17-18).
>
> **4.** We also must remember that *imprecations are nothing more than human prayers based on divine promises.* One is simply asking God to do what he has already said he will do. . . .
>
> **5.** Imprecations are expressions provoked by the horror of sin. [Writers] prayed this way because of [their] deep sensitivity to the ugliness of evil. . . . It is frightening to think that we can stand in the presence of evil and not be moved to pray as [authors of Scripture] did.
>
> **6.** The motivation behind such prayers is zeal for God's righteousness, God's honor, God's reputation, and the

triumph of God's kingdom. Is our willingness to ignore blasphemy and overlook evil due to a deficiency in our love for God and his name? . . .

7. Another factor to keep in mind is that David [in particular], being king, was God's representative on earth. Thus, an attack on David was, in effect, an attack on God. . . .

8. The prayers of imprecation are rarely, if ever, for the destruction of a specific individual but almost always of a class or group, namely, "the wicked" or "those who oppose [God]."

9. We must keep in mind that in most instances these prayers for divine judgment come only after extended efforts on the part of the psalmist to call the enemies of God to repentance. These are not cases of a momentary resistance to God but of unrepentant, recalcitrant, incessant, hardened and haughty defiance of him. . . .

10. David knows that he needs spiritual protection lest he "hate" God's enemies for personal reasons. That is why he concludes Psalm 139 with the prayer that God purify his motives and protect his heart. . . . Therefore, when David speaks of "hatred" for those who oppose God's kingdom he is neither malicious nor bitter nor vindictive, nor moved by self-centered resentment. But he most certainly is jealous for God's name and firmly at odds with those who blaspheme. (Storms, "10 Things"; emphasis in original)

As we already noted, Psalm 137 is a composite of lament (vv. 1-4), commitment (vv. 5-6), and imprecation (vv. 7-9). It also is one of the easiest psalms to date, being written during the Babylonian exile. Its history is far from us, but the expressions of pain and sorrow are as fresh and real as any today. There are three principles we can learn from our ancestors when agony and tragedy have virtually overwhelmed us.

A Time for The Lord's People to Mourn
PSALM 137:1-4

Judah had been invaded and conquered by Nebuchadnezzar and the Babylonians, finally falling in 586 BC. The city and temple were destroyed, and many of the brightest and best citizens were taken into exile to Babylon. Most of those exiled would never see their much-loved homeland again. Heartbreak and despair overwhelmed them like a flood. At such a time, mourning was an appropriate (and maybe the only) response.

We Mourn When We Experience Loss (137:1)

The psalmist is "by the rivers of Babylon," the Tigris and Euphrates. Walking or resting beside a river is usually relaxing and refreshing but not for this songwriter. Here he, along with others ("we"), "sat down and wept" when they "remembered Zion." Reflecting on what once was and now was lost, they cried in despair and sorrow. Thinking about Zion or Jerusalem (mentioned five times in the psalm), about home, brought these Hebrew exiles to tears and mourning. And it should. The sins of Judah against God and one another brought God's just judgment on his people. It hurt. The pain and sense of loss were almost unbearable. But if the discipline of the Lord brought them to repentance, it would be worth it. Hebrews 12:10 reminds us, "But [the Lord] disciplines us for our good, that we may share his holiness" (ESV).

We Mourn When Taunted by the Wicked (137:2-4)

These songwriters and singers continue their mourning and lament. They hang up their lyres, their harps, on the poplar trees (v. 2). There would be no singing today—maybe never again. But things become worse. Their captors, the Babylonians, begin to harass and taunt them. "Sing us a song," they say. With glee and sarcasm, they pour salt in their wounds and shout, "Sing us one of the songs of Zion!" (v. 3). Allen Ross pinpoints what was behind their mocking and lack of sincerity: "[They] were not interested in hearing their songs. They were simply mocking the Jews by demanding that they sing one of their victory songs. It is as if they were saying, 'Where is your God now?'" (*Psalms 90–150*, 790). These Jewish exiles are no doubt hurt and embarrassed by these taunts, but they will not be manipulated by their oppressors. "How can we sing the LORD's song on foreign soil?" (v. 4) means there will be no singing today by this choir. They were not there for the Babylonians' amusement and frivolity! They were there because they dishonored and disobeyed their Lord. Sinful people should not be singing a song of celebration and victory—maybe someday but not today. We rightly mourn over our sin, but our hope is still in the Lord as the following verses make clear.

A Time for the Lord's People to Renew Their Faith in God
PSALM 137:5-6

Despair need not lead to defeat. Being down does not mean you are out. Renewal, restoration, and reviving are always in the realm of possibility with our God. Remember what God has done in the past. He can do it again in the future. Just 70 years after the fall of Jerusalem in 586 BC, Babylon, the greatest empire the world had known up to that time, would fall (516 BC), never to rise again. The Jews, on the other hand, would begin to make their way back home to Jerusalem. We renew our faith today and watch our God begin to respond if not today, then tomorrow. What is essential to renewal? The psalm gives two instructions.

Remember What God Has Done (137:5)

Willem VanGemeren says 1 Kings 8:48-49 could have been in the minds of these exiles as they penned these words (*Psalms*, 951). That is certainly a possibility. In 1 Kings 8:46-53 we read words that are so appropriate to the Jews' plight in Babylon:

> *When they sin against you—for there is no one who does not sin—*
> *and you are angry with them and hand them over to the enemy, and*
> *their captors deport them to the enemy's country—whether distant or*
> *nearby—and when they come to their senses in the land where they were*
> *deported and repent and petition you in their captors' land: "We have*
> *sinned and done wrong; we have been wicked," and when they return*
> *to you with all their heart and all their soul in the land of their enemies*
> *who took them captive, and when they pray to you in the direction of*
> *their land that you gave their ancestors, the city you have chosen, and*
> *the temple I have built for your name, may you hear in heaven, your*
> *dwelling place, their prayer and petition and uphold their cause. May*
> *you forgive your people who sinned against you and all their rebellions*
> *against you, and may you grant them compassion before their captors,*
> *so that they may treat them compassionately. For they are your people*
> *and your inheritance; you brought them out of Egypt, out of the middle*
> *of an iron furnace. May your eyes be open to your servant's petition*
> *and to the petition of your people Israel, listening to them whenever they*
> *call to you. For you, Lord God, have set them apart as your inheritance*
> *from all peoples of the earth, as you spoke through your servant Moses*
> *when you brought our ancestors out of Egypt.*

These Hebrew exiles recommit themselves to God in striking and picturesque language. "Jerusalem" here is symbolic of Yahweh's gracious covenant with Israel and all the blessings and obligations included in the covenant. To "forget" Jerusalem is to renounce that relationship. Conversely, to "exalt" Jerusalem (v. 6) is to embrace it. If they forgot their home, their God, and all he gave them, then they pronounce this oath: "May [our] right hand forget its skill." "Let it become paralyzed and lose its usefulness" could be in the psalmist's mind. Or perhaps the idea is related to his skill in playing the harp (Broyles, *Psalms*, 479). In either case his affirmation is strong. Better to lose something physically valuable than to forget my God and his holy city Jerusalem. Exile will not result in spiritual amnesia! How interesting it is, in this context, that Psalm 137 is sandwiched between Psalms 136 and 138, psalms that praise God and recount his faithfulness.

Rejoice in Where God Dwells (137:6)

Verse 5 parallels verse 6 in thought. Forget God? Better to lose the use of our hands (v. 5) and our tongues (v. 6). Better to lose the skill to play the harp and to sing (things that would especially devastate a musician), "If I do not remember you, if I do not exalt Jerusalem as my greatest joy!" Charles Spurgeon writes, "The singers imprecate eternal silence upon their mouths if they forget Jerusalem to gratify Babylon" (*Treasury*, vol. 3a, 228). Today we might say, "I would rather lose an arm or a leg than walk away from my God. I would rather die than betray him. This world and this life are not 'my greatest joy.' God is. His kingdom is." Like father Abraham, we are "looking forward to the city that has foundations, whose architect and builder is God" (Heb 11:10). The Hebrews of old did not want to lose sight of old Jerusalem. Those in Christ do not want to lose sight of New Jerusalem (Rev 21–22). That is where our God will dwell for all eternity. This is where we should long to be.

A Time for the Lord's People to Commit
Final Judgment to God
PSALM 137:7-9

Verses 7-9 contain the imprecatory portion of this psalm. Two enemies of the people of God are in the crosshairs of the songwriter: the Edomites (v. 7) and the Babylonians (vv. 8-9). Both brought pain and sorrow to the Hebrews. Both dealt ruthlessly with Judah. God is both merciful and just. It is time for his justice.

Commit to God Those Who Want Your Total Destruction (137:7)

The psalmist asks God to remember "what the Edomites said that day at Jerusalem." Ross notes,

> According to the biblical records, the Edomites had sided with the Babylonians against Judah and had taken great pleasure in the destruction of Zion (see Obadiah, Lam. 4:21; and Ezek. 25:12f, 35:5f). They had shouted for the Babylonians to tear the city down to its foundations. (*Psalms 90–150*, 792)

We see this reflected in our text: "Destroy it! Destroy it down to its foundations!" They wanted the total destruction of Jerusalem: its physical, social, spiritual, and cultural foundations and all the city represents. The Edomites, descended from Jacob's twin brother Esau, were closely related to the Jews, which only accentuated the Edomites' treachery. The exiled Jews want justice, but they will leave that in the hands of the Lord.

Commit to God Those Who Have Treated You with Great Evil (137:8-9)

The psalmist now turns his attention to "Daughter Babylon." No one had ever, to that point in history, treated Israel with such destruction and slaughter. But they, just like Judah and Israel, would have their day of judgment (e.g., Isa 13:16; Hab 1). They are "doomed to destruction" according to the word of the Lord. "Happy [or "blessed"] is the one who pays you back what you have done to us" (ESV). "Happy [or "Blessed"] is he who takes your little ones and dashes them against the rocks." Strong language. Striking language. Startling language that challenges our modern sensibilities. Was this, in part, to prevent future retaliation? Was it some type of judgment that God would bring that matched what Babylon had done to Jerusalem? Those of us who have never experienced such pogroms and holocausts should not be too quick to judge the depth of feeling here. Like the writer of Psalm 137, we will commit the whole matter to God. This is not personal revenge. This is a national prayer for God to punish the heartless and ruthless enemies of God's people. We will trust Deuteronomy 32:35 and Romans 12:19. Vengeance belongs to the Lord. He will repay.

Conclusion

Babylon was such an evil and wicked empire it became symbolic of the godless kingdoms of this world that stand in unrepentant and steadfast opposition to God. Revelation 18–19 makes this clear. That is why when our gracious Savior, the Lord Jesus, comes again, he will bring this "notorious prostitute" to judgment and avenge "the blood of his servants that was on her hands" (Rev 19:2). And on that day, "her smoke [will ascend] forever and ever" as a sign of God's just and righteous judgment (Rev 19:3). Our Lord is a merciful Savior. He is also a righteous Judge. May we know him as the former.

Reflect and Discuss

1. Which of the 10 principles on imprecatory psalms was particularly helpful to you? Why?
2. What does the psalmist's imprecatory prayer reveal about his faith and belief in God?
3. Have you ever prayed an imprecatory prayer? Where do you think those around you need God's justice? How can you pray for those according to the principles in this psalm?
4. Is mourning discussed frequently in your context? Why do many Christians seek to avoid mourning? What do Christians lose if they neglect to mourn?
5. Is mourning a sign of unbelief? In what ways can mourning be an act of faith? How does one practically mourn in faith?
6. Does loss ever cause you to examine your own life for sin? Is this important to consider? Does tragedy mean that God is always disciplining us for sin?
7. What should Christians remember about God during their mourning?
8. What were the most helpful ways other Christians interacted with you during a time of mourning? What was unhelpful?
9. What must one believe about God and about oneself in order to commit to him people who have treated him or her unjustly?
10. How can one pray in a way that reflects both Psalm 137 and Matthew 5:44?

God Knows What He Is Doing— Beautifully Exemplified in the Life of Sarah Hall Boardman Judson

PSALM 138

Main Idea: We can give thanks to our great Lord because he knows the humble, will keep his promises, and will complete his purpose in our lives.

I. Thank God for Who He Is before the Nations (138:1-2).
II. Thank God That He Answers Prayer as We Witness (138:3).
III. Thank God That He Blesses the Humble but Rejects the Proud (138:4-6).
IV. Thank God That He Will Fulfill His Purpose in Your Life (138:7-8).

Sarah Hall Boardman Judson (1803–1845) was a remarkable Christian missionary who faithfully served King Jesus in Burma (modern Myanmar) for over 20 years. She married and buried one missionary husband (George Boardman) and then remarried and was buried by another (Adoniram Judson). Her life was a marvelous witness both to the grace of God and to the wisdom of God. Her life testifies that our God knows what he is doing even during the greatest difficulties and trials. Her life is also a beautiful commentary on a thanksgiving psalm of King David, Psalm 138, a psalm with messianic overtones (VanGemeren, *Psalms*, 955).

This psalm has four movements. It will be a journey of joy and sorrow to see the life of Sarah B. Judson reflected in its truth. Sarah's life was one of absolute confidence in a sovereign Savior, a confidence that enabled her to pen this hymn:

> Proclaim the lofty praise of Him who once was slain,
> But now is risen, through endless days, to live and reign.
> He lives and reigns on high, who bought us with His blood,
> Enthroned above the farthest sky, our Savior, God. (Burrage,
> *Baptist Hymn Writers and Their Hymns*, 302) [4]

---

[4] Concerning this hymn's origin, Burrage writes, "By Dr. Hatfield, the well known hymnologist, this hymn is ascribed to Mrs. Sarah B. Judson, but on what grounds I am not informed."

Thank God for Who He Is before the Nations

PSALM 138:1-2

David sounds the praise of thanksgiving from the beginning of this psalm: "I will give you thanks with all my heart." And where will David herald his thanksgiving? He says, "I will sing your praise before the heavenly beings." The meaning of this last phrase is not clear and is also translated as "before the gods" (so ESV) or "before judges" or "before kings" (see the translation note in the CSB). Allen Ross favors the translation "before the gods" and writes,

> Other passages in this part of the Psalter refer to pagan gods as well (Pss 95:3; 96:4-5; and 115:3-8). The psalmist praises the greatness and glory of Yahweh "in the face"—so to speak, of false gods. (*Psalms 90–150*, 804)

We prefer this understanding. Verse 2 expands the thought of verse 1, explaining just how David will testify and sing his thanksgiving of the Lord before these false gods. He will "bow down toward [God's] holy temple" (ESV) in Jerusalem. There he will "give thanks to [the LORD's] name for [his] constant love [Hb *chesed*] and truth [Hb *emeth*, ESV "faithfulness"]." And why will he bow down and sing of the Lord's love and truth, his "constant love and faithfulness"? Because "[the Lord has] exalted [his own] name and [his] promise above everything else." Commenting on this verse Charles Spurgeon writes,

> The name of the Lord in nature is not so easily read as in the Scriptures, which are a revelation in human language, specifically adapted to the human mind, treating of human need, and of a Saviour who appeared in human nature to redeem humanity. Heaven and earth shall pass away, but the divine word will not pass away, and in this respect especially it has a pre-eminence over every other form of manifestation. Moreover, the Lord lays all the rest of his name under tribute to his word: his wisdom, power, love, and all his other attributes combine to carry out his word. It is his word which creates, sustains, quickens, enlightens, and comforts. As a word of command it is supreme; and in the person of the incarnate Word it is set above all the works of God's hand. . . . Let us adore the Lord who has spoken to us by his word, and by his

Son; and in the presence of unbelievers let us both praise his holy name and extol his holy word. (*Treasury*, vol. 3a, 244–45)

If ever there was a follower of the Lord Jesus who praised the name of the Savior and extolled his gospel before the lost and their false gods, it was Sarah B. Judson. Sarah was born on November 4, 1803, in Alstead, New Hampshire. She was the oldest of 13 children in an extremely poor family. At 17, she professed faith in Christ and was baptized. She felt the call to missions immediately and wished "to follow in the footsteps of her heroine Ann Judson, who visited America in 1823" (Beck, "More Than Rubies"). In the book *Missionary Biography: The Memoir of Sarah B. Judson, Member of the American Mission to Burmah,* Emily Judson (who used the pen name Fanny Forester), and who was the third and last wife of Adoniram Judson, includes an entry from Sarah's journal written less than a month after her baptism. There Sarah writes,

> While I have this day had the privilege of worshipping the true God in solemnity, I have been pained by the thoughts of those who have never heard the sound of the gospel. When will the time come that the poor heathen, now bowing to idols, shall own the living and true God? Dear Saviour, haste to spread the knowledge of thy dying love to earth's remotest bounds! (Forester, *Missionary Biography*, 11).

Her passion for the lost would continue to grow. She became involved in tract distribution and established a prayer meeting. All but one who attended became Christians. However, her heart for the nations would not wane. In a letter to a dear friend, she would write,

> "It is my ardent desire . . . that the glorious work of reformation may extend till *every knee* shall bow to the living God. For this expected, this promised era, let us pray earnestly, unceasingly, and with faith. How can I be so inactive, when I know that thousands are perishing in this land of grace; and millions in other lands are at this very moment kneeling before senseless idols!"
> And in her journal—"Sinners perishing all around me, and I almost panting to tell the far *heathen* of Christ! Surely this is wrong. I will no longer indulge the vain foolish wish, but endeavor to be useful in the position where Providence has

placed me. I can *pray* for deluded idolaters, and for those who labor among them, and this is a privilege indeed." (Stuart, *Lives of the Three Mrs. Judsons*, 135; emphasis in original)

Sarah, however, could not shake loose her concern for the lost who were far away. Her heart for international missions would find a companion in a man named George Boardman. Moved by a poem he read on the death of a missionary named Colman, who died in Chittagong after only two years on the field, Boardman tracked down its author, who happened to be Sarah Hall. He proposed to her almost immediately, and she accepted. Initially, her friends and family discouraged her in this action, with her parents withholding their consent. Eventually, however, they gave their permission. George and Sarah wed on July 4, 1825. They would leave for Burma the same month, and the voyage would take 127 days. The moving scene of their departure, for the trip from which they would never return, is one of the most heart-wrenching in all missionary lore:

We recollect that when she left her paternal home, to reach the ship which was to convey her "over the dark and distant sea," after she had taken her seat in the stage coach with her chosen companion . . . and had bestowed her last farewell upon the family group—as though she felt that she had not obtained that free and full consent to her abandonment of home and country which her filial heart craved, she looked out at the coach window and said, "Father, are you willing? Say, father, that you are willing I should go." "Yes, my child, I am willing." "Now I can go joyfully!" was the emphatic response; and the noble wanderer went on her way with cheerful composure.

Of this scene [Sarah] writes to her husband's parents, "My mother embraced me as tenderly, when she whispered, 'Sarah, I hope I am willing,' as she did one month before, when she wildly said, 'Oh! I cannot part with you!'" (Forester, *Missionary Biography*, 24–25)

Fanny then adds to this sorrowful scene:

And so the fond child's heart was made glad even in the moment of its agony; for something of the previous reluctance of the sorrow-stricken parents to resign their treasure may be gathered from such pleadings as these [from Sarah].

"Let us, my dear parents, go to Calvary; let us behold for a few moments, the meek, the holy Lamb of God, bleeding for our transgressions. Then let us inquire, 'Shall I withhold from this Saviour any object, however dear to my heart? Shall I be unwilling to suffer a few short years of toil and privation for his sake?' Let us call to remembrance those days of darkness through which we passed before Jesus lifted upon us the light of his countenance. We have, I trust, each of us, seen our lost and ruined condition by nature, have seen ourselves exposed to the righteous indignation of our Creator, have felt ourselves sinking into endless despair and ruin, and all this is merited. But oh, amazing love! at that desperate moment the Saviour smiled upon us. He opened his arms of compassion, all polluted as we were with iniquity, he received us, forgave our sins, and bade us hope for joy unutterable beyond the grave. Did we not, then, surrender *all* into his hand? Was not this the language of our hearts,

'Had I a thousand lives to give,
    A thousand lives should all be thine!'

And has not the precious Redeemer as strong claims upon us now as he had then?" (Forester, *Missionary Biography*, 25–26; emphasis in original)

May we, like David and like Sarah, thank God and proclaim his love and faithfulness before the nations and their false gods so that they too may worship and sing praises to our Lord!

Thank God That He Answers Prayers as We Witness
PSALM 138:3

Verse 3 naturally flows out of verses 1-2. David praised and thanked God for his constant love and faithfulness because, at an unspecified time when David sought the Lord, the Lord answered. Furthermore, the answer "increased strength within [him]." Alec Motyer words this verse as, "You invigorate me with strength in my soul" (*Psalms by the Day*, 396). The Lord gave David spiritual strength, courage, and boldness as he rejoiced in the Lord before pagan gods and their idolatrous followers. This type of work is certainly something God did for Sarah Boardman Judson.

Unsurprisingly, Sarah would experience many hardships on the mission field. More than once she nearly died from severe sickness. Giving birth to three children during her marriage to George, Sarah saw only one (George Jr.) survive infancy. On more than one occasion, her life was put in danger by robbery of her home, riots, and rebellions. Indeed, she was warned by an English general of "lawless men and the wild beasts of the jungle" in Burma (Forester, *Missionary Biography*, 44). Yet in her journal Sarah would write,

> We trembled when we thought of the disturbances in Burmah, and there was only one spot where we could find peace and serenity of mind. That sweet spot was the throne of grace. [There] we would often [go] and lose all anxiety and fear respecting our dear friends, our own future prospects, and the Missionary cause in Burmah. It was sweet to commit all into the hands of God. . . . We considered it our duty to supplicate for grace to support us in the hour of trial, and for direction in time of perplexity. (Stuart, *Lives of the Three Mrs. Judsons*, 147)

And after the robbery in their home while they lay in bed at night, Sarah would recount the kind provision and protection of God in their lives:

> I saw the assassins with their horrid weapons standing by our bedside, ready to do their worst had we been permitted to wake. Oh how merciful was that watchful Providence which prolonged those powerful slumbers of that night, not allowing even the infant at my bosom to open its eyes at so critical a moment. If ever gratitude glowed in my bosom, if ever the world appeared to me worthless as vanity, and if ever I wished to dedicate myself, my husband, my babe, my *all*, to our great Redeemer, it was at that time. . . .
>
> Yes, my beloved friend, I think I can say, that notwithstanding our alarms, never did five months of my life pass as pleasantly as the last five have done. The thought of being among this people whom we have so long desired to see, and the hope that God would enable me to do some little good to the poor heathen, has rejoiced and encouraged my

heart. I confess that once or twice my natural timidity has *for a moment* gained ascendancy over my better feelings. . . . But these fears have been transitory, and we have generally been enabled to place our confidence in the Great Shepherd of Israel who never slumbers or sleeps, assured that he would protect us. . . .

And we have also felt a sweet composure in the reflection that God has marked out our way; and if it best accord with his designs that we fall prey to these blood-thirsty monsters, *all will be right.* (Stuart, *Lives of the Three Mrs. Judsons,* 154; emphasis in original)

Thank God That He Blesses the Humble but Rejects the Proud
PSALM 138:4-6

Verses 4-6 contain what Allen Ross calls "a prophecy concerning the nations" (*Psalms 90–150,* 806). I call it a missionary promise! All the nations, represented by their kings, "will give you thanks, LORD, when they hear what you have promised" (v. 4; see also Pss 68:29-32; 72:10-11; 102:15-16). This language anticipates and echoes Isaiah 52:15 and the great Suffering Servant song (Isa 52:13–53:12). When the kings of the earth hear of the great salvation of God on their behalf through his Servant, "they will sing of the LORD's ways," joyfully acknowledging that "the LORD's glory is great" (v. 5). Here are salvation and adoration beautifully woven together.

The glory of the Lord is further made known when you consider that "though [he] is exalted, he takes note of the humble" (v. 6; cf. Phil 2:9-11). The Lord sees the down and out, the nobodies of this world, and they become the objects of his saving goodness and grace. In contrast, "he knows the haughty from a distance." God *is* great, and the arrogant only *think* they are great. The humble he knows lovingly and intimately. The arrogant, the prideful, and the self-righteous he keeps at arm's length. "A glance from afar," says Spurgeon, "reveals to him their emptiness and offensiveness . . . he has no respect unto them, but utterly abhors them" (*Treasury,* vol. 3a, 246).

The Burmese, awash in pagan religions, were proud and self-righteous. It would take a patient, steady stream of gospel truth to break through this barrier. God sent the Judsons and Boardmans to do just that. God brought a notorious criminal and murderer among the Karen people—it is reported he was involved in more than 30 murders—Ko Thah-Byoo to faith in Jesus. George Boardman would baptize him, and Ko Thah-Byoo would become a famous and successful evangelist among the Karen people. The gospel began to go forth in great power. It appears God had prepared the Karen for the day of their salvation. In their tradition, "they believe in a God who is denominated Yu-wah" (Stuart, *Lives of the Three Mrs. Judsons,* 160). Though they recognized that their wickedness had separated them from this God, they believed "God will again have mercy upon us, God will save us again" (ibid.). When would that day come? In one of their traditional songs, we read this verse: "When the Karen King arrives, / Everything will be happy; / When Karens have a king, / Wild beasts will lose their savageness" (ibid.). Reflecting on the grace of God among the Karen but recognizing there was still much work to be done, Sarah would write to a beloved sister in 1828:

> We have to suffer many little inconveniences in this country;
> but have no disposition to complain. We rejoice in the
> kind providence that has directed our steps, and would not
> exchange our condition. Our desire is to labor among the
> poor heathen until called to our eternal home. (Ibid., 163)

God would indeed answer this desire of Sarah's heart. Both George and she would die on the mission field, never having returned to America. Thank God he blesses humble servants.

Thank God That He Will Fulfill His Purpose in Your Life
PSALM 138:7-8

This psalm concludes with a powerful confession of confidence in the providence, protection, and grace of a sovereign God. Five affirmations are made concerning the God who is with us. "If I walk into the thick of danger" (v. 7), God will "not abandon the work of [his] hands" (v. 8). What does David declare in terms of his confidence in the Lord?

> *You will preserve my life from the anger of my enemies.*
> *You will extend your hand* [i.e., your power and strength]*;*
> *your right hand will save me.*
> *The Lord will fulfill his purpose for me.*
> *Lord, your faithful love endures forever.*

These faithful promises apply so appropriately and beautifully to the life of Sarah Boardman Judson. God would spare her life on more than one occasion from serious illness. He would sustain her heart upon the death of her little daughter Sarah on July 8, 1829—she was two years and eight months old. And he would preserve her as she watched her husband slowly descend into death from tuberculosis. Of this time she would write to her mother,

> Oh, my dear mother, it would distress you to see how emaciated he is!—and so weak, that he is scare able to move. God is calling to me in a most impressive manner to set my heart on heavenly things. Two lovely infants already in the world of bliss—my beloved husband suffering under a disease which will most assuredly take him from me—my own health poor, and little Georgie [their son] often ill. (Forester, *Missionary Biography*, 82–83)

George Boardman would die on February 11, 1831, at the age of 30. Of her first husband Sarah said,

> He exhibited a tenderness of spirit, a holy sensibility, such as I never witnessed before. He seemed to see the goodness of God in everything. He would weep while conversing on the love of Jesus; and words cannot describe to you the depth of feeling with which he spoke of his own unworthiness. (Stuart, *Lives of the Three Mrs. Judsons*, 86)

As he neared death, he said this:

> You know, Sarah, that coming on a foreign mission involves the probability of a shorter life than staying in one's native country. And yet obedience to our Lord, and compassion for the perishing heathen, induced us to make this sacrifice. And have we ever repented that we came? No; I trust we can both say that we bless God for bringing us to Burmah, for directing our footsteps to Tavoy, and even for leading us hither. (Forester, *Missionary Biography*, 90)

After George's death, Sarah at first considered returning to America with her young son, but her love for the Burmese compelled her to stay. She wrote,

When I first stood by the grave of my husband, I thought I
must go home with George. But these poor, inquiring, and
Christian Karens, and the school-boys, and the Burmese
Christians, would then be left without any one to instruct
them; and the poor, [ignorant] Tavoyans would go on in the
road to death, with no one to warn them of their danger. How
then, oh, how can I go? We shall not be separated long. A few
more years, and we shall all meet in yonder blissful world,
whither those we love have gone before us. I feel thankful that
I was allowed to come to this heathen land. Oh, it is a precious
privilege to tell idolaters of the Gospel; and when we see them
disposed to love the Saviour, we forget all our privations and
dangers. My beloved husband wore out his life in this glorious
cause; and that remembrance makes me more than ever
attached to the work, and the people for whose salvation he
laboured till death. (Forester, *Missionary Biography*, 106–7)

Three years after her husband's death, Sarah Boardman would
marry Adoniram Judson. She had not returned home to America as
many friends counseled her to do. However, she would, with a broken
heart, eventually send her young son George back to America because
of health concerns. He would become the much-respected pastor of
First Baptist Church, Philadelphia (1864–1894), and a well-known oppo-
nent of slavery. Sarah would remain in Burma, continuing the work,
making evangelistic tours, preaching the gospel to men and women
when no qualified man was available, and supervising the numerous
schools she helped establish. She would translate *The Pilgrim's Progress*
into Burmese. She would translate tracts, including the tract "Life of
Christ" that her husband Adoniram wrote, and the New Testament into
Peguan. Concerning her preaching to both men and women, a point
of controversy in her day and ours, her biographer Fanny Forester puts
things in their proper perspective:

But now she sat in the zayat, which had been erected for
her husband, at the foot of the mountain, and in others,
wherever a little company of worshippers could be collected,
and performed even weightier offices than those of Miriam
and Anna . . . but meek, and sometimes tearful, speaking in
low, gentle ascents, and with a manner sweetly persuasive.
In several instances she thus conducted the worship of

two or three hundred Karens, through the medium of her Burmese interpreter; and such was her modest manner of accomplishing the unusual task, that even the most fastidious were pleased; and a high officer of the English Church, which is well-known to take strict cognizance of irregularities, saw fit to bestow upon her unqualified praise. These acts, however, were not in accordance with her feminine taste or her sense of propriety. The duty, which called her to them, was fashioned by peculiar circumstance; and, as soon as opportunity offered, she gladly relinquished the task in favour of a person better suited to its performance. (Forester, *Missionary Biography*, 122)

Conclusion

Sarah Boardman Judson would be married to missionary Adoniram Judson for 11 years. She would love him and labor alongside him faithfully as she had her first husband George. She would have eight children with him. Five would survive into adulthood (Pierard, "The Man Who Gave the Bible to the Burmese"). Her obituary faithfully captures Judson's loving opinion of his second wife:

The Memoir of his first beloved wife [Ann] has been long before the public. It is, therefore, most gratifying to his feelings to be able to say in truth, that the subject of this notice was, in every point of natural and moral excellence, the worthy successor of Ann H. Judson. He constantly thanks God that he has been blest with two of the best of wives; he deeply feels that he has not improved those rich blessings as he ought; and it is most painful to reflect, that from the peculiar pressure of the missionary life, he has sometimes failed to treat those dear beings with that consideration, attention, and kindness, which their situation in a foreign heathen land ever demanded. (Forester, *Missionary Biography*, 174–75)

Sarah became deathly ill, and her plan was to go home to America with the hope she might recover. It was not to be. Adoniram, Sarah, and three of their small children set sail. Although she briefly rebounded, she lapsed in health once again, and it was obvious she would soon die. Sarah went to be with the Savior she so dearly adored and loved at St.

Helena in the South Atlantic on September 1, 1845. She was not quite
42 years old. Biographer Fanny Forester records the final words shared
between Adoniram and Sarah:

> A few days before her death, [Adoniram], called her children
> to her bedside, and said, in their hearing, "I wish, my love,
> to ask pardon for every unkind word or deed of which I have
> ever been guilty. I feel that I have, in many instances, failed of
> treating you with that kindness and affection which you have
> ever deserved." "Oh!" said she, "you will kill me if you talk so. It
> is I that should ask pardon of you; and I only want to get well,
> that I may have an opportunity of making some return for all
> your kindness, and of showing you how much I love you."
>
> This recollection of her dying bed leads me to say a few
> words relative to the closing scenes of her life. . . . Her hope
> had long been fixed on the Rock of Ages, and she had been
> in the habit of contemplating death as neither distant nor
> undesirable. As it drew near, she remained perfectly tranquil.
> No shade of doubt, or fear, or anxiety, ever passed over her
> mind. She had a prevailing preference to depart, and be
> with Christ. "I am longing to depart," and "what can I want
> besides?" (Forester, *Missionary Biography*, 175–76)

A few days later the time of her departure to go be with Jesus
arrived. Her husband provides the details of their joyful and sorrowful
separation:

> At two o'clock in the morning, wishing to obtain one more
> token of recognition, I roused her attention, and said, "Do
> you still love the Saviour?" "Oh, yes," she replied, "I ever love
> the Lord Jesus Christ." I said again, "Do you still love me?" She
> replied in the affirmative, by a peculiar expression of her own.
> "Then give me one more kiss," and we exchanged that token
> of love for the last time. Another hour passed,—life continued
> to recede,—and she ceased to breathe. For a moment I traced
> her upward flight, and thought of the wonders which were
> opening to her view. I then closed her sightless eyes, dressed
> her, for the last time, in the drapery of death, and being quite
> exhausted with many sleepless nights, I threw myself down
> and slept. On awaking in the morning, I saw the children

standing and weeping around the body of their dear mother.
(Ibid., 177)

Sarah would be buried in St. Helena next to another missionary from
Ceylon, a Mrs. Chater.

We would be remiss if we did not note that Sarah was an accomplished poet. Thinking in her last days that she might yet cheat death
again, it was determined that she would proceed to America with
the children and her husband would return to the work in Burma.
Contemplating their forthcoming years of separation, perhaps their
permanent separation in this life, she wrote the last words she would
ever pen to her husband on a scrap of broken paper. Thankfully, they
survived and have become famous in the history of missions.

The Parting

We part on this green islet, love,—
    Thou for the eastern main,
I for the setting sun, love—
    Oh, when to meet again!

My heart is sad for thee, love,
    For lone thy way will be;
And oft thy tears will fall, love,
    For thy children and for me.

The music of thy daughter's voice
    Thou'lt miss for many a year,
And the merry shout of thine elder boys
    Thou'lt list in vain to hear.

When we knelt to see our Henry die,
    And heard his last faint moan,
Each wiped the tear from other's eye—
    Now each must weep alone.

My tears fall fast for thee, love,
    How can I say farewell!
But go, thy God be with thee, love,
    Thy heart's deep grief to quell.

Yet my spirit clings to thine, love,
    Thy soul remains with me,

And oft we'll hold communion sweet,
  O'er the dark and distant sea.

And who can paint our mutual joy,
  When, all our wanderings o'er,
We both shall clasp our infants three,
  At home, on Burmah's shore.

But higher shall our raptures glow,
  On yon celestial plain,
When the loved and parted here below
  Meet, ne'er to part again.

Then gird thine armor on, love,
  Nor faint thou by the way—
Till the Boodh shall fall, and Burmah's sons
  Shall own Messiah's sway. (*Judson Offering*, 213–14)

Forester records this word about Sarah's poem: "'In all the missionary annals,' says the editor of the 'New York Evangelist,' 'there are few things more affecting than this'" (*Missionary Biography*, 169–70).

Success in missions is defined by faithfulness, not numbers. But the faithfulness of Sarah Broadman Judson did result in much fruit. Today there are over two and a half million Protestant Christians in Myanmar (Burma); there are almost five thousand churches in Myanmar; and Myanmar holds one of the world's largest Baptist communities in the world (*Myanmar [Burma] Joshua Project*; Barrett, "Baptist Church Restoration a Mixed Blessing for Myanmar"). Yes, our God knows what he is doing!

Reflect and Discuss

1. What is the Christian's primary motivation for missions? What motivated Sarah to give her life as a missionary?
2. How can knowing the lives of missionaries like Sarah help you follow Christ?
3. What about Sarah's life encouraged or challenged you? Why?
4. What is different about Sarah's life as a missionary from what would be true of a missionary life today? What access do you have to the nations that was not true during Sarah's time?
5. Should danger ever deter Christians from serving where God calls them? What hope do Christians have that can give boldness in the face of danger?

6. Explain verse 6 in your own words. In what ways is God great that makes it unexpected that he takes note of the humble?
7. Did God fail to keep the promises of Psalm 138 to Sarah? What Scripture can you use to answer this?
8. What was Sarah's view of the tragedy and difficulty she faced while a missionary? What contributed to the view she had?
9. Why should the gospel motivate all Christians to participate in missions? What are the various roles in Christian missions?
10. What is your local church doing to reach the nations? Have you prayed that God would use you to reach the nations? If so, what role will you play?

You Are Fearfully and Wonderfully Made

PSALM 139

Main Idea: God is the all-knowing, always-present Creator who will judge both the righteous and the wicked.

I. God Knows Everything (139:1-6).
- A. He knows my heart (139:1).
- B. He knows my actions (139:2-3).
- C. He knows my words (139:4).
- D. He knows my life (139:5-6).

II. God Is Everywhere (139:7-12).
- A. God is with me above or below (139:7-8).
- B. God is with me in the east or the west (139:9-10).
- C. God is with me in the dark or the light (139:11-12).

III. God Can Do Anything (139:13-18).
- A. The Lord formed my body (139:13-15).
- B. The Lord foreordained my life (139:16-18).

IV. God Will Deal with Everyone (139:19-24).
- A. God will deal with the wicked who hate him (139:19-22).
- B. God will lead the humble who trust him (139:23-24).

Whenever I (Danny) teach Bible interpretation, I always encourage my students to ask two particularly important questions of the passage they are studying: (1) What does this text teach us about God? (2) What does this text teach us about humanity? If we ask those two questions about Psalm 139, the simple answer is, "A lot!" The sixteenth-century Reformer John Calvin (1509–1564) understood this truth; he began his classic *Institutes of the Christian Religion* by saying, "Our wisdom, insofar as it ought to be deemed true and solid wisdom, consists almost entirely of two parts: the knowledge of God and of ourselves" (*Institutes*, 1960, 4). Psalm 139 provides for us this true and solid wisdom. This psalm sings the truth of Hebrews 4:13: "Nothing in all creation is hidden from God's sight. Everything is uncovered and laid bare before the eyes of him to whom we must give account" (NIV).

Psalm 139 includes diverse genres, including praise, thanksgiving, lament, confession, meditation, and prayer. It has the characteristics of both a didactic psalm (how to teach) and a wisdom psalm (how to live). It teaches us how to think wisely about our God, ourselves, and our lives. The psalm divides into four stanzas of six verses each in our English text. Some form of the word *know* dominates the whole passage, occurring seven times (vv. 1,2,4,6,14,23). King David, who penned this psalm, boldly and joyfully declares that God knows everything (vv. 1-6), that God is everywhere (vv. 7-12), that God can do anything (vv. 13-18), and that God will deal with everyone (vv. 19-24).

David knew, as we must know, that wrong ideas about God will inevitably lead to wrong ideas about ourselves. Wrong thinking can tragically lead to wrong decisions, leading to the wrong path, resulting in the wrong eternal destiny. This psalm, then, has a lot to teach us. It has a lot to say about the greatness of our God. It also has a lot to say about the importance and sanctity of every human life from the moment of conception to the moment of death. As Hassell Bullock well says, "Psalm 139 puts God's claim on every nook and cranny of the universe" (*Psalms*, 511).

God Knows Everything
PSALM 139:1-6

The Bible teaches that the one true God is an "omni God." He is omniscient (he knows everything), he is omnipresent (he is everywhere), and he is omnipotent (he can do anything). David applies these wonderful truths specifically to himself. The pronouns "I" and "me" occur almost 50 times. Stanza one begins with the theme of God's omniscience. Simply put, God knows everything about you. Some form of the word *know* occurs four times in verses 1-6. What is it that God knows?

He Knows My Heart (139:1)

David begins by noting that the covenant Lord (Yahweh) has an intimate and personal knowledge of him. He has "searched me and known me." The Lord's knowledge of us is penetrating and precise. Our hearts and souls are laid bare before the Lord's X-ray vision of who we truly are. Charles Spurgeon writes, "The Lord knows us thoroughly as if he had examined us minutely, and had pried into the secret corners of our being" (*Treasury*, vol. 3b, 258). He then adds, "This infallible knowledge has always existed" (ibid.). The Lord has always known everything about me and you.

He Knows My Actions (139:2-3)

God knows your character (v. 1). He also knows your conduct and actions. The Lord knows when you sit down and stand up. He knows you outside and inside ("You understand my thoughts from far away"). Distance is no hindrance or problem for our God (v. 2). Verse 3 reinforces the idea of verse 2. God knows where you go ("my travels") and when you lie down ("my rest"). Indeed, he is "aware of all [our] ways." In the daytime or nighttime, all that we do is before his ever-watching eyes.

He Knows My Words (139:4)

God knows all our conversations. Even before we say a single word, we can say with the psalmist, "You know all about it, LORD." We may, in an unguarded moment, blurt out something foolish. We may say something we did not think we would say. But God was not surprised. He saw it coming. Even before you formed the word on your tongue, God already knew exactly what you would say.

He Knows My Life (139:5-6)

These verses form a fitting conclusion to the first stanza. God knows the entire course of our lives. He has you surrounded, "encircled" (CSB), hemmed in (ESV). You cannot escape his knowledge of you (vv. 1-6), nor can you escape his presence (vv. 7-12). The Lord has placed his sovereign, providential hand on each and every one of us (v. 5).

God's omniscience overwhelms King David (v. 6). It is more than he can handle. This knowledge of an omniscient God is too wonderful and too high. It is "full of wonder, surpassing, extra-ordinary . . . incomprehensible" (Ross, *Psalms 90–150*, 822). It scares him. And it amazes him. It is not human; therefore, it is unattainable. It is otherworldly. In A. W. Tozer's classic book, *The Knowledge of the Holy*, he helps us understand what David is saying:

> To say that God is omniscient is to say that He possesses perfect knowledge and therefore has no need to learn. But it is more: it is to say that God has never learned and cannot learn.

The Scriptures teach that God has never learned from anyone. . . . From there it is only a step to the conclusion that God cannot learn. Could God at any time or in any manner receive into His mind knowledge that He did not possess and had not possessed from eternity, He would be imperfect and less than Himself. To think of a God who must sit at the feet of a teacher, even though that teacher be an archangel or seraph, is to think of someone other than the Most High God, maker of heaven and earth. . . .

God perfectly knows Himself and, being the source and author of all things, it follows that He knows all that can be known. And this He knows instantly and with a fullness of perfection that includes every possible item of knowledge concerning everything that exists or could have existed anywhere in the universe at any time in the past or that may exist in the centuries or ages yet unborn.

God knows instantly and effortlessly all matter and all matters, all mind and every mind, all spirit and all spirits, all being and every being, all creaturehood and all creatures, every plurality and all pluralities, all law and every law, all relations, all causes, all thoughts, all mysteries, all enigmas, all feeling, all desires, every unuttered secret, all thrones and dominions, all personalities, all things visible and invisible in heaven and earth, motion, space, time, life, death, good, evil, heaven, and hell.

Because God knows all things perfectly, He knows no thing better than any other thing, but all things equally well. He never discovers anything. He is never surprised, never amazed. He never wonders about anything nor (except when drawing men out for their own good) does He seek information or ask questions. (*A. W. Tozer: Three Spiritual Classics in One Volume*, 99–102)

God Is Everywhere
PSALM 139:7-12

Stanza one (vv. 1-6) focused on God's omniscience. Stanza two (vv. 7-12) focuses on God's omnipresence. When I (Danny) was a little boy, I went off with some older boys down by a creek without my mother's knowledge. As we were returning home, we met a search party of men looking for me! When I returned home, I found an angry, hysterical mother who quickly informed me of her unhappiness in up-close and personal terms to my backside. Later I went into my bedroom, got in bed, and hid under the covers because I was heartbroken over her displeasure and the spanking. I did not realize I had done anything wrong. However, I soon discovered I could not hide from my mom under the covers. Trying to hide from God would also be like trying to hide under the covers. Has it ever occurred to you that God never goes anywhere? He is already there! He is simply inescapable. He is everywhere, even under the covers.

God Is with Me Above or Below (139:7-8)

Verse 7 uses two rhetorical questions that anticipate a clear answer. They are a beautiful example of Hebrew parallelism because the two questions complement each other. "Where can I go to escape your Spirit?" Answer: nowhere! "Where can I flee from your presence?" Same answer: nowhere! "If I go up to heaven, you are there; if I make my bed in Sheol [the grave, the place of the dead], you are there" (v. 8). God is up and down and everywhere in between. God comprehends space!

God Is with Me in the East or the West (139:9-10)

God comprehends time. The ESV and CSB contain the same message, but their wording differs slightly:

> *If I take the wings of the morning and dwell in the uttermost parts of the sea* (ESV)

> *If I fly on the wings of the dawn and settle down on the western horizon* (CSB)

A literal translation would be "I take up the wings of the dawn; I dwell at the end of the sea." The word *dawn* implies "east," since the sun rises in the east. Since the Mediterranean Sea formed the western border of Israel, the word *sea* was used for "west." The idea is that if we go east or west, then "even there [God's] hand will lead me; [his] right hand will hold on to me." It also means that from morning to evening, from dawn to dusk, the Lord will direct us ("lead me") and protect us ("hold on to me"). We cannot escape his presence, and we cannot outrun it. No matter how far we go and no matter how fast we run, he is already there!

God Is with Me in the Dark or the Light (139:11-12)

The Lord comprehends space and time. He also comprehends light. David contemplates hiding from God in the dark at night (v. 11). What a foolish thought! Darkness is not dark to the God who sees everywhere and everything. For God, "night shines like the day; darkness and light are alike" (v. 12). Turn off the lights. Pull the drapes. Close the blinds. Retreat to your closet. You may hide from man, but you cannot hide from God. Just ask Adam and Eve. Just ask Jonah. C. S. Lewis is spot on: "We may ignore, but we can nowhere evade, the presence of God. The world is crowded with Him. He walks everywhere incognito" (*Letters to Malcolm*, 101).

God Can Do Anything
PSALM 139:13-18

Omniscience and omnipresence are wed to omnipotence in stanza three in the most intimate and personal way: our development in the wombs of our mothers. These verses give a biblical perspective on the tragedy of abortion. Life is sacred from the moment of conception to our final breath. God is pro-life.

Jeremiah 1:4-5 says, "The word of the LORD came to me: I chose you before I formed you in the womb." God saw us and loved us before he made us and as he made us. Omnipotence knits us together in the dark and secret place of our mothers' wombs. Before our mothers knew they were pregnant, the Lord was busy shaping and forming us in their wombs. He was already laying out the particulars of our lives. David wants each one of us to know that God cares about our beginning (vv. 13-15) and that he cares about our future (vv. 16-18). Ross is exactly right: "The third strophe of the psalm explains the first two: God knows everything about us and is always present with us because he made us" (*Psalms 90–150*, 826).

The Lord Formed My Body (139:13-15)

The word "for" connects stanza three with stanzas one and two. The Lord has "created" us. The word *you* is emphatic. He and no other created us, even our inward or inmost parts (lit. "kidneys"). All that we are inwardly, body and soul, he made.

God was involved in the intricate details of our conceptions and development. As a skilled craftsman would knit a piece of cloth or weave a beautiful basket, God made us with such focused care. James Merritt helps put in perspective how intricate and detailed God's creation is:

A single thread of DNA from one human cell contains information equivalent to a library of 1,000 volumes or 600,000 printed pages with 500 words on every page. At conception, one embryo has the equivalent of 50 times the amount of information contained in the entire Encyclopedia Britannica. ("The Mystery of Creation")

David rightly marvels over the mysterious process of a baby developing inside his or her mother. He can only break out in praise, knowing we are "remarkably and wondrously made" (v. 14). He is awestruck with wonder, amazement, and reverence at God's magnificent creation. David stands amazed in his presence, and so should we! He sees the works of this great Creator God as marvelous, "wondrous." He affirms, "I know this very well" (v. 14). He has no doubts about either the greatness of the Creator of the universe or the value of the tiny creation in the mother's womb. There is human life in that womb, put there and knit together by God.

God's omniscience makes another appearance in verses 15-16. David says, "My bones were not hidden from you when I was made in secret." The Lord sees everything, and he knows everything. He saw David growing and developing inside his mother. In the secret, hidden place within his mother, he was skillfully wrought (ESV, "intricately woven"). *The Message* has this: "You know exactly how I was made, bit by bit, how I was sculpted from nothing into something." Chip McDaniel notes that the Hebrew word could be translated "embroidered" and that the other eight times the verb is used in the Old Testament describe the needlework in the tabernacle and clothing described in Exodus (26:36; 27:16; 28:39; 35:35; 36:37; 38:18,23; 39:29) ("The Psalms," 40).

The phrase "in the depths of the earth" is a figure of speech. It points to the darkness, hiddenness, and secrecy of the mother's womb. Even with 4D sonograms, we do not know all that is going on in a mother's womb. Our knowledge of all that is unfolding and developing is so small and insignificant in comparison to what our God sees and knows. Not only did he form your body, but also he foreordained your life.

The Lord Foreordained My Life (139:16-18)

Once more omniscience and omnipotence come together, working hand in hand. God saw us at the moment of conception as an unformed substance. Even when we were not much, we were still something to him. He prerecorded and set out all our days in advance. God wrote all the details of our lives down in his book, and he fashioned and formed all the days of our lives when none of them yet existed (v. 16). God had a plan for David. God has a plan for each of us. He plans both the length and the specifics of life. God has his purposes and plans.

Once more these truths inspire David to break out in praise to his God (vv. 17-18). I like to paraphrase these verses like this:

> Your thinking of me down to the last detail is so precious to me, my God. The vastness and greatness of their total are so great that they are more than every grain of sand on the earth. Trying to count them all exhausts me, and I fall asleep. Yet when I wake, you are there as you are every day of my life.

Some Bible teachers believe the phrase "when I awake, I am still with You" (v. 18 NASB) may be alluding to another waking—waking up from death in the presence of the Lord (Kidner, *Psalms 73–150*, 467). Unlike the wicked who are slain by the Lord (v. 19), the believer in the resurrected Jesus has a different destiny altogether. No wonder the New Testament repeatedly refers to the death of the child of God as "sleep." He closes his eyes one moment and wakes up in the presence of Jesus, his Creator and Savior, the next. The God who made him is the God who saved him. The God who gave him life is the same God who gives him eternal life. He is the God who will never leave us or abandon us (Heb 13:5).

God Will Deal with Everyone
PSALM 139:19-24

The fourth and final stanza constitutes what could be called "a dangerous prayer." It takes the psalm in a new and unexpected direction. Our great God is a good God, a just God, and a righteous God. Nothing is beyond his knowledge, presence, or power. He is indeed an omnicompetent God. Here we see his competency applied to the moral order of things. There is coming a day when God will make all things right (cf. Gen 18:25). David notes the heart and mind of those who oppose God and are his enemies (vv. 19-22) in stark contrast with those who seek God and are his children (vv. 23-24). Our Lord knows everything that is going on with each and every one of us, both the good and the bad. He will deal justly with us all.

In an imprecatory psalm, a psalm that vividly calls on God to judge the wicked who do great evil, David asks God to slay the wicked. But at the same time he pleads with the Lord to search his own heart, knowing the utter depravity of man apart from God's saving grace. He is not looking down his nose at others. He knows his own sin too. Thus, he commits all action to God. God must act. David will not take things into his own hands.

God Will Deal with the Wicked Who Hate Him (139:19-22)

David's description of the wicked is striking and unnerving. These men are wicked murderers ("bloodthirsty men") who rightly deserve God's judgment (v. 19). David does not want to have anything to do with them ("stay away from me"). They are evil in their actions. These men are also evil with their words (v. 20). They use religion in their evil schemes. They use the name of God for false and deceptive purposes. They are religious liars and hypocrites. These men are evil in their agenda (v. 21). To put it simply, they hate the Lord. Their plans and goals are not his. They "rebel" against the Lord.

These men are David's enemy because they are God's enemy. As a result, David hates them with complete, or extreme, hatred (v. 22). What should we do with this idea of hatred in verses 21-22? Did not Jesus tell us to love our enemies (Matt 5:44)? The context can help us understand what David means. Hate, in this context, means to reject and oppose. Emotions are involved, but David's response is reasoned and volitional. David asks God to deal with the wicked whom he rejects and opposes. John Piper is helpful here:

> There is a kind of hate for the sinner that may coexist with pity and even a desire for their salvation. You may hate spinach without opposing its good use.
>
> But there may come a point when wickedness is so persistent and high-handed and God-despising that the time of redemption is past and there only remain irremediable wickedness and judgment. . . . We will grant to the psalmist (usually David), who speaks, under the guidance of the Holy Spirit, as the foreshadowed Messiah and Judge, the right to call down judgment on the enemies of God. This is not personal vindictiveness. It is a prophetic execution of what will happen at the last day when God casts all his enemies into the lake of fire (Rev 20:15). We would do well to leave such final

assessments to God, and realize our own corrupt inability to hate as we ought. . . . Let us tremble and trust God, lest we fail, and find ourselves on the other side of the curse. ("Do I Not Hate Those Who Hate You, O Lord?")

God Will Lead the Humble Who Trust Him (139:23-24)

David concludes this psalm with a prayer of humility and introspection. He knows the truth expressed in Jeremiah 17:9 very well: "The heart is more deceitful than anything else, and incurable—who can understand it?" In light of his passionate words in verses 19-22, he knows that he needs his own heart examined by the Lord, not by himself. He pleads with the Lord to "search" (the same word as in v. 1) him, know him, try him, and lead him. He asks God to examine his heart, his thoughts, and his ways. He wants God to see if he finds anything grievous or offensive, anything that will bring pain to him or others. In other words, he says, "Lord, give me a completely honest examination and evaluation. Hold nothing back. Tell it like it is! Tell me exactly what you see. Then, lead me and guide me in a different and better direction. Lead me in the everlasting way—the way that pleases you and the way that will endure forever."

Five Applications from Psalm 139

In addition to what the psalm has taught us so far, there are five applications we can take from it. First, even before you were conceived in your mother's womb, the Lord had planned your size, your shape, and the specific makeup of your body and soul. With the precision of a skilled artisan, he made you exactly as you are for his purposes and glory. Second, from the moment of conception and throughout the entirety of your life, each and every day was ordained and planned by him and written down in his "book." This is how the Father planned the life of his Son. This is how he planned the life of each of us. Third, from the moments we were conceived to the last breaths of life, there is no such thing as fate, fortune, luck, or coincidence. The sovereign God who made us is the sovereign God who planned out our lives for us. He planned our beginnings, our ends, and everything in between. Fourth, the fact we have been made and ordained by this omniscient, omnipresent, and omnipotent God should remind us that nothing we do is hidden from him and nothing we do can ultimately thwart his plan. Fifth, we are fearfully and wonderfully made by an awesome and wonderful

God. He made us, knows us, and is with us. Unlike the wicked who are his enemies and hate him, we Christ-followers are his friends who worship him.

Two thousand years ago, a woman named Mary conceived a baby who was knit together wonderfully by the Holy Spirit of God. That baby came into the world to live and die as God planned. His heart, words, actions, and life were completely pleasing to God, and he was willing to give his life that we might have life. His death proves that every life is valuable from the womb to the tomb and beyond into eternity!

Reflect and Discuss

1. What does this psalm teach about the nature and character of God?
2. If wrong ideas about God will inevitably lead to wrong ideas about ourselves, then what are some wrong ideas about God that one could have? How would these ideas affect how you view yourself?
3. How does the truth that God knows everything you think, speak, and do both encourage and challenge you? Why do you think it led David to praise?
4. How is the teaching that God is everywhere (omnipresent) different from the teaching that God is in everything (panentheism)?
5. Why would you never want to be in a place where God is not?
6. What does it mean that God foreordained your life?
7. How does Scripture's teaching that God plans a person's life work together with the teaching that he judges people for their decisions?
8. How can remembering that God planned your size, shape, and mental abilities help you view your own physical appearance and mental capabilities rightly? How does this help you view others as God does?
9. Why would David want God to search him for anything grievous in his life?
10. How can God's omniscience, omnipresence, and omnipotence aid your prayers?

When God Comes to the Rescue

PSALM 140

Main Idea: Those who trust in God can call on him to save them from the wicked.

I. We Can Call on God to Save Us (140:1-5).
II. We Can Trust That God Will Hear Our Cries (140:6-8).
III. We Can Ask God to Judge the Wicked (140:9-11).
IV. We Can Know That God Will Defend the Righteous Who Are Hurting (140:12-13).

It is not difficult at all to imagine the Lord Jesus praying this song of David on the night of his betrayal and the beginning of his passion. In this psalm of lament, the writer is "being wrongly accused of something serious by malicious slanderers bent on ruining him" (Ross, *Psalms 90–150*, 840). This was true of King David. It would be true of King Jesus (Matt 26:59-61). It may also be our experience as those who desire to live godly lives in Christ Jesus (2 Tim 3:12). When "evil men," "violent men," and those "who plan evil in their hearts" (vv. 1-2) come after us both in action and in word, what is our proper response? Psalm 140 provides four biblical truths to believe and hold to in such trying times.

We Can Call on God to Save Us

PSALM 140:1-5

When we are pursued and persecuted by evil, violent, and wicked men, our first impulse should not be to defend ourselves. Our first response should be to pray to the Lord we know personally and intimately. David refers to his personal, covenant-keeping God—"the Lord" (Yahweh)—seven times in Psalm 140. To this God he cries out, "Rescue me" (v. 1), "Keep me safe" (vv. 1,4) "Protect me" (v. 4). From whom does David need to be saved and rescued? It is evil and violent men (v. 1), men who "plan evil in their hearts" and "stir up wars all day long" (v. 2; cf. Jas 4:1-3). Their primary weapon is the tongue (cf. Jas 3:5-12). David says their tongues are "as sharp as a snake's bite; viper's venom is under their lips.

Selah" (v. 3).[5] Because his enemies are so skilled in verbal warfare, David again pleads to the Lord, "Protect me" (v. 4). These wicked and violent and proud men, who are powerful and persuasive, "plan to make [him] stumble." They want to trap David with ropes. He says, they "spread a net along the path and set snares for me" (v. 5). These soldiers of Satan want only evil and David's downfall.

Michael Wilcock notes, "In Romans 3:13, Paul quotes verse 3, the poison of vipers is on their lips . . . to help show that evils of this kind are endemic to [fallen] human nature" (*Message: Songs*, 263). Evil men are often intelligent. They are often skilled orators who are excellent at verbal combat. They are good at setting traps with their words. Too often they are far superior to us in this warfare. However, they are weaklings in comparison to our God! What is our best weapon against them? Prayer. Who needs to fight this battle? Our Lord, the "captain" of our salvation (Heb 2:10 KJV). Selah! Think and meditate on that wonderful truth when you are wrongly and maliciously attacked for your devotion to the Lord Jesus.

We Can Trust That God Will Hear Our Cries
PSALM 140:6-8

Verses 6-8 are extremely personal, as David references Yahweh (the Lord) four times. Through a continuation of the prayer of verses 1-5, this section begins with a short and concise declaration of faith: "I say to the Lord [Yahweh], 'You are my God.'" The Lord is David's God, and because of that foundational truth, he can cry out, "Listen, Lord, to my cry for help" (ESV, "my pleas for mercy"). Verse 7 conveys the confidence David has in the Lord his God: "Lord [Yahweh], my Lord [*Adonai*], my strong Savior [*Yeshuah*], you shield my head on the day of battle." As our strong deliverer, our saving strength, God shields and protects us like a sturdy helmet. Since he's our divine warrior and guard, we can know we will be saved when the battle comes. Spurgeon speaks about this truth beautifully: "The shield of the Eternal is better protection than a helmet of brass. When arrows fly thick and the battle-axe

---

[5] Regarding the meaning of "Selah," Jim Shaddix writes, "While its exact meaning is unknown, it's generally thought to indicate a pause or interlude in a musical presentation of the psalm. The term often corresponds to structural divisions within a text and can help us understand the various components of a poem" (Platt et al., *Exalting Jesus in Psalms 51–100*, 30).

crashes right and left, there is no covering for the head like the power of the Almighty" (*Treasury*, vol. 3a, 296).

Confident in the truth that the Lord will advance his righteous cause, David concludes the second movement of this psalm in verse 8 by praying, "LORD, do not grant the desires of the wicked; do not let them achieve their goals. Otherwise, they will become proud. *Selah*." David asks the Lord to frustrate their plans so that they do not become more arrogant and puffed up than they already are. Warren Wiersbe wisely writes, "Our prayers for godless people must focus on changing their character, and not just stopping their persecution of believers" (*Bible Exposition Commentary*, 369).

We Can Ask God to Judge the Wicked
PSALM 140:9-11

Verses 9-11 are an imprecatory prayer. David asks God to judge the wicked for their evil against him. To put it in contemporary language, he says, "These men must have their deserts, and taste their own medicine" (Kidner, *Psalms 73–150*, 469). Some find these types of prayers inconsistent with Jesus's telling us to love and pray for our enemies (Matt 5:44). However, there are several reasons David's prayer does not contradict Jesus's teaching. First, and most importantly, David commits the matter completely to the Lord. He does not take matters into his own hands. We are to love our enemies in our actions as we entrust them to God, the righteous Judge. Second, mercy and justice always go hand in hand. You cannot have one without the other. To uphold justice for the poor and needy (vv. 12-13), the wicked must be held accountable. Third, imprecatory psalms foreshadow the end-time judgment of the wicked by God himself (see Rev 20:11-15). God will be the righteous Judge of all people, so David's prayer aligns with our future hope. Fourth, our Lord himself pronounced in harsh language woes of judgment on the evil men of his day (see Matt 23). Finally, these imprecatory prayers are almost always in the Psalms. So the issues of poetic language like hyperbole should also guide our reading of these verses.

David asks the Lord to deal with his adversaries and persecutors when they surround him (v. 9). When they attack him with their words, David asks that God would turn their words back on them: "May the trouble their lips cause overwhelm them" (cf. v. 3). Verse 10 has an eschatological judgment in view. In language that recalls the judgment of Sodom and Gomorrah (see Gen 19), David asks God to "let hot coals fall on them." In language that anticipates eternal condemnation for those who reject God and the salvation he offers in Jesus, David prays, "Let them be thrown into the fire, into the abyss, never again to rise" (v. 10; cf. Rev 14:9-11; 20:10,14-15; 21:8). This is David's way of saying, "Lord, stop what these evil and wicked men say and do now and forever." Calvin observes at this point, "David cuts off the reprobate from the hope of pardon, as knowing them to be beyond recovery. Had they been disposable to repentance, he would have been inclinable on his part to mercy" (*Psalms 93–150*, 2005, 231). Verse 11 concludes the section with David asking the Lord to remove these wicked persons and their influence: "Do not let a slanderer stay in the land." Send them away, he says. Let them be hunted by the evil with which they have hunted. "Let evil relentlessly hunt down a violent man." It is sobering to think these verses describe everyone separated from Christ. It once described each of us in our unredeemed and unrepentant state. We may rightly ask God to judge the wicked, but we would be wise to examine our own lives before we do.

We Can Know That God Will Defend the Righteous Who Are Hurting
PSALM 140:12-13

Verses 12-13 move away from judgment on the wicked to hope for the hurting (v. 12) and the righteous (v. 13). Four words in these verses describe the identity of God's people in contrast to the wicked in the prior verses: "poor," "needy," "righteous," and "upright." The psalmist is confident ("I know") that "the LORD" will defend the cause of those who have been unjustly treated by wicked and evil men. Ross notes that David applies legal terms to what the Lord will do for those who are his (*Psalms 90–150*, 848). The Lord "upholds the just cause of the poor." He will provide "justice for the needy" (v. 12). Evil, violent, and wicked men may abuse, hound, and mistreat God's people. But we must not return evil for evil. Remain silent. Commit the matter to the Lord. He will defend you.

The psalm that began with a cry of desperation ends on a note of praise and confidence. In the end our God will make all things right (see Gen 18:25). Justice will prevail. Therefore, those who trust in this God as their Lord ("the righteous" and "the upright") "will praise [his] name," and they "will live in [his] presence." They will joyfully sing of who he is and what he has done for them. They will live forever in his presence, enjoying safety and security. These wonderful truths do not make the difficulties and trials of this life easy. They do, however, give us the faith and strength to endure them.

Conclusion

The song "Have Faith in God" could have been written as a response or reflection on Psalm 140. The third stanza is especially appropriate for these 13 verses. For those who have fled to Jesus for salvation, no matter what they may endure in this life, these words provide a wonderful reminder of how great is his care for his children.

> Have faith in God in your pain and your sorrow;
> His heart is touched with your grief and despair.
> Cast all your cares and your burdens upon Him;
> And leave them there, oh, leave them there.
> Have faith in God, He's on His throne;
> Have faith in God, He watches o'er His own.
> He cannot fail, He must prevail;
> Have faith in God, have faith in God. (B. B. McKinney)

Reflect and Discuss

1. Why should your first response be prayer to the Lord instead of defending yourself when persecuted? What must we believe about prayer in order for this to be the first response?
2. In what ways can Christians be tempted to respond to hurtful speech? How does Jesus respond to hurtful speech in the Gospels?
3. If Christians should pray in response to hurtful speech, what should they pray? What are the various aspects of David's prayer in this psalm?
4. What do David's descriptions about God reveal about his beliefs?
5. Is the Christian's primary goal in persecution to pray for it to stop? Why or why not? What other goals might Christians have?
6. How are justice and mercy related? Why can you not have one without the other?
7. How does the gospel inform how Christians pray for justice?
8. Can Christians use the pursuit of justice now to be a witness to God's future justice? If so, how?
9. Where else does Scripture speak about the presence of God as a promise for his people? Why is God's presence important?
10. Can justice exist without God? How can the hope for justice help you witness about the good news of the gospel?

The Man Who Will Not Compromise

PSALM 141

Main Idea: Ask the Lord to help you avoid sin and to protect you from sinners.

I. Ask the Lord for Help (141:1-2).
II. Ask the Lord for Wisdom (141:3-4).
III. Ask the Lord for Good Friends (141:5a).
IV. Ask the Lord for Vindication (141:5b-7).
V. Ask the Lord for Protection (141:8-10).

Prayer is a difficult Christian discipline. It is also an essential Christian discipline for a healthy spiritual life. Jesus gives us a model for prayer in the greatest sermon ever preached, his Sermon on the Mount (Matt 6:9-13; Luke 11:2-4). There are also other places in the Bible where we receive instruction in the discipline of prayer. Such a place is King David's quartet of prayers in Psalms 140–143.

Psalm 141 is "a Psalm of petition, a prayer for sanctification and protection" (Ross, *Psalms 90–150*, 853). David asks the Lord for guidance and deliverance as he seeks to live life to the glory of God. He knows he needs God's help. He knows he needs the correction of good friends. He knows all of this help is essential if he is to live a life of wisdom and not foolishness (cf. Matt 7:24-28; Jas 3:13-18). The person who will stay true to his Lord, no matter what, needs a consistent and intentional prayer life. Five particulars of prayer occur in Psalm 141, a psalm in which every word in every sentence is a prayer.

Ask the Lord for Help
PSALM 141:1-2

One who has a life without compromise will run to the Lord. Such a person will ask the Lord to run to him (v. 1). This person recognizes his need for the Lord if he is to stand strong and courageous, especially in times of trouble and temptation.

Twice David calls to the Lord in verse 1. This is an example of Hebrew poetic parallelism where line two adds specificity to line one.

There is desperation and urgency in his voice as he asks the Lord to "hurry to help [him]" and "listen to [his] voice." This urgency and desperation are complemented by worship in verse 2. The Lord he runs to is the Lord he worships. He desires for his prayer to be a sweet aroma and a pleasing offering. Warren Wiersbe notes, "Incense is a picture of prayer going up to the Lord (Rev 5:8; 8:4)" (*Bible Exposition Commentary*, 370).

"The raising of my hands" (cf. Ps 134:2) demonstrated worship and adoration (see also 28:2; 63:4; 1 Tim 2:8). The "evening offering" may indicate this was prayed at evening worship or even at night as David prepared for bed. Perhaps it was voiced after a long and difficult day. Patrick Reardon makes a beautiful Christological connection with the evening offering or "sacrifice" (ESV) when he writes,

> The Old Testament's "evening sacrifice" was a type of and preparation for that true oblation rendered at the evening of the world, when the Lamb of God, nailed to the Cross, lifted his hands to the Father in sacrificial prayer for the salvation of mankind. This was the true lifting up of the hands, the definitive evening sacrifice offered on Golgotha, by which God marked His seal on human destiny. (*Christ in the Psalms*, 281–82)

Ask the Lord for Wisdom
PSALM 141:3-4

James 1:5 says, "Now if any of you lacks wisdom, he should ask God—who gives to all generously and ungrudgingly—and it will be given to him." Wisdom is something we should ask the Lord for daily and specifically. It is the ability to see life as God sees it and then respond as he would. David highlights several areas in which wisdom from above is essential (cf. Jas 3:13-18). First, he asks God to give him wisdom with his words (v. 3). With beautiful Hebrew poetic parallelism, David asks God to temper his tongue and muzzle his mouth: "Lord, set up a guard for my mouth; keep watch at the door of my lips." James 3:1-12 provides an expanded commentary on the trouble with the tongue. It informs us that without the Lord's help, it is "set on fire by hell" (3:6).

Second, David asks the Lord to give him wisdom in his heart (v. 4): "Do not let my heart turn to any evil thing." The Bible repeatedly addresses the importance of the heart. Proverbs 4:23 reminds us, "Guard your heart above all else, for it is the source of life." And Jeremiah 17:9 says, "The heart is more deceitful than anything else, and incurable—who can understand it?" The real you and I are on the inside. David knew, as must we, the deceptive power of the heart. He knew he could not trust it. He needed the Lord to transform and guard it. He knew we all need a "spiritual heart transplant," which only the gospel of Jesus Christ can give us.

Third, David asks for wisdom in his actions (v. 4). He points out the close connection between what we think and what we do (cf. Jesus's words in Mark 7:21-23). If, for instance, your heart is leaning or turning toward evil, it will eventually do evil. David prays, "Do not let my heart . . . perform wicked acts with evildoers. Do not let me feast on their delicacies." He asks the Lord to protect his heart, to direct his actions, and to keep him away from bad influencers no matter how enticing and attractive they are. Satan often tempts us through our companions, the people we spend time with. He also makes their sin look fun and harmless. He never shows us its dark side.

David warns us concerning those who are wicked and sinful. He warns us that their evil can be camouflaged with delicacies. These may be men of influence and status, popular and powerful, whose wealth and position allow them to enjoy the finer things of life as the world measures things. If we resist temptation in our own strength and willpower, we will not resist long. We must ask the Lord not to allow our hearts to have any inclination in this direction. Proverbs 14:12 is a wise warning: "There is a way that seems right to a person, but its end is the way to death."

Ask the Lord for Good Friends
PSALM 141:5A

One of the great blessings of life is good friends, friends you can trust with your life. The longer I (Danny) live, the more I realize such friends are few in number, valuable beyond words, and essential to a consistent walk with God over a lifetime. Friends influence you. No debate. The wicked and sinful men of verse 4 contrast sharply with the influence of righteous friends who act in "faithful love" in verse 5. David says he will seek out friends who love him enough to rebuke him. The image of correction is powerful: "Let the righteous one strike me." You need friends who will strike you with hard but healing words. It is actually an act of *chesed* (NASB, "kindness"; CSB, "faithful love"). The *Jesus Storybook Bible* calls such love, whose origin is always from God, a "Never Stopping, Never Giving Up, Unbreaking, Always and Forever Love" (Lloyd-Jones, *Jesus Storybook Bible,* 36). We all need rebuke and correction from friends who love us.

It is not easy for any of us to receive rebuke, however. David was no different. So David asks the Lord to help him in this: "Let me not refuse it." David is asking God to let him see it as *chesed.* In other words, he essentially says, "Lord, let me receive it as excellent oil and an act of honor and respect. My brother and my sister love me enough to tell me the truth and make me better for you. Thank you! Praise the Lord! Do not let me refuse it. Help me to receive it. Help me remember Proverbs 27:6, 'Faithful are the wounds of a friend'" (ESV).

Ask the Lord for Vindication
PSALM 141:5B-7

In verses 5-7 we encounter an imprecatory passage where the psalmist prays in strong language for God to judge his enemies. Because of their evil, they are the enemies of God. These are men of power and authority: "judges" or "rulers" (VanGemeren, *Psalms*, 973). David's words may strike and startle our modern sensibilities. But do not miss the redemptive note in this stanza tucked away at the end of verse 6.

David will continually pray against evil and those determined to do evil (v. 5b). His prayer "anticipates the destruction of the wicked rulers" in verses 6-7 (Ross, *Psalms 90–150*, 860). They "will be thrown off the sides of a cliff" (v. 6). God will scatter their bones so that they do not even receive a decent burial (v. 7) (VanGemeren, *Psalms*, 973). In this context the word "Sheol" means the grave. This lack of burial reveals that the wicked are under God's curse and judgment. Here one can/should hear the terrors of the end-time judgments so graphically depicted in the apocalypse of Revelation 6–19, a judgment poured out by none other than the Lord Jesus Christ himself.

David's harsh words have a redemptive goal. He prays so that "the people will listen to [his] words," find them pleasing, and come to their spiritual senses (v. 6). Derek Kidner says the verse reinforces "the resolve to strike no bargains with evil, by looking ahead to the time when such a stand will prove its point and win its following" (*Psalms 73–150*, 472). Alec Motyer adds, "When the stresses and strains are over, then will be the time to speak. Not gloatingly or in a triumphalist fashion, but soothing words that make for peace" (*Psalms by the Day*, 403).

Ask the Lord for Protection
PSALM 141:8-10

David sees life as a titanic battle between good and evil, right and wrong, godliness and ungodliness. He knows that engaging in this battle exposes him to danger. Yet, as a man who will not compromise, he has no choice but to engage. He also knows he dare not engage this battle without the help and protection of the Lord. Verses 8-10 begin with a confession, but they end with a petition.

David will keep his eyes on his King, Yahweh his Lord (CSB, "Lord, my Lord"; NIV, "Sovereign Lord"). He will strive in all circumstances to maintain a Godward, heavenly perspective (cf. Col 3:1-4). And he will "seek refuge," protection and safety, in the Lord. This desire moves him to pray, "do not let me die" (ESV, "leave me not defenseless"; lit. "do not lay bare my life"). Ross notes that the phrase is used "for physical death in Isaiah 53:12" (*Psalms 90–150*, 861). David depends on the one true God, Yahweh, to preserve his life.

David continues his prayer in verse 9 by asking the Lord to "protect [him] from the trap they have set for [him], and from the snares of evildoers." He concludes in verse 10 by asking that those who plot to destroy him will be ensnared by their own evil devices. That like a boomerang, their wicked plans will return on them. God allows us, in grace, to safely escape these devices. This judgment is the Lord's doing. Romans 12:19 provides a helpful New Testament insight on all of this: "Friends, do not avenge yourselves; instead, leave room for God's wrath, because it is written, Vengeance belongs to me; I will repay, says the Lord."

Conclusion

The person who will not compromise is a rare and unique individual. I am not sure I have ever met such a person who completely fulfills the portrait we see in Psalm 141. But then I turn to Jesus, and I do meet such a Person. Here I discover a man who in times of trouble . . .

- Asked the Lord for help:

During his earthly life, he offered prayers and appeals with loud cries and tears to the one who was able to save him from death, and he was heard because of his reverence. (Heb 5:7)

• Asked the Lord for wisdom:

Very early in the morning, while it was still dark, he got up, went out, and made his way to a deserted place; and there he was praying. (Mark 1:35)

• Asked the Lord for good friends:

During those days he went out to the mountain to pray and spent all night in prayer to God. When daylight came, he summoned his disciples, and he chose twelve of them, whom he also named apostles. (Luke 6:12-13)

• Asked the Lord for vindication:

Father, the hour has come. Glorify your Son so that the Son may glorify you. (John 17:1)

Jesus also depended on the Lord for protection. He, of course, died. But he continued to trust the Lord who would raise him from the dead: "Father, into your hands I entrust my spirit" (Luke 23:46). And God came through! Here in Jesus is the man who would not compromise! Here is the man we have as our Savior and our example. Here is the One who enables us to live as we ought. Here is the God we honor, worship, and run to so that we too may live without compromise.

Reflect and Discuss

1. Why do Christians pray? What beliefs are at the foundation of our reasons for praying?
2. Why is prayer sometimes a difficult act for Christians? What happens when we pray consistently and desperately?
3. Does one's physical posture in prayer matter? Why or why not?
4. What does David's physical posture (raising his hands in prayer) tell you about him and his prayer?
5. This section defines *wisdom* as "the ability to see life as God sees it and then respond as he would." What about this definition stands out to you? How does it compare/contrast with how your culture defines *wisdom*?

6. Are a Christian's pursuit of wisdom and avoidance of sin connected? If so, how?
7. What other Scripture passages help you understand how Christians are to correct and rebuke one another?
8. How is God's judgment of evil consistent with his character of love? In what ways would God be unloving if he did not judge evil?
9. How does leaving judgment/vengeance to God show your faith in him?
10. What promises does Scripture give us to hold onto when it seems we are not protected from evil?

The Lord Is My Refuge—Plainly Put on Display in the Life of Ann Hasseltine Judson

PSALM 142

Main Idea: The Lord knows our needs and promises to be our refuge.

I. God Hears the Cries of Your Heart (142:1-2).
II. God Knows What You Are Going Through (142:3-4).
III. God Will Deliver You as Your Refuge (142:5-7).

Ann ("Nancy") Judson has rightly been called "the mother of modern missions" (Robert, "The Mother of Modern Missions"). This title is all the more amazing when you consider she died from cerebral meningitis at the young age of 37 in the Southeast Asian country of Burma, modern-day Myanmar. Her grave, along with that of her little daughter Maria, is located there under what her husband Adoniram called "the hope tree." Ann did not have a long life, but it was a full life used in service to King Jesus.

Psalm 142 is a psalm of lament written by David from a cave (either Adullam in 1 Sam 22 or En-gedi in 1 Sam 24). It could easily have been written by Ann Hasseltine Judson on numerous occasions as she served King Jesus and labored among the Burmese people for their salvation. It is a psalm filled with "great distress" (VanGemeren, *Psalms*, 974). The honesty of the psalm in its cries for help should instruct us about the realities of forsaking everything to follow Jesus. The hope that arises even amid difficult and painful circumstances should inspire us. Three movements will be examined in our study of these seven verses.

God Hears the Cries of Your Heart
PSALM 142:1-2

The first two verses flow with words of passionate verbal petition to the Lord (Yahweh): "I cry"; "I plead"; "I pour out"; "I reveal." Aloud David pleads "for mercy" from the Lord. Aloud he complains and tells his troubles to the One who is his "shelter," "portion," and rescuer (vv. 5-6). This crying is not a one-time event. The crying and pleading are continuous.

Spurgeon wisely points out, "We do not show our trouble before the Lord that *he* may see *it*, but that *we* may see *him*. It is for *our* relief, and not for his information" (*Treasury*, vol. 3b, 324; emphasis in original).

Ann Judson, of all those who followed the Lord's call to the international mission field, knew we have a God who anywhere, anytime, and under any circumstances hears our prayers. She learned this truth early in her life, and it sustained her until her death. Ann was born just before Christmas in 1789 in Bradford, Massachusetts. She was the youngest of five children. She was cheerful, popular, intelligent, and beautiful. During her first 16 years, she seldom felt any real conviction concerning salvation. God, however, used Hannah More's *Strictures on the Modern System of Female Education*, John Bunyan's *Pilgrim's Progress*, and a visit to an aunt to stir her heart and bring her to Christ. Her own words from her journals beautifully describe her conversion as she cried out and fled to Jesus:

> I longed for annihilation; and if I could have destroyed the existence of my soul, with as much ease as that of my body, I should quickly have done it. But that glorious Being, who is kinder to his creatures than they are to themselves, did not leave me to remain long in this distressing state. I began to discover a beauty in the way of salvation by Christ. He appeared to be just such a Savior as I needed. I saw how God could be just, saving sinners through him. I committed my soul into his hands, and besought him to do with me what seemed good in his sight. When I was thus enabled to commit myself into the hands of Christ, my mind was relieved from that distressing weight which had borne it down for so long a time. . . . A view of his purity and holiness filled my soul with wonder and admiration. I felt a disposition to commit myself unreservedly into his hands, and leave it with him to save me or cast me off, for I felt I could not be unhappy, while allowed the privilege of contemplating and loving so glorious a Being.
>
> I now began to hope, that I had passed from death unto life. When I examined myself, I was constrained to own, that I had feelings and dispositions to which I was formerly an utter stranger. I had sweet communion with the blessed God, from day to day; my heart was drawn out in love to Christians of whatever denomination; the sacred Scriptures were sweet to my taste; and such was my thirst for religious knowledge, that I

frequently spent a great part of the night in reading religious books. O how different were my views of myself and of God, from what they were, when I first began to enquire what I should do to be saved! I felt myself to be a poor lost sinner, destitute of everything to recommend myself to the divine favour; that I was, by nature, inclined to every evil way; and that it had been the mere sovereign, restraining mercy of God, not my own goodness, which had kept me from committing the most flagrant crimes. This view of myself humbled me in the dust, melted me into sorrow and contrition for my sins, induced me to lay my soul at the feet of Christ, and plead his merits alone, as the ground of my acceptance. (James, *Ann Judson*, 24–25)

In 1806, at the age of 16, Ann publicly confessed Christ at a revival. During the same revival, her entire family also was converted. God quickly developed a missionary heart in Ann. Somewhere around the age of 19 she wrote,

March 17 [probably 1809]. Have had some enjoyment in reading the life of David Brainerd [pioneer missionary to the North American Indians]. It had a tendency to humble me, and excite desires to live as near to God, as that holy man did. Have spent this evening in prayer for quickening grace. Felt my heart enlarged to pray for spiritual blessings for myself, my friends, the church at large, the heathen world, and the African slaves. Felt a willingness to give myself away to Christ, to be disposed of as he pleases. Here I find safety and comfort. Jesus is my only refuge. (Ibid., 33)

By the age of 21, Ann was determined to become a missionary. The same was true of a young Congregational minister named Adoniram Judson who was smitten the first time he saw Ann. On February 5, 1812, they married. Twelve days later they, along with Samuel and Harriet Newell, set sail for India on a ship called the *Caravan* as the first commissioned missionaries from America. God had heard the cries of Ann's heart in salvation and the cries of her heart to know and do his will. Again her journals give a glimpse into God's powerful work in her:

Aug. 8, 1810. Endeavoured to commit myself entirely to God, to be disposed of, according to his pleasure. . . . I do feel, that his service is my delight. Might I but be the means of converting a single soul, it would be worth spending all my days to accomplish.

Sept. 10. For several weeks past, my mind has been greatly agitated. An opportunity has been presented to me, of spending my days among the heathen, in attempting to persuade them to receive the Gospel. Were I convinced of its being a call from God, and that it would be more pleasing to him, for me to spend my life in this way than in any other, I think I should be willing to relinquish every earthly object, and in full view of dangers and hardships, give myself up to the great work.

A consideration of this subject has occasioned much self-examination, to know on what my hopes were founded, and whether my love to Jesus was sufficiently strong to induce me to forsake all for his cause.

Oct. 28. I rejoice, that I am in his hands—that he is every where present, and can protect me in one place as well as in another. He has my heart in his hands, and when I am called to face danger, to pass through scenes of terror and distress, he can inspire me with fortitude, and enable me to trust in him, Jesus is faithful; his promises are precious. . . . If I have been deceived in thinking it my duty to go to the heathen, I humbly pray, that I may be undeceived, and prevented from going. But whether I spend my days in India or America, I desire to spend them in the service of God, and be prepared to spend an eternity in his presence. O Jesus, make me live to thee, and I desire no more.

Sabbath [undated]. Blessed Jesus, I am thine forever. Do with me what thou wilt; lead me in the path in which thou wouldest have me to go, and it is enough. (James, *Ann Judson*, 39–42)

God Knows What You Are Going Through
PSALM 142:3-4

Verses 3-4 contain "the lament proper" (Ross, *Psalms 90–150*, 870). David's trials are weighing him down. Yet, even in his distress, David is confident the Lord knows his way and sees everything he is going through. Still, what he is experiencing is almost overwhelming.

If we are honest, we have all been where David is. This is how we feel when times are tough and when service to Jesus is excruciatingly difficult. Again, few people who have followed in the footsteps of our Lord Jesus have known hardship better than Ann Judson. Just reflect on the following:

- On the way to India, she and her companions became convinced of believer's baptism and had to forgo all support from the Congregationalists who sent them.
- They would be denied entry into India and forced to go to Burma, which was extremely hostile to Christianity.
- Harriett Newell, Ann's dearest friend, would die in childbirth (as would the child) when Harriet was only 19, never making it to the mission field.
- Ann's first child was stillborn.
- Her second child, a boy named Roger, died before his first birthday.
- In 1820, after six years on the field, Ann nearly died and had to go to Calcutta, and eventually back to America, to recover. She would be separated from her beloved husband for two years.

When Ann returned to Burma in 1824, she became pregnant. Soon thereafter, Adoniram and fellow missionary Jonathan Price were imprisoned for 17 months. The conditions were beyond brutal. Adoniram nearly died several times and considered suicide. During this period, Ann gave birth to a baby girl named Maria, pleaded repeatedly for her husband's release, and daily walked two miles to supply him and others with water and food. Of this time she would write,

> Sometimes for days and days together, I could not go into the prison, till after dark, when I had two miles to walk, in returning to the house. O how many, many times, have I returned from that dreary prison at nine o'clock at night, solitary and worn out with fatigue and anxiety. . . . My prevailing opinion was, that my husband would suffer violent death; and that I should, of course become a slave, and languish out a miserable though short existence in the tyrannic hands of some unfeeling monster. But the consolations of [Christ], in these trying circumstances, were neither "few nor

small." It taught me to look beyond this world, to that rest, that peaceful happy rest, where Jesus reigns, and oppression never enters. (James, *Ann Judson*, 191–92)

During this time Ann again became seriously ill and nearly died, as did little Maria. Her own words are truly more than one can fathom both in terms of her suffering and in her faith in God's providence:

Our dear little Maria was the greatest sufferer at this time, my illness depriving her of her usual nourishment and neither a nurse nor a drop of milk could be procured in the village. By making presents to the jailers, I obtained leave for Mr. Judson to come out of prison [in fetters] and take the little emaciated creature around the village, to beg a little nourishment from those mothers who had young children. Her cries in the night were heart-rending, when it was impossible to supply her wants. I now began to think the very afflictions of Job had come upon me. When in health I could bear the various trials and vicissitudes, through which I was called to pass. But to be confined with sickness, and unable to assist those who were so dear to me, when in distress, was almost too much for me to bear: and had it not been for the consolations of [my Lord], and an assured conviction that every additional trial was ordered by infinite love and mercy, I must have sunk under my accumulated suffering. (Ibid., 213–14)

God knows what we are going through. Any pain, any suffering, and any trial must first pass through the hands of an infinitely wise and loving heavenly Father.

God Will Deliver You as Your Refuge
PSALM 142:5-7

Despite his dire circumstances, David is confident the Lord will meet his needs. James Boice helpfully identifies four things God was for David (and for us) in verses 5-7 (*Psalms 107–150*, 1232–33). First, God is our **refuge** (v. 5). In verse 4, as David looked around he saw no refuge. Now, as he looks up, he sees God as his refuge. He shouts, "You are my shelter." You are "a trustworthy place of safety" (Motyer, *Psalms by the Day*, 405).

Second, God is our **portion** in the land of the living." He is our living inheritance, an inheritance far more valuable than any earthly possession. Third, he is our **Savior**. In our broken, weak, and humbled condition, those who persecute and pursue us are too strong. They are too much for us to handle. Only God can deliver us. Only he can rescue us. Only he can save us. Fourth, he is our **liberator**. He is the one who can set us free literally and figuratively from prison. In response to this truth, the psalmist says he will "praise [the LORD's] name." He continues, "The righteous will gather around me because [God deals] generously with me." Interestingly, the verb "gather around" could possibly mean, in this context, "put a crown on me" (Motyer, *Psalms by the Day*, 405).

Ann Judson would experience the truth of verse 7 in an unexpected way. Adoniram would be released from prison, and he and Ann would be joyfully reunited. However, it would last for only two weeks. Adoniram would be called away on business for the Burmese government. While he was away, Ann died on October 24, 1826, from cerebral meningitis. Her body had been broken from the ordeal and sufferings of the previous two years. Tragically, little Maria would follow her mother in death to glory six months later. Concerning his losses, Adoniram would write to Ann's mother:

> The next morning we made [Maria's] last bed in the small
> enclosure that surrounds her mother's lonely grave. Together
> they rest in hope, under the hope tree, which stands at the
> head of the graves, and together, I trust, their spirits are
> rejoicing after a short separation of precisely six months. And
> I am left alone in the wide world. My own dear family I have
> buried; one in Rangoon, and two in Amherst. What remains
> for me but to hold myself in readiness to follow the dear
> departed to that blessed world, "Where my best friends, my
> kindred dwell, Where God, my Saviour, reigns"? (Anderson, *To
> the Golden Shore*, 380–81)

Conclusion

It is difficult to summarize all that this amazing woman accomplished in her short life. Her story and writings alone mobilized untold numbers of women to go to the nations for the cause of Christ and the Great Commission. And to this accomplishment we may add the following:

- She modeled joint ministry partnership with her husband. In a letter to her sister in 1812, she wrote, "Good female schools are extremely needed in this country. I hope no missionary will ever come out here without a wife, as she, in her sphere, can be equally useful with her husband" (Robert, "The Mother of Modern Missions," 24). They were truly a dynamic duo in ministry.

- She was an evangelist, taught women the gospel, adopted orphans, and started schools for children.
- She was a superb linguist and translator who learned spoken Burmese and Siamese better than her husband. She translated tracts, a catechism, the Gospel of Matthew, Daniel, and Jonah into Burmese.
- She wrote a history of their mission work entitled "A Particular Relation of the American Baptist Mission to the Burmese Empire" (1823). Her plan was to use the proceeds to redeem little girls sold into slavery. (Ibid.)

In an appeal to American women, "Address to Females in America, Relative to the Situation of Heathen Females in the East," she closes with these powerful words:

Shall we, my beloved friends, suffer minds like these to lie dormant, to wither in ignorance and delusion, to grope their way to eternal ruin, without an effort on our part, to raise, to refine, to elevate, and to point to that Saviour who has died equally for them as for us? Shall we sit down in indolence and ease, indulge in all the luxuries with which we are surrounded, and which our country so bountifully affords, and leave beings like these, flesh and blood, intellect and feeling, like ourselves, and of *our own sex*, to perish, to sink into eternal misery?'
No! By all the tender feelings of which the female mind is susceptible, by all the privileges and blessings resulting from the cultivation and expansion of the human mind, by our duty to God and our fellow creatures, and by the blood and groans of him who died on Calvary, let us make a united effort; let us call on all, old and young, in the circle of our acquaintance to join us in attempting to meliorate the situation, to instruct, to enlighten and save females in the Eastern world; and though time and circumstances should prove that our united exertions have been ineffectual, we shall escape at death that bitter thought, that Burman females have been lost, without

an effort of ours to prevent their ruin. (James, *Ann Judson*, 259; emphasis in original)

Ann Judson was a remarkable woman of God, of that there can be no doubt. May our great God multiply her kind ten thousand times over so that his name might be made famous among the nations for their eternal good and for his eternal glory.

Reflect and Discuss

1. What does the psalmist's honest expression of distress teach you about prayer? Are you honest with God in your prayers?
2. If God knows our prayers, why should one's cries and pleadings to the Lord be continuous? How does ongoing prayer help us see God as Spurgeon says?
3. What parts of Ann's prayers stand out to you? Why?
4. What parts of Ann's life are challenging or encouraging to you? Why?
5. Ann and Adoniram gave up financial support because they changed their theological convictions on baptism. What does this choice reveal about their beliefs about God and themselves?
6. How could Ann say, "His service is my delight. Might I but be the means of converting a single soul, it would be worth spending all my days to accomplish"? Do you know one person who needs the gospel that you can commit to pray for daily?
7. What all did Ann give up by choosing to be a missionary? What promises of God in Scripture can you match with these things that show she would actually experience gain and not loss in the long run?
8. What was Ann's primary goal in her life and mission work?
9. Were Ann's missionary efforts a success? How should we define success in missions?
10. Is God calling you to go somewhere? How might you begin praying about where you can serve God?

My Soul Thirsts for You

PSALM 143

Main Idea: In this desperate prayer David teaches us about the basis for prayer, the nature of spiritual warfare, and the need to make specific petitions.

I. **A Plea on the Basis of the Gospel (143:1-2)**
II. **A Plan for Spiritual Warfare (143:3-6)**
   A. Acknowledge your condition (143:3-4).
   B. Meditate on God's work (143:5).
   C. Yearn for God's presence (143:6).
III. **A Pattern for Presenting Requests (143:7-12)**
   A. "Renew me" (143:7-8a).
   B. "Guide me" (143:8b,10).
   C. "Deliver me" (143:9,11-12).

Traditionally, this psalm has been classified as one of the penitential psalms (a psalm of confession). This is because of the confession of universal guilt in verse 2b; however, that's the only reference to sin in this psalm (Kidner, *Psalms 73–150*, 475). It's really an individual lament. David's main concern has to do with his desperate situation. He's troubled by his enemies and troubled in spirit. Psalm 143 gives us a picture of a godly man in desperate prayer.

What makes David such a giant in the faith? Certainly, he was a gifted man. He was also a tender man. And he was a tough man. But what made him unlike other gifted, tender, and tough men? We can't say that he was sinless because he certainly wasn't! David did some horrible things! I submit that the most important practical lesson we can learn from David is the depth of his devotional life. Kidner says, "It is this personal devotion that was David's greatness and is the continuing greatness of his psalms" (ibid., 476). David was a worshiping man. He was a praying man. He was a repenting man. Psalm 143 demonstrates some of this spiritual vitality. Here we find him pleading with God. He's pursuing God. He thirsts for God. If you're interested in cultivating a deep devotional life with God, there are three dynamics to learn from this psalm.

A Plea on the Basis of the Gospel
PSALM 143:1-2

David begins his prayer with a plea (v. 1a; cf. 5:1; 17:1; 28:2; 54:2; 64:1).
He wants God's attention and God's answers (v. 1b; cf. 5:2; 4:1; 13:3;
86:1). Later, David will make particular appeals for God to answer his
petitions (vv. 7-12), but those petitions are delayed for the time being.
First, we have some important lessons to consider.

The first lesson involves *the basis for prayer*. David roots his prayer in
God's character. Notice the emphasis on God's faithfulness, righteousness, mercy, and grace in these opening verses. David knew that God
had made a covenant with his people. God would be *faithful* to it. God's
perfect *righteousness* provided David with additional assurance that God
would uphold it. God is perfectly righteous. Since God said he would
be faithful to the covenant, David could pray with confidence. David
banked his hope on God's commitment to his people. Regardless of
what he was feeling personally at the time, David could expect God to
hear and answer him because of this covenantal relationship to God.

In verse 2 David also highlights God's covenantal *mercy* and *grace*.
He does so by pointing out mankind's universal guilt before God (cf.
130:3). On what basis does David come to God? Can he make his plea
to God based on his own works? No. Can he make his plea to God based
on his own acts of justice? No. He knows that God has been gracious and
merciful to him. God has not treated him as his sins deserve. David has
his relationship with God based on grace, not performance. His appeal
to mercy was an appeal for God's acceptance of him.

This psalm, then, opens with a powerful gospel statement. It
reminds us that we have no right to be in the presence of God apart
from God's faithfulness and righteousness, his grace and mercy (Rom
3:20-26; Gal 2:15-21). In God's faithfulness he kept his word and brought
forth the Messiah. In God's mercy he grants sinners the righteousness of
Jesus. We are accepted on the basis of grace, not works.

You know that feelings come and go. But if you are in Christ, your
position in him never changes. We pray in the name of Jesus. That's the
only way we can come to God. We come because of the work of another.
Christ's faithfulness, righteousness, and gift of salvation enable us to pray.

On what should we bank our hope when it comes to prayer? Rest
everything in Christ. Because of Christ's work on our behalf, we can
come to God with our desperate pleas.

A Plan for Spiritual Warfare
PSALM 143:3-6

Before arriving at David's specific petitions that he wants God to answer, we learn another valuable lesson related to spiritual warfare. We see a picture of David's external and internal battle in verses 3-6. David exposes his present crisis to us (as he expresses it to God) and provides a helpful pattern for us. Consider three instructions for engaging in spiritual warfare.

Acknowledge Your Condition (143:3-4)

David doesn't temper his words. David has an enemy who's attacking him (v. 3; cf. 7:5; 88:3-6). This enemy is stated generally, making it easily applicable for us. Whoever the enemy is, he has been successful, "crushing" David to the ground. As a result, David sits in "darkness" (cf. 88:6; Mic 7:8) and feels like a "dead" man (cf. Lam 3:6). Internally, he has been brought low. He has a weak spirit and despairing heart (cf. Ps 77:3).

Kidner says of this description,

> Every phrase here is so heavy with distress, that no sufferer
> need feel unique in what he experiences. And the similarity of
> those terms to those that describe our Lord's emotions (cf. Matt
> 26:37; Heb 4:15ff) remind [*sic*] us that none need feel himself
> alone, or less than fully understood. (*Psalms 73–150*, 475)

Amen! You aren't unusual if you have an enemy, if you feel crushed, if you're experiencing despair, or if you're spiritually weak. Further, Jesus understands our weakness and stands ready to grant us grace. Don't hide your weaknesses. Admit them. Go to the Father with them.

At this point you might wonder, *Doesn't God already know my condition? Why tell him about it?* Don't think that. Prayer is about communicating with your Father. Open up your heart and express your weakness to him. Tell him about your predicament. You aren't giving him new information but expressing intimacy and honesty in communication.

I (Tony) love how Ligon Duncan described the prayer life of one of my Christian heroes, the mighty theologian Francis Schaeffer. Pastor Duncan highlighted the specificity and intimacy of Schaeffer's prayers:

> One of the things that I used to do when C. Everett Koop was
> still coming to the meetings of The Alliance of Confessing

Evangelicals in Philadelphia is I would take him to the airport
after the meeting was over. And it was fascinating hearing him
telling stories of traveling around the country with Frances
Schaeffer. . . . [O]ne of the most interesting things he said
was it was always an experience to pray with Frances Schaeffer
in the various hotel rooms around the country because
when Frances Schaeffer was in private, his prayers were very
direct and very intimate and very frankly a little bit eccentric.
They would get in a hotel room after they had settled in and
Schaeffer and his wife, Edith, and C. Everett Koop and the
companions that would be with them would get ready to pray
and Schaeffer would turn around and kneel at the bedside
or at a chair or at the sofa and he would say, "Well, Lord, it's
Fran." And C. Everett Koop was thinking, "Well, Fran, don't
you know that He already knows it's Fran who's praying to
Him?" And he'd say, "We're here in room 516 in the such-
and-such hotel." And Koop was thinking, "God already knows
that, Fran! Why are you praying that to Him?" But he'd
be very, very specific about these incidental little details. If
Frances Schaeffer could be that specific about those kinds
of incidental details, don't you think you need to be specific
about the predicament that you're in when you're praying to
the Lord? David did. He tells the Lord exactly how he feels,
exactly where he is, exactly what's going on. The Lord knows
it already, but by following the example of Scripture, we learn
that we need to spell it out. David spells out his situation to the
Lord. (Duncan, "Lord, Have Mercy")

The prayer life of Schaeffer challenges me. The prayer life of David
challenges me. Let's learn from them about the need to cultivate a
deep, intimate, direct communion with God.

What can David do about his present crisis? He responds with God-
centered meditation and yearning.

Meditate on God's Work (143:5)

David teaches us to meditate on what God has done in the past. Memory
has the ability to increase our faith in God. It can lift our spirits (cf.
Ps 42). We have already studied several historical psalms that magnify
God's work in creation and redemption (Pss 105–107). It's incredibly
important to deal with your present crisis by considering God's past

deeds (cf. Ps 77). Reflecting on what God has done inspires us to say, "Do it again, Lord!" (Williams, *Psalms 73–150*, Kindle).

David is not filling his mind with nostalgia. He does not want to go back to the "glory days," which Kidner calls "that fruitless yearning for other times and places" (*Psalms 73–150*, 475). This is a big problem for many Christians. Don't have a fruitless longing for other times and places. Instead, recall what God has done and ask God to do a fresh, new work in your life right where you are!

See the value here of mediating on Scripture and also God's work throughout history. The Bible is filled with examples of how God has worked. Church history contains more examples. Our own lives also are filled with instances in which the Lord has blessed us in particular ways. Allow reflecting on them to bring you hope in the present and ask God to do a fresh work.

Yearn for God's Presence (143:6)

In an attitude of desperation for God, David spreads out his hands to God (cf. 28:2; 44:20; 88:9; Lam 1:17); this is a posture of prayer (cf. Exod 9:29; 1 Kgs 8:22,54; Ezra 9:5). What's most important, though, is the attitude of his heart. David is longing for *God* more than anything, even more than getting *answers* from God! David's soul is thirsty. He knows only God will satisfy that thirst. He admits his spiritual dryness and asks God to come and satisfy his thirst with his presence. This kind of pursuit of God is expressed powerfully in two previous psalms:

> As a deer longs for streams of water,
> so I long for You, God.
> I thirst for God, the living God. (Ps 42:1-2 HCSB)

> God, You are my God; I eagerly seek You.
> I thirst for You;
> my body faints for You
> in a land that is dry, desolate, and without water. (Ps 63:1 HCSB)

David knows that his greatest need is not answers. It's not deliverance. It's God himself. He needs to know the nearness of God.

In God's presence we find joy, strength, and renewal (16:11; 90:14; 63:3). When we experience his presence in close, powerful ways, we will begin to recover from spiritual darkness and dryness.

When I travel, people often ask when I return, "What was the best part of the trip?" I always say, "Coming home." I just want to be with my bride. I want to be with my family. I want to be in my home. David is expressing spiritual homesickness. His soul is in a parched land. He wants to return to his soul's resting place in God's presence. Can you identify with this longing?

Our spiritual lives have ups and downs. We go through seasons of deep intimacy with God and seasons of spiritual depression. Learn to yearn for God.

A Pattern for Presenting Requests
PSALM 143:7-12

After this expression of longing for God's presence more than anything, David enters into a time of supplication. There are about 11 petitions in this section. We may group these prayers in three categories: (1) renewal, (2) guidance, and (3) deliverance. We will find ourselves presenting these types of requests at various times in our Christian pilgrimages.

Though David is despairing, his petitions are filled with expressions of confidence in God. He trusts in God (v. 8b), he appeals to God (v. 8b), he's hidden in God (v. 9b), he belongs to God (v. 10), and he's confident that God will deal with his enemies because he's a servant of God (v. 11). Out of this dynamic relationship with God, he can offer his petitions boldly.

"Renew Me" (143:7-8a)

In verse 7 David admits his need for spiritual renewal. He wants God to hear and answer him, confessing that his own "spirit fails" (cf. 84:2; Jonah 2:7). This is an expression of despair and need. He seeks God's "face" (cf. 27:9; 102:2) because apart from God's favor he is like those who go down to "the Pit" (cf. 28:1; 88:4). They're spiritually dead, but he wants spiritual vitality. He knows theologically that God is with him and for him, but he wants to "experience" God's "faithful love" (v. 8). He asks in particular for God to meet him afresh "in the morning" (cf. 30:5; 90:14; 130:6; Lam 3:23) and increase his sense of God's presence and power. This may be a figure of speech for the passing of darkness or literally for God to appear in power in the morning to him. Either way, he knows God can renew him, as he confidently says, "For I trust in you."

Is your spirit failing? Do you need to experience God's love afresh? Pray for the Holy Spirit to come and renew you (Eph 3:14-21; 2 Cor 4:16-18).

"Guide Me" (143:8b,10)

David prays for guidance in three ways. In the second line of verse 8 he emphasizes **the mind**—that is, his need for *spiritual discernment* (cf. 25:4; 32:8). We are all called to follow Jesus according to God's revealed will in Scripture. Yet the Lord puts us in particular contexts. Recall how Jesus explained to Peter and John that each of them would follow him, but they would do it in different contexts (John 21:20-22). Ask the Lord to show you how best to live out his Word.

In the first part of verse 10, David emphasizes **the will**, that is, the need to be *obedient to God's revealed will*. Ask yourself, "Am I doing what's clear in Scripture?" Start here before seeking out particulars. This may mean obeying God's will in small matters, like serving in your local church, being a good steward of money, caring for the poor and afflicted, mentoring a young person, or praying for your pastors and leaders. You never know where God may lead you once you start obeying him on the basic matters of the faith.

Finally, David emphasizes **the heart**, that is, the *humility* we need to follow God's guidance. David prays that the Spirit would incline his heart to follow God's leadership. David expresses a humble attitude, admitting that he needs the Shepherd to guide him by his "gracious Spirit" (cf. Neh 9:20). He not only needs to know which way to go but also needs someone to shepherd him to get there. The plea for "level ground" implies that David knows he may stumble (Kidner, *Psalms 73–150*, 476). He humbly asks God to lead him by the Spirit. As you seek God's will, don't merely seek answers. Cultivate a life of humility and holiness so that you are prepared to hear and do God's will once it's made clear.

David doesn't merely want to survive this situation; he wants to know and do God's will. What good is living if there's no purpose for it? Seek God's will for a meaningful life. Do you desire to do God's will? What proof do you have to demonstrate that you desire to do it? Are you searching out God's revealed will in Scripture? Are you asking God for guidance for doing his will in your particular situation? Are you asking for the Spirit's guidance?

"Deliver Me" (143:9,11-12)

In the remaining verses we read of David's great need for deliverance. He first mentions *the gift of God's deliverance* (v. 9; cf. 31:15; 59:1; 142:6). It's a simple prayer. He looks to God—not to weapons, horses, or other human resources—to rescue him.

Next, David speaks of *the goal of God's deliverance* (v. 11; cf. Pss 30:3; 119:25). He wants God's name to be honored in this deliverance (cf. 31:3; 106:8). He roots his prayer again in God's "righteousness" (cf. v. 1). When our righteous God grants deliverance, he alone deserves the glory.

Finally, David highlights *the basis of confidence in God's deliverance* (v. 12). We have come full circle now, ending where we began, with the gospel. David's confidence comes in the character of God and in his relationship to God that he obtained through grace. David knows God's faithfulness. David knows that God will fulfill his promises and deal with David's adversaries (cf. 54:5; 73:27; 94:23). David knows that he is God's "servant."

We should remember that while we may or may not be delivered from every trial in this fallen world, we will ultimately be delivered from our greatest enemies because of Jesus's death and resurrection. Salvation is a gift from God (Eph 2:8-10). Praise God that Jesus said to the Father, "Not what I will, but what you will" (Mark 14:36), and followed through with perfect and costly obedience, which included his atoning death on the cross. Someone has said that when you read the Psalms, you should imagine sharing a hymnbook with Jesus. Our Lord loved the Psalms. Of course, he would have applied them differently at various points. He took the "judgment" (v. 2) for unrighteous sinners, though he never sinned, pouring out his soul unto death so that sinners like us could receive God's righteousness (v. 11) by faith. Jesus solved our greatest problem. We should endure all other trials with this gigantic fact in mind.

Reflect and Discuss

1. What strikes you the most about David's devotional life in the Psalms (his prayers, songs, etc.)?

2. What does this psalm teach us about the gospel, particularly in verses 1-2?

3. Explain David's situation in Psalm 143. Why was he desperate for God?

4. What does this psalm teach us about our weakness and the reality of spiritual warfare?

5. How can Christians today meditate on God's work in the past (v. 5)?

6. In this psalm, how do you see David pursuing God more than anything (including answers from God)?

7. Read Psalms 42:1-2 and 63:1 along with Psalm 143:6. Can you identify with this spiritual longing? Explain.

8. In verses 7-12, how do you see David expressing confidence even though he's in a time of desperate need?

9. What does this passage teach us about God's guidance? What strikes you the most about this particular concept?

10. Take a few moments to pray through this psalm, seeking renewal and guidance.

The Song of a King for Himself and His People

PSALM 144

Main Idea: God protects and blesses those who call on him as their God.

I. **Look at Who Our God Is (144:1-2).**
   A. He is our rock (144:1).
   B. He is our faithful love (144:2).
   C. He is our fortress (144:2).
   D. He is our stronghold (144:2).
   E. He is our deliverer (144:2).
   F. He is our shield (144:2).
   G. He is our refuge (144:2).
II. **Look at What Our God Does (144:3-11).**
   A. He has come down to rescue lowly humanity (144:3-8).
   B. He gives victory to King David his servant (144:9-11).
III. **Look at Who Our God Blesses (144:12-15).**
   A. He blesses our sons (144:12).
   B. He blesses our daughters (144:12).
   C. He blesses our produce (144:13).
   D. He blesses our livestock (144:13-14).
   E. He blesses all his people (144:14-15).

It is good for our spiritual life and health when we know who God is, who we are, and what we can trust God to do for us. Psalm 144 helps us gain clarity in each of these areas while pointing us to the final, climactic, and eschatological victory of the Davidic Messiah, King Jesus. Our Lord is a warrior and a blessing to his people.

Psalm 144 is something of a mixture; it looks forward and it looks back, drawing significantly from earlier psalms, especially Psalm 18. Richard Belcher points out,

> Psalm 144 is placed in the final Davidic collection of the
> Psalter (138–145), keeping alive the hopes of the post-exilic
> community for a Davidic king [v. 10]. Thus, the psalm looks
> forward and expresses the hope of victory and blessing

through him. . . . The final victory of God's people will result
in an outpouring of eschatological blessings (144:12-15) and
the participation of all creation in the praise of God (150).
(*Messiah and the Psalms*, 154)

The flow of the psalm can be seen in three movements. First, we
see who God is for the king and for those who follow this king (vv. 1-2).
Second, we see what God does for the king and for those who reside
in his kingdom (vv. 3-11). Finally, we see who God blesses (vv. 12-15).
The expected and wonderful answer is this: "the people whose God is
the LORD."

Look at Who Our God Is
PSALM 144:1-2

With language borrowed from Psalm 18, "a thanksgiving song," David
blesses the Lord (Yahweh), who has prepared him for battle and war
(Ross, *Psalms 90–150*, 895). Yahweh "trains [his] hands for battle
and [his] fingers for warfare" (v. 1). He is ready to fight for the Lord
because the Lord has made him ready to fight. But who is this God
who has prepared him? Who is this God who "subdues . . . people
under [him]" (v. 2)? Who gives the king his kingdom and defeats his
enemies? Seven powerful images tell us exactly who this God is. Note
how often the word *my* appears. These affirmations are intimate and
personal for David. ·

He Is Our Rock (144:1)

The Lord is strong and immovable, solid and dependable (cf. 18:31,46;
19:14; 28:1; 31:3). Jesus says the wise man builds his house on the rock,
which is the Word of God (Matt 7:24-25). The Lord is our rock, a solid
foundation.

He Is Our Faithful Love (144:2)

The Lord is our *chesed*, "[our] faithful love." The Lord is "mercy" (one
meaning or nuance of *chesed*), "my loving God" (NIV), "my steadfast
love" (ESV), "my lovingkindness" (NKJV). My Lord is the faithful God of
covenant love and loyalty. He will not leave or abandon me (Heb 13:5).

He Is Our Fortress (144:2)

The Lord is "[our] fortress," a strong place of safety when we are pursued or under attack. We can run to our Lord, and he will protect us and put our souls at rest.

He Is Our Stronghold (144:2)

This idea builds on the previous one of God as our fortress. The NKJV translates the word as "high tower." The idea is that the Lord is a safe and secure place to flee to when we are assaulted and attacked by the enemy.

He Is Our Deliverer (144:2)

The Lord helps me escape harm, as if he's a firefighter rescuing someone from a fiery building (cf. 18:2; 40:17; 70:5). The Lord comes to my rescue when I am hounded and pursued by my enemies.

He Is Our Shield (144:2)

The Lord protects me when I am attacked. He keeps me from harm and injury (Ross, *Psalms 90–150*, 896). Paul reminds us to put on the "shield of faith with which [we] can extinguish all the flaming arrows of the evil one" (Eph 6:16). What a great protector is Yahweh!

He Is Our Refuge (144:2)

The Lord is the place of supreme protection and safety. The psalms especially love this image, using it over and over (2:12; 5:1,11; 7:1; 9:9; 11:1; 14:6; 16:1; 17:7; 18:2,30; 25:20; 31:1,2,4,19; 34:8,22; 36:7; 37:39,40; 43:2; 46:1; 52:7; 57:1; 59:16; 61:3-4; 62:7-8; 64:10; 71:1,3,7; 73:28; 90:1-2,4,9; 94:22; 104:18; 118:8-9; 141:8; 142:4).

The language of these verses echoes Psalm 18. They also echo 2 Samuel 22 when David sang to the Lord for rescuing "him from the grasp of all his enemies and from the grasp of Saul" (2 Sam 22:1). There he sang,

> *The LORD is my rock, my fortress, and my deliverer, my God, my rock where I seek refuge. My shield, the horn of my salvation, my stronghold, my refuge, and my Savior, you save me from violence.*
> (2 Sam 22:2-3)

Psalm 144 teaches us that David never forgot who the Lord is. Neither should we.

Look at What Our God Does
PSALM 144:3-11

Verses 3-11 make an amazing turn. The God who trains the Davidic king for war is actually the Lord who fights for him and rescues him (vv. 10-11). This is all the more amazing when we recognize who God is and who man is.

He Has Come Down to Rescue Lowly Humanity (144:3-8)

Verse 3 draws from Psalm 8:4. David is amazed the Lord condescends and pays any attention at all to lowly humans. What could we do for the formidable God of verses 1-2? We are "a breath" and our "days are like a passing shadow" (v. 4). We are brief and fleeting, here today and gone tomorrow. Still we look to our Lord and pray. We petition him and ask him to do for us what we cannot do for ourselves. The language that follows is almost apocalyptic. It again draws from Psalm 18 and is reminiscent of Mount Sinai. Ross perceptively notes,

> The psalmist was praying for some immediate deliverance. But the final answer to this prayer will undoubtedly be at the second coming of the Lord, when he does actually come down and destroy the wicked. So here is another case of a messianic interpretation that uses a type to point to the time when the poetic language will become historically literal. (*Psalms 90–150,* 898)

Lord, the psalmist appeals, intervene. "Part your heavens and come down." Show your awesome power. "Touch the mountains, and they will smoke" (v. 5). Bring divine judgment. "Flash your lightning and scatter the foe," the enemy. "Shoot your arrows and rout them" (v. 6). David speaks personally: "Reach down from on high; rescue me from deep water, and set me free from the grasp of foreigners whose mouths speak lies, whose right hands are deceptive" (vv. 7-8). David is deep in trouble, and only God can save him. He may have been trained for battle, but he is no match for his many enemies. They are outside invaders who are liars in word and deed. Warren Wiersbe writes, "They told lies and took oaths they never meant to keep. When they lifted their right hand in an oath, it was only deception" (*Bible Exposition Commentary*, 375). David faced an enemy that was cruel, deceptive, and powerful. He needed his Lord to come down and save him. We are no different. We need our God to come down and "rescue . . . and deliver" us (NKJV). Praise God he has done so in the coming of Jesus.

He Gives Victory to King David His Servant (144:9-11)

These verses sing of messianic hope and expectation. The king is confident that the Lord will come to his rescue. He is so confident that he says, "God, I will sing a new song to you" (v. 9). In context, this is a new song of salvation and victory. He will sing this song and "play on a ten-stringed harp." The one to whom he will play and sing is the Lord "who gives victory to kings, who frees his servant David from the deadly sword" (v. 10).

Verse 11 repeats the refrain of verses 7-8. They frame verses 9-10 and add intensity to the king's desperate plea for rescue and deliverance. Spurgeon writes,

> Oh to be delivered from slanderous tongues, deceptive lips, and false hearts! No wonder these words are repeated, for they are the frequent cry of many a tried child of God—"*Rid me and deliver me*." The devil's children are strange to us: we can never agree with them, and they will never understand us, they are aliens to us, and we are despised by them. O Lord, deliver us from the evil one, and from all who are of his race. (*Treasury*, vol. 3b, 358; emphasis in original)

Look at Who Our God Blesses
PSALM 144:12-15

The blessings God bestows on the Davidic king, the Messiah King, now overflow to the people of God. The rescue and deliverance of the king result in abundant blessings for "the people whose God is the LORD" (v. 15). What God does for the sovereign he also does for the sovereign's subjects.

He Blesses Our Sons (144:12)

The "sons will be like plants nurtured in their youth." They will flourish, mature, and become strong as they put down their roots (Ross, *Psalms 90–150*, 902). Strength is given by the Lord to the men of the nation.

He Blesses Our Daughters (144:12)

The daughters will be "like corner pillars that are carved in the palace style." They will be like "polished gracefulness . . . they will be flourishing in full vigor and wonderous beauty into the next generations" (Ross, *Psalms 90–150*, 902). They will be beautiful, statuesque, and elegant.

He Blesses Our Produce (144:13)

The "storehouses will be full, supplying all kinds of produce." Famine will not be a concern in this kingdom (cf. Deut 28:4). The barns in the land will be overflowing with more than enough for everyone.

He Blesses Our Livestock (144:13-14)

God will also bless the livestock in great abundance. The "flocks will increase by thousands and tens of thousands in our open fields" (v. 13). "Cattle will be well fed" (ESV, "may our cattle be heavy with young"; NIV, "our oxen will draw heavy loads"). All we need to prosper and flourish in the land will be provided in super-abounding quantity. As one beautiful hymn well says, in that day "there shall be showers of blessing."

He Blesses All His People (144:14-15)

The song concludes with its climax. In the eschatological kingdom, there are safety and blessings for "the people whose God is the LORD" (Yahweh). First, "there will be no breach in the walls, no going into captivity." (The ESV understands the phrase to refer to the cattle and translates it, they will suffer "no mishap or failure in bearing." We follow here the CSB reading.) No army will break down the walls and invade our city. Never again will we be exiled to a foreign land and enslaved to foreign rulers (cf. Amos 4:3). Second, and as a result of this promise, there is "no cry of lament in our public squares" (cf. Jer 14:2). Never again will God's people wail and cry out in lament and sorrow because foreign enemies have invaded the land and carried loved ones into captivity. God has come down and rescued his people. And this rescue is permanent and everlasting! Such a promise of victory calls for a shout of praise: "Blessed are the people to whom such blessings fall! Blessed are the people whose God is the Lord" (ESV).

Conclusion

Michael Wilcock provides a fitting word to conclude our study. May we reflect on what he says.

> Then and now, whenever God's people are under assault they do well to remind themselves of all that their *loving God* has done for them in the past, insignificant though they are. They can quite properly ask him to act in ways that even in modern times might be described as the rending of the heavens, a bolt of lightning, rescue from a sea of troubles. They know that his, and their, chief weapon is the truth of the gospel, to destroy the lies which . . . are the secret of the enemy's great strength. They are sure that nothing but good can result, even from the most disastrous circumstances, when God's people are taking refuge in the Rock. (*Message: Songs*, 271; emphasis in original)

Reflect and Discuss

1. What do the metaphors for God in this psalm have in common? Using the metaphors like the psalmist, what lies are you often tempted to believe about God?
2. Why is it significant that the psalmist recalls the nature both of God (vv. 1-2) and of man (vv. 3-4)?
3. If God is the deliverer and shield, as the psalmist describes, why do Christians have trouble? What other passages of Scripture can help you answer this question?
4. David sang this psalm when God rescued him. What does this action teach us about the role of singing in our lives and in the church?
5. Do you, like David in verses 5-8, ask God to act on your behalf? How would you describe the manner in which David speaks to God?
6. Lying by the wicked frequently appears in the psalms. Why would this be a danger to David? Is this a danger to us still? Why or why not?

7. How might you describe God's promise of blessing in verses 13-14 using modern terms?

8. David places his request to God between his blessing of God and his hope in God. What does this teach you about how to interact with God? How would including blessing and hope in your prayers shape how you make requests to God?

9. What happens when we forget who we are (vv. 3-4)? How would forgetting who we are affect our prayers?

10. According to the Scriptures, what does it mean to be blessed?

Unsearchable Greatness, Abundant Goodness

PSALM 145

Main Idea: In his last recorded hymn in the Psalter, David magnifies the greatness and goodness of God, which should kindle in us God-centered hope, peace, and awe.

I. **Praise God for His Unsearchable Greatness (145:1-3).**
II. **Praise God for His Abundant Goodness (145:4-9).**
    A. Commend God's goodness to the next generation (145:4-7).
    B. Cherish God's goodness in salvation (145:8).
    C. Consider God's goodness in creation (145:9).
III. **Praise God for His Kingly Greatness (145:10-13a).**
IV. **Praise God for His Satisfying Goodness (145:13b-21).**
    A. The Lord helps the weak (145:14).
    B. The Lord provides food for all creatures (145:15-16).
    C. The Lord answers prayer (145:18-19).
    D. The Lord protects his people (145:20).

Several years ago I (Tony) made the decision to memorize various psalms in order to rejuvenate my weak devotional life. One of the first psalms I chose was Psalm 145. Day after day, usually on my back porch, I would recite it out loud, meditate on its truths, and pray through it. I think it impacted me to the extent it did because this psalm magnifies the greatness and goodness of God, and I need to be reminded of these realities daily! Why does everyone need an elevated vision of God's greatness and goodness? A vision of God's greatness and goodness will help us overcome despair, anxiety, and apathy.

It's easy to *despair* or grow hopeless in this life. Negative cynicism and hopeless despair are everywhere today. Many of these feelings grow out of a doubt in the goodness of God and a disbelief in the greatness of God. Cynics live with a sense of "defeated weariness" (Paul Miller, *Praying Life*, 77). They doubt if God will do anything great or good. But when you read Psalm 145, your cynicism gets attacked. Your despair gets confronted. If you will lift your eyes to this King, whose "greatness is unsearchable," you can learn to hope again. You can learn to believe that "this is my Father's world" and I have every reason to hope. Psalm 145 is not teaching naïve optimism but God-centered optimism.

It's also easy to be *anxious* in this life. Fearful or paralyzing anxiety robs you of joy and turns you inward. But Psalm 145 shows us that God sustains and satisfies every living thing. He is worthy of our trust. We can rest in his care.

How about *apathy*? One of the problems many Christians face is familiarity with the things of God. As a result of being around religious things, many Christians can slowly lose an awe of God. I experienced this when I was a PhD student. And there's nothing more dangerous than for a believer to lose his or her awe. If you don't live with a sense of awe before God, it will negatively affect every aspect of your life. Relationships will suffer. You will spend money wrongly. You will make bad decisions. You will drift into idolatry. We were made for wonder. Paul Tripp states, "Every human being has been hardwired by God to live in daily awe of God" (*Dangerous Calling*, 117). So Psalm 145 is important, as Tripp calls this psalm "one of the Bible's awe passages" (ibid., 114). Allow this text to reignite childlike wonder in you.

My prayer as we consider this psalm is that it will confront your despair, anxiety, and apathy, and ignite God-centered hope, peace, and awe.

Derek Kidner calls this psalm "An Alphabet of Praise" (*Psalms 73–150*, 480). That's because it is an alphabetic acrostic. That is, each verse begins with a consecutive letter in the Hebrew alphabet. This is the last of eight acrostics in the book of Psalms (see Pss 9–10; 25; 34; 37; 111–112; and 119). David penned five of these acrostics; he obviously valued this rhetorical device. (Verse 13b provides the *nun* or "n" in the acrostic, which is found in the documents discovered at Qumran and is found in other ancient translations as well.)

Psalm 145 is one of the most beautiful hymns in the Psalter. Some in the Jewish tradition believed that if one would recite it three times a day, with heart and lips, one would experience spiritual happiness and enjoy blessings in the world to come (Calvin, *Commentary*, 4:271). Indeed, every believer in Christ today would benefit from committing it to memory.

This psalm is the last in the Psalter attributed to David. Perhaps even more surprising is that this is the only inscription in the Psalter that calls the psalm a hymn or "A Song of *Praise*" (ESV; emphasis added). In the psalms following Psalm 145 (Pss 146–150), each begins and ends with "Hallelujah!" So you could call Psalm 145 the preface or introduction to the praise songs. David provides this introduction as he focuses our attention on the object of our praise. He gives an awe-inspiring description of both the *greatness of God* and the *goodness of God*, who is our *King.* We see a mingling of God's majesty and grace, righteousness and kindness, kingship and fatherly generosity. Indeed, the wonder of this psalm revolves around David's vision of God, not his use of the Hebrew alphabet! I have chosen an (imperfect) outline that draws attention to God's greatness and goodness. (For a more structural breakdown, see VanGemeren, "Psalms," 860.)

Praise God for His Unsearchable Greatness
PSALM 145:1-3

David wouldn't agree with Christopher Hitchens's book *God Is Not Great.* To the contrary, David magnifies the "unsearchable greatness" of God. God's greatness serves as the fuel for praise.

The tone is set in verse 1. David, an earthly king, recognizes that ultimately there's only one King. The power and sovereignty of earthly kings is limited, but God the King reigns over all (cf. Ps 93). The glory of earthly kings is fleeting, but God's glory endures "forever and ever." Consequently, it's fitting to exalt God and to bless his name now and forever. These expressions of praise are the first of many in this psalm. David's personal praise is intended to stir up others to do the same.

Perhaps you've been asked, or have asked, "What are the plans today?" "What should we do today?" We may do a number of things, but one thing we should do every day is bless the Lord (v. 2). We should bless him daily and forevermore.

Notice in verses 1-2 the emphasis on "I will." As they join in the song, each member of the congregation is committing to praise. Praise involves an act of the will. We must decide to praise the Lord instead of other substitute gods. Everyone will praise something. It's not like the Psalms are only speaking to a small subset of religious people who are interested in the topic of praise. They are addressing every person that has ever lived. The issue is how you finish this sentence: "I will praise _____." We were made for praise—and that praise belongs only to God, the King.

Can you say he is your King (v. 1a)? You can if you have bowed to Jesus Christ and submitted your life to him. He's the reigning King who died and rose for sinners like us, who make substitute gods. The only King with all power and glory died for sinners? What kind of King does that? There's only one true saving King, and his name is Jesus.

David continues to talk about the stunning nature of God (v. 3). Here's a great reason to praise the Lord: the Lord is great. His greatness is unsearchable (cf. 48:1; 96:4; 147:5).

Great is a word that is overused in our day. People use the term for things like deodorant, hamburgers, cities, and athletes. Some have even used this adjective as part of their names, like "Alexander the Great." Sometimes you hear people say, after talking with a famous political leader, for instance, "I have been in the presence of greatness." I don't want to downplay the significance of influential and gifted people, but all human displays of greatness pale in comparison to the greatness of God. Only of God can we say, "How great thou art!" When we've been extolling him, we can truly say, "I was in the presence of greatness."

Sometimes people wonder, "Doesn't it get old to exalt the Lord every day?" Not if you see that his greatness is "unsearchable" (cf. Eph 3:8). The best of minds from all ages, using the most advanced technology, can't come close to capturing the glory of God (Storms, "Unsearchable"). What we know of the majesty of God is a gift; God has chosen to reveal himself to us. David reminds us that for all of eternity we will marvel at God's splendor, majesty, and greatness. We can't fully fathom the depth of his majesty (cf. Job 5:9; 9:10; Isa 40:28).

The question is, Does your praise of God do honor to his greatness? David says that God is "highly praised" (v. 3). He doesn't say, "He's worthy of half-hearted praise." Do you get more excited about great plays on the football field or great movies than you do at the privilege you have of giving praise to the great God? If none compare to him, our praise to him should be deeper and more passionate than our praise of other things.

Praise God for His Abundant Goodness
PSALM 145:4-9

Here's the good news: this infinitely great and majestic and powerful God is also *good*. Imagine if this great God were also *bad*! The psalmist helps us ponder and apply aspects of God's goodness.

Commend God's Goodness to the Next Generation (145:4-7)

David looks ahead to the coming generations giving praise to the Lord for his greatness and goodness. David had no idea how many millions would declare God's praise in the coming generations! John says that no one will be able to number the people—a people from every tribe and tongue—that will sing praise unto the Savior (Rev 7:9-12).

Verse 4 shows us *the need to pass on* the story of redemption to the next generation (cf. Gen 18:19; Exod 12:26-27; 13:8; Deut 6:1-9; Ps 78:4). John Piper reminds us of our responsibility:

> It is the Biblical duty of every generation of Christians to see to it that the next generation hears about the mighty acts of God. God does not drop a new Bible from heaven on every generation. He intends that the older generation will teach the newer generation to read and think and trust and obey and rejoice. It's true that God draws near personally to every new generation of believers, but he does so through the Biblical truth that they learn from the preceding generations. ("One Generation")

David tells us *what to pass on,* namely, the saving activity of God. In the Old Testament these "mighty acts" (v. 4) remind us of the exodus event, the great display of God delivering his people from bondage. In the New Testament we have an even greater display of God's mighty acts in the story of Jesus's death and resurrection. We must continue to teach the coming generations about the gospel of Jesus.

In addition, David tells us *how to pass on the gospel.* He doesn't merely say, "Impart truth to the next generation," though that's part of it. He says that one generation will "commend" (ESV) or "praise" (NKJV) or "declare" (CSB) God's works to the next generation. This involves not just a commitment to the truth but a love for the truth. It involves not merely transferring information but demonstrating adoration. In other words, the next generation needs to see their parents and teachers praise God with passion. We need to say, "Taste and see that the LORD is good" (Ps 34:8) as people who have found the satisfying pleasure of knowing God personally.

We must cherish the gospel. We won't commend what we don't cherish. So verse 5 reminds us that we need to *meditate on the gospel* (ESV). We must daily ponder what God has done in redemptive history so that our hearts may overflow with public acts of praise and proclamation. The reason the gospel doesn't get passed on to the next generation is largely because God's people fail to fill their affections with the good news. They fail to meditate on it. Remember, we are always one generation away from losing the gospel. Meditate on it, that you may know it, be edified by it, and teach it to the next generation.

In verse 6 the responsibility of passing on the story of God's mighty acts continues. David shows us the way multiplication works. One declares, and others follow.

Verse 7 has become a personal prayer of mine for my kids. Here's *the goal of passing on the gospel* with passionate adoration. David longs for the next generation not only to speak about the Lord but also to gush out praise! Do you long for this in your children and in the children of your church, that they would pour forth the fame of God's abundant goodness? I long for a lot of things in my children—that they would do well in school, stay out of trouble, get good jobs, and more. But this should be at the top of our list: that our children may pour forth praise to God! We should long for them to know the essentials of the faith, but that's not our only goal. We want them to speak of God's awesome deeds. We should long for them to pour forth the praises of God. The goal isn't merely to train up civil little kids who know Bible answers. This psalm is pushing us further—to train up God-exalting missionaries!

There are several ways we may teach the coming generations: through preaching, teaching, writing, singing, small groups, one-on-one discipleship, and helping them practice spiritual disciplines. But our teaching should always be infused with passion and zeal for the King. Otherwise, there's a great disconnect. Our words say one thing, but our emotions portray another. Effective discipleship involves both information and adoration.

The church supports this discipleship and helps equip parents to do it better (Eph 4:11-12), but the primary responsibility for training the next generation falls on parents (Deut 6:4-7; Ps 78:5-7; Eph 6:1-4). Let's not cease commending God's works to the next generation!

Cherish God's Goodness in Salvation (145:8)

In verse 8 David's words of praise about God's grace and compassion echo God's self-revelation at Sinai in Exodus 34:6, which God provided to Moses in response to his prayer. It's one of the most quoted statements in the Old Testament (Kidner, *Psalms 73–150*, 481). Jonah cited it in anger when the Ninevites repented (Jonah 4:2,11) because the reluctant missionary didn't think the Ninevites deserved God's salvation. Jonah wanted to preach to his own people, not "those people." But God's saving goodness extends to all sinners who repent (see also Neh 9:17,31; Pss 86:15; 103:8; Joel 2:13). We should never imagine that we have been saved by our own goodness. We have been saved because God is good. Paul writes to Titus,

For we too were once foolish, disobedient, deceived, enslaved by various passions and pleasures, living in malice and envy, hateful, detesting one another.

But when the kindness of God our Savior and his love for mankind *appeared, he saved us—not by works of righteousness that we had done, but* according to his mercy—*through the washing of regeneration and renewal by the Holy Spirit. He poured out his Spirit on us abundantly through Jesus Christ our Savior so that, having been* justified *by his grace, we may become heirs with the hope of eternal life.* (Titus 3:3-7; emphasis added)

For all eternity we will be singing of the Lord's goodness, mercy, and grace, which he has shown to us in Christ Jesus. Cherish God's goodness.

Consider God's Goodness in Creation (145:9)

God's goodness extends in common grace to all creation. Think about the wonder of God's goodness displayed to evil men. Even the vilest of sinners—serial killers, rapists, wicked tyrants, sexual perverts, liars—get to see and experience the goodness of God in creation. Nero got to eat delicious steak. Hitler got to see the Alps. Manson saw sunsets. Pol Pot smelled flowers. Stalin breathed cool air. Each of these evil men experienced God's goodness in creation. Jesus said of the Father in heaven, "He causes his sun to rise on the evil and the good, and sends rain on the righteous and the unrighteous" (Matt 5:45; cf. Jas 1:17). Sadly, these men, and every other unrepentant person, only get to enjoy God's goodness for a moment—this life is a vapor—but for all who have entered into Christ, all who have become new creations in Christ Jesus, we will enjoy God's goodness for all eternity.

Many have difficulty with the Christian faith because of the "problem of evil." They ask, "How could a good, loving, and powerful God allow evil to exist?" But no one seems to have difficulty with the problem of good. No one wakes up with this question on their mind: How could a holy God allow sinful people to experience any of his goodness? We don't ask that question because we have presumed upon God's goodness. We think we're entitled to his goodness. We're not! We don't deserve any of his grace. We deserve judgment. So then, let's not take his goodness for granted. Recognize his goodness expressed widely and rejoice in it personally.

Praise God for His Kingly Greatness
PSALM 145:10-13A

Verse 10 picks up the train of thought in verse 9. All that God has made should give thanks to him for his common goodness (vv. 9b-10a). And God's "saints" (v. 10b ESV) or "faithful" (CSB) should give thanks to God for his saving goodness (vv. 9a,10b). From there, the psalmist describes God's kingship, using the term *kingdom* four times in verses 11-13.

In verses 11-12 David explains the verbal responsibility of the saints. They will "speak" of the glory of God's kingdom (v. 11). They will "declare" God's might (v. 11). They will inform people of God's mighty deeds and of the glorious splendor of his kingdom (v. 12).

Kingdom people are talking people. We must never stop exalting our King, whose "everlasting kingdom" endures throughout all generations (v. 13). His kingdom will never be overthrown from the outside by human dynasties, nor will it ever collapse from within due to poor leadership. There are no successors to God's reign! There's no "Yahweh II." There's just Yahweh! His reign endures forever.

Interestingly, verse 13 reappears on the lips of Nebuchadnezzar in Daniel 4:3, when this earthly king confesses God's universal rule. Nebuchadnezzar's expression of praise to God, the true King, illustrates God's sweeping sovereignty over every kingdom of man.

When basketball superstar LeBron James returned to play for Cleveland, after leaving the city for his championship run in Miami, Cleveland fans rejoiced with hope, saying, "The king is returning!" They believed King James would bring victory to the city. James may bring a championship, but the believer's hope is in the return of another King. Jesus Christ, who in his first coming proclaimed the kingdom and previewed the glory of the culminated kingdom, will return to fulfill this biblical theme and satisfy the believer's hope. King Jesus will set all things right, make all sad things come untrue, and put all enemies under his feet, and we will dwell in that eternal kingdom. You can, and should, trust in this King.

Praise God for His Satisfying Goodness
PSALM 145:13B-21

God is not only the sovereign King but also the gracious King. The following verses show how the Lord sustains the world. As the sovereign King, his rule extends throughout the entire creation. As the gracious King, he sustains his creation with kind provisions. This gracious King cares for creation in general, and he has special care for those who are in relationship with him.

Verses 13 and 17 show us the character of God from which these works of grace flow. God's provisions flow from his faithful, gracious, and righteous character. In the King's graciousness he preserves his creatures, especially his people. Consider four ways in which the Lord satisfies the needs of all who look to him.

The Lord Helps the Weak (145:14)

The Lord's kindness is displayed in the way he restores the fallen. He "helps" all who are falling. He "raises up" the "oppressed," or the bowed down. Richard Sibbes says, "Christ refuses none for weakness . . . but accepts none for greatness" (*Bruised Reed*, 26). Your weakness isn't a limitation but an opportunity to experience the Savior's grace.

Indeed, the Lord is mindful of the oppressed. He's mindful of those who are crushed in spirit. David says elsewhere, "The LORD is near the brokenhearted; he saves those crushed in spirit" (34:18). The weary believer can say with David, "But you, LORD, are a shield around me, my glory, and the one who lifts up my head" (3:3).

When I (Tony) played baseball as a kid and then into high school, my dad was my coach. He was a very encouraging coach. When I played in college, he would take his vacation days to watch me play, often arriving in the stands before the team showed up to road games! I'll never forget this support. My dad knew that my tendency was to get down emotionally after making an error or striking out. He would often say to me as I returned to the dugout things like, "Head up, six!" (That was my number.) Good dads help their sons pick their heads up. They encourage and lift. That's what our God does. We have the King who says, "Get your head up! I'm with you and for you." What kind of King is mindful of the brokenhearted, beaten, and bruised? Our God is. Are you weak? Are you falling? Has sin overwhelmed you? Has someone oppressed you? Look to this God for help. He is our glory and the lifter of our heads. This is not naïve optimism; this is God-centered truth.

The Lord Provides Food for All Creatures (145:15-16)

David describes how all creation looks to God for provision (v. 15). A similar expression is found in Psalm 104, where the psalmist describes how the eyes of every donkey, bird, cow, stork, goat, hyrax, lion, sea creature, and more depend on the Creator (104:10-27). The Lord's royal love for his creatures is expressed in intimate terms, as David goes on to say (v. 16). The Lord opens his hand like a person feeding animals, giving them as much as they desire. The King is generous, not dispensing in small, measured amounts but providing abundantly (Goldingay, *Psalms*, 703).

The Lord Answers Prayer (145:18-19)

After making a statement about the Lord's "righteous" and "faithful" character in verse 17, David rejoices in God's willingness to hear and answer the cries of his people. In whatever situation, one may call out to the Lord. Whether one is in danger, hunger, sickness, panic, or fear, simply call out to the Lord "with integrity" (v. 18b) or "in truth" (ESV). Because God is sovereign, he's *able* to carry your burden. Because God is gracious, he's *willing* to carry your burden. Give it to him.

The emphasis is on not wavering in your crying. In Israel's context David may have something like this in mind: "Don't cry out to the Lord for help but be secretly trusting in Baal." While we may not trust in Baal, we may trust in human ingenuity or worldly wealth to get out of a predicament, all the while "praying about it."

The Lord is near to those who are *sincerely* seeking him alone as one's ultimate help (John 4:24). Don't worry about impressing God with eloquence. Some think, *My prayers are not worth writing home about.* That's OK because you're not writing home but heaven (Jared Wilson, *Pastor's Justification*, 69). Speak sincerely to the Father.

Verse 19 links with verse 18 as David speaks again of God's hearing prayers. The people who call on the Lord "with integrity" (v. 18) are the people who "fear him" (v. 19). Those who submit to God and walk in his ways are his people (cf. 25:14). And they can cry out to God for help, knowing God is faithful to respond. But "he knows the haughty from a distance" (138:6). How do people enter a relationship with God and continue that intimate relationship? They humble themselves before the Lord (cf. Luke 14:11; 18:13-14).

Be encouraged here. Pray sincerely. Pray dependently. Pray humbly. The Lord hears his people when they cry out to him like this.

The Lord Protects His People (145:20)

Those who receive God's protection are the people who "love him" (v. 20a). This is a simple expression of a Christian. When talking about God guarding his people by his power (1 Pet 1:5), Peter says that though we have not seen him, we "love him" (1 Pet 1:8). Those who love King Jesus belong to him forever. Jesus will protect, guard, preserve, and sustain them until the God of all grace brings them into his eternal kingdom (1 Pet 5:10). This doesn't mean his people will have easy lives, but they will have eternally secure ones (Luke 21:16-18).

The wicked share no such assurance (v. 20b). All who fail to submit to the King in repentance and faith will perish (1:6; 104:35; 143:12; cf. 7:12-16).

Therefore, look to King Jesus. He saves sinners from the wrath to come. He graciously attends to the needs of all who look to him. To enter into a saving and satisfying relationship, all you need is *need*. Sadly, many don't have it. They want to live life apart from Jesus. But those who admit their need find rest for their souls—not only rest in this life but also eternal rest in the coming kingdom. Jesus said, "Blessed are the poor in spirit, for the kingdom of heaven is theirs" (Matt 5:3). Do you feel too afflicted to cry out for help? Too sinful? Too poor? Think again. You're a great candidate for the King's grace.

The psalmist concludes with the only logical response to God's goodness and greatness, along with his sovereignty and sustaining grace: praise (v. 21). Kidner says that this note of praise is "as wide as mankind and as unfading as eternity" (*Psalms 73–150*, 483). David thus ends where he began (vv. 1-2), with a commitment to praise the Lord forever. He has given us a whole alphabet of reasons to praise the Lord! So let us join in this song of praise to our God, the King whose goodness is abundant and whose greatness is unsearchable.

Reflect and Discuss

1. How can Psalm 145 help us overcome the problems of anxiety, despair, and apathy?
2. How is the greatness of God expressed in this passage?
3. How is the goodness of God expressed in this passage?
4. How does Psalm 145 promote next-generation discipleship?
5. What does the psalmist say about God's "common grace," that is, his goodness displayed to creation in general?
6. Why should this passage encourage a person doubting God's provision?
7. How does this passage encourage the weak and the oppressed?
8. How does this passage encourage us to pray?
9. How does Psalm 145 introduce the psalms that follow (Pss 146–150)?
10. Take a few moments to pray through Psalm 145.

Our God Is an Awesome God

PSALM 146

Main Idea: God's faithful character and righteous conduct are eternal reasons for praising, trusting, and hoping in him.

I. **I Will Praise the Lord (146:1-2).**
II. **I Will Trust the Lord (146:3-4).**
III. **I Will Hope in the Lord (146:5-9).**
    A. He helps his covenant people (146:5).
    B. He made everything (146:6).
    C. He keeps his word (146:6).
    D. He helps the oppressed (146:7).
    E. He feeds the hungry (146:7).
    F. He frees prisoners (146:7).
    G. He gives sight to the blind (146:8).
    H. He exalts the humble (146:8).
    I. He loves the righteous (146:8).
    J. He cares for the foreigners (146:9).
    K. He sustains the fatherless and widows (146:9).
    L. He frustrates the way of the wicked (146:9).
IV. **I Will Exalt the Lord (146:10).**

One of the greatest musical works ever written is George Frederic Handel's (1685–1759) *Messiah*. The most famous song of that oratorio is the "Hallelujah" chorus. The text of the song comes from Revelation 11:15; 19:6,16. The song both begins and ends with the word "Hallelujah." It would not have been surprising to find Handel had drawn inspiration from the closing psalms of the Hebrew hymnbook. The final five songs all begin and end with the word "Hallelujah," which is translated "Praise the Lord" in several English versions.

Psalm 146 is the first psalm of this hallelujah quintet. It is appropriate that the Psalter ends in this way. Two other sections of psalms bring *hallel* or *hallelujah* psalms together. Psalms 113–118 are Egyptian Hallel psalms and Psalms 120–136 are the Great Hallel (VanGemeren, *Psalms*, 992). Now we come to the end of our journey through the psalms

343

with the double hallelujah psalms, which begin and end with the word "Hallelujah." Those who have experienced the grace and goodness of God recognize that our God is an awesome God. Our world is filled with sin and sorrow, but we serve a great God who made everything (v. 6), keeps his word (v. 6), does what is right (v. 7), and helps those who are hurting (vv. 7-9). For such a God, we can say "Hallelujah!" For such a God, we can say, "Praise the Lord!"

What exactly does this unknown psalmist (146–150 are all anonymous) model for us in terms of the proper response to our great God? The psalm provides us with four responses from its ten verses.

I Will Praise the Lord
PSALM 146:1-2

The psalm begins literally, "Praise Yah," a word in Hebrew that uses a shortened form of the Lord's divine name (Yahweh). It is pronounced *hallelujah*. The psalmist vows to praise the Lord "all [his] life" and "as long as [he lives]." "LORD" appears 11 times in this psalm (counting the occurrences in the word "Hallelujah"), and "God" appears four times—a total of 15 references to God in 10 verses. A joyful life will be a theocentric life, a God-centered, God-focused, God-intoxicated life. From the depths of our souls and with all that we are, we should praise the Lord. And what lives in our souls will find its way to our lips (v. 2). We must determine to praise the Lord with our singing "as long as [we] live." Such praise and singing are not always easy, but they are absolutely necessary to our spiritual health and vitality.

Genuine praise to our God will engage the mind, stir the emotions, and move the will. It will build its foundation on the Word of God, and it will engulf the whole person. All of the psalmist ("my soul") will praise this great God as long as he lives and for all of eternity.

I Will Trust the Lord
PSALM 146:3-4

The psalmist calls us to trust the Lord, but he does so by a negative example. His example highlights the finitude, impotency, and transitory nature of human life. It intentionally aims to humble us.

Kings and "nobles" (v. 3), presidents and governors, are powerful and influential. By the command of their voices and the power of their pens, they can make decisions that influence thousands, millions, even billions. Still they are mere mortals. They are flesh and blood like you and me. Ultimately, they "cannot save" us either in this life or in the life to come. "Do not trust" in them, the psalmist says. Sadly, many put more hope in Capitol Hill than Calvary's hill! They put more hope in a government than they do in God! They trust in those who are not awesome rather than in the One who is.

Mere mortals cannot save us. They cannot even save themselves. Verse 4 tells us that when this leader's "breath leaves him, he returns to the ground; on that day his plans die." Here today, gone tomorrow, and soon to be forgotten as a historical footnote; that is a powerful man's destiny.

Death comes to us all. Presidents, princes, and the powerful are not exempt. Genesis 3:19 is a sober reminder to us all: "You will eat bread by the sweat of your brow until you return to the ground, since you were taken from it. For you are dust, and you will return to dust." We are *adam* (man), and to the *adamah* (ground) we must return. First Maccabees 2:63, an intertestamental Hebrew writing, says it well: "Today they will be elevated, but tomorrow they will not be found, because they will have returned to their dust and their counsels will be lost" (NETS). If these men cannot save themselves, why would we trust them to save us? We should only trust in the Lord.

I Will Hope in the Lord
PSALM 146:5-9

These verses are the heart of the psalm. They inform us about the character and conduct of our God—who he is and what he does. There is a similar theme in the messianic text of Isaiah 61:1-3 as well as in the words of Jesus in Luke 4:18-19 and 7:22-23 (Kidner, *Psalms 73–150*, 484).

Psalm 146 charges us to find our help and our place of hope in the "God of Jacob," the "LORD his God" (v. 5). The "God of Jacob" reminds us that our God is a covenant-keeping God who helped the patriarchal schemer in his times of need and even desperation (see Gen 25–35). The title "God of Jacob" appears numerous times in Psalms (e.g., 20:1; 24:6; 46:7,11), and the beatitude or blessing of verse 5 is the last of 25 blessings in the Psalms that began with Psalm 1:1 (Wiersbe, *Bible Exposition Commentary*, 378). There are 12 glorious affirmations in verses 5-9 that teach us why this God is the only God we should hope in. The psalmist builds a powerful case.

He Helps His Covenant People (146:5)

The God of the fathers, "the God of Jacob," is faithful to his people even when his people are unfaithful. He helps us, and we rightly and wisely hope in him.

He Made Everything (146:6)

He is the "Maker of heaven and earth." The Creator God of Genesis 1–2 and the covenant God of Genesis 12 and 2 Samuel 7 are the same. As the Maker of everything, including "the sea and everything in [it]," he has omnipotent power to meet any and every need we may have. The people of the psalmist's day feared the sea and saw it as dangerous and uncertain. But the Hebrews' God is the one who made it, and they (and we) can trust him.

He Keeps His Word (146:6)

Our God "remains faithful forever." Other translations read, "Who keeps truth forever" (NKJV); "Who keeps faith forever" (ESV; NASB); "Who remains faithful forever" (NIV); "He always does what he says" (*The Message*). You can trust Yahweh to keep his word. You can trust his promises. He will not fail you.

He Helps the Oppressed (146:7)

Our God is continually "executing justice for the exploited." Those who would abuse the oppressed should recognize they make God their enemy. He will bring wicked oppressors who push down and hold down others to justice. Some meet his justice in this life. All unbelievers will face his justice at the great white throne judgment of Revelation 20:11-15; believers will face the judgment seat of Christ mentioned in 2 Corinthians 5:10.

He Feeds the Hungry (146:7)

Our Lord is "giving food to the hungry." Allen Ross notes, "[God] may intervene directly, but he often chooses to use his covenant people as the agents, especially in championing justice for those who are oppressed and for feeding the hungry" (*Psalms 90–150*, 925). Through his body on earth, the church, he dispenses both physical bread and spiritual bread (the bread of life of John 6:35). Jesus speaks to this idea in Matthew 25:34-46.

He Frees Prisoners (146:7)

Working for justice, our Lord sets free those whom evil and unjust rulers wrongly imprison. Again, he often uses his people to do so. William Wilberforce (1759–1833), who led the movement to abolish the slave trade in England, is one example. The greatest liberation is that by the Lord Jesus, who through his cross and resurrection sets us free from sin, Satan, death, hell, and the grave. John 8:36 is a wonderful promise: "So if the Son sets you free, you really will be free."

He Gives Sight to the Blind (146:8)

"The LORD opens the eyes of the blind." In the ministry of Jesus, he healed both physical and spiritual blindness (see John 9). Jesus came as the "light of the world." Giving physical healing to some, he gives spiritual healing to all who call on him, for, "Anyone who follows [him] will never walk in the darkness but will have the light of life" (John 8:12).

He Exalts the Humble (146:8)

"The LORD raises up those who are oppressed." He raises those who are humbled and brought low in this life to a new status as they place their hope in him (cf. Jas 1:9-11). Consider the rich man and Lazarus in Luke 16:19-31. Our God is the God of great reversals. What counts for much in this world counts for little or nothing in the kingdom of God. James 4:6 is instructive: "But [God] gives greater grace. Therefore, he says: 'God resists the proud but gives grace to the humble.'"

He Loves the Righteous (146:8)

The Lord loves "the righteous," those who are made righteous in Christ and pursue righteousness in all they do. They are not carnal pragmatists who believe the ends justify the means. No, they know and understand as those who trust and hope in a righteous God that we promote righteous means as well as righteous ends.

He Cares for the Foreigners (146:9)

God protects foreigners. God cares for the stranger, the resident alien, the sojourner, the outsider, the minority, the immigrant. He has a unique and particular concern for them. Do you? Do I?

He Sustains the Fatherless and Widows (146:9)

Have you lost a father or mother? Are you an orphan in this world? God will sustain and uphold you. He will help you. Allow him, ask him, and he will become your parent, your perfect Father (John 1:12). Have you lost a spouse by death, desertion, or divorce? He knows. He cares. He will help you make it. He will give you the strength you need to continue.

He Frustrates the Way of the Wicked (146:9)

God ruins the way of the wicked (ESV); he "frustrates" their ways, their plans. They think they have it all figured out and, in a heartbeat, it all falls apart. Proverbs 14:11-12 teaches us,

> The house of the wicked will be destroyed, but the tent of the upright will flourish. There is a way that seems right to a person, but its end is the way to death.

I Will Exalt the Lord

PSALM 146:10

The psalm ends as it began with the high note of "hallelujah," or "praise the LORD." But a new word about Yahweh's eternal kingship and reign is added: "The LORD reigns forever." Wiersbe notes,

> "This statement comes from the song of victory that Israel sang at the Exodus (Ex. 15:18). 'The Lord reigns' is found in 93:1; 96:10; 97:1; and 99:1" (*Bible Exposition Commentary*, 378).

Earthly rulers come and go. They are like an early morning fog burned off by the blazing heat of the sun. Regardless of their wisdom, power, personality, and influence, they eventually pass off the scene. They die. This is true of every king but one: our King, the Lord who is King, our King Jesus. As Revelation 11:15 says,

> The seventh angel blew his trumpet, and there were loud voices in heaven saying, The kingdom of this world has become the kingdom of our Lord and of his Christ, and he will reign forever and ever!

Conclusion

The Lord reigns from Zion "for all generations." Zion is the earthly home of the King. Echoes of Psalm 2:6-8 can be heard in the corridors of heaven! The Lord's anointed King, his anointed Son, will sovereignly reign over all that he has purchased with his blood. His reign is total. His reign is forever. What can we say to this? "Hallelujah!" "Praise the LORD!" Truly, our God is an awesome God. The question we must each answer is this: Is he my awesome God through repentance and personal faith in his Son, King Jesus?

This humble Galilean, the Lord Jesus Christ, is worthy of our trust. He is an awesome Savior. He is an awesome God.

Reflect and Discuss

1. Why will a God-focused life be a joyful life? In what ways does a God-centered life bring more joy than a self-centered life? Does this mean non-Christians are less happy than Christians?

2. How does the Word of God fuel and assist our praise of God? How are you already incorporating the Word of God into your worship of him? What other ways can you incorporate his Word?

3. How can trust in man replace one's trust in God? How does one use human resources for help and aid while continuing to trust in God?

4. In what ways does the psalmist contrast nobles (vv. 3-4) and God (vv. 5-10)? What does this contrast teach us?

5. How does God's character as Creator and covenant maker (vv. 5-6) shape how he acts (vv. 7-9)? What does God's work for the exploited and oppressed tell you about his character?

6. Where do you see God's concern for the poor and lowly in the New Testament? What does the New Testament teach about how the church should care for and love this group?

7. This psalm teaches that God often uses his covenant people as his agents to care for the lowly. Who are the lowly around you? What can you do to be an agent of God's care to them?

8. How are both words and deeds vital to the church's work in the world? What happens if the church loses either words or deeds?

9. How can God's eternal reign give you hope for his work in the present?

10. How does your relationship with God affect your ability to praise him?

The Uniqueness of God

PSALM 147

Main Idea: It is good and right to praise our incomparable God, the Creator and Redeemer, who delights in his people.

I.   Praise God because His Commands Lead Us into Joy (147:1).
II.   Praise God because He Heals the Brokenhearted (147:2-3).
III. Praise God because He Creates and Rules Nature (147:4-5).
IV.   Praise God because He Lifts and Punishes (147:6).
V.   Praise God because He Provides (147:7-9).
VI.   Praise God because He Takes Pleasure in His People (147:10-11).
VII. Praise God because He Blesses His People (147:12-14).
VIII. Praise God because He Commands the Weather (147:15-18).
IX.   Praise God because He Instructs by His Word (147:19-20).

This hymn in Psalm 147 (probably written after the exile; see vv. 2,13-14) magnifies the uniqueness of God. Yahweh alone is God. He's in a category by himself. He stands alone. The psalmist weaves together two main themes that magnify God's incomparable nature: God's power over creation and his redeeming love for his people. Reflecting on God as Creator and Redeemer, the psalmist speaks of God's power, wisdom, and transcendence. He also speaks of God's care, compassion, and generosity. God is majestic and merciful, kind and King, powerful and gracious. The psalmist gives many illustrations of these wonderful truths.

As a result of God's unrivaled glory, we should praise him! The psalm gives an exhortation to praise God three times (vv. 1,7,12). In between these exhortations, reasons to praise God are provided. These reasons highlight the character and works of our Creator and Redeemer. I want to walk through the psalm and highlight nine reasons we should praise God wholeheartedly.

Praise God because His Commands Lead Us into Joy
PSALM 147:1

Over and over in the Psalms we're called to praise God. Why? Is God narcissistic? No. God is worthy of praise, so we should praise him. But in addition to this truth, in commanding us to praise him, God is inviting us to experience true and lasting joy, for our greatest good and highest joy comes in praising God. God's commands are always for our good and our joy.

The psalmist reminds us in verse 1 not only that God is good but also that it's good to praise him. It's fitting. It's right. It's pleasurable. It's beautiful.

Do you feel this way about worship? Do you delight in both personal and corporate worship? Compare it to entertainment: Do you enjoy sports, movies, or recreation more than the praise of God? Can you say, "It is good to praise God! There's *nothing like* being with God's people singing God's praise"? I (Tony) couldn't always say that. Not at all! Before Jesus changed my life, it was drudgery to assemble at a local church on a Sunday. Of course, it's fine to delight in gifts like sports and food. But our greatest delight will be found in God himself, since the more valuable the object, the more intense the delight there is (Lewis, *Reflections*, 46). Because God is the most valuable of all sources of joy, we will not find the depth of delight that we find in him anywhere else.

The true believer knows that to release affection Godward in worship is more satisfying than anything this world has to offer. Knowing that the Spirit of God is working in our lives, in our midst as a church, is beautiful, powerful, and pleasurable (cf. 133:1).

God commands us to experience this pleasure! What a God to command what we most desire! We're made for beauty, for delight, and for community, and in worshiping God we find what we were made for. Lewis says, "In commanding us to glorify him, God is inviting us to enjoy him" (ibid., 41).

So don't reject God's commands. John says, "His commands are not a burden" (1 John 5:3). The true saints delight in the law of the Lord. They delight in praising the Lord. We need to remind our non-Christian friends that if you turn to God, you aren't giving up pleasure; rather, you will find true and lasting pleasure. The pleasures of sin are "fleeting" (Heb 11:25), but the pleasures of worshiping God are fulfilling.

Praise God because He Heals the Brokenhearted
PSALM 147:2-3

Who is this God that we worship? Verse 2 suggests that this psalm was written during the rebuilding of Jerusalem, after the Jewish exiles returned home from Babylon (Neh 12). God in his grace brought his people, the outcasts, back home (Isa 40:1-11).

Verse 3 highlights the condition of the people's hearts prior to this restoration. The brokenhearted reentered a broken city, and God cared about his people's brokenness. While our context is different today than Israel's, the Lord still cares for the brokenhearted (Ps 145:14; cf. 34:18).

The Lord heals the wounded (Jer 30:17; Hos 6:1; 7:1; 14:4). In his kindness, he rebuilds broken lives. He restores families. He heals bodies. If you're grieving, the Lord knows. Don't run from him in grief, but rather run to him. Look to him for healing. If you're crushed in spirit, look to the One who was crushed for you.

In Isaiah we see the Suffering Servant of the Lord accomplishing this healing work. We read, "[God] has sent me to heal the brokenhearted, to proclaim liberty to the captives and freedom to the prisoners" (Isa 61:1). Jesus used this text to announce his ministry in Luke 4:18. Jesus knows suffering. He knows brokenness, not simply because he knows all things but because he entered into it. He can sympathize with the weak. He can bring healing, and one day he will bring ultimate healing. Because Jesus was wounded for us, we can have our wounds mended.

We're quick to care for physical injuries—and rightly so. We need to treat broken legs, open wounds, and other emergencies. But what if we had that same concern for spiritual injuries? What would happen if we went to the Great Physician as we experienced despair, bitterness, guilt, shame, anxiety, desertion, bereavement, apathy, and so on? Don't neglect to care for your inner person. The writer of Proverbs puts the priority there: "A person's spirit can endure sickness, but who can survive a broken spirit?" (Prov 18:14). The Lord restores the crushed in spirit. Don't go another day without looking to the Savior. There's no deficiency in him. He stands ready to restore the broken.

Praise God because He Creates and Rules Nature
PSALM 147:4-5

The psalmist reminds the brokenhearted of the Creator's glory (v. 4). Spurgeon says that he counts stars like a merchant counts coins (*Treasury*, vol. 3, 415)! Israel would have encountered astrologers in Babylon. The psalmist says Yahweh, not some Babylonian astrologer, controls the stars (Williams, *Psalms 73–150*, Kindle).

Scientists can't give us a precise number of the stars (cf. Gen 15:5), but God knows them all. He even names them (see Isa 40:26)! To name them implies that he rules them and that he cares for them. Further, these stars are intended to glorify God. Job says, "The morning stars sang together" during creation week (Job 38:7). In Psalm 19 we read that the heavens are proclaiming the glory of God.

The fact that God rules nature witnesses to the following affirmation (v. 5). God is almighty. God's wisdom is infinite. Truly, there's no one like him. Since this is true, his people shouldn't fear. We shouldn't despair. We shouldn't become anxious. We should rest in his power and wisdom. We should align ourselves with his ways.

The God who knows the stars by name is the God who restores the broken. He is the one who renews our strength like the eagles (Isa 40:26-31). Listen to Spurgeon:

> What a change is here from the preceding verse [v. 3]! Read the two without a break, and feel the full force of the contrast. From stars to sighs is a deep descent! From worlds to wounds is a distance which only infinite compassion can bridge. Yet he who acts a surgeon's part with wounded hearts, marshals the heavenly host, and reads the muster-roll of suns and their majestic systems. O Lord, it is good to praise thee as ruling the stars, but it is pleasant to adore thee as healing the broken heart! (*Treasury*, vol. 3, 415)

The next time you see the stars, remind yourself not only of God's power and wisdom but also of his care for the broken. Truly, there is none like him.

Praise God because He Lifts and Punishes
PSALM 147:6

This great God is gracious to the needy, but he's also just to the wicked. He will punish the unrepentant. This verse resembles the previous psalm: "The LORD protects resident aliens and helps the fatherless and the widow, but he frustrates the ways of the wicked" (146:9). The Lord sustains, blesses, and upholds those in need (cf. 145:20; 146:8; 113:5-9). What grace!

This passage should remind us that to imitate God (Eph 5:1), we too should seek to lift up the afflicted. Just as the Lord watches over the sojourner, the widow, the fatherless, the afflicted, the prisoners, the blind, and the hungry, so his people should put his care on display with practical acts of mercy and justice (Mic 6:8; Jas 1:27). One may look at the hurting around the world today and wonder, "Where is God?" But the question we should ask is, "Where are God's people?" God's plan has always been to use his people to display his love and righteousness in this broken world. Let's be quick to be about the Father's business. Look for opportunities to lift up others and supply basic needs to the hurting.

God's grace and justice were put on full display in Christ. He humbled himself as an act of grace. He died for the wicked that we may be declared righteous. And one day we know he will bring perfect justice to this broken world. We who have experienced this grace and share this hope should seek to put God's love on display.

Deep within the human heart is a desire for justice. Remember this: our longing for justice is ultimately a longing for Jesus. He will set all things right one day. So look to him now for grace. Humble yourself before him and confess him as Lord. You will experience not only the joy of knowing him now but also the promise of a peaceful and just world to come.

Praise God because He Provides
PSALM 147:7-9

The second exhortation to praise God appears in verse 7. In light of verses 1-6, how could we not give him thanks? If the Lord has saved you, restored you, and drawn near to you, then the appropriate response to him is gratitude. With a stringed instrument much like a harp, they are to praise God and make it beautiful!

In verses 8-9 the psalmist gives us further reason to praise God by speaking of how God provides for creation. God feeds both birds and animals (cf. Ps 104; Job 38). Baal doesn't cause the rain. Mother Nature doesn't supply the earth with rain. God does. Mother Nature doesn't cause the grass to grow for animals; God does!

N. T. Wright says of these verses,

> God feeds the animals, then, and is kind to those who call
> upon him. God may be building up Jerusalem (147:2,13), but
> he is also out there in the wild, making the grass grow on the

hills and feeding the young ravens when they call to him. (*Case for the Psalms*, 147)

Indeed, God is in the wild! Marvel at the Creator's wisdom, power, and grace when you behold the existence of his creatures scattered around God's earth.

Praise God because He Takes Pleasure in His People
PSALM 147:10-11

The next awe-inspiring truth about God is that he values or delights in his people. He's not impressed with the power of this world. The mighty empires of this world do not impress him. His deepest delight doesn't come when he watches horse racing or football! This awesome God, who names the stars and feeds all creation, actually takes delight in *us*. Those who fear him receive his particular attention. God takes joy in his people! He loves his people!

Tim Keller says, "This unimaginably immense God is given *pleasure*, real joy and delight, when human beings put their life's hope in his gracious love" (*Songs of Jesus*, 360; emphasis in original). Keller goes on to pray this:

> Lord, it is astonishing that I can bring *you* delight. And this delight does not wax and wane depending on my performance but is unvarying because I am in Jesus Christ (Ephesians 1:3-4). Let me start every day from the platform that "the only eyes in the universe that count are delighted in me." Amen. (Ibid.; emphasis in original)

Let that sink in. The Lord does delight in you if you're in Christ Jesus. Why? Because the Father has perfect delight in his Son. Through our union with Christ, the Father is pleased with us. We have been caught up in divine delight. And let this fact free you from trying to please people. The one that matters most takes pleasure in you. He hates sin, but he takes pleasure in his people. Now, out of this assurance, let us pursue holy lives for his glory.

How does one enjoy such a relationship with God? You come to God humbly. God rejects the proud and powerful that rely on themselves, but he receives all who "put their hope in his faithful love" (v. 11). His faithful love has been displayed in Christ Jesus. Look to him to begin this relationship.

Praise God because He Blesses His People
PSALM 147:12-14

The third exhortation to worship comes in verse 12 (cf. Ps 132:13-16). Why should God's people praise him? More reasons are given in verses 13-14.

Consider the blessings the psalmist reminds the people of on this particular occasion. He says God makes the city secure with steel bars (v. 13; cf. Neh 3:3,6,13-15; Ps 127:1b). God defends and protects his people. He uses just governments and officials to oversee matters. Next, God blesses his people with children—here, increasing the population of the gathered exiles (v. 13b). And then God grants peace along Jerusalem's borders and provides his people with the finest of wheat (v. 14). So peace, provision, and prosperity all come from God. In this season of blessing and abundance, the people are exhorted to exalt the Lord.

This psalm helps us understand not only the doctrine of *providence* but also the doctrine of *vocation*. Luther used Psalm 147 to help Christians understand how God uses various vocations to accomplish his work in the world (Luther, *Exposition*). God doesn't always drop manna from heaven! Food doesn't miraculously appear on our dinner plates each night. So, how does God provide ordinarily? God provides for creation in verses 8-9, but man has to do the work of cultivation in order to live. In verses 13-14 God provides security, but man has to make the steel bars and set up government, order, rulers, etc. Luther writes,

God could easily give you grain and fruit without your plowing and planting. But He does not want to do so. . . . What else is all our work to God—whether in the fields, in the garden, in the city, in the house, in war, or in government—but just such a child's performance, by which He wants to give His gifts in the fields, at home, and everywhere else? These are the masks of God, behind which He wants to remain concealed and do all things. . . . We have the saying: "God gives every good thing, but not just by waving a hand." God gives all good gifts; but you must lend a hand and take the bull by the horns. . . . Make the bars and gates, and let Him fasten them. Labor, and let Him give the fruits. Govern, and let Him give His blessing. Fight, and let Him give the victory. Preach, and let Him win hearts. Take a husband or a wife, and let Him produce the children. Eat and drink, and let Him nourish and strengthen you. And so on. In all our doings He is to work through us, and He alone shall have the glory from it. (Luther, *Exposition*)

God works through our works. God provides for our civic needs through the civic work of people. God provides food for us by using farmers, bakers, truck drivers, retailers, and computer programmers (Keller, *Every Good Endeavor*, Kindle).

How should this affect our perspective of work? It should help us in at least two ways. This reality *dignifies* work. Even small work matters. Think about it. Cleaning your house doesn't require a master's degree, but if someone doesn't clean the house, you may very well die (Keller, "Our Faith"). Even small jobs matter.

An implication of the dignity of work for the local church is that we should not be snobby toward anyone who may have a "lesser job" in the eyes of the world. God uses all kinds of people to sustain his creation. They matter to God and they should matter to us.

Second, seeing the relationship between God's providence and our human labors provides additional *meaning* to work. Most Christians think that the only way they can honor God at work is by being good witnesses. They should be good witnesses; their coworkers need the gospel. But in addition to this mindset, you should also see that your work is an expression of *neighbor love*. You're an agent of God's common grace to the world. So make good food. Make good products. Dig good ditches. Pave good roads. Land the plane every time! Your work matters. If you're a lawyer, God wants to work his justice through you. If you're a farmer, God wants to provide daily bread to people through you. If you're a builder, God may use you to create security and peace for others. See all your work in view of God. Do your job for the good of people and the glory of God.

Praise God because He Commands the Weather
PSALM 147:15-18

These verses pick up the previous thought of God's power over creation (vv. 4-5,8-9). When God speaks, creation obeys. God throws the snow like confetti. He says, "Let there be frost!" and there's frost. The hail falls at his word. He can cause the temperatures to rise and fall. In the book of Job, Elihu says,

> For [God] says to the snow, "Fall to the earth,"
> and the torrential rains, his mighty torrential rains,
> serve as his sign to all mankind,
> so that all men may know his work.
> The wild animals enter their lairs
> and stay in their dens.
> The windstorm comes from its chamber,
> and the cold from the driving north winds.
> Ice is formed by the breath of God,
> and watery expanses are frozen.
> He saturates clouds with moisture;
> he scatters his lightning through them.
> They swirl about,
> turning round and round at his direction,
> accomplishing everything he commands them
> over the surface of the inhabited world.
> He causes this to happen for punishment,
> for his land, or for his faithful love. (Job 37:6-13)

God can make things freeze or thaw, the winds to blow, and the waters to flow. God commands the weather (cf. Job 37–38; Isa 55:10-11). The psalmist and Elihu help us look at the weather and marvel at God's sovereignty, majesty, power, justice, and love. Spurgeon says, "It is wise to see God in winter and in distress as well as in summer and prosperity" (*Treasury*, vol. 3, 419).

As I (Tony) write this commentary, the northeastern part of the United States is enduring winter snowstorm Jonas. The effects of this storm have reached our home in North Carolina. Schools are closed, and games are canceled as ice and snow continue to fall. How do you respond to such snowstorms? There are various ways we should respond. Obviously, we should pray for people who find themselves in desperate situations. We should help the homeless and the needy. But we should also marvel at the power of God. We should stand amazed by his authority. He can send the freezing ice, and he can then melt it. And we should see our need for his mercy. No one can stand up against his power.

Praise God because He Instructs by His Word
PSALM 147:19-20

Finally, the psalmist speaks of God's written Word. God revealed his Word to his people (v. 19). God did this for no other nation (v. 20). God chose Israel to be the first recipient of his Word. As such, the people were recipients of great grace. With that privilege came the responsibility of making his Word known. Now, by God's providence, the nations can know his Word, and indeed, we should desire the world to hear it and know it!

God didn't program us like computers. Instead, he addresses us relationally through his Word (Kidner, *Psalms 73–150*, 486). We open up the Scriptures daily because the Father speaks to us there. Nothing else in the world is like this gift.

One of the best things we could do for our unbelieving friends is to invite them to study Scripture with us. God speaks to people and draws people to himself through the gospel.

When my friend Kevin (now a pastor) was in high school, he couldn't understand the Bible. He was a bright student. In fact, he was accepted into Yale. Only after a friend invited him to read through the Gospel of Matthew could Kevin say, "By the time I got to Matthew 28, I believed."

What a privilege to have a copy of the Bible! What a privilege to understand who God is! In fact, if we didn't have it, we wouldn't be able to look at this particular psalm that tells us so many important truths about God! Don't take Scripture for granted. Read it. Meditate on it. Treasure it. Spread it.

In light of all these wonderful truths about God, the psalmist ends where he began: "Hallelujah!" (v. 20). No one is like our God. No one is like our Savior. He has not dealt with us as our sins deserve. Instead of judgment, he has given us saving grace. Exalt him with thanksgiving!

Reflect and Discuss

1. Why does God command us to praise him?
2. How does this psalm encourage the brokenhearted?
3. How are God's power and wisdom described in this psalm?

4. How do we see both God's justice and his grace in this passage? How do these attributes of God point to Jesus?
5. Why do you think the psalmist includes the exhortation to praise God with the lyre?
6. What does this passage teach us about God's providence? How do our vocations and God's providence work together?
7. According to Psalm 147, in what does God delight?
8. What does this psalm say about the weather? How should we respond to the types of weather conditions described in this psalm?
9. How should we respond to the privilege of having God's Word?
10. Take a few moments to pray through this psalm.

All Creation Praise the Lord

PSALM 148

Main Idea: God should receive praise from everyone and everything because he is the Creator, Sustainer, and Savior.

I. **Praise the Lord from the Heavens (148:1-6).**
   A. Who praises him (148:1-4)?
   B. Why praise him (148:5-6)?
II. **Praise the Lord from the Earth (148:7-14).**
   A. Who praises him (148:7-12)?
   B. Why praise him (148:13-14)?

Psalm 148 is a magnificent psalm of creation that calls on the choir of creation to "praise the name of the Lord" (vv. 5,13) for his magnificent work. Concerning this psalm, Charles Spurgeon writes,

> The song is one and indivisible. It seems almost impossible to expound it in detail, for a living poem is not to be dissected verse by verse. It is a song of nature and of grace. As a flash of lightning flames through space, and enwraps both heaven and earth in one vestment of glory, so doth the adoration of the Lord of this Psalm light up all the universe and cause it to glow with a radiance of praise. (*Treasury*, vol. 3b, 437)

The psalm naturally divides into two parts. Verses 1-6 call on the heavens and all that are in them to "praise the Lord." Verses 7-14 call on the earth and all who dwell there to "praise the Lord." The word "praise" (also "hallelujah" in verses 1 and 14) occurs 13 times in 14 verses. Those who rightly perceive the vastness and greatness of what God has made cannot help but join in singing his praises with this majestic hymn.

Praise the Lord from the Heavens

PSALM 148:1-6

Only one Creator God reigns sovereignly over and outside of his creation. This theme resonates from Genesis to Revelation. Genesis 1–2 and Job 38–42 especially stand out for their descriptions of God as the Creator (see also Ps 19). In the New Testament, John 1, Colossians 1, and Hebrews 1 attribute creation to the Son. Trinitarian categories can help us understand the role of each Person of the Godhead in creation: the Father is the author of creation, the Son is the architect of creation, and the Holy Spirit is the agent of creation. Psalm 148 raises and answers two questions concerning the praise of the Lord.

Who Praises Him? (148:1-4)

Psalms 146–150 begin the same way: "Hallelujah!" (ESV, "Praise the Lord!"). The Hebrew word for "Lord" (Yahweh) appears six times, counting "Yah" in the opening and closing "Hallelujah." The psalmist draws attention to *who* praises the Lord beginning in the highest possible realm: "the heavens . . . the heights" (v. 1). Who in the heavenly and stellar realms should praise the Lord? Everyone and everything! Animate and inanimate. Those who can give verbal expression, "his angels . . . his heavenly armies," should praise him (v. 2). Those that cannot speak can still declare his praise by their beauty and design. They should praise him too. These celestial objects include the "sun and moon . . . all you shining stars" (v. 3). It also includes the "highest heavens . . . you waters above the heavens" (v. 4). Derek Kidner notes, "*Highest heavens* is literally 'heaven of heavens', a similar superlative to 'holy of holies' . . . the *waters above the heavens* are a poetic or popular term for the rain clouds; cf. Genesis 1:6-8" (*Psalms 73–150*, 487–88; emphasis in original). All of these references echo Psalm 19, and they are a powerful polemic to counter the pagan religions of the ancient world that deified creation, worshiping the things of creation rather than the Creator (cf. Rom 1:18-25). Allen Ross helpfully writes, "A fine piece of craftsmanship brings glory to the one who made it. Each part of creation tells of the sovereign power and glory of the creator" (*Psalms 90–150*, 946).

Why Praise Him? (148:5-6)

Verses 5-6 tell us why we should "praise the name of the Lord." The answer is grounded in his powerful word: he spoke, and it was done. He is not only the Creator but also the sustainer: he established the heavens and the waters, placed them, and causes them to stand and stay in place "forever and ever." And he is the Ruler: he sovereignly and providentially is in charge over all he has made. John Piper makes valuable application here:

[An] implication of the doctrine of creation is that everything that exists has a purpose, a goal, a reason for being. If God did not create the world then any man's goal is as good as another. There are no absolutes and everything is aimless and absurd. The only meaning in life is what you arbitrarily create by doing your own thing. But if God did create the world then it has an absolute purpose and goal, for God is not whimsical or frivolous. Nor is his purpose ever in jeopardy, for he says in Isaiah 46:10, "My counsel shall stand and I will accomplish all my purpose." ("He Commanded and They Were Created")

This is what God has done, and this is what God is doing. This is why the heavens praise him.

Praise the Lord from the Earth
PSALM 148:7-14

Those on earth are now invited to join the choir of creation. No person or thing is to be left out. Like verses 1-6, verses 7-14 raise and answer both the *who* and the *why*.

Who Praises Him? (148:7-12)

Those called to praise the Lord in these verses are representative of that which Yahweh has created in the earthly sphere (Ross, *Psalms 90–150*, 947). "All sea monsters [ESV, "you great sea creatures"] and ocean depths" are called to praise the Lord (v. 7). Elements under God's control like "lightning and hail, snow and cloud, powerful wind that execute his command" (ESV, "fulfill his word") are called to praise the Lord (v. 8 HCSB). The "mountains and all hills, fruit trees and all cedars" are called to praise the Lord (v. 9). "Wild animals and all cattle" and "creatures that crawl and flying birds" are likewise called to praise the Lord (v. 10). But in verses 11 and 12 there is a shift to the pinnacle of God's creation: those who bear his image (Gen 1:26-27), the divine imprint, are called to praise the Lord. Human beings of various stations in life are called to join the angelic choir in heaven. This includes "kings of the earth and all peoples." This includes "princes and all judges of the earth." The "young men as well as young women, old and young together" are called to praise the Lord who brought them into existence. No object is left out. No person is left out. Angels in heaven and humans on earth unite in a chorus of praise to the great Creator God. Kidner says it well:

> Starting with the angelic host, and descending through
> the skies to the varied forms and creatures of earth, then
> summoning the family of man and finally the chosen people,
> the call to praise unites the whole creation. If any notion of a
> colourless or cloistered regime were associated with the name
> of God, this glimpse of His tireless creativity would be enough
> to dispel it. (*Psalms 73–150*, 487)

Why Praise Him? (148:13-14)

All of creation is to "praise the name of the LORD." Why? First, "his name alone is exalted" (cf. Phil 2:9-11). There is no God like our God. Second, "his majesty covers heaven and earth." *The Message* paraphrases: "His radiance exceeds anything in earth and sky." There is a splendor about our God that covers all of creation like a beautifully made quilt. Third, "he has raised up a horn for his people." The horn is a symbol of power (cf. Rev 5:6). Ross notes, "In many places it refers to kings who had power (see Ps. 78:6 and 132:17)" (*Psalms 90–150*, 948). Psalm 132:17 says, "There I will make a horn grow for David."

Is there a messianic impulse in verse 14 that we should not pass over too quickly? If there is a missions impulse in verse 11, there may also be a messianic impulse here. The horn of strength and power that the Lord will raise up in Messiah Jesus is a horn of salvation that all the earth is called on to praise and exalt. The horn God has raised up for his people evokes "praise to all his faithful ones" (ESV, "his saints"). This praise especially is the appropriate response for "the Israelites, the people close to him." Theirs is a particularly special and tender relationship. They, of all people, should praise the Lord and exalt his name for all that he has done to make them his covenant people. John Piper again puts it so well:

> The foundation of all redemptive history is that God the
> Father, through the agency of his eternal Son, created out of
> nothing all that is not God by his word of command, and by
> that same word he upholds all things so that the emergence of
> every new being is his peculiar creation. Therefore, God owns
> everything that exists. We and all our so-called possessions
> are his to do with as he pleases. What pleases him is the

achievement of his ultimate purpose to fill the earth with his glory. Therefore, the all encompassing life-goal of every creature should be to display the value of God's glory. But since we are helpless and absolutely dependent on God for everything, the only way this can be done is by becoming like little children who are not anxious for anything, but entrust their souls to the faithful Creator (1 Peter 4:19). (Piper, "He Commanded and They Were Created")

There is just one thing left to say: "Hallelujah!" Praise the Lord!

Conclusion

One of the most beautiful songs in the Baptist hymnal is anonymous, appearing first "in 1796 in a collection put together for use in one of the charitable institutions of the day, the Foundling Hospital in London," a home for abandoned children (Wilcock, *Message: Songs*, 282). Its inspiration was Psalm 148. Its title is "Praise the Lord! Ye Heavens, Adore Him."

Praise the Lord! ye heav'ns, adore Him;
Praise Him, angels, in the height.
Sun and moon, rejoice before Him;
Praise Him, all ye stars of light.
Praise the Lord! for He hath spoken;
Worlds His mighty voice obeyed.
Law which never shall be broken
For their guidance hath He made.

Praise the Lord! for He is glorious;
Never shall His promise fail.
God hath made His saints victorious;
Sin and death shall not prevail.
Praise the God of our salvation!
Hosts on high, His power proclaim.
Heav'n and earth and all creation
Laud and magnify His name.

Worship, honor, glory, blessing,
Lord, we offer unto Thee.
Young and old, Thy praise expressing,
In glad homage bend the knee.

All the saints in heav'n adore Thee;
We would bow before Thy throne.
As Thine angels serve before Thee,
So on earth Thy will be done.

Reflect and Discuss

1. What does it mean to "praise" God?
2. How often do you think about God as the Creator? How would regularly meditating on God as Creator shape other areas of your faith?
3. The first chapter of three New Testament books (John, Colossians, Hebrews) describe Jesus's role in creation. Why do you think the authors begin in this way? How does beginning with this teaching affect everything else in those books?
4. In what ways does the beauty and design of creation bring praise to God?
5. How can the truth that God sustains creation increase your confidence and faith in him?
6. How does sin distort everyone's praise of God? In what ways has sin affected your praise in particular? How has God worked in your life to restore your praise of him?
7. Can praising God help you fight sin? Why or why not?
8. How can this psalm's call for everyone to praise the Creator God help you think better about Jesus's command in the Great Commission (Matt 28:18-20)?
9. In addition to God's past work in creation and salvation, what are other reasons (present and future) you can praise God?
10. How can Christians help one another praise God?

In the End Our God Wins

PSALM 149

Main Idea: Praise God because of his character, his present and past work in your life, and his future fulfillment of his promises.

I. **Praise the Lord for What He Is Doing Now (149:1-4).**
    A. Praise the Lord in song, for he is our Creator (149:1-2a).
    B. Praise the Lord with dancing, for he is our King (149:2b-3).
    C. Praise the Lord for his victory, for he is our Savior (149:4).
II. **Praise the Lord for What He Will Do in the Future (149:5-9).**
    A. The Lord will give his people peace (149:5).
    B. The Lord will give his people justice (149:6-9a).
    C. The Lord will give his people honor (149:9b).

A drian Rogers, a spiritual hero to me (Danny) and to many others, was the pastor of the historic Bellevue Baptist Church in Memphis, Tennessee, and a three-time president of the Southern Baptist Convention. He was often referred to as the "Prince of Preachers" among Southern Baptists and was famous for his witticisms, which his friends called "Adrianisms." One Adrianism that is particularly appropriate to Psalm 149 is, "What is the world coming to? It's coming to Jesus!" (Rogers, *Adrianisms*, 329). Rogers is right. The world is going somewhere with what R. C. Sproul called "an ultimate *telos*—a culmination of purpose, aim, or goal" ("How Should Christians View World History?").

Psalm 149 is an eschatological psalm that "celebrates a victory," the victory of the Lord, "the King of Zion" (VanGemeren, *Psalms*, 1005). Some hold the date of its writing to be after the Babylonian exile during the time of Nehemiah, as the Hebrew people returned to the land of Israel. It may have originated there, but its gaze stares into the future. As Allen Ross writes, "The hymn celebrated a recent saving victory, perhaps the deliverance from exile; but it replaces the normally expected existing cause for praise with a section of future hope" (*Psalms 90–150*, 953).

The psalm progresses in two movements, which instruct us on how to praise the Lord for what he is doing now and what he will do in the future. Our God has won victories for us in the past, he is winning victories for us in the present, and he will win a climactic victory for us in the future.

Praise the Lord for What He Is Doing Now
PSALM 149:1-4

This psalm begins and ends like its companions (Pss 146–150), with a note of praise: "Hallelujah!" (ESV, "Praise the Lord"). This praise is expressed by singing to the Lord a new song (cf. Pss 96:1; 98:1). A new song is a song of salvation, a song of celebration and hope. Some see Psalm 149 emerging from a seed planted in 148:14, which speaks of the power and salvation of the Lord on behalf of "his people," "his faithful ones." This song of praise is to be sung "in the assembly of the faithful," the *chasidim*. Michael Wilcock notes the word "means being loved by God with his covenant love (*ḥesed*) and so being devoted to him with a love of the same kind" (*Message: Songs*, 282). Our God loves us, and we love him in return. His love has been made known time and time again through his mighty acts of salvation.

After the call to praise, the psalmist expresses the nature and character of God in three ways in verses 2-4. They help us understand why we sing this new song of salvation and why we delight in our Lord.

Praise the Lord in Song, for He Is Our Creator (149:1-2a)

The gathered people of God worship the Lord and "celebrate" the fact that he is their "Maker." The focus is on the nation of Israel and not the material creation of Genesis 1–2. The Lord brought Israel into existence and established her as a nation and his people. It was completely his doing and not theirs. Grace produced the celebration that makes their hearts "glad" (ESV).

Praise the Lord with Dancing, for He Is Our King (149:2b-3)

"Children of Zion" is similar in meaning to "Israel," but that phrase perhaps emphasizes "the true worshipers of the Lord" (Ross, *Psalms 90–150*, 955). The object of their worship is clear and exclusive: "their King," the Lord their Maker. The expression of their worship in song is to be complemented "with dancing" and making music to the Lord "with tambourine and lyre" (a harplike instrument). VanGemeren notes, "The people of God regularly celebrated the Lord's victory and blessing in dance (cf. Ex. 15:20; Jdg. 11:34; 2 Sam. 6:14; Jer. 31:4)" (VanGemeren, *Psalms*, 1006). The words of Charles Spurgeon fittingly explain the role of dance in praise to God:

> Let them repeat the triumph of the Red Sea, which was ever the typical glory of Israel. Miriam led the daughters of Israel in the dance when the Lord had triumphed gloriously; was it not most fit that she should? The sacred dance of devout joy is no example, nor even excuse, for frivolous dances, much less for lewd ones. Who could help dancing when Egypt was vanquished, and the tribes were free? Every mode of expressing delight was bound to be employed on so memorable an occasion. Dancing, singing, and playing on instruments were all called into requisition, and most fitly so. There are unusual seasons which call for unusual expressions of joy. When the Lord saves a soul its holy joy overflows, and it cannot find channels enough for its exceeding gratitude: if the man does not leap or play or sing, at any rate he praises God, and wishes for a thousand tongues with which to magnify his Saviour. Who could wish it to be otherwise? Young converts are not to be restrained in their joy. Let them sing and dance while they can. How can they mourn now that their Bridegroom is with them? Let us give the utmost liberty to joy. Let us never attempt its suppression, but issue in the terms of this verse a double license for exultation. (*Treasury*, vol. 3b, 453)

Praise the Lord for His Victory, for He Is Our Savior (149:4)

The people of God truly experience showers of blessing from the Lord. The psalmist tells us our Lord continually delights in his people, adorning "the humble with salvation." The word *adorn* has the meaning of "glorify" or "beautify" (cf. Isa 55:7,8; 60:7,9,13) (Ross, *Psalms 90–150*, 956). Those who trust in the Lord receive his salvation, his victory. Those who humble themselves before King Jesus in faith and repentance are blessed with victory over sin, Satan, death, and hell. James Boice says, "We express delight in God because he first took delight in us and saved us from sin" (*Psalms 107–150*, 1280). That God would take pleasure in saving rebellious sinners who were his enemies is remarkable evidence of his grace and kindness. The blind hymn writer Fanny Crosby eloquently captures this wonderful truth in a line from her hymn "He Hideth My Soul": "A wonderful Savior is Jesus my Lord, A wonderful Savior to me; . . . I sing in my rapture, 'Oh, glory to God For such a Redeemer as mine!'"

Praise the Lord for What He Will Do in the Future

PSALM 149:5-9

When we think of prophetic books of the Bible, the ones that usually come to mind are Isaiah, Daniel, Ezekiel, Micah, and Zechariah in the Old Testament. In the New Testament we think of Jesus's Olivet Discourse (Matt 24–25), the Thessalonian letters, and Revelation. Psalms is usually not on our list. Yet numerous psalms point to the future: our Lord's final and climactic victory over evil and the drawing of the nations to his exalted Messiah King (see Pss 2; 22; 24; 45; 83; 96–99; 110). The last five verses of Psalm 149 are prophetic and eschatological in focus. They highlight three aspects of the Lord's final victory as he draws to a close the curtain on history.

The Lord Will Give His People Peace (149:5)

The praise by God's people continues in verse 5. How and where should the "faithful" celebrate? They should "shout for joy on their beds." This last phrase could either mean they are lying down at night in restful peace or they are "reclining at a festal meal . . . especially if the theme of such a festival was the final victory of God" (Kidner, *Psalms 73–150*, 489). Either is possible, and both would be true. In God's final victory, the Prince of peace will reign (Isa 9:6-7; Ps 110:4-7). The people of God will enjoy perfect and eternal *shalom*. The victory celebration will be the climax of history. The rest enjoyed by the people of God under King Jesus will be forever! Hallelujah!

The Lord Will Give His People Justice (149:6-9a)

Patrick Reardon summarizes verses 5-9 well:

> Exaltation of the saints in the victory of Christ, their
> evangelical struggle for the Gospel, and the ultimate judgment
> of the world thereby are the themes of Psalm 149. . . . Combat
> and invocation, battle and blessing, are inseparable in the
> evangelical life. (*Christ in the Psalms*, 299)

The saints are resting peacefully on their beds praising the Lord in verse 5. But they also are exalting the Lord with a "double-edged sword in their hands" in verse 6. This praise and exaltation of God in their mouths has the future and final victory of God in view. Although they have swords in their hands, it must be the Lord who fulfills the judgment of verses 7-9. These verses are a prophetic anticipation of Revelation 19:11-16, where the saints follow Christ as he returns in judgment. We are spectators, not participants, in his judgment against the nations. Christ alone will inflict vengeance, bind kings, and carry out judgments. Justice is coming to the world, and all of it will be the Lord's doing.

The Lord Will Give His People Honor (149:9b)

Verse 4 teaches us the Lord takes pleasure in giving his people salvation. Verse 9 affirms that the final victory honors "all his faithful people." Ross writes, "The final victory will be the most spectacular glory for the beloved people of God" (*Psalms 90–150*, 958). Our God truly is a God of salvation. He saved the nation of Israel repeatedly throughout Old Testament history. Today he is saving individuals from every tribe, tongue, people, and nation. As history draws to a close and as the antichrist and his evil empire appear to have won the day, our Lord will come again from heaven and destroy them all with the power of his word. His people will share in his glorious victory. What an honor this will be. To all of this, there is only one appropriate word. "Hallelujah!" Praise the Lord!

Conclusion

Psalm 149 finds its climactic fulfillment in the last book of the Bible: Revelation. There the godly cry out in Revelation 6:10, "Lord, the one who is holy and true, how long until you judge those who live on the earth and avenge our blood?" The answer comes in Revelation 19:11: "Then I saw heaven opened, and there was a white horse. Its rider is called Faithful and True, and with justice he judges and makes war." That rider on the white horse is Jesus. His coming is imminent. His victory is certain. On that day "the children of Zion [will] rejoice in their King" (Ps 149:2). That will be for you a day of victory and not a day of vengeance because in the end our God wins.

Reflect and Discuss

1. Why should the nature of God (e.g., Creator, King, Savior) cause us to praise him?

2. What might the use of dancing and music express about our love for God?

3. What is the role of singing in your local church and your discipleship? In what ways can singing help us believe the truths of Scripture better? Are there other areas in your life in which you can sing more praise to God?

4. What does it mean that God gives honor to his people? Why does he do this?

5. Read 2 Corinthians 5:9. How do we understand God's pleasure as something that is already ours because of Christ and as something to pursue continually?

6. Of the peace, justice, and honor that God will bring in the future, which one do you most look forward to? Why?

7. Describe the peace, justice, and honor the world pursues. In what ways are the peace, justice, and honor God will bring better?

8. What forms of justice can the Christian pursue now in order to witness to the ultimate justice God will accomplish when Jesus returns?

9. Why is final justice necessary when Christ returns? Can there be peace without justice? Why or why not?

10. What are some other promises in Scripture that give you reasons to praise God?

Let Everything That Breathes Praise the Lord!

PSALM 150

Main Idea: God should be praised by all people, at all times, and in all places because of his great works and abundant mercy.

I. Where Should We Praise the Lord (150:1)?
II. Why Should We Praise the Lord (150:2)?
III. How Should We Praise the Lord (150:3-6)?
IV. Who Should Praise the Lord (150:6)?

For many Christians, Psalms is the richest and the most comforting portion of the Old Testament, if not the whole of God's Word. Therefore, it is appropriate that it concludes on a "Hallelujah" note with a psalm completely dedicated to the praise of our good, great, and gracious God. The psalmist exclaims with exuberance in verse 6: "Let everything that breathes praise the LORD. Hallelujah!"

Psalm 150 is the grand finale of the book of Psalms. It functions like a climactic doxology. If Psalm 1 is an appropriate introduction, then Psalm 150 is an equally appropriate conclusion. The first four books of the Psalter end with doxologies and words of praise (see 41:13; 72:18-19; 89:52; 106:48). Allen Ross notes, "Book V ends with this elaborate doxology, because it brings to a conclusion the entire collections of psalms" (*Psalms 90–150*, 962).

Psalm 150 is brief (only six verses), but it is exhilarating from start to finish. It encourages us eschatologically because it informs us how God's redemptive story will end. It will end on a note of praise to our Lord. In this psalm we will see that worship is a universal privilege, worship is always and only for our God, worship is the result of who God is and what he has done, and worship should be an exciting and soul-moving experience (Storms, "Praise Him! Praise Him! (Psalms 148–150)").

Praising God should change us. It should transform us. We should leave corporate worship different from how we came. Our minds should become more informed, our hearts more tender and thankful toward God, and our wills more determined to live for the glory of this most excellent and great God (v. 2). Psalm 150 helps us think well theologically. It helps us know where we should praise the Lord, why we should praise the Lord, how we should praise the Lord, and who should praise the Lord.

Where Should We Praise the Lord?
PSALM 150:1

The psalm begins and concludes in the same way as Psalms 146–149: with the word "Hallelujah," meaning "Praise Yah." The word *Yah* is a shortened form of the covenant and personal name of Israel's God, Yahweh. Counting "Hallelujah," the word *praise* occurs 13 times in the psalm. Over and over again, this psalm encourages us to praise the Lord, with whom we have a personal and intimate relationship. He is our covenant God, and we are his new covenant people.

Following quickly on this verbal command are instructions specifying where the Lord, the abundantly great God (v. 2), should be praised. First, we should praise him "in his sanctuary," his holy place. The earthly tabernacle or temple in Jerusalem is in view. Second, those "in his mighty expanse," his mighty firmament, should also praise him. All the vast universe and what God created is in view. Derek Kidner writes,

> So the call is to God's worshippers on earth, meeting at His chosen place, but also to His heavenly host . . . to mingle their praises with ours. Earth and heaven can be utterly at one in this. His glory fills the universe; His praise must do no less. (*Psalms 73–150*, 491)

The voices of earth and heaven join in perfect harmony in praise of the Lord. From below and from above, God is to be praised. By humans and by angels, the Lord is to be praised. Whether they are gathered today on earth in the place set aside for worship or throughout the expanse of the universe, our most excellent God is to be praised!

His greatness and glory fill the universe, and so must his praise. There is no place where praise is not welcomed and rightly voiced. Church buildings are good but not necessary. Church buildings are never essential. We can praise God anywhere and anytime. Praise can happen in a simple building like a small church, in a magnificent European cathedral, under a tree with South Americans along the Amazon, in prison like Paul and Silas, in a hiding place like the catacombs as our first brothers and sisters in Christ experienced, or in a house church in China or Afghanistan. Anyplace and anytime are where and when it is right to praise the Lord.

Why Should We Praise the Lord?

PSALM 150:2

Scripture does not call us to blind or uninformed worship. Faith does not call us to pretend to believe in a God who is not there. No, the Bible calls us to embrace an informed faith, a reasoned faith. We do not check our brains at the door as we enter the room of faith and worship. On the contrary, we come in faith to a living God who has done "powerful acts" and is abundant or excellent in his greatness. We engage our minds to grasp something of the powerful God who has done powerful things.

"Powerful acts" speak of what God has done. They include his great acts of salvation, his mighty work of creation, and his sovereign reign over all that he has made. Warren Wiersbe notes that in the Old Testament one cannot help but think of the "exodus from Egypt, the conquest of the promised land, the expansion of the Davidic Kingdom, the deliverance of the Jews from Babylon, and the restoring of the nation" (*Bible Exposition Commentary*, 385). In the New Testament one cannot help but think of the miracles of Jesus, his cross and the empty tomb, the gift of the Holy Spirit, and the explosive growth of the church.

"Abundant greatness" speaks of who he is. To praise God we must know God. He is not the god of deism, pantheism, polytheism, or finite theism. He is not the god we create in our minds that we are comfortable with, that we wish him to be. No, he is the God who has revealed himself as he truly is in his Word.

We must know, acknowledge, and praise the God who is omnipotent, omniscient, and omnipresent. His holiness, love, mercy, grace, righteousness, justice, and faithfulness must continually be before our minds' eyes. We need twenty-twenty spiritual vision when it comes to our God. We see what he has done with one eye and who he is with the other.

How Should We Praise the Lord?

PSALM 150:3-6

The simple answer to this question is, with everything we are and with everything that we have. The psalmist, however, has some particular instructions for God's people as they come together for worship. These verses can help us put to rest some aspects of the unfortunate "worship wars" that have been raging for centuries.

The worship of the Lord is properly accompanied by a variety of musical instruments. Several are listed in verses 3-5, though the list is most certainly representative, not exhaustive. Wind instruments, string instruments, and percussion instruments are welcome in a symphony of praise to the abundantly great God. Anything that rightly honors God should be welcome. The first four instruments are the "ram's horn," the "harp and lyre"—these are stringed instruments and are similar if not identical—and the "tambourine." "Dance" also accompanies the tambourine. We find this pairing of the tambourine and dance in Exodus 15:20-21, which celebrates the exodus from Egypt. There the Bible says,

> Then the prophetess Miriam, Aaron's sister, took a tambourine in her hand, and all the women came out following her with tambourines and dancing. Miriam sang to them: Sing to the LORD, for he is highly exalted; he has thrown the horse and its rider into the sea.

The last four praise instruments are "strings," which is probably a general term that includes all stringed instruments; the "flute," which Ross says is a shepherd's flute or pipe; "resounding cymbals," which are perhaps small percussion instruments that had a clear sound; and "clashing cymbals," which were larger, loud cymbals with a deeper and louder sound (*Psalms 90–150*, 967). In verse 6 the psalmist adds to the instruments of praise the praise from voices. All are a part of this choir! "Let everything that breathes praise the LORD." C. S. Lewis wisely reminds us, "Let choirs sing well or not at all!" (*World's Last Night*, 86). A great God deserves excellence in our worship. Ultimately, how we praise the Lord is a matter of the heart. Nevertheless, our God of "abundant greatness" always deserves the best we can give him.

Who Should Praise the Lord?
PSALM 150:6

This final question receives an easy and expected answer in verse 6. Everything and everyone that breathes should praise the Lord. This is a fitting answer for Psalm 150 and the entire Psalter. If you can breathe, you should "praise the LORD." This theme finds ample support in both the Old and New Testament (Ps 148:7-14; Rev 5:13). Charles Spurgeon challenges us well: "Join all ye living things in the eternal song. Be ye least or greatest, withhold not your praises. What a day will it be when all things in all places unite to glorify the one and only living and true God"

(*Treasury*, vol. 3b, 464). To all of this only one word seems appropriate: "Hallelujah!" Praise the Lord!

Conclusion

In 1695 an Anglican bishop named Thomas Ken (1637–1711) penned a hymn that continues to be sung around the world every Lord's Day. Orphaned in childhood and raised by his older sister Ann, he would serve as chaplain to the king of England, Charles II. The words of the hymn were first published in 1709, but they are actually the last verse of a longer hymn entitled, "Awake, My Soul, and with the Sun." We know the hymn as "The Doxology," and what a fitting commentary it provides on Psalm 150.

> Praise God from whom all blessings flow;
> Praise Him, all creatures here below.
> Praise Him above, ye heavenly host;
> Praise Father, Son, and Holy Ghost.

Hallelujah! Praise the Lord!

Reflect and Discuss

1. Why are worship and praise such an integral part of the Christian life?
2. What does the location of God's praise ("in his sanctuary" and "in his mighty expanse") reveal about the nature of God?
3. Is it possible for someone to live their Christian life without praise? Why or why not?
4. What does it reveal about a person's heart if he or she is not concerned with the praise of God?
5. If non-Christians do not praise God, are they devoid of praise? Why or why not?
6. How has God acted powerfully in your life and shown you his goodness?
7. What roles do faith and reason play in the Christian life?
8. Does praising God require a certain emotion?
9. Why are music and singing important parts of one's praise to God? Does praise always require music and singing? Why or why not?
10. What is the place of corporate and individual praise in the Christian life?

WORKS CITED

Alcorn, Randy. "Consequences of a Moral Tumble." *CT Pastors*, n.d. Accessed July 13, 2018. https://www.christianitytoday.com/pastors /1988/winter/88l1046.html.

Allen, Leslie C. *Psalms 101–150*. Word Biblical Commentary 21. Waco, TX: Word, 1983.

Anderson, A. A. *Psalms 73–150*. Grand Rapids: William B. Eerdmans, 1972.

Anderson, Courtney. *To the Golden Shore: The Life of Adoniram Judson*. Boston, MA: Little, Brown & Company, 1956.

Augustin. *Augustin: Expositions on the Psalms*. Edited by Philip Schaff. Vol. 8. Nicene and Post-Nicene Fathers. Peabody, MA: Hendrickson, 1994.

Barrett, Ken. "Baptist Church Restoration a Mixed Blessing for Myanmar." *Nikkei Asian Review*, December 24, 2017. Accessed January 16, 2020. https://asia.nikkei.com/Life-Arts/Life/Baptist -church-restoration-a-mixed-blessing-for-Myanmar2.

Beale, G. K. *We Become What We Worship*. Downers Grove: InterVarsity Press, 2008.

Beck, Rosalie. "More Than Rubies." *Christian History Institute*, n.d. Accessed January 16, 2020. https://christianhistoryinstitute.org /magazine/article/more-than-rubies.

Belcher, Richard P., Jr. *The Messiah and the Psalms: Preaching Christ from All the Psalms*. Fearn, Ross-shire: Mentor, 2006.

Bird, Michael. *Evangelical Theology: A Biblical and Systematic Introduction*. Grand Rapids: Zondervan, 2013.

Boice, James Montgomery. *Psalms: Psalms 42–106*. Vol. 2. Grand Rapids: Baker, 2005.

———. *Psalms: Psalms 107–150*. Vol. 3. Grand Rapids: Baker, 2005.

Bonhoeffer, Dietrich. *Life Together: The Classic Exploration of Christian Community*. New York: HarperCollins, 1954.

————. *Psalms: The Prayer Book of the Bible.* Minneapolis: Augsburg Fortress, 1970.

Bratcher, Robert G., and William David Reyburn. *A Translator's Handbook on the Book of Psalms.* UBS Handbook Series. New York: United Bible Societies, 1991.

Broyles, Craig C. *Psalms.* Grand Rapids: Baker, 1999.

Brueggemann, Walter. *Praying the Psalms: Engaging Scripture and the Life of the Spirit.* 2nd ed. Eugene, OR: Cascade, 2007.

Bullock, C. Hassell. *Psalms (Volume 2: Psalms 73–150).* Teach the Text. Grand Rapids: Baker, 2017.

Burrage, Henry S. *Baptist Hymn Writers and Their Hymns.* Portland, ME: Brown Thurston & Co., 1888.

Calvin, John. *Commentary on the Book of Psalms Vol IV: Psalms 93–150.* Calvin's Commentaries 6. Reprint. Grand Rapids: Baker Books, 2005.

————. *The Institutes of the Christian Religion.* Vol. 1. Edited by John T. McNeill. Louisville: Westminster John Knox Press, 1960, reissued 2006.

————. *Institutes of the Christian Religion.* Revised ed. Peabody, MA: Hendrickson, 2007.

————. *Psalms 93–150.* Translated by James Anderson. Calvin's Commentaries 6. Grand Rapids: Eerdmans, 1949.

Carson, D. A. *For the Love of God.* Vol 1. Wheaton, IL: Crossway, 1998.

————, R. T. France, J. A. Motyer, and C. J. Wenham, eds. *New Bible Commentary.* 4th ed. Downers Grove, IL: InterVarsity Press, 1994.

Chambers, Oswald. *My Utmost for His Highest.* Westwood, NJ: Discovery House, 1963.

Chantry, Walter J. *Praises for the King of Kings.* Oxford: Banner of Truth, 1991.

Collins, C. John. "Psalms." *ESV Study Bible.* Wheaton, IL: Crossway, 2008.

Collins, Jim. *Good to Great: Why Some Companies Make the Leap and Others Don't.* New York: HarperBusiness, 2001.

deClaissé-Walford, Nancy L., Rolf A. Jacobson, and Beth LaNeel Tanner. *The Book of Psalms.* New International Commentary on the Old Testament. Grand Rapids: Eerdmans, 2014.

Dowling, John, ed. *The Judson Offering, Intended as a Token of Christian Sympathy with the Living and a Memento of Christian Affection for the Dead.* New York: Lewis Colby & Co., 1850. Accessed March 27, 2020. http://baptiststudiesonline.com/wp-content/uploads/2018/05/The_Judson_Offering.pdf.

Duncan, Ligon. "Determined to Worship." Accessed March 28, 2016. Sermon available online at http://ligonduncan.com/determined-to -worship-432.

———. "Grace" Accessed March 24, 2016. Sermon available online at http://ligonduncan.com/grace-734.

———. "Greatly Afflicted." Accessed March 28, 2016. Sermon available online at http://www.fpcjackson.org/resource-library/sermons /greatly-afflicted.

———. "Living in the Right Kind of Fear." Accessed March 28, 2016. Sermon available online at http://ligonduncan.com/living-in-the -right-kind-of-fear-460.

———. "Lord Have Mercy." Accessed March 28, 2016. Sermon available online at http://www.fpcjackson.org/resource-library/sermons/lord -have-mercy–2.

———. "Non Nobis Domine (Not to Us, O Lord)." Accessed March 28, 2016. Sermon available online at http://ligonduncan.com/non -nobis-domine-not-to-us-o-lord-468.

———. "Our Help Is in the Name of the Lord." Accessed March 28, 2016. Sermon available online at http://www.fpcjackson.org /resource-library/sermons/our-help-is-in-the-name-of-the-lord.

———. "Our Story." Accessed March 28, 2016. Sermon available online at http://ligonduncan.com/our-story-743.

———. "A Prayer in Affliction." Accessed March 24, 2016. Sermon available online at http://ligonduncan.com/a-prayer-in-affliction-733.

Elliot, Elisabeth. A Path through Suffering. Grand Rapids: Revell, 2003.

Ferguson, Sinclair. "Do Dreams Come True?" Accessed March 28, 2016. Sermon available online at http://mp3.sa-media.com/filearea/fpc -092706/fpc-092706.mp3.

Flavel, John. The Method of Grace. New York: American Tract Society, 1845.

Forester, Fanny. Missionary Biography: The Memoir of Sarah B. Judson, Member of the American Mission to Burmah. London: Aylott & Jones, 1848.

Foster, Richard. Celebration of Discipline. San Francisco: HarperCollins, 1978.

Goldingay, John. Psalms. Vol 3: Psalms 90–150. Baker Commentary on the Old Testament Wisdom and Psalms. Grand Rapids: Baker Academic, 2008.

Greidanus, Sidney. Preaching Christ from Psalms. Grand Rapids: Eerdmans, 2016.

James, Sharon. *Ann Judson: A Missionary Life for Burma*. Darlington, UK: Evangelical Press, 2015.

Keil, C. F., and Franz Delitzsch. *Commentary on the Old Testament: Psalms*. Translated by Francis Bolton. Peabody, MA: Hendrickson, 2011.

Keller, Timothy. *Center Church*. Grand Rapids: Zondervan, 2012.

———. *Counterfeit Gods*. New York: Dutton, 2009.

———. *Every Good Endeavor*. New York: Dutton, 2012. Kindle.

———. *King's Cross*. New York: Dutton, 2011.

———. "Our Faith and His Work." Accessed March 28, 2016. Sermon available online at http://pcpceveningsermons.s3.amazonaws.com /20140122_wintergrace_keller-52e1dc2c35969.mp3.

———. *Preaching*. New York: Viking, 2015.

———. *The Songs of Jesus*. New York: Viking, 2015. Kindle.

———. *Walking with God through Pain and Suffering*. New York: Dutton, 2013.

Kidner, Derek. *Psalms 1–72: An Introduction and Commentary*. Tyndale Old Testament Commentaries. Downers Grove, IL: IVP Academic, 1973.

———. *Psalms 73–150: An Introduction and Commentary*. Tyndale Old Testament Commentaries. D. J. Wiseman, general editor. Downers Grove, IL: IVP Academic, 1973

Kuyper, Abraham. *Abraham Kuyper: A Centennial Reader*. Edited by James D. Bratt. Grand Rapids: Eerdmans, 1998.

"Latest Bible Translation Figures Show Progress." *Wycliffe Bible Translators*, n.d. Accessed February 11, 2020. https://www.wycliffe .org.uk/resources/press-releases/latest-bible-translation-figures.

Lawson, Steven J. *Psalms 1–75*. Holman Old Testament Commentary. Nashville: B&H, 2003.

———. *Psalms 76–150*. Holman Old Testament Commentary. Nashville: B&H, 2003.

———. "Trusting God." Accessed March 28, 2016. Sermon available online at https://www.monergism.com/topics/mp3-audio-multi media/00-old-testament-sermons-book/psalms/5-books-psalms -audio/book-5-psal-18.

Leupold, H. C. *Exposition of the Psalms*. Grand Rapids: Baker, 1979.

Lewis, C. S. *Letters to Malcolm, Chiefly on Prayer*. Reissue ed. San Francisco: HarperOne, 2017.

———. *Mere Christianity*. New York: MacMillan Pub. Co., 1952.

———. *Reflections on the Psalms*. Preprint. Seattle, WA: CreateSpace Independent Publishing, 2014.

———. *The World's Last Night: And Other Essays*. San Francisco: HarperOne, 2017.

Lloyd-Jones, Sally. *The Jesus Storybook Bible: Every Story Whispers His Name*. Grand Rapids: ZonderKidz, 2007.

Luther, Martin. *Exposition of Psalm 147*. Quoted by J. D. Greear, "Martin Luther on 'The Masks of God.'" Accessed March 28, 2016. Article online at http://www.jdgreear.com/my_weblog/2013/08/martin-luther-on-gods-masks.html.

———. *First Lectures on the Psalms II: Psalm 76–126*. Edited by Hilton C. Oswald. Vol. 11. Luther's Works. St. Louis, MO: Concordia, 1976.

Manton, Thomas. *Psalm 119*. Vol. 2. Oxford: Banner of Trust, 1990.

McDaniel, Chip. "The Psalms." Class Notes. Southeastern Baptist Theological Seminary, 2019.

Merritt, James. "The Mystery of Creation." *Touching Lives*, October 27, 2017. Accessed March 2, 2020. https://www.touchinglives.org/devotionals/the-mystery-of-creation.

Merton, Thomas. *Praying the Psalms*. Collegeville, MN: Liturgical, 1956.

Miller, Paul. *A Praying Life*. Colorado Springs: NavPress, 2009.

Motyer, Alec. *Psalms by the Day: A New Devotional Translation*. Fearn, Ross-shire: Christian Focus, 2016.

"Myanmar (Burma) | Joshua Project." Accessed January 16, 2020. https://joshuaproject.net/countries/BM.

Newell, Harriet. *Delighting in Her Heavenly Bridegroom: The Memoirs of Harriet Newell, Teenage Missionary Wife*. Edited by Jennifer Adams. Forest, VA: Corner Pillar, 2011.

Newell, Marvin J. *Expect Great Things: Mission Quotes That Inform and Inspire*. Pasadena, CA: William Carey Library, 2013.

O'Flaherty, William. *The Misquotable C. S. Lewis: What He Didn't Say, What He Actually Said, and Why It Matters*. Eugene, OR: Wipf and Stock, 2018.

Packer, J. I. *Knowing God*. Downers Grove: InterVarsity, 1973.

Peterson, Eugene. *Answering God: The Psalms as Tools for Prayer*. New York: HarperCollins, 1989.

———. *A Long Obedience in the Same Direction: Discipleship in an Instant Society*. Downers Grove, IL: InterVarsity Press, 2000.

———. *Working the Angles*. Grand Rapids: Eerdmans, 1987.

Pierard, Richard V. "The Man Who Gave the Bible to the Burmese." *Christian History & Biography Magazine*, 2006. Accessed January 24,

2020. https://christianhistoryinstitute.org/magazine/article/the-man -who-gave-the-bible-to-the-burmese.

Piper, John. "Do I Not Hate Those Who Hate You, O Lord?" *Desiring God*, October 3, 2000. Accessed March 28, 2016 and October 2, 2018. Article online at http://www.desiringgod.org/articles/do-i -not-hate-those-who-hate-you-o-lord.

———. "Don't Eat the Bread of Anxious Toil." Accessed March 28, 2016. Sermon available online at http://www.desiringgod.org/messages /dont-eat-the-bread-of-anxious-toil.

———. "Everlasting Truth for the Joy of All Peoples." *Desiring God*, October 26, 2003. Accessed July 17, 2018. https://www.desiringgod .org/messages/everlasting-truth-for-the-joy-of-all-peoples.

———. *Future Grace: The Purifying Power of the Promises of God*. Revised ed. Colorado Springs: Multnomah, 2012.

———. "He Commanded and They Were Created." *Desiring God*, October 4, 1981. Accessed October 23, 2019. https://www.desiring god.org/messages/he-commanded-and-they-were-created.

———. *Let the Nations Be Glad!: The Supremacy of God in Missions*. 2nd ed. Grand Rapids: Baker, 2007.

———. *Let the Nations Be Glad!: The Supremacy of God in Missions*. 3rd ed. Grand Rapids: Baker Academic, 2010.

———. "One Generation Shall Praise Your Works to Another." Accessed March 28, 2016. Sermon available online at http:// www.desiringgod.org/messages/one-generation-shall-praise-your works-to-another.

———. "The Pleasure of God in All That He Does." *Desiring God*, February 1, 1987. Accessed January 23, 2020. https://www.desiring god.org/messages/the-pleasure-of-god-in-all-that-he-does.

———. "The Pleasure of God in His Creation." Accessed March 28, 2016. Sermon available online at http://www.desiringgod.org/messages /the-pleasure-of-god-in-his-creation.

———. *The Pleasures of God*. Revised ed. Colorado Springs: Multnomah, 2012.

———. *When I Don't Desire God*. Wheaton: Crossway, 2004.

———. "Where the Great King Keeps His Wine." *Desiring God*, November 19, 1990. Accessed March 24, 2016. http://www.desiringgod.org /articles/where-the-great-king-keeps-his-wine.

Platt, David, Jim Shaddix, and Matt Mason. *Exalting Jesus in Psalms 51–100*. Nashville, TN: Holman Reference, 2020.

Reardon, Patrick Henry. *Christ in the Psalms.* Ben Lomond, CA & Chesterton, IN: Conciliar, 2000.

Robert, Dana L. "The Mother of Modern Missions." *Christian History and Biography* 90, April 1, 2006: 22–24.

Rogers, Adrian. *Adrianisms: The Collected Wit and Wisdom of Adrian Rogers.* Collierville, TN: Innovo, 2015.

Ross, Allen P. *A Commentary on the Psalms: Volume 1 (1–41).* Kregel Exegetical Library. Grand Rapids: Kregel Academic, 2012.

————. *A Commentary on the Psalms: Volume 3 (90–150).* Kregel Exegetical Library. Grand Rapids: Kregel Academic, 2014.

————. "Psalms." In *The Bible Knowledge Commentary: Old Testament,* edited by John F. Walvoord and Roy B. Zuck, 779–899. Wheaton, IL: Victor, 1985.

Sanders, J. Oswald. *Spiritual Leadership: Principles of Excellence for Every Believer.* Chicago: Moody, 2017.

Sibbes, Richard. *A Bruised Reed.* Revised ed. Carlisle, PA: Banner of Truth, 1998.

Sproul, R. C. "How Should Christians View World History?" *Ligonier Ministries,* June 8, 2015. Accessed October 23, 2019. https://www.ligonier.org/blog/christians-view-world-history.

Spurgeon, C. H. *The Metropolitan Tabernacle Pulpit: Sermons Preached and Revised.* Vol. 21. London: Passmore & Alabaster, 1876.

————. *The Treasury of David.* Vol 2. Psalms 58–110. Peabody, MA: Hendrickson, 1988.

————. *The Treasury of David.* Vol 3. Psalms 111–150. Peabody, MA: Hendrickson, 1988.

————. *The Treasury of David: Psalms 58-110.* Vol. 2b. Grand Rapids: Zondervan, 1979.

————. *The Treasury of David: Psalms 111–150.* Vol. 3a. Grand Rapids: Zondervan, 1979.

————. *The Treasury of David: Psalms 111–150.* Vol. 3b. Grand Rapids: Zondervan, 1979.

Storms, Sam. "10 Things You Should Know about the Imprecatory Psalms." *Crosswalk,* n.d. Accessed December 20, 2019. https://www.crosswalk.com/faith/bible-study/10-things-you-should-know-about-the-imprecatory-psalms.html.

————. "Praise Him! Praise Him! (Psalms 148–150)." *Sam Storms,* n.d. Accessed October 1, 2019. https://www.samstorms.com/all-articles/post/praise-him-praise-him–psalms-148-150-.

————. "The Unsearchable Splendor of God." Article online at http://www.samstorms.com/all-articles/post/the-unsearchable-splendor-of-god–psalm-145-. Accessed March 28, 2016.

Stuart, Arabella W. *Lives of the Three Mrs. Judsons.* Charleston, SC: BiblioBazar, 2007.

Thomas, I. D. E. *The Golden Treasury of Puritan Quotations.* Accessed March 28, 2016. Book available online at http://www.wtsbooks.com/common/pdf_links/9780851512495.pdf.

Tozer, A. W. *A. W. Tozer: Three Spiritual Classics in One Volume: The Knowledge of the Holy, the Pursuit of God, and God's Pursuit of Man.* Combined edition. Chicago: Moody, 2018.

Tripp, Paul. *Dangerous Calling.* Crossway: Wheaton, 2012.

VanGemeren, Willem A. "Psalms." In *Psalms, Proverbs, Ecclesiastes, Song of Songs.* Vol 5. The Expositor's Bible Commentary. Frank E. Gaebelein, general editor. Grand Rapids: Zondervan, 1991.

————. *Psalms.* Edited by Tremper Longman III and David E Garland. Revised Edition. The Expositor's Bible Commentary. Grand Rapids: Zondervan, 2008.

Warren, Rick. *The Purpose Driven Life.* Grand Rapids: Zondervan, 2002.

Wiersbe, Warren W. *The Bible Exposition Commentary: Old Testament Wisdom and Poetry.* Colorado Springs: Victor, 2003.

Wilcock, Michael. *The Message of Psalms 73–150.* The Bible Speaks Today. Leicester, England: Inter-Varsity Press, 2001.

————. *The Message of Psalms 73–150: Songs for the People of God.* Downers Grove, IL: IVP Academic, 2001.

Williams, Donald. *Psalms 1–72.* The Preacher's Commentary 13. Nashville: Thomas Nelson, 1986. Kindle Edition.

————. *Psalms 73–150.* The Preacher's Commentary 14. Nashville: Thomas Nelson, 1989. Kindle Edition.

Wilson, Jared C. *The Pastor's Justification.* Wheaton: Crossway, 2013.

Wright, N. T. *The Case for the Psalms.* New York: HarperCollins, 2013.

SCRIPTURE INDEX